From its flamboyant beginning in the second half of the third century BCE, through the late republic and into the early empire, Roman tragedy was at the centre of the city's cultural and political life. A. J. Boyle's landmark introduction is the first detailed cultural and theatrical history of this major literary form. Professor Boyle not only plots the history of Roman tragic techniques and conventions, of generic formation and change, of the debt of Rome to Greece and text to text, but also traces the birth, development and death of Roman tragedy within the context of the city's evolving institutions, ideologies and political and social practices.

Each Roman tragedian whose works survive in any substance is discussed and analysed in detail, including the early republican dramatists Ennius, Pacuvius and Accius, as well as Seneca and his post-Neronian successors. Attention is given both to tragedy proper and to the historical drama (*fabula praetexta*) which the Romans allied to tragedy. The book is addressed to students of theatre and of Roman political and cultural history, and, with parallel English translations to Latin quotations, is accessible to all those interested in the social dynamics of writing, spectacle, ideology and power.

A. J. Boyle is Professor of Classics at the University of Southern California, Los Angeles, and editor of the classical literary journal, *Ramus*. His previous publications include: *The Eclogues of Virgil*, *Seneca Tragicus*, *The Chaonian Dove*, *Seneca's Phaedra*, *The Imperial Muse*, *Roman Epic*, *Seneca's Troades*, *Roman Literature and Ideology*, *Tragic Seneca*, *Ovid and the Monuments*. He has also co-edited, with J. P. Sullivan, *Roman Poets of the Early Empire* and *Martial in English*, with R. D. Woodard, *Ovid's Fasti*, and with W. J. Dominik, *Flavian Rome*.

AN INTRODUCTION TO ROMAN TRAGEDY

A. J. Boyle

Routledge
Taylor & Francis Group

LONDON AND NEW YORK

First published 2006
by Routledge
2 Park Square, Milton Park, Abingdon, Oxon, OX14 4RN

Simultaneously published in the USA and Canada
by Routledge
270 Madison Ave, New York, NY 10016

Routledge is an imprint of the Taylor & Francis Group

Typeset in Garamond by Taylor & Francis Books
Printed and bound in Great Britain by MPG Books Ltd, Bodmin

British Library Cataloguing in Publication Data
A catalogue record for this book is available from the British Library

Library of Congress Cataloging-in-Publication Data
Boyle, A. J. (Anthony James)
Roman tragedy / Anthony J. Boyle.
p. cm.
Includes bibliographical references and index.
ISBN 0-415-25102-8 (hardback : alk. paper) -- ISBN 0-415-
25103-6 (pbk. : alk. paper) 1. Latin drama (Tragedy)--History
and criticism. 2. Literature and society--Rome. 3. Theater--
Rome. I. Title.
PA6068.B69 2005
872'.0109--dc22

2005006892

1005457678

ISBN 0–415–25102–8 (hbk)
ISBN 0–415–25103–6 (pbk)

T&F informa

Taylor & Francis Group is the Academic Division of T&F Informa plc.

FOR HELEN MORALES

CONTENTS

Preface   ix

Part I
The birth of Roman drama   1

1 Staging Rome   3

Part II
The evolution of Roman tragedy   25

2 Founding fathers: the appropriation of Greece   27

3 The second wave: generic confidence   56

4 Tragic apex: poetic form and political crisis   109

5 Canonisation and turmoil: the end of
   the republic   143

6 *Roma theatrum*: the early empire   160

7 Seneca's tragic theatre   189

CONTENTS

Part III

The death of tragedy at Rome   219

8 Tragedy and autocracy: the liberty of silence   221

Notes   239
Select bibliography   278
Index   292

PREFACE

This book requires little justification. Roman tragedy was at the centre of Rome's performative life, cultural and political, from its flamboyant beginning in the second half of the third century BCE, through the late republic and into the early empire, but until 2004 there was no monograph in English even attempting to address the evolution of Roman tragedy and its literary, theatrical and cultural importance. The standard book on (at least a substantial part of) the subject was published 130 years ago in Leipzig: Otto Ribbeck's *Die Römische Tragödie im Zeitalter der Republik* (1875). In the last fifty years there have been several useful studies of Roman drama, entertainment, spectacle and theatricality, and a plethora of studies of Roman comedy and of the comic dramatists Plautus and Terence. Seneca, too, has received significant critical and scholarly attention, especially in the last twenty years, and there have been signs of burgeoning interest in the early Roman tragedians. But Roman tragedy, despite its cultural importance and the increasing emphasis in Classical Studies on cultural history and analysis, still awaits a detailed theatrical and cultural account of its history and evolution. Both the global inquiry of Dupont (*L'acteur-roi: le théâtre dans la Rome antique*, Paris 1985) and the stimulating metatheatrical study of Erasmo (*Roman Tragedy: Theatre to Theatricality*, Austin 2004), from whose confrontation with the early tragic fragments I learned much, contain elements of such a history but cannot be said to perform this task.

The subject, of course, poses special difficulties because of the fragmentary nature of the plays of the early Roman tragedians; but such difficulties are partially offset by several recent excellent editions and, though they pose limitations on what may be said, entail neither silence nor neglect. What has been needed for some time is a cultural and theatrical history of Roman tragedy which not only plots the history of theatrical techniques and conventions, of generic formation and change, of the debt of playwright to playwright and text to text, but traces the birth, development and death of Roman tragedy within the context of Rome's evolving institutions, ideologies and political and social practices. This is what is attempted in this 'Introduction', which is somewhat longer than other volumes in the series, because of the unfamiliarity of much of the primary material and the relative paucity and inaccessibility of scholarship in the field. I hope that this study may prove of interest, not only to students of theatre and of Roman political and cultural history, but to all interested in the societal interplay of writing, spectacle, ideology, performance and power.

For the text of the fragmentary Roman tragedians (i.e. for all except Seneca and the authors of *Hercules Oetaeus* and of *Octavia*) and of their *praetextae*, I have used the editions of Klotz (Munich 1953) and (for the fragments of Ennius' tragedies only) Jocelyn (Cambridge 1967). Minor changes in punctuation and orthography to those editions are not noted, but major emendations are. I have also followed Klotz and Jocelyn in the spelling of the various play titles but have generally not followed either editor's arrangement of the fragments of a given play. For Seneca's tragedies, the *Hercules Oetaeus* and *Octavia*, I have used the OCT of Zwierlein (1986), except for citations from *Phaedra* and *Troades*, where I have used my own editions (Liverpool 1987, Leeds 1994). All translations in the book are my own and follow the principles outlined in my editions of *Phaedra* and *Troades*, from which my translations of passages from those plays in Chapter 7 derive. Throughout the book conventional spellings of the names of tragic characters have been adopted, except where a Latinised version (e.g., Antiopa for Antiope) seemed more appropriate.

I have several debts. To Routledge for permission to reuse some material from my *Tragic Seneca: An Essay in the Theatrical Tradition* (1997) in Chapter 7; to my own university, USC, for the provision of sabbatical and study leave which enabled me to begin and complete this project, and for a decade and a half of strong institutional support; to Cambridge University Classics Faculty for permission to use on a regular basis their library's unsurpassed Classics collection, without which this book would have taken twice as long to complete. The following friends and scholars read the book in an earlier draft and offered advice: Elaine Fantham, John Henderson,

John Penwill, Alessandro Schiesaro and Joseph Smith. Joseph Smith also assisted with the proofs. I thank all the above sincerely.

I dedicate the book to my partner, Helen Morales, who has given me a remarkable world to live in.

A. J. Boyle
USC, Los Angeles
Thanksgiving 2004

Part I

THE BIRTH OF ROMAN DRAMA

1

STAGING ROME

populi sensus maxime in theatro et spectaculis
perspectus est.

(Cicero *Ad Atticum* 2.19.3)

The will of the people is most clearly seen in the
theatre and at the shows.

Theatricality and power

Rome was always already theatrical. As an Etruscan city in the sixth century BCE and an independent state in the fifth and fourth centuries BCE, Rome from its genesis was shaped by institutions, religious rituals and social practices that involved complex performances by political and religious leaders before an engaged audience of citizens and slaves. Public celebrations, sacrifice, divination, communal prayer, political and military oration, legal trials and executions, marriage, funerals, religious and triumphal processions, even a magistrate's movement through the city streets, as later his departure for or return from provincial office, involved self-conscious (re-)enactment of a social script. The re-enactments served several functions, among the more important of which was an acting-out of relations of power. Thus Polybius' account in the mid-second century BCE of the typical funeral of a Roman aristocrat (6.53):

> When a prominent man dies, he is carried into the forum to the so-called rostra, sometimes in an upright, conspicuous position, more rarely in a reclining one. Encompassed by the whole people standing, an adult son (if one survives and is present) or another relative climbs the rostra and speaks on the virtues and achievements of the dead man.

The result is that the crowd, both those who participated in the achievements and those who did not, as they recall and visualise the past, are drawn to such sympathy that the loss seems not a private one for the mourners but a public one affecting the people. Then after the interment and the customary rites they put the image of the dead man in the most conspicuous place in the house, enclosed in a wooden shrine. This image is a mask (*prosopon*) which reproduces the deceased's features and colouring with remarkable likeness. These images, honorifically adorned, are displayed at public sacrifices, and, when a prominent family member dies, are taken to the funeral procession and put on men whose stature and general appearance most resemble those of the different ancestors. The men wear togas – with a purple border if the ancestor had been a consul or praetor, whole purple if he had been a censor, embroidered with gold if he had celebrated a triumph or had accomplished something similar. The men parade in chariots, and before them are carried rods and axes and the other magisterial insignia according to the status of the offices of state held by each during their lifetime. And when they reach the rostra, they all sit in a row on chairs of ivory. It would be difficult to find a more glorious spectacle (*theama*) for a young man who aspires to fame and nobility. For who would not be stirred by the images of men renowned for their virtue, all together, as if alive and breathing? What could be a more glorious spectacle?

The funeral as political theatre: audience, dialogue, action, actors, costumes, masks, props, stages – one of the stages being the processional route through Rome itself, another the rostra in the place which became the principal site of Rome's early 'literary' drama: the Roman Forum. Like a stage play, this theatrical procession was accompanied by music (omitted by Polybius) played loudly on the flute, trumpet and sometimes horn by musicians who led the way, and was accompanied, too, by a dirge from professional mourners, who sometimes interspersed and/or followed the funeral oration with a 'chorus' of lamentations, orchestrated by their own 'chorus-leader', the *praefica*.[1] The inspirational force of the event for the young elite Roman is well observed by Polybius; it was a function of aristocratic Rome's obsessive, competitive culture. The funeral not only paraded the achievements of an individual aristocratic family, but furnished in the parade the grounds for that family's superior social and political position.[2] Collectively, such funerals celebrated the values and traditions of the political elite and sustained its hegemony, employing the artifice of theatre to naturalise the past in justification of the existing social order.

More obviously directed to the validation of social supremacy was that coveted pinnacle of Roman military achievement, the triumph. Here is Silius Italicus' account (some three hundred years after the event) of the triumphal procession of Scipio Africanus in 201 BCE:

> mansuri compos decoris per saecula rector,
> deuictae referens primus cognomina terrae,
> securus sceptri, repetit per caerula Romam
> et patria inuehitur sublimi tecta triumpho.
> ante Syphax feretro residens captiua premebat
> lumina et auratae seruabant colla catenae.
> hic Hannon clarique genus Phoenissa iuuenta
> et Macetum primi atque incocti corpora Mauri,
> tum Nomades notusque sacro, cum lustrat harenas,
> Hammoni Garamas et semper naufraga Syrtis.
> mox uictas tendens Carthago ad sidera palmas
> ibat et effigies orae iam lenis Hiberae,
> terrarum finis Gades ac laudibus olim
> terminus Herculeis Calpe Baetisque lauare
> solis equos dulci consuetus fluminis unda,
> frondosumque apicem subigens ad sidera mater
> bellorum fera Pyrene nec mitis Hiberus,
> cum simul illidit ponto quos attulit amnes.
> sed non ulla magis mentesque oculosque tenebat
> quam uisa Hannibalis campis fugientis imago.
> ipse adstans curru atque auro decoratus et ostro
> Martia praebebat spectanda Quiritibus ora:
> qualis odoratis descendens Liber ab Indis
> egit pampineos frenata tigride currus;
> aut cum Phlegraeis, confecta mole Gigantum,
> incessit campis tangens Tirynthius astra.
> salue, inuicte parens non concessure Quirino
> laudibus ac meritis non concessure Camillo.
> nec uero, cum te memorat de stirpe deorum,
> prolem Tarpei mentitur Roma Tonantis.
> (*Punica* 17.625–54)

Possessed of eternal glory, the first ruler
To carry the name of a conquered land,
Confident of power, crosses the sea to Rome
And enters his ancestral home in a soaring triumph.
Before him Syphax on a litter held captive eyes
Downcast, and chains of gold guarded his neck.
There was Hanno and Carthage's noble youth
And Macedon's chiefs and black-bodied Moors,
Numidians and the Garamantes, whom sacred Ammon
Sees scouring the desert, and ship-wrecking Syrtis.
Soon Carthage passed, stretching conquered hands
Starward, and a model of Spain now peaceful,
Of Gades the world's end, Calpe once the limit
Of Hercules' fame and the Baetis which bathes
The sun's horses in its sweet river waters –
And, pushing her forested height starward, that fierce
Mother of wars, Pyrene, and the ungentle Ebro,
When it crashes the ocean with all its streams.
But no picture held their minds and eyes more
Than that of Hannibal fleeing the field.
Standing in his chariot, clothed in purple and gold,
Scipio gave Romans the spectacle of Mars' face:
So looked Liber when he drove from perfumed India
His vine-leafed chariot with bridled tigers;
So looked Hercules on Phlegra's plain when the Giants
Were destroyed and he touched the stars as he walked.
Hail, unconquered father unsurpassed by Quirinus
In glory, unsurpassed by Camillus in deeds.
Truly Rome tells no lie when she calls your stock divine,
And names you child of the Capitoline Thunderer.

Again the theatrics are undisguised – audience (at first the reader, and finally the Romans of 201 BCE); a stage (Rome); players, including a cast of former warriors, now costumed in golden chains and paraded in their role of defeated foes; painted scenery and props (images of conquered territories and rivers) which themselves present the 'plot' of Scipio's all-conquering campaigns, culminating in the climactic scene of the defeated general in flight; the whole accompanied, like the funeral procession, by music (the flourish of trumpets, again omitted),[3] and modulated to include scenes of pathos and awe and to lead to, as dramatic finale and closure, the *deus ex machina* Scipio, who in his triumphal chariot, costumed in purple and gold, acts out through the *triumphator*'s 'red mask' his role as Mars and/or Jupiter. This 'red mask' was the *triumphator*'s face, painted red, which seemed to cast the Roman general in the role of Jupiter, whose cult image in the Capitoline temple, to which the *triumphator* made his ascent, was similarly painted, or, as in Silius' account (for the red on the general's face might signify, too, the blood of enemies), seemed to cast him in the role of Mars. Certainly the comparison with the gods – Mars, Liber, Hercules, Quirinus, Jupiter – underscores the prime political and social function of the triumph, its demonstration of the superiority of the *triumphator*. The triumph's theatricalised celebration of Rome, its gods, its army, its conquering might, arouses the 'patriotic' emotions of the citizen-audience, reinforcing community, solidarity and collective identity in the face of the enemy 'other'. But those emotions are made instruments of individual acclamation.[4]

Rome's funerary and triumphal rituals, and the *pompa circensis* or 'procession to the circus' with which they are frequently compared, seem to modern scholars to have been Etruscan in origin,[5] and were held by the writers of the classical period to have originated in the earliest period of the city. Their authority derived in part from their very antiquity, although their precise age is difficult to guess. There are some pointers to the age of the triumph, which is represented in classical texts as monarchic. The Triumphal *Fasti*, for example, record triumphs from the regal and the early republican period, Festus (504L) confirms the antiquity of the triumph, and Livy (2.16.1) assigns a triumph in the first decade of the republic to the consuls of 505 BCE, Marcus Valerius and Publius Postumius. The theatrics of Rome's social institutions and their political force were certainly well established before the city's first attested drama was produced.[6] Spectacle was always already both the display and the agent of power.

Drama and archaic Rome

Whether such spectacle included unattested 'dramatic' entertainment is debated. Reliable evidence for the detailed cultural practices of archaic Rome is scarce. Rational hypotheses rule. It is now generally supposed that Rome had a flourishing culture of poetry and song well before the third century BCE, associated primarily with the aristocratic symposium.[7] It seems reasonable to think that another aspect of archaic Roman culture, especially in a highly theatricalised society influenced by both Etruria and Greece, was some kind of formal drama, the existence of which would then have preceded not only the traditional date of 240 BCE, assigned by the ancient *testimonia* to the appearance of the city's first performed play with a plot (written by Livius Andronicus),[8] but also Livy's much quoted mid-fourth century date for the introduction of theatrical entertainment to Rome. Livy's notice, which probably owes its controversial date to the first century BCE antiquarian Varro, who seems to have promoted a rustic origin for Roman drama, especially its derivation from the festivities of the *Liberalia*,[9] emphasises the religious motivation of the *ludi scaenici* ('theatrical shows') and their foreign derivation, especially their origin in Etruria. The *ludi* themselves in Livy's account are primarily perfor- mances of music and dance.

The famous passage deserves substantial quotation, at least in translation.[10] The year is that of the consulship of Gaius Sulpicius Peticus and Gaius Licinius Stolo, i.e. 364 BCE:

When the force of the pestilence was alleviated neither by human strategies nor by divine help, they were over- whelmed by superstitious fears and are said to have also instituted theatrical shows (*ludi scenici*), a new phenomenon for a warlike people (for their only spectacle was the circus), among other efforts to appease the wrath of the gods. But this was a small thing, as almost all things are initially, and it was imported from abroad. Without any singing, without imitating songs, players (*ludiones*) who had been summoned from Etruria danced to the strains of the piper and performed not ungraceful movements in the Etruscan fashion. Next the young men started to imitate them, at the same time exchanging jokes in uncouth verses; nor were their movements out of harmony with their words. And so it was adopted and sustained through frequent use. The native performers, because a player (*ludio*) was called *ister* in Etruscan, were given the name of *histriones*, 'actors'; they did not, as before, take turns in hurling rushed and crude verses like the Fescennines, but performed *saturae* (medleys?) full of tunes with song now written for the flute and with appropriate movement. Some years later (they say) Livius, who was the first to move from *saturae* and compose a play (*fabula*) with a plot (*argumentum*) – like everyone then, he was an actor of his own pieces – when frequent calls upon his voice had dulled it and he had got permission for a boy to stand before the flautist and do the singing, acted a monody with increased vigour of movement because he was unrestrained by the need to use his voice. From that moment actors (*histriones*) started to have the singing done to their gestures, and reserved just the dialogue for their own voices. As this type of play moved away from merriment and loose jokes and a 'show' (*ludus*) had gradually become art, the young men abandoned the acting of plays to 'actors' (*histriones*) and began to revive the antique custom of hurling silly verses at each other. Whence arose what were later termed 'after-pieces' (*exodia*) and were most often joined with Atellan plays. The latter – a type of show (*ludus*) acquired from the Oscans – was kept by the young men, and they would not let it be polluted by actors (*histriones*): hence the tradition that performers of Atellan plays are not disfranchised and serve in the army as if they had no connection with the theatrical arts (*ars ludicra*). It has seemed worthwhile to position the prime origin even of shows among the small-scale beginnings of other things, so that one can see the sober start of a phenomenon which has now reached a madness scarcely able to be supported by opulent kingdoms.

(Livy 7.2.3–13)

The focus in Livy on the Etruscan origin of both the form and the vocabulary of Roman drama (a vocabulary which seems to derive from Etruscan adaptations of Greek),[11] reinforced by the evidence of Etruscan vase- and tomb-painting, have prompted some scholars to infer that drama came to Rome from Greece via Etruria and most probably at the time of Etruria's greatest influence on the city, i.e. during the sixth or fifth centuries BCE.[12] What this hypothesised drama might have been – and it needs to be underscored that Attic tragedy only reached its maturity in the fifth century – is unclear. Livy's comments indicate that no oral tradition concerning any pre-fourth-century drama existed and that the *ludi scaenici* of the mid-fourth century were thought of as primitive.

Archaic Rome is a barely documented society, and even in the case of the late fourth century, when a vigorous interest in the viewing of spectacle, including presumably *ludi*, is signalled by Gaius Maenius' addition of spectator balconies (*maeniana*) to the shops of the Roman Forum (318 BCE: Festus 120L), the city has left little trace of its theatrical interests. And if it seems reasonable to assume that some form of non-literary archaic drama existed of which inevitably no traces have survived, conjectures to the effect that such Roman drama constituted a celebration of 'civic identity' by means of the performance of national myths have not automatically commanded assent.[13] Certainly when Roman drama begins (from 240 BCE) to generate texts to index both its existence and its nature, a number of the (tragic) titles show a potentially aetiological preoccupation with Troy and the Trojan cycle, and a few extant titles (*Romulus* or *Lupus, Sabinae*) indicate an overt interest in theatricalising myths of 'national significance'. Clearly, too, issues of civic identity would have been embedded in the performance of all early Roman plays through the social cohesiveness of the theatrical gathering, the plays' validation of Latin as the 'prestige language',[14] and the ambivalent spectacle of Rome's appropriation of Greek culture.[15] But the collective impetus of post-240 BCE attested early Roman drama – tragedy, comedy, 'history plays' (*praetextae*) (to which may be added Atellan farce, of which we possess scant but telling knowledge) – seems directed less to the glorification of the *populus Romanus* (although that is certainly involved), more to the celebration of members or families (*gentes*) of the Roman elite, especially the magistrates and the *gentes* of the magistrates who commissioned and financed the actual plays performed. More persuasive is the idea – supported by the passage from Livy,[16] by Fabius Pictor's description of a chorus of 'satyric' dancers in the *pompa circensis* at the end of the third century BCE (DH *Ant. Rom.* 7.72.5),[17] by Etruscan wall-paintings and the likelihood of an Etruscan theatrical tradition[18] – that some form of 'comic' satyric drama, filled with jesting, music and dance, existed alongside the other entertainments which accompanied the festivals of archaic Rome.

Dramatic kinds

When attested Roman drama emerged in the second half of the third century BCE it manifested itself in a variety of literary modes, influenced by both native Italian traditions and Greek literary forms. The Greek influence was clearly related to Rome's substantial exposure to Hellenistic culture in the first half of the third century BCE through her almost continuous contact with the Greek cities of southern Italy and Sicily during a series of military engagements which culminated in the First Punic War of 264–41 BCE. Rome's contact with the Greek cities of Italy is evident throughout the whole of her republican history, but there had never been anything on this scale or of such continuous duration. It resulted in a circulation (albeit small) at Rome of Greek literary texts. Furthermore, the increasing power of the Roman *plebs* had produced a body of influential Romans not averse to the pleasures of art and the crafts, areas of human achievement traditionally viewed with suspicion, if not with outright contempt (*poeticae artis honos non erat*, 'no esteem was attached to poetry'),[19] by the city's landed aristocracy. Rome's competitive instincts also must have been triggered by the huge disparity in theatrical culture between the cities she had taken and the conquering city itself. She lacked the theatrical finery adorning the sophisticated Greek cities of the south, which, like other Greek cities in the Mediterranean world, projected their theatrical institutions as a defining constituent of an urban identity modelled on that of Athens (without its democracy). The Greek cities were not slow to advertise their cultural superiority.[20] Horace with Augustan hindsight and prejudice inverts late third-century Roman ideology to present the city captured by Greece:

> Graecia capta ferum uictorem cepit et artes
> intulit agresti Latio.
>
> (*Epistles* 2.1.156–7)
>
> Enslaved Greece enslaved her savage victor and brought
> The arts to rustic Latium.

Most conspicuous among Rome's newly flaunted dramatic modes were tragedy and comedy, the latter modelled substantially (at least from Naevius' time)[21] on the third-century Greek New Comedy of manners (hence its descriptor, *fabula palliata*, 'Play in a *pallium* or Greek cloak') but influenced also by such local traditions as Fescennine jesting (ribald, versified abuse at weddings and similar events),[22] the Roman *Saturnalia*,[23] and the parodies of tragic themes apparent in the so-called *phlyakes* farces, which were popular in the Greek communities of southern Italy during the fourth and third centuries BCE.[24] Like its Greek progenitor, Roman comedy was essentially domestic and bourgeois, generally concerned with the removal of barriers to young love, but in the hands of Plautus and Terence it achieved (in the case of the former) a precocious metatheatrical dimension and (in the case of the latter) a level of social criticism at odds with generic expectation. Roman tragedy (*fabula* – more precisely, to use the term of the grammarians, *fabula crepidata* – or *tragoedia*) was similarly oriented towards Greece. Like comedy, it remodelled and 'Romanised' the dramas of the Greek mainland, but its predilection was for Attic drama of the fifth century, even if modulated (perhaps substantially) in and by Hellenistic and south Italian theatrical practice.

This Roman remodelling of Greek comedy and tragedy was nothing like our idea of translation. Described by the ancients through the concepts of *contaminatio* ('combination'), *aemulatio* ('rivalry') and *imitatio* ('imitation'), it generally involved a substantial reframing and reworking of the Greek play or plays in a competitive attempt to rival or, preferably, outdo the 'source-text'. The texts of the Greek plays available to the early Roman dramatists may have already been substantially reworked by the Greek 'actor-interpolators' of the travelling Dionysiac guilds. The cuts, expansions, insertions and remodelling of the Roman playwrights, their 'translations', were perhaps an extension of current non-Roman theatrical practice.[25] The Roman dramatists are, however, unlikely to have altered such matters as the scenic location or the scenic and temporal unity (or occasional disunity) of their 'source-texts'.

Often accompanying a tragedy or comedy, from early on, was a performance of an Atellan farce (*fabula Atellana*), a knockabout style of unscripted comic drama, featuring clown-like stereotypes with exaggerated masks, engaging in slapstick humour and horseplay, often of a sexual nature.[26] This kind of dramatic entertainment was associated with the Oscan town of Atella in Campania and seems much older than the late third-century explosion of literary tragedy and comedy. Such is clearly implied by the passage of Livy quoted above (7.2.12), where it is also stated that later they functioned as *exodia* or 'after-pieces'. By the early first century BCE a literary form of the *Atellana* had been developed.

Another mode of drama evident in the late third century is the historical play known as the *fabula praetexta*, which derived its name from the purple-bordered toga (*toga praetexta*) worn by a Roman magistrate and which dramatised an event in Roman history. This most interesting dramatic form was designed according to Varro to 'teach the people' (*docuit populum*, *LL* 6.18), and would have had a potent impact on Rome's *pueri nobiles*, 'boys of high birth', also wearers of the *toga praetexta*.[27] It began its attested literary life in the late third century BCE with the epic poet and dramatist Gnaeus Naevius, who directed the form's focus not only to distant, defining events in Rome's history (such as Romulus' foundation of the city), but to more immediate contemporary events. Partly aetiological, partly celebratory of Rome's history, success (especially military success) and divine favour, the *praetexta* functioned also on notable occasions as political acclamation of particular contemporary (or recently deceased) Romans.[28] It was (in its earlier and in its later but more aetiological instances) perhaps more likely than any other kind of drama to have been produced in an overtly religious context such as the dedicatory games of a temple, and was thus perhaps in its early instances the most sacral of Rome's dramatic forms. Allied with tragedy in form and language from the start, and identified by some later grammarians as a subspecies of that genre,[29] the *fabula praetexta* within a century of its birth had begun to tackle such 'tragic' subjects as the rape and suicide of Lucretia and the self-sacrificing death-in-battle (*deuotio*) of Decius Mus at Sentinum.[30]

Indeed in the mid-second century BCE, even as tragedy was dividing itself into mythological (*fabula crepidata*) and historical (*fabula praetexta* – although not all *praetextae* were 'tragic'),[31] comedy bifurcated into the traditional *fabula palliata* and the new *fabula togata*,[32] which, as *togata* implies, dealt with specifically Roman or at least Italian characters, transferring the comic situations of the bourgeois *palliata* to the lower-class citizens (even manual labourers) of the country towns of Italy.[33] But whereas tragedians wrote both *fabulae crepidatae* and *praetextae*, no comic dramatist seems to have written both *palliatae* and *togatae*. No complete *fabula togata* is extant. Nevertheless, ancient witnesses suggest that it could be obscene (Quint. *Inst.* 10.1.100) and it could be moralistic (Sen. *Ep. Mor.* 8.8). Recent commentators also suggest that a recurring contrast in the *togata* was between the (decadent) 'Greecising' ways of the town and the (truer) Italian ways of the country.[34] Surviving fragments indicate that some of its creative practices were not dissimilar to those of the *palliata*.[35] There may also have been a third kind of comic drama, viz. that suggested above for archaic Rome: the satyr play. Certainly Vitruvius (5.6.9) and Horace (*AP* 220–50 – a much debated passage) seem to imply this for the Augustan stage, and, although Diomedes talks only of Greek satyr plays, a plausible argument can be mounted to suggest the existence of satyr plays in late republican Rome, perhaps in the form of (topical?) 'satyric comedy' or 'satyric mime'.[36]

Ludi scaenici

The social context of Roman plays varied. By the late republic, if not earlier, elite Romans might arrange for a private performance of a play or other theatrical show in their own houses as part of the entertainment accompanying a banquet.[37] The normal context, however, for dramatic performance was that of the official *ludi*, the 'games' or rather 'shows' which accompanied one of the great religious festivals held annually at Rome in honour of Jupiter, Flora, Apollo, Magna Mater (the 'Great Mother'), and Ceres. These 'games/shows' featured a variety of entertainments, including boxing-matches, chariot-races, animal hunts (*uenationes*), tightrope-walking, juggling, and all kinds

of 'circus' acts – as well as, increasingly, plays. The different entertainments were spread over a number of days and involved a variety
of venues or sites. By the end of the third century BCE the major *ludi*
were six in number, although in some cases 'dramatic shows', *ludi
scaenici*, were not included until the second century.

The six major *ludi* were, in order of institution: *Ludi Romani*
('Roman Games/Shows', also called *Ludi Magni*, 'Great Games/
Shows'), the most ancient of Rome's festivals, held annually in
September in honour of Jupiter, Juno and Minerva (the 'Capitoline
Triad'), with *ludi scaenici* attested from 364 BCE and tragedies/comedies
from 240 BCE; *Ludi Florales*, celebrated in honour of the goddess Flora
from 241 or 238 BCE (Vell. Pat. 1.14.8; Pliny *HN* 18.286) but not
made annual until 173 BCE (Ovid *Fasti* 5.295–330), when the festival
was held in April–May and included dramatic shows; *Ludi Plebeii*
('Plebeian Games/Shows'), instituted in 220 BCE with plays attested
from 200 BCE, when Plautus' *Stichus* was presented at them, and held
annually in November in honour of Jupiter; *Ludi Apollinares*, held in
July in honour of Apollo from 212 BCE (annually from 208 BCE), with
ludi scaenici from the start; *Ludi Megalenses*, held in April in honour of the
Great Mother, *Magna Mater*, from 204 BCE, with plays from 194 BCE
(Livy 34.54), performed from 191 BCE in front of the goddess' newly
dedicated temple on the Palatine; *Ludi Ceriales*, attested from 201 BCE
(Livy 30.39.8) and held annually in April in honour of Ceres, Liber
and Libera, with *ludi scaenici* later attached. Theatrical shows seem also
to have been part of the *Liberalia* of March 17, at least in the late third
century, when they were famous for their liberty of speech:

> libera lingua loquemur ludis Liberalibus.
> (Naevius *Incerta* frag. v Ribbeck)

We will speak with free tongues at the shows of Liber.

But during the second century, probably as a result of the repression
of Bacchic cults evidenced by the senate decree of 186 BCE, these
ludi were amalgamated with those of the *Cerialia* in April.[38]

Ludi scaenici were not of course restricted to comedies, tragedies and
Atellan farces, but included music, dancing, and mime, all intermingling
in the carnivalesque atmosphere of the Roman religious festivals.
Unlike at Athens, comedies and tragedies were not performed on sepa-
rate days. Occasionally, too, there were performances of Greek plays by
Greek actors, and (perhaps as early as the Second Punic War) plays in
Italian languages other than Latin.[39] Mime (*mimus*) was to prove espe-
cially important. Despite its name, mime was not mute, but a lively,

maskless, initially unscripted farce or vaudeville, featuring women 'actresses' (*mimae*) in the female roles and uninhibited in its staging of sexual activity and display of female nudity. Introduced in its erotic form at the early *Ludi Florales*, with which it remained associated, it had by the late republic coupled its obscenity with a strong vein of sententiousness, and occasionally revealed a sharp political edge.[40] Like the *Atellana*, the mime became scripted and 'literary' in the first century BCE, even employing comic metres.

The religious nature of the *ludi scaenici* merits emphasis. Polybius, writing in the middle of the second century BCE, was impressed by the religious convictions of the Romans and the penetration of those convictions into both public and private life (Polyb. 6.56.6–8). The *ludi* were in no sense secular events framed by religious ritual. Included (along with the *ludi circenses*, 'Circus shows') as a religious institution in Varro's monumental work, *Antiquitates Rerum Diuinarum*, the *ludi scaenici* enacted collective homage to the various deities, in most cases initially to secure, and later to offer thanks for, their assistance in national crises. The *Ludi Apollinares* and the *Ludi Megalenses*, for example, were inaugurated during the strains and pressures of the Second Punic War. Although clearly part of an aristocratic strategy to create social cohesion in the face of the threat from Hannibal, they were highly charged religious occasions designed to enlist and then preserve the gods' favour in the struggle against Carthage. And the fact that in the case of these *ludi* the religious observance was of a foreign deity, worshipped in accordance with the prescriptions of an alien cult,[41] underscored the religiosity of the occasion even as it signalled the imperialist appropriation of both ritual and god and the evolving transformation of Rome.

All *ludi* began with a sacrifice to the appropriate deity and a procession from the cult temple to the theatre, where the ritual of the *sellisternium* took place – viz. the placing of the special chair (*sella*), decked with emblems of the relevant deity, in a position of honour in the theatre from where the god could view the plays.[42] Frequently, the theatre was erected near the temple of the deity. The plays themselves were technically a religious ceremony performed in homage to the respective deity and subject to religious rules governing their completion. If a play was interrupted, for example, by the observation of religious *prodigia* or simply through audience desertion for more attractive entertainment (see the prologue of Terence's *Hecyra*), or if it suffered a mishap and was in some way incomplete, the rule of religious *instauratio* was invoked and the play was repeated from the beginning. This often occasioned the addition of an extra day of *ludi* or more.[43]

The days devoted to *ludi scaenici* would vary from year to year and increased considerably in the first half-century following Livius Andronicus' debut. Four days were allocated to *ludi scaenici* at the *Ludi Romani* of 214 BCE (Livy 24.43.7), but by 190 BCE perhaps some seventeen official days each year were devoted to them.[44] To these should be added an unknown number of days given over to the repetition of improperly performed or interrupted plays and to the performance of plays in other less regular contexts: at the triumphs or funerals of distinguished citizens (in the latter case the shows were called *munera*, 'Duty-Shows'), and at the dedication of temples, spectacular occasions which the spectacle of theatre appropriately enhanced. Occasionally also there were 'great votive shows', *ludi magni uotiui*, in honour of Jupiter, vowed by a Roman military commander in battle or by the consuls instructed by the senate.[45]

Munera were organised by private individuals to pay tribute to a recently – or not so recently[46] – dead relative, and could feature plays and other entertainments, including from 264 BCE (at funeral celebrations) gladiatorial bouts.[47] The annual *ludi*, on the other hand (*ludi sollemnes*), were organised by Roman magistrates,[48] who used them to impress their peers, clients and the citizen body as a whole, often – and increasingly so in the late republic – for specific political goals, most obviously for election to higher office.[49] The plays produced at the *ludi* were not part of a dramatic competition, as in Athens; they were, however, competitive in the sense that the magistrate who commissioned them was competing with his peers for the favour of the citizen body seated in the theatre. And that citizen body became increasingly to feel the provision of extravagant spectacles and *ludi* its due, an appropriate tribute from one of Rome's elite to its own civic status and *dignitas*.[50]

Playwrights and actors

Accordingly, initially and into the late republic, the bulk of the credit or odium for a performance went not to the playwrights, actors or other theatrical personnel, but to the magistrate who chose and bought the plays, contracted their staging and arranged the *ludi*, sometimes (despite occasional attempts to control this)[51] at great expense as a result of personal supplementation of the funds (*lucar*) allocated by the state. The earliest playwrights themselves were of low social status and were paid employees of the commissioning magistrate. The existence by the end of the third century of a 'Guild of Writers and Actors', a *collegium* based from *c.* 207 BCE in the plebeian stronghold of the Temple of Minerva on the Aventine (Festus 446–8L), confirmed their banausic status.[52]

The situation began to change somewhat during the second century BCE, when the reputation of Roman playwrights spread beyond Rome to the theatrical centres of southern Italy, which may have commissioned repeat performances of the successful plays of the capital.[53] By the middle of the second century, as the prologues of Terence reveal, playwrights were becoming major bearers both of credit and of odium. Early in the following century the existence of a *collegium poetarum*, a 'Guild of (Dramatic) Poets', is attested quite separate from the previous joint *collegium* with actors; it seems to have contained patrician members.[54] And later in that century it is clear that the early writers of Roman drama were regarded as the founders of an important indigenous literature. In fact there was no major poet between the end of the First Punic War and the time of the Gracchi who did not write drama, which clearly surpassed in its diversity and popular appeal the other literary forms, including epic. The tragedians were later occasionally thought even to excel their Greek counterparts (Cic. *Tusc.* 2.49).

Tragic and comic actors, however, were from the beginning socially stigmatised, and, at least from the late republic, legally marginalised:

> praetoris uerba dicunt: 'infamia notatur qui ab exercitu ignominiae causa ab imperatore eoue cui de ea re statuendi potestas fuerit dimissus erit; qui artis ludicrae pronuntiandiue causa in scaenam prodierit; qui lenocinium fecerit ...'
>
> (Justinian *Digest* 3.2.1)

> The praetor's words declare: 'The following are branded with *infamia*: one who has been discharged from the army for disgraceful conduct by the general or the person with appropriate authority; one who has appeared on stage for acting or recitation; one who has maintained a brothel ...'

> ait praetor: 'qui in scaenam prodierit, infamis est.'
>
> (Justinian *Digest* 3.2.2.5)

> The praetor rules: 'Whoever has appeared on stage incurs *infamia*.'

The first passage is from Julian's edition of the praetor's edict (131 CE), the second from that of Ulpian (213–17 CE), but it is clear that the praetor's ruling dated from the republic. Roman writers and inscriptions from the late republic onwards draw attention to the *infamia* that attends acting.[55]

Many actors were either slaves or non-citizens; in the late third century several were probably Greeks previously associated with the itinerant actors, writers and theatricals known as the 'Artists' or better 'Artisans' of Dionysus (*technitai Dionusou*), who performed in the Greek theatres of southern Italy and throughout the Greek world and organised themselves into Guilds on the model of city-states.[56] But even those who were Roman citizens were legally classified as *infames*, 'infamous', banned apparently from the army and disfranchised, removed from the higher social orders of which they were members,[57] liable in the late republic to be flogged by Roman magistrates anywhere,[58] unable (by Augustan times) to marry freeborn citizens, and subject along with prostitutes and gladiators to a large range of other restrictions.[59] The Atellan farce seems to have been exempt from these restrictions, if Livy is to be believed (7.2.12: quoted above). There were distinguished actors who managed to escape the various bans, including the great comic actor of the first century BCE, Roscius, raised to equestrian status by the dictator Sulla and regarded by Cicero as a friend (Macr. *Sat.* 3.14.11ff.). But, on the whole, actors (*histriones*), like gladiators, were Rome's celebrities and its dregs, a social contradiction, penalised by Roman law and adored by Rome's citizens, who 'loved those they punished': *amant quos multant* (Tertullian *Spec.* 22.2). Their employment by Rome's elite in something so prestigious as a great statesman's funeral procession changed nothing (Diod. Sic. 31.25.2). The guilds in which actors and other theatricals organised themselves, unlike their Greek Dionysiac counterparts, seem to have had no political clout.[60]

Staging

As to how early Roman drama was staged, much remains obscure. Clearly, however, Roman productions were more operatic than their Greek predecessors. Lyric sections, which are prominent in Plautine comedy and take up a far greater proportion of the surviving lines of Roman republican tragedy than of extant Attic tragedy, were accompanied by a piper or flute-player, *tibicen*, whose importance to the production is indicated by the practice (unknown in the Greek tradition) of the recording of his name in the play-notices. Both comedy and tragedy featured three distinct kinds of verbal performance, corresponding to different metres: simple dialogue (in iambic senarii) unaccompanied by music; recitatives (in trochaic septenarii, iambic octonarii and related systems), accompanied by music; and *cantica*, arias sung to music by actors in complex lyric metres. Unsurprisingly, given that Roman playwrights, unlike those of Greece, frequently wrote both tragedy and comedy, the sharp metrical distinctions that exist between Greek tragedy and Greek comedy are not manifested in Roman drama.[61] One generic distinction, however, in Roman drama was that tragedy – but not comedy – featured passages of choral lyric, sung by a dramatic chorus.[62] Although some ancient scores for the plays of the Greek tragedians existed in the second century BCE, the music composed for the double piped reed instrument of the Roman *tibicen* was probably not only original, but quite different from that written for the Athenian *aulos*.[63]

At least by the first century BCE actors were wearing the tragic and comic mask (Cic. *De Or.* 2.193, 3.221), and generically appropriate footwear: the *coturnus* or raised boot for tragedy, the *soccus* or slipper for comedy. Some have suggested that masks were worn from the beginning of Roman drama.[64] From 56 BCE there is evidence of a stage-curtain (*aulaeum*), which was rolled down at the beginning of a performance and raised to conceal the stage at the end.[65] An acting company (*grex*, literally 'flock') seems to have included a *choragus*, responsible for the costumes (and possibly also the props).[66] Elaborate costuming was normal in tragedy; the *fabula praetexta* featured characters wearing the purple-bordered toga of a Roman magistrate. In the *fabula palliata*, those taking the roles of free men wore the *pallium* or 'Greek cloak' over a tunic, slave characters wore a sleeveless tunic, short cloak and red wig, and 'free-born women' a full-length tunic or gown beneath a woman's cloak or *palla*. Little is known of the costuming of the *fabula togata*, but apparently the Roman toga was worn by appropriate figures. In both tragedy and comedy, specialist roles (soldiers, sailors, travellers, shepherds, kings, queens) required specialist costuming. All actors in tragedy, comedy, *praetextae* and the Atellan farce seem to have been male. Frequently, too, the same actors performed both tragedy and comedy; these forms were never the separate institutions they were in Greece. The plays (especially the prologues of Terence) provide evidence of considerable theatrical rivalry between companies or *greges* of actors, managed by their leading actor, whose slaves in some cases they may have been (Plaut. *Cist.* 782–5) .

Acting itself seems to have been a virtuoso performance in a self-consciously 'grand' or 'comic' style, involving highly expressive movement, stance and gesture, as well as power and nuance of voice. They, like the dramatists themselves, played for the favourable judgement of an audience, who were quite explicitly represented by the comic writers as 'judges' (*iudices*) of the performance (e.g. Ter. *Ad.* 4). Claques (*fautores*) supporting particular actors are known from Plautus' day (*Amph.* 65–85), and audience response was often noisy and disruptive. The Latin word for that 'audience', *spectatores* (*spectatores, plaudite*, 'audience, your applause', Plaut. *Curc.* 729),[67] defines it as a body of 'viewers' not 'listeners'. And what those Roman *spectatores* necessarily wanted and received in increasing quantity and splendour – at the theatre, amphitheatre and triumphal or funeral procession – was spectacle:

> si foret in terris, rideret Democritus, seu
> diuersum confusa genus panthera camelo
> siue elephans albus uulgi conuerteret ora;
> spectaret populum ludis attentius ipsis,
> ut sibi praebentem nimio spectacula plura;
> scriptores autem narrare putaret asello
> fabellam surdo. nam quae peruincere uoces
> eualuere sonum referunt quem nostra theatra?
> Garganum mugire putes nemus aut mare Tuscum,
> tanto cum strepitu ludi spectantur et artes,
> diuitiae peregrinae, quibus oblitus actor
> cum stetit in scaena, concurrit dextera laeuae.
> 'dixit adhuc aliquid?' 'nil sane.' 'quid placet ergo?'
> 'laena Tarentino uiolas imitata ueneno.'
>
> (Horace *Epistles* 2.1.194–207)

> Were he on earth, Democritus would laugh, whether
> Some mongrel breed of camel-crossed-with-panther
> Or a white elephant enticed the crowd's eye;
> He'd watch the people more keenly than the shows
> As providing far the greater spectacle;
> He'd think the playwrights were telling their tale
> To a deaf ass. For what voices have prevailed
> To drown the din echoing from our theatres?
> You'd think the Garganus forest or Tuscan sea roared,
> So great is the noise when they view the shows, art-works
> And foreign finery, plastered with which the actor
> Steps on stage to the crashing of right hand with left.
> 'Has he said something yet?' 'Nothing.' 'Why the applause?'
> 'It's that violet cloak dyed in Tarentum.'

The Horatian commentary is prejudicial. But it points to a consistently attested emphasis in Roman cultural and theatrical practice.

Cicero reported to his friend Marcus Marius that, at the opening of Pompey's theatre, the entrance of Agamemnon in Accius' *Clytaemestra* was accompanied by 600 mules and in *Equos Troianus*, 'Trojan Horse' (by Naevius?), 3,000 wine-bowls were used (*Fam.* 7.12). The audience, if not Cicero, loved it. A generation later Livy, as observed above, writes of the theatre's 'madness (*insania*) scarcely able to be supported by opulent kingdoms' (7.2.13).

The theatrical space

Yet for almost two centuries after Rome's first attested drama, until 55 BCE, all plays performed at the *ludi* in Rome were staged on temporary wooden structures, erected for the duration of the *ludi scaenici* (Tac. *Ann.* 14.20) in the Roman Forum or at the site of the appropriate temple (that of Magna Mater, Flora or Apollo), or, occasionally, in the Circus Maximus.[68] Both the wide, deep, raised stage (*pulpitum*)[69] and the stage-building (*scaena*) with its roofing and painted scenery-panels would have been of wood. The facade of the stage-building (*scaenae frons*) featured (generally) three doorways, which not only led conveniently to the actors' quarters but could represent three houses, with the central door (*ualua regia*) often indicating in tragedy the main entrance to the royal palace. Tiers of wooden seating would have been erected for the audience, some members of which might sit on the ground or watch the play standing. The wealthier Greek cities of southern Italy and Sicily had stone theatres dating from the fifth or fourth centuries, and by the end of the second century BCE several Italian towns had acquired their own permanent stone-built theatre.[70] But Rome had to wait until the dying days of the republic for its 200-year dramatic tradition to receive a permanent theatre.

Even so, aristocratic competitiveness ensured that some of the temporary theatrical structures were extremely lavish and ornate, and by the late republic such features as *trompe l'oeil* scene-painting and awnings (*uelaria*) to protect the audience from the sun were common. The erection of temporary wooden theatres continued even after the construction of Pompey's theatre (Vitr. 5.5.7) – and not simply because of the volume of theatrical business. Indeed immediately upon the construction of Pompey's theatre (52 BCE) Curio's double wooden theatre was erected, consisting of two hinged theatres arranged back to back. Spectators could see dramatic performances in the morning, and in the afternoon, when the theatres had been turned around to form an amphitheatre, they could watch gladiatorial fighting (Pliny *HN* 36.116–20). This novel concept ensured that Curio's wooden theatre lasted longer than most: certainly at least for a year (Cic. *Fam.* 8.2.1).

The delay in the introduction of the stone theatre to Rome requires comment. Attempts were made to build a permanent theatre at Rome in 179, 174 and 154 BCE.[71] They all failed. The censorial commission of 154 BCE almost succeeded. The stone theatre commissioned near the Lupercal (Vell. Pat. 1.15.3) was reaching completion three years later when it was knocked down by order of the senate.[72] It would be a hundred years before the next (and successful) attempt was made. The reasons for this reluctance on the part of Rome's elite to accept a permanent theatre in Rome are not difficult to divine. Although the annual recurrence and frequency of the *ludi scaenici* underscored their centrality to Roman culture, they constituted in that culture an ambiguous social force.[73] They may have served to ensure the linguistic hegemony of Latin and, through the works of certain playwrights, even promoted the values of Rome's elite,[74] but the theatres in which the *ludi* were performed became places associated, in the rigid ideology of Rome's aristocracy, with immorality and idleness. A stone theatre, it was claimed, would provide a permanent breeding-ground for vice.[75]

Perhaps more to the point is what remained unsaid: a stone structure would diminish the senate's control over the theatre itself. The constant construction and enforced dismantling of theatrical structures confirmed the senate's authority in theatrical matters.[76] A permanent theatre or group of theatres might not only erode that authority but damage the senate's authority *per se*. Theatres were places where 'the judgement and will of the Roman people in public matters' (*de re publica populi Romani iudicium ac uoluntas*, Cic. *Sest.* 106) could be, and in the late republic often were,[77] directly expressed. Inevitably, the resistance of Rome's elite to the construction of a permanent context for such expression was long and hard.

A further problem of control arose from the nature of the audience. Admission to the scenic games was free. The membership of Rome's theatrical audience, unlike that of Athens, came from all sections of the urban community: patrician, plebeian, aristocratic, base, free-born, slave, male, female, Roman, Italian, non-Italian – Asian, African, Gallic, Greek.[78] Its size is much disputed. A lower estimate restricts it in the early period to perhaps 1,600 to 2,000 per performance,[79] especially in the cases of those plays performed in the more restricted acting spaces in front of Rome's temples. The late republican Theatre of Pompey and the Augustan Theatre of

Marcellus seated (at the most conservative estimate)[80] 11,000 and 13,000 *spectatores* respectively. The temporary Theatre of Scaurus erected in 58 BCE seated even more.[81] But even in the late third and early second century BCE, since plays were often repeated, a much larger audience than the conjectured 2,000 could be reached. Initially the audience were seated unselfconsciously without regard for social status, but at the *Ludi Romani* of 194 BCE, on instructions from the censors and at the instigation of Scipio Africanus, special seating was set aside by the curule aediles for members of the senate (in the orchestra, between the stage and the wooden tiers), to the dismay of the plebeian *spectatores*.[82]

From that point onwards the theatre was a mirror of the city's social hierarchy. Laws were passed at different times restricting various sections of the theatre to particular social groups, the most famous being the Roscian Law of 67 BCE assigning the first fourteen rows in the theatre to members of the equestrian class. Although the Roscian Law was unpopular (Plut. *Cic.* 13), Augustan and later legislation went further, transforming the theatre into a place where Rome's complex structures of power were visibly – and, because visibly, vulnerably – made manifest. Such legislation made more visible and more vulnerable the very social hierarchy it was designed to confirm. The legal restrictions placed (perhaps from the early days of the Roman theatre) on actors, whose lines sometimes mentioned and in the late republic targeted prominent political figures, especially in the audience itself (Pompey, Julius Caesar, Nero),[83] were only one of the overt displays of deep cultural anxiety about the political and social power of the theatre itself. At Rome plays were never simply just plays. They were regular exhibitions of a complex political, social and religious system, defined by patronage and unequal distributions of power, the very structures of which became more patently, completely and strictly displayed as Rome's dominion expanded and her political and social institutions weakened and (in some prominent instances) collapsed.

Part II

THE EVOLUTION OF
ROMAN TRAGEDY

2

FOUNDING FATHERS

The appropriation of Greece

Livius Andronicus

> nam et Odyssia Latina est sic tamquam opus aliquod
> Daedali et Liuianae fabulae non satis dignae quae
> iterum legantur.
>
> (Cicero *Brutus* 71)

> For the Latin *Odyssey* is like a work of Daedalus and
> the plays of Livius are not worth a second reading.

The father of Roman tragedy was a Greek. Livy's attempts to make
this fact invisible underscore Augustan discomfort.[1] The post-
Augustan Suetonius has no difficulty in calling Roman drama's
founding father (and Ennius) at least *semigraecus*, 'half-Greek' (*Gram.*
1.2). Lucius Livius Andronicus was born in the Greek area of southern
Italy known as Magna Graecia perhaps *c.* 290 BCE.[2] Captured at
Tarentum in 272 BCE during Rome's 'conquest' of the area,
Andronicus became a slave in the household of the Livii Salinatores,
apparently serving as tutor to the children. After manumission he
acquired the status of *ciuis libertinus*, 'freedman-citizen', and took the
nomen Livius and the *praenomen* Lucius. Perhaps at this time he established his own school, since Suetonius talks of him teaching both at
home (*domi*) and outside (*foris*).[3] At what stage he wrote his way into
Roman celebrity by authoring that 'most antique poem',[4] his epic,
Odusia, a Latin adaptation of Homer's *Odyssey* in (native Italian)[5]
Saturnian verses, is unknown. If, as most think and the ancient testimony implies, *Odusia* precedes the dramas, Livius' epic constitutes the
first attested literary translation of a literary work.[6]

The cultural and literary significance of Livius' *Odusia* was substantial and wide-ranging. Prior to the time of Livius, in so far as there
was a circulation of books in Rome, that circulation would have been

small and of Greek, not Latin, books. *Odusia* began the process which changed all that, and not only fostered a specifically Roman literary culture, while simultaneously celebrating Greek texts, but promoted the hegemony of Latin as the local literary language. And, through its archaising and poetising diction, it established the alterity of Latin poetic language, its separation from everyday writing and discourse. *Odusia*'s success as a school text (it was used even in Horace's day: *Ep.* 2.1.69–75) made its cultural impact secure, and complemented the analogous impact of his dramatic work, all of which assumes a high level of cultural literacy in the audiences of Rome. Unfortunately, like his dramatic work, Livius' epic survives only in fragments.

The year 240 BCE is the traditional date for the beginning of Roman drama, since this was the performance date of the first attested Roman play. That play (*fabula* – most likely a tragedy)[7] was scripted by Livius (Cic. *Brut.* 72),[8] who clearly translated in a more than literal sense the theatrical traditions of Tarentum to Rome.[9] The play was produced presumably at the *Ludi Romani* held in 240 BCE to celebrate Rome's victory in the long war with Carthage, known as the First Punic War (264–41 BCE). The *fabula* probably featured Livius as one of the actors, since Livy tells us that he acted in his own plays (*suorum carminum actor*, 7.2.8),[10] and that he continued to do so even when his voice had lost some of its clarity. Although the title of the 240 BCE work is not known, several titles of both tragedies and comedies have survived to provide some indication of Livius' literary range and focus. Among the titles are those of (possibly) ten tragedies: *Achilles, Aegistus, Aiax Mastigophorus* ('Ajax the Whip-Bearer'), *Andromeda, Antiopa* (?), *Danae, Equos Troianus* ('Trojan Horse'), *Hermiona, Ino* and *Tereus*. Varro also testifies to an eleventh tragedy by Livius featuring the Greek hero, Teucer (*LL* 7.3), and his return to Salamis.

The tragedies were all Latin adaptations of Greek originals, an appropriation of Greek plots, dramatic forms and metres for a Roman audience. The appropriation of dramatic subjects was highly selective. There is a marked preference for plays concerned with the Trojan cycle (six out of the eleven), as if Livius were writing dramatic additions to, or expansions of, his *Odusia* (which itself offered a more dramatic narrative than was to be found in Homer), and appealing to a burgeoning interest at Rome in the city's mythical Trojan origins. Rome's myth of Trojan origin was archaic (it may go back to the sixth century BCE),[11] and had recently been used politically (in 263 BCE) to secure an alliance with the Sicilian town of Segesta against Carthage (Zonaras 8.9.12). The *Equos Troianus* may even have been chosen as a subject (and Naevius was to choose this subject, too) because of a purported connection between the Trojan Horse and the contemporary Roman ritual of the 'October Horse' (Festus 190L).[12] Two of the remaining five plays are bound up with Perseus: *Andromeda* and *Danae*, and the latter certainly had aetiological and cultural potential (see discussion of Naevius' *Danae* below). The titles of Livius' plays alone dictate that love, lust, rage and madness were dominant themes – together with their attendant conflicts and disasters.

Livius' favourite tragic models seem to have been Sophocles and Euripides, although what kinds of texts of the various plays were in circulation and available to him (and his immediate successors), whether they derived from the Dionysiac actors' guilds complete with interpolations,[13] and what kinds of performance of Greek tragedy he might have witnessed in or outside Rome (in the Greek cities of southern Italy or Sicily), is unknown. What is known is that at most one of his attributed plays (the doubtful *Antiopa*) addressed that perennial subject of Greek, especially Sophoclean, tragedy: Thebes.

Whether Livius was the first to have composed Latin verses in Greek metres is unclear,[14] but the surviving tragic fragments reveal his successful Latin adaptation of Greek iambic and trochaic verses in dialogue and the use of trochaic and cretic patterns in what seems to be an actor's monody. Indeed one of the differences between Livius' plays and those of his Greek models seems to have been the larger presence of *cantica* or sung monodies for his actors. Livy's brief notice on Livius' role in early Roman drama underscores the monodic element, since he comments on the early dramatist's fading voice and his resulting introduction of a boy to sing the actor's own *cantica* while Livius himself performed the gestures to it (7.2.8–9). This increased monodic element in Roman tragedy (in comparison with Greek tragedy) is probably due less to Livius' own taste, more to the already existing musical emphasis in the *ludi scaenici*. Livius seems to have enhanced this musical emphasis by retaining in his tragedies something jettisoned in Roman comedy, a chorus: his *Ino*, for example, is reported to have contained a chorus who sing a hymn to Diana.[15] Naevius, Ennius and the rest were to continue the musical emphasis and retain the chorus.

Fragments survive from eight of Livius' tragedies. All Roman tragic texts prior to Seneca are fragmentary. The reader needs to be aware that the reconstruction of tragic action, even in the case of plays or playwrights where substantial fragments exist, is necessarily conjectural. Assistance is sometimes provided by such ancient summaries of mythic narratives as are to found in Hyginus' *Genealogiae* (usually titled *Fabulae*) or Apollodorus' *Library*, but the problem of deciding

the relevance of such narratives is always substantial, as is that of determining the staged tragic action. Fragments from four of Livius'
tragedies follow. Notable immediately is the variety in Livian tragic
style from the plain to the self-consciously 'high'.

Achilles

The plot of the play is unknown. It could have concerned any of the
myths surrounding Achilles. Some suggest the play dealt with the
conflict between Agamemnon and Achilles in Homer's *Iliad*; others
with the Deidamia episode on Scyros.[16]

Frag. 1

si malas imitabo, tum tu pretium pro noxa dabis.

If bitches are my model, you'll pay for the wrong.

The metre is iambic senarius, the standard dialogue line of Roman
plays. If Achilles is speaking, the context is possibly a scene on Scyros
or the quarrel with Agamemnon as narrated by Homer in *Iliad* 1 and
9. Such are, of course, mere guesses. Little can be gleaned here except
Livius' insertion of the Roman legal term *noxa* with its firm nuance
for a third-century audience,[17] the writer's penchant for alliteration
(common in early Latin verse), the plain diction, the stylised nature of
the line (note the balance: *m...m...t...t...pr...pr...*), and the staccato effect which would have attended its delivery.

Frag. 2

haut ut quem Chiro in Pelio docuit ocri

Not like the man Chiron taught on craggy Pelion

Again, plain diction, but this time a more nuanced alliterative
pattern produces a vigorous and speakable line. The metre is again
iambic senarius. The allocation of the line to Livius is sure, but to
Achilles uncertain.

Aegistus

The plot of *Aegistus* seems to have concerned the return of
Agamemnon to his kingdom and wife Clytemnestra after the Trojan

war, and his subsequent murder at the hands of his wife and her usurping lover, Aegisthus. The most celebrated dramatisation of this plot was Aeschylus' *Agamemnon*. The *Aegisthus* or a possible *Clytaemestra* of Sophocles may also have been a 'source-text'. Frag. 7 below is positioned as frag. iii in Klotz.

Frags 1 and 2

> nam ut Pergama
> accensa et praeda per participes aequiter
> partita est

> For after Pergamum
> Was torched and the prizes parcelled fairly
> Among the participants

> tum autem lasciuom Nerei simum pecus
> ludens ad cantum classem lustratur ...

> Then the playful snub-nosed herd of Nereus
> Circles the fleet frolicking to our song ...

The subject matter of the above iambic senarii and the reminiscences of the lines in Seneca's *Agamemnon* (421–2, 449–55) point to their likely origin in a messenger's speech describing the storm which hit the Greek fleet after its departure from Troy. Again an archaic poet's penchant for pronounced alliterative patterning is evident, sometimes pursued with resulting redundancies or (more positively) etymological play, and sometimes of a mannered chiastic kind – *l...c...c...l* (frag. 2, line 2). The periphrastic description of dolphins, with its series of modifiers, indexes a self-consciously tumid style. It was later imitated and transcended by Pacuvius (*Teucer* frag. 9).

Frag. 3

> nemo haece uostrum ruminetur mulieri.[18]

> None of you should rehash this to the woman.

Perhaps the 'woman' is Cassandra, and Agamemnon is giving instructions that she be spared overt recollections of the Greek sack of Troy. *Ruminetur*, 'rehash' – literally 'chew the cud', is a striking word, which occasioned comment from the grammarians and ensured the line's survival.

Frag. 4

sollemnitusque deo dicat laudem et lubens.

Solemnly and gladly let him praise the god.

The text is uncertain (I have combined the emendations of Mueller 1885 and Bothe 1834), but the line may concern Agamemnon's ritual thanksgiving to the gods for his safe return.

Frags 5 and 6

... in sedes conlocat se regias:
Clutemestra iuxtim, tertias natae occupant.

... He seats himself on the royal throne:
By him Clytemnestra; the daughters take third place.

ipsus se in terram saucius fligit cadens.

The man himself falls wounded, crashing to the ground.

These two fragments seem to come from a description of Agamemnon's murder in the palace probably (given Aeschylean precedent and Senecan *imitatio*) spoken by Cassandra during a vision of the bloody events taking place inside the palace. The lines show that, when the occasion demanded it, Livian language could be concrete, sharp, evocative, without any trace of tragic tumidity.

Frag. 7

iamne oculos specie laetauisti optabili?

Have you now pleasured your eyes with the desirable sight?

The context is uncertain, but the desirable sight seems to be that of Agamemnon's corpse. The speaker is perhaps Aegisthus, addressing Clytemnestra, or Clytemnestra, addressing Aegisthus.

Frag. 8

quin quod parere <mihi> uos maiestas mea
procat, toleratis temploque hanc deducitis?

Endure the orders my majesty demands
And lead this woman from the sacred precinct.

Presumably Aegisthus is speaking, instructing his men to take Cassandra or Electra from the altar or sacred precinct (*templum*) where she has taken refuge. Notice again (see *Achilles* frag. 1) the importation of a Roman concept, that of *maiestas* – the 'majesty' of a Roman magistrate or of the Roman people or state, the diminution or violation of which constituted high treason. The periphrastic language seems self-consciously grand, even pompous.

Aiax Mastigophorus

Livius' play may well have been based on Sophocles' *Ajax*, to which the Greek word *Mastigophoros* was attached in some manuscripts. The plot presumably dealt with the anger of Ajax over (as he saw it) the injustice of not being awarded the arms of Achilles and with his subsequent madness and suicide. Both fragments below are in dialogue iambic senarii.

Frag. 1

mirum uidetur quod sit factum iam diu?

Does it amaze because it's now an ancient deed?

Plain language for a plain question? This fragment may well have been part of a denigration of Ajax' accomplishments in the Trojan War, now regarded as ancient history.

Frag. 2

praestatur uirtuti laus, set gelu multo ocius
uerno tabescit.

Praise is vouchsafed to virtue, but melts far quicker
Than ice in spring.

This fragment, on the other hand (the text of which however is uncertain), seems positive towards Ajax, apparently lamenting the disappearance of the esteem accorded the great hero's *uirtus*. The line is perhaps spoken by Teucer, Ajax' brother, and seems to be a 'translation' of Sophocles' *Ajax* 1266–7, where Teucer, before Ajax' dead body, laments 'how quickly gratitude (*charis*) to the dead vanishes among men'. Livius' line is both more imagistic and more overtly emotional than the restrained Sophoclean words, and more self-consciously homiletic. And its homiletic quality focuses on a core Roman aristocratic value. Of course, *uirtus* in the Latin of any period is a wide-ranging term, as well as a core value of the Roman male elite. It would certainly have included martial valour as displayed by Ajax, his endurance, bravery, constancy, but it also connoted in a larger sense 'manliness' and aristocratic 'nobility'. The best commentary on its role as core value for the aristocracy and the state may found in the monody of Alcumena in Plautus' tragicomedy, *Amphitruo* (648–53), written perhaps c. 190 BCE. In it *uirtus* is represented as protecting *libertas*, *salus*, *uita*, *res*, *parentes*, *patria*, *prognati* ('liberty', 'security', 'life', 'property', 'parents', 'fatherland', 'progeny').[19] Livius' own *Ajax* may well have been a celebration of aristocratic *uirtus* through a dramatisation of the consequences of its disesteem. The homiletic quality of Roman tragedy, which was to reach its climax and mature dramatic deployment in Senecan *sententiae*, is already evident in these early fragments.

Equos Troianus

The play dealt with the famous story of the Trojan Horse, which was pulled into Troy by the Trojans themselves and brought about the downfall of the city.

Frag. 1

Da mihi hasce opes,
Quas peto, quas precor:
Porrige, opitula!

Give to me this help here,
Which I seek, which I beg.
Provide it, assist me.

The lyric outburst above (a combination of cretics and trochaics) is probably from an actor's monody. The metre is Greek, but the language, repetition, synonyms, alliteration and colon structure derive from the rituals of Roman prayer.[20]

Most of Livius' plays were presumably written and performed during the two decades between the First and Second Punic Wars. Whether they were part of the reason behind the visit of Hiero II of Syracuse to Rome in 237 BCE for the express purpose of 'viewing the shows' (*ad ludos spectandos*, Eutropius 3.1–2) is unclear.[21] They were clearly sufficiently successful not to interfere with the political career of a later member of Livius' patronal household (perhaps the son or even grandson of his original patron), Marcus Livius Salinator, who was elected consul in 219 BCE on the eve of Rome's momentous conflict with Hannibal. The next evidence we have concerning Livius concerns an important appearance in the year 207 BCE. This was the year of the second consulship of Marcus Livius Salinator, who was about to face Hannibal's brother, Hasdrubal, in battle at the River Metaurus in the north-east of Italy. Prior to Salinator's departure a religious procession took place at Rome designed to appease and win the favour of Juno Regina, at which thrice nine virgins sang an expiatory hymn, a *partheneion*, composed by Salinator's protégé (and probably ex-tutor), Livius Andronicus (Livy 27.37.11–15), *Livius poeta*, as Livy calls him (27.37.7). The historian's disparaging comments on this hymn (Livy 27.37.13) –

carmen ... illa tempestate forsitan laudabile rudibus ingeniis, nunc abhorrens et inconditum, si referatur

a song ... meriting praise perhaps to the untrained minds of that period, but, if repeated today, abhorrent and uncouth

– reflect the self-congratulatory prejudices of the Augustan era. Clearly the song was deemed a material success (the expiation of Juno was attested by Salinator's victory over Hasdrubal), and Andronicus himself received public acknowledgement through the allocation – in his honour – of Minerva's Temple on the Aventine for the official meetings of the *Collegium* or 'Guild' of *scribae* (writers) and *histriones* (actors) (Festus 446–8L).

This organisation of 'writers' (playwrights, certainly, but also 'government clerks', *librarii*) and 'actors', the foundation of which seems to predate the 207 event, was remarkable for (apparently) being free of individual private patronage. It seems to have been modelled to some extent on the contemporary Greek Guilds of the 'Artisans of Dionysus', which, like the *Collegium*, included actors and authors but, unlike the *Collegium*, included every other type of 'theatrical' as well (flautists, cithara players, mask-makers, costumiers, etc.).[22] Although such a union of playwrights and actors would have indicated to Roman eyes an artisan status for the dramatic poet (notably, the later *Collegium Poetarum* seems to have excluded actors), the honorific allocation of Minerva's temple for its meetings, enacted through senatorial decree, was no small index of contemporary respect for Livius himself. Livy's comments, however, do reflect a negative evaluation of Livius' poetic works by the intellectual elite of late republican and Augustan Rome, which includes both Cicero and Horace (*Ep.* 2.1.69–75). Cicero's comments in this chapter's epigraph seem to suggest that Livius' plays were not performed in his day.[23] Livius even failed to make the list of the top ten Roman comic dramatists compiled about 100 BCE by Volcacius Sedigitus (Gellius 15.24). But Horace also points to his own contemporaries' admiration of Livius and the latter's canonic status in the schools of the *grammatici*. Virgil seems to have had several debts to Livius, including to his tragedies.[24] His tragedies – or at least their reputation – sufficiently impressed Suetonius for the Hadrianic biographer in *De Poetis* to call him *tragoediarum scriptor clarus*, 'a distinguished writer of tragedies' (Jer. *Chron.* ad Ol. 148, 1–2).

Gnaeus Naevius

> immortales mortales si foret fas flere,
> flerent diuae Camenae Naeuium poetam.
> itaque postquam est Orci traditus thesauro,
> obliti sunt Romae loquier lingua Latina.
> (Aulus Gellius *Noctes Atticae* 1.24.2)[25]

> If immortals were allowed to mourn mortals
> The divine Camenae would mourn poet Naevius.
> So, after his delivery to the vault of Death,
> They forgot in Rome how to speak in Latin.

The second father of Roman tragedy and the founder of the *fabula praetexta*, Gnaeus Naevius, was not a Greek. He was a Campanian from Capua or the Capua region, a plebeian with Roman citizenship (*sine suffragio*, without a vote)[26] or at least Latin rights. He tells us in his epic *Bellum Poenicum* ('Punic War'), that he fought on the side of Rome in the First Punic War (Gell. 17.21.45). That military service puts his birth date perhaps *c.* 280 BCE; and, since the confused story of his altercation with the Roman aristocratic family of the Metelli and subsequent punishment by them (perhaps exile) locates that punishment and his death in the last few years of the third century, likely dates for his life are *c.* 280–01 BCE. The testimony of Jerome's *Chronicle*, which is generally unreliable but seems in this case to derive ultimately from Varro's *Liber de Poetis*,[27] records his death in exile at Utica on the north coast of Africa in the year 201 BCE. Like Livius, Naevius was also the author of comedies and of an epic in Saturnians, and it was as an epicist and a comic dramatist that he was later primarily celebrated. Indeed whereas only some six or seven titles of tragedies and two of *praetextae* are known, thirty-four titles of comedies have survived. In the canon of Volcacius Sedigitus he appears as the third best comic writer, and it is as a *comicus* and an enemy of the Metelli that Suetonius remembers him in *De Poetis* (Jer. *Chron.*, ad Ol. 144, 3).

Naevius may have been a member of the audience watching Livius' first play at the *Ludi Romani* of 240 BCE. At any rate from Varro we learn that Naevius' earliest dramatic production took place a mere five years later, in 235 BCE (Gell. 17.21.45). Clearly influenced by Livius' dramatic compositions, especially his predecessor's predilection for *cantica*, Naevius nevertheless was responsible for two major innovations: first, the practice of *contaminatio*, the fusion of two or more 'source plays' into one – a practice on which Terence (*And.* 18) comments in respect of Naevius' comedies, but which is reflected in his epic (which combines Homer's *Iliad* and his *Odyssey*) and surely in his tragedies too; second, his creation of a new kind of serious drama, the historical play known as the *fabula praetexta* and classified by later grammarians as a subspecies of tragedy itself.

In a sense Naevius did to Livian tragedy what he did to Livian epic: he Romanised it. But he Romanised not simply its subject matter (as he did in epic), dramatising in his *praetextae* Roman history itself, but also (at least in some of his *tragoediae*) its form: for *contaminatio* is a thoroughly Roman practice, signalling the city's predilection for merging diverse ethnicities into one Roman state or diverse items of cultural plunder into single tokens of power. And just as in his *Bellum Poenicum* he epicised both legendary and contemporary history, so in his *praetextae* he dramatised not only Rome's foundation myth in his *Romulus* or *Lupus* ('Wolf'), but also a contemporary historical event, the defeat of the Gallic Insubres at Clastidium (modern Casteggio) in northern Italy in 222 BCE by Marcus Claudius Marcellus, who also performed the rare feat of winning the *spolia opima* by killing the enemy commander in single combat.[28] Theatricalising contemporary historical figures was an even bolder move than transforming them into epic heroes. At least in a triumphal procession the *triumphator* was to a large extent his own playwright with substantial control (especially in the planning stages) of the spectacle. In a *fabula praetexta* representation of the *triumphator* was in the hands of others.

The titles of six tragedies of Naevius are known: *Aesiona*, *Danae*, *Equos Troianus* ('Trojan Horse'), *Hector Proficiscens* ('Hector Departing'), *Iphigenia* and *Lucurgus*. A seventh play, *Andromacha*, is less securely attributed to Naevius.[29] Again the majority of the plays (five out of seven) feature plots from the Trojan cycle. This may be bound up not only with dramatic rivalry with Livius but with increased Roman interest in the city's Trojan origins. The interest in Troy may have peaked during the Second Punic War (218–01), which involved a sustained conflict with the Macedonian king, Philip V, a self-proclaimed descendant of Achilles, and with Greek cities in Italy sympathetic to Hannibal. Under the year 212 BCE Livy (25.12.3–8) reports an oracle specifically addressing the Romans as *Troiugenae*, 'Troy-born'. Naevius' own *Bellum Poenicum*, which deals with the First Punic War, includes a section on 'Trojan' Aeneas, from whom the patrician families of the Iulii and the Aemilii were to claim descent,[30] and whose connection with Rome, as already noted, may have been established three hundred years earlier. Fabius Pictor's Greek history of Rome (Cic. *Div.* 1.43), Ennius' *Annales*, and Cato's *Origines*, written in the decades following Naevius' death, similarly reference Aeneas. But, while both historians (Fabius and Cato) postulate several generations between Aeneas and Rome's foundation, the poets Naevius and Ennius, in whose epics Aeneas figures as Romulus' grandfather (Serv. Auct. *ad Aen.* 1.273), present Aeneas as much closer to the city's 'beginnings'.

Two Naevian titles, *Equos Troianus* and *Danae* (the latter may also have been concerned with 'origins', see below), were titles of plays by Livius, and, unless there has been some confusion in the *testimonia* here, indicate something of a theatrical rivalry between Naevius and his predecessor – one which the evidence suggests that Naevius may have won. His *Equos Troianus* was probably the version restaged at one of the great cultural moments of the late republic, the dedication of Pompey's Theatre in 55 BCE. If so, it was an extraordinary tribute to the third-century dramatist.

Most of the 70 or so lines to have survived come from two plays, *Danae* and *Lucurgus*. Commentary on the fragments from these plays follows. The place of the fragments in the dramatic action of each play is uncertain. The reader should note that I have included in *Lucurgus* a line (frag. 19) attributed to Naevius, but not specifically to that play.

Danae

The myth dramatised in this play concerned the seduction of Danae, daughter of Acrisius, king of Argos, by Jupiter in the form of a shower of gold. Acrisius, in fear of an oracle which foretold that he would be slain by his grandson, imprisoned his daughter Danae. Jupiter visited her in her prison, and she conceived a son, Perseus, by him. Mother and son were then cast out to sea in a chest and drifted to the island of Seriphus, where they were rescued. Possible sources for this play are the *Acrisius*, *Danae* and *Larisaei* ('Larissans') of Sophocles and the *Danae* of Euripides – and, of course, the *Danae* of Livius. It is probably a 'contaminated' play.[31]

As with Livius, the subject of Danae may have had aetiological and political import. According to some accounts (Virg. *Aen.* 7. 409–10 and Servius *ad loc.*, Sil. It. 1.660–1), Danae was credited with founding Ardea just south of Rome, and was also associated (through the death of her son Argus) with the Argiletum, the main street which leads from the Subura into the Roman Forum (Serv. Auct. *ad Aen.* 8.345). Immigrants from Ardea made up a substantial section of the citizens of Saguntum, the Spanish city taken by Hannibal in 219 BCE (Sil. It. 1.660–1). A recent speculative interpretation of the *Danae* fragments would have the play set on Seriphus or (better and more radically) in Latium, and ascribe to the play an overtly political function of galvanising Roman public opinion in the aftermath of the fall of Saguntum.[32] Others, more conventionally, set the play in Argos. The order of these fragments is totally uncertain.

Frag. 1

omnes formidant homines eius ualentiam.

All mankind dreads his power.

This strong iambic line is generally taken to refer to the power of Jupiter or of Amor, the god of love. Some think that it may come from a divine prologue, perhaps spoken by Mercury.[33] If so, the prologue of Plautus' *Amphitruo* may be alluding to it.[34]

Frag. 2

suo sonitu claro fulgoriuit Iuppiter.

Jupiter flashed with his own loud noise.

This standard dialogue line could come from anywhere. Again it might be early in the play, perhaps from a prologue describing Jupiter at the beginning of his erotic visit, or it might be a description of a response by Jupiter to Danae's plea for help (frag. 10),[35] or ...

Frag. 3

... quae quondam fulmine icit Iuppiter

Which Jupiter once struck with his thunderbolt

The reference is unclear. Some emend *quae* to *quam* to make the allusion one to the Theban queen Semele, penetrated by Jupiter as a thunderbolt.

Frag. 4

contemplo placide formam et faciem uirginis.

I calmly examine the virgin's form and face.

Some conjecture that this might have been spoken by the divine speaker of the prologue (Mercury?), or by Jupiter himself.[36] The 'virgin' is presumably Danae. Typical of archaic verse is the use of alliterative and assonantal effects *(pla...pla...f...f)* to bind the line. They give it a tensile dramatic strength.

Frag. 5

eam nunc esse inuentam probris compotem scis.

You know that she was found now engaged in filth.

The subject is clearly the discovery of Danae's 'lewdness'. If the metre is bacchiac, the line presumably comes from a *canticum* or actor's monody.

Frag. 6

desubito famam tollunt, si quam solam uidere in uia.

If they have seen a woman alone in the street,
They raise a scandal at once.

Another line (an iambic octonarius) accompanied by music, drawing attention to the ease with which a woman's reputation is destroyed. Assonance and alliteration are again strongly evident.

Frags 7 and 8

excidit orationis omnis confidentia.

All confidence of speech fell away.

... auri rubeo fonte lauere <me> memini manum.

... I remember washing my hand in a red fountain of gold.

These two trochaic septenarii would have been delivered, but not sung, to the accompaniment of music. Fragment 7 may refer to the speechlessness of Danae before her father, or before Jupiter during his erotic visit. Female speechlessness became something of a topos in descriptions of rape (see, e.g., Ovid *Fas.* 2.613–14,797–8). This and fragment 8 may have come from a speech or speeches of Danae describing her experience of Jupiter's sexual onset. It may even have been presented as a dream after the 'model' of Sophocles' *Acrisius*.[37] Again worthy of note is the sonal play: the chiastic force of fragment 7 *...c...o...o...c*, and the run of fragment 8: *ri...ru...me...memi...man.* Emotionally disturbing events are given mannered form.

Frag. 9

... indigne exigor patria innocens.

... undeservedly I'm thrust from my fatherland – innocent.

Certainly spoken by Danae after her father's decree of punishment. The metre is uncertain (either iambic or trochaic).

Frag. 10

... manubias suppetat
pro me ...

... Let him request the thunderbolts
For me ...

In this obscure line *me* is perhaps Danae, seeking Jupiter's assistance.

Frag. 11

quin, ut quisque est meritus, praesens pretium pro factis ferat.[38]

Let each by his deserts receive present reward for his deeds.

Delivered again to music, the line (a trochaic septenarius) may have been delivered by Acrisius with reference to the punishment about to be meted out to Danae and her son. But the line could have been spoken by almost any of the play's characters, even Danae herself. Some boldly speculate on a reference here to Hannibal's capture of Saguntum, for which the Carthaginian will pay.[39] Notice the heavy alliteration (*q...q...p...p...p...f...f*), reminiscent of legal formulae which the line seeks to imitate and appropriate to the line's portentous tone. The ambivalence of *praesens* ('present', meaning both 'immediate' and 'in person') increases the injunction's force.

Naevius' dramatisation of the Danae myth shows an interest in moral dilemmas and the abuse of power, reflected in the surviving fragments, in which issues of sexual morality, reputation, moral deserts, justice, crime and punishment figure prominently. The dramatic diction used by Naevius is sharp and concrete, and alliterative and assonantal effects, not all of which have been explicitly noted above, have force and purpose. There are also issues of Roman collective identity involved in the playwright's decision to dramatise a Greek myth in which Rome's history and (possibly) current pressing military and political events are implicated. Certainly an aetiological and political approach to this play accords with Naevius' predilection to Romanise both epic and tragedy (the latter in the form of the *praetexta*), using inherited literary forms to focus on issues of national achievement and identity.

Lucurgus

The dramatic action of this play concerned the opposition of Lycurgus, a Thracian or Hellespontine king, to Liber/Dionysus and his Bacchic followers, as they travelled from Asia into Europe. Lycurgus captured or (in another version of the myth) killed the Bacchantes, and was punished horrifically for this. Aeschylus' tetralogy, *Lycurgeia*, probably provided source play(s) for Naevius' drama. The tetralogy concluded with a satyr play, entitled *Lycurgus*. Naevius' play seems to have featured a chorus of Bacchantes, with the action taking place before the palace of Lycurgus.

Frags 1 and 2

> tuos qui celsos terminos tutant ...
> Men who guard your border garrisons ...

> alte iubatos angues inlaesae gerunt.
> They hold high up crested snakes – unharmed.

The fragments above seem to come from a speech or speeches describing to Lycurgus the advance of the Bacchantes into his kingdom.

Frag. 3

... quaque incedunt, omnis aruas opterunt.[40]

... wherever they advance, they crush all the fields.

This may well belong to the same context as above. The line certainly seems to refer to the Bacchantes in their advance.

Frag. 4

suauisonum melos

mellifluous song

An apparent reference to the song of the Bacchantes and/or Liber, probably from a chorus.

Frags 5–7

uos, qui regalis corporis custodias
agitatis, ite actutum in frondiferos locos,
ingenio arbusta ubi nata sunt, non obsitu.

You to whom protection of the royal body
Falls, go at once to the leafy places
Where trees have grown by nature, not by sowing.

ducite
eo cum argutis linguis mutas quadrupedis.

Lead
Them there as mute beasts for all their sharp tongues.

alis sublimen altos saltus
inlicite ubi bipedes uolucres lino linquant lumina.[41]

Draw them on wings up high to other glades
Where two-legged birds are trapped and leave the light.

A series of instructions by Lycurgus to his bodyguard and others to find the Bacchantes, and to bind, gag, and ensnare them. Perhaps from the same speech or at least the same scene. The Greecising, periphrastic language and strong imagery are aspects of a deliberately pursued high tragic style.[42]

Frag. 8

utin uenatu uitulantis ex suis
lucis nos mittant poenis decoratas feris?

To expel us from their woods exulting
In the hunt, smartened by savage punishment?

The Bacchantes react to the news of Lycurgus' plans against them.

Frag. 9

pergite thyrsigerae Bacchae modo
Bacchico cum schemate.

Forward, Bacchantes with your wands,
In Bacchic manner and mien.

From a lyric passage (the metre is dactylic and trochaic tetrameters), perhaps from a choral passage delivered by the Bacchantes themselves or from a monody sung by Liber.

Frag. 10

ignotae iteris sumus,
tute scis.

We do not know the way,
You know it.

The Bacchantes ask the way.

Frag. 11

dic quo pacto eum potiti: pugnan an dolis?

Tell how you overpowered him: by fighting or guile?

Lycurgus asks his men how they captured Liber. The line would have been delivered to the accompaniment of music.

Frag. 12

ne ille mei feri ingeni <iram> atque animi acrem acrimoniam.

> He should not stir my savage nature's wrath and my mind's
> acrid acrimony.

The 'savage nature' above is presumably that of the tyrant-figure
Lycurgus, who most probably speaks this line concerning Liber
(= 'He').

Frag. 13

> caue sis tuam contendas iram contra cum ira Liberi.

> Please beware of matching your wrath with Liber's wrath.

Spoken to Lycurgus (accompanied by music – the metre is trochaic
septenarius) either by Liber himself or by another character, perhaps
a royal adviser. It could well have been a response to frag. 12 (also a
trochaic septenarius).

Frag. 14

> oderunt di homines iniuros.
> > egone an ille iniurie
> facimus?

> Gods loathe unjust men.
> > Is it me or him acting
> Unjustly?

The second part of the fragment seems attributable to Lycurgus in
response to the moral pronouncement of another character.

Frags 15–19

> sed quasi amnis celeris rapit, sed tamen inflexu flectitur

> But as a swift stream rushes but yet bends and twists

> iam ibi nos duplicat aduenientis ... timos pauos.[43]

> Then there terror, dread doubles us up as we approach.

Or (supplying *Liberi* with Warmington 2.128)

> Then there terror, dread of Liber's approach doubles us up.

nam<que> ut ludere laetantis inter se<se> uidimus
praeter amnem aquam creterris sumere ex fonte ...

For as we saw them playing joyfully among themselves
Across the stream, drawing water in bowls from the spring ...

pallis patagiis crocotis malacis mortualibus

In robes, gold stripes, saffron dresses, soft clothes of death

diabathra in pedibus habebat, erat amictus epicroco.

He had slippers on his feet, he wore a saffron dress.

The secure location of these fragments is especially difficult.
Warmington (2.132–5) refuses to place fragment 15 and assigns
16–19 to a description by the guards of the capture of the
Bacchantes earlier in the play. Fragments 16–19 certainly refer to
Lycurgus' men coming upon the Bacchantes, but the lines may
concern the later encounter when they are defeated by Liber and his
followers. Fragments 18 and 19 depict the Bacchantes and Liber in
their defining dress. Fragment 19 is not specifically attributed to
Lucurgus by the source, but may well be from this play.

Frag. 20

sine ferro pecua manibus ut ad mortem meant

As cattle go to death with no goad, led by hands

Perhaps a description of Lycurgus' men led to their death,
although Warmington (2.130–1) interprets this fragment as a
reference to the capture of the Bacchantes and thus places it earlier
in the play.

Frag. 21

ut uideam Volcani opera haec flammis fieri
flora

To see all this flowering in flame, courtesy
of Vulcan

Presumably spoken by Liber as he articulates his plans for the
punishment of Lycurgus.

Frag. 22

proinde huc Triante regem prognatum patre
Lucurgum cette!

Then bring here the king, son of his father Trias,
Lycurgus!

Probably again spoken by Liber, as he summons Lycurgus for punishment. Again alliteration gives the line a legal ring, as does the genealogical formula, *prognatum patre*. Some take the line to be the opening of a messenger's speech earlier in the play, but the imperious tone tells against this, unless the messenger is to be envisaged as quoting the instructions of another (Liber?).

Frags 23 and 24

iam solis aestu candor cum liquesceret

Now when the whiteness began melting from the sun's heat

late longeque transtros nostros feruere.[44]

Far and wide our wood-beams glow.

Iambic dialogue lines again, of which the second has sometimes been interpreted as a description of the burning of Lycurgus' palace.

Frag. 25

uos qui astatis obstinati ...

You who stand steadfast by him

An address (by Liber?) to the bodyguard of Lycurgus.

The fragments of *Lucurgus* prove revealing in terms of an evident concern on the part of Naevius, as in *Danae*, with the tyrannical abuse of power, with *ira*, wrath, and its control, with justice and the appropriate treatment of the gods. But what is most interesting about *Lucurgus* is the god at the centre of the play: Liber, here identified with Bacchus, the god whose cult permeated the whole of the Italian peninsula, embraced Roman, Latin and allied cities, and 'cut across all the usual boundaries between social groups',[45] uniting slave and free, poor and rich, woman and man, but whose worship was most violently suppressed by the Roman senate just over a decade after Naevius' death (186 BCE: Livy 39.8–19). The late third and the second centuries at Rome show a concern on the part of the Roman elite to define more clearly what was Roman and what non-Roman, and to control the spread of 'non-Roman' religion.[46] The year 215 BCE had witnessed the dedication on the Capitol at Rome of a temple to Venus of Eryx from Sicily, in fulfilment of a vow made in 217 BCE after the disaster of Lake Trasimene. But, just two years later in 213 BCE, a senatorial decree and an edict of the praetor forbade sacrifice according to 'strange or foreign rites' (*nouo aut externo ritu*, Livy 25.1.12). The final years of the Second Punic War, however, witnessed quite different behaviour on the part of the Roman elite, prompted (again) by consultation of the Sibylline books and (perhaps) in response to popular pressure. In 205–4 BCE they imported the goddess Magna Mater, the 'Great Mother', from Asia Minor, into the city and began the building of an impressive temple to her in the heart of Rome on the Palatine, and inaugurated annual games in her honour. A decade later (194 BCE) the games even included plays.[47]

The treatment of Venus of Eryx and of Magna Mater were exceptions which proved the rule: the worship of Magna Mater, most especially, was subject to the most stringent controls.[48] Of course *Lucurgus* could have been performed at any time between 235 and 204 BCE, although recent commentators have favoured a date in the last years of the third century, even in 204 itself.[49] But, whatever the play's production date, its general subject matter and Naevius' apparent treatment of it would have constituted some kind of intervention in this larger cultural debate. The identification in the play of the Roman and Italian god, Liber, a vegetation and fertility god, who had inhabited a temple on the Aventine since 493 BCE, with Bacchus/Dionysus, the Greek god of passionate ecstasy, may well have shocked. How a Roman audience would have responded is impossible to know. Most Roman citizens had a personal association with Liber, since it was usually at his festival on March 17, the *Liberalia*, that Roman youths received the toga of manhood, the *toga uirilis*.[50] The *toga uirilis* was sometimes known as the *toga libera*, and to some Romans it must have signified a form of 'liberation'. Two centuries later Ovid specifically mentions the connection between *Liber*, the *toga uirilis* and *libertas* (*Fas.* 3.777–8), and notably Naevius, too, in an unplaced fragment, underscores the association between Liber, his festival, and *libertas*:

> libera lingua loquemur ludis Liberalibus
> (*Incerta* frag. v Ribbeck)

We will speak with free tongues at the shows of Liber.

In *Lucurgus* the Campanian playwright may well be advocating a far greater inclusiveness in Roman religion and a tolerance of different gods, their worshippers and rituals, even a larger and more generous concept of *libertas*, than seems to have been the norm in late third-century conservative Rome.

Naevius' most innovative move in the area of serious drama was the creation of the Roman historical drama known as the *fabula praetexta* (or *praetextata*),[51] the subject matter of which was taken from both ancient ('mythological') and contemporary history. This form of drama took its name from the purple-bordered toga worn by Roman magistrates and by the actors who played them, and was heralded with pride by Horace as a distinctively Roman literary form.

> nil intemptatum nostri liquere poetae,
> nec minimum meruere decus uestigia Graeca
> ausi deserere et celebrare domestica facta,
> uel qui praetextas uel qui docuere togatas.
>
> (*Ars Poetica* 285–8)

> Our poets have left nothing untried,
> And have earned no slight praise for their courage
> To leave Greek paths and celebrate events at home
> By producing either *praetextae* or *togatae*.

Although Horace exaggerates slightly (the Greeks did produce historical tragedies, such as Aeschylus' *Persae*, Phrynichus' *Sack of Miletus*, and the fourth-century Moschion's *Themistocles* and *Pheraeans* – and some scholars speculate on an Etruscan origin for the form),[52] the Romans thought of the *praetexta* as essentially theirs. Later commentators such as Donatus (*De Com.* 6.1) and Lydus (*Mag.* 1.40.13–16) allied the form to tragedy.[53] Diomedes (*Ars Gram.* 3, *GL* 1. 489 Keil) notes that, while the subject matter of the *praetexta* consists of the 'business of generals and public affairs' (*imperatorum negotia ... et publica*) and it brings on stage 'Roman kings or generals' (*reges Romani uel duces*), the treatment of the characters is similar to that of tragedy in the representation of their 'social standing and high rank' (*dignitas et sublimitas*).

Written only by dramatists who also wrote tragedy proper, the *fabula praetexta* which Naevius introduced seems to have taken its language, motifs and dramatic form (including the chorus)[54] from tragedy and applied them to a plot wholly created by the dramatist from (an ideological version of) the chosen historical event. The *praetexta* which directed itself to contemporary or recent historical events seems to have functioned in signal part as political laudation of a living or recently deceased member of the Roman elite. It was perhaps influenced substantially by the visual acclamation and drama of the Roman triumphal procession, with its paraded paintings of the *triumphator*'s victories, defeated enemies and conquered territories,[55] and by the political theatre of the aristocratic Roman funeral. It influenced in its turn, and was influenced by, the politico-historical epics of the authors of the early *praetextae* (Naevius' *Bellum Poenicum* and Ennius' *Annales*) and the (prose) annalistic histories of such authors as Fabius Pictor and the elder Cato.

Concerning the occasions on which *fabulae praetextae* were performed, we are without specific evidence. There is no convincing argument to exclude any of the usual dramatic contexts in third-century republican Rome: public festivals, votive games, temple dedications, funeral games, or triumphs.[56] *Praetextae* were more likely than *tragoediae* to have been commissioned by an individual member of Rome's aristocratic elite, and such apparently 'triumphal' *praetextae* as *Clastidium* may well have been performed as part of the triumphal celebrations of the Roman general involved, or at votive games or temple dedications for which he or his family were responsible – or, indeed, at the great man's funeral. Possible production dates for *Clastidium* might be: the celebrations accompanying Marcellus' triumph following his victory in 222 BCE at Clastidium and his winning of the *spolia opima*; funeral games for Marcellus in 208 BCE; games accompanying the dedication of the Temple of Honos et Virtus in 205 BCE near the Porta Capena at Rome by the son of Marcellus in fulfilment of the vow his father made before the battle of Clastidium.[57]

The last-mentioned context is especially attractive,[58] since it cloaks (at least thinly) the politics of the performance with religious aetiological respectability and immediately precedes the young Marcellus' election to the plebeian tribunate (Livy 29.20.11), for which *Clastidium* would then function as pre-electoral canvassing. A clear advantage of a performance date after Marcellus' death would lie in the representation of the great general himself, who could have been 'played' by a (silent?) actor wearing the *imago* or 'mask' (*prosopon*) of the deceased, like the actors who donned ancestral masks in the aristocratic funeral procession. A posthumous production would also have accorded with Cicero's belief that the ancient Romans did not approve of a living person (*uiuus homo*) being praised or abused on stage (*Rep.* 4.12).

The *praetextae*, however, on more 'national' topics such as Naevius' *Romulus*, may well have been taken up by the aediles and performed at the *Ludi Romani* or any of the other great festivals. Some have argued that *Clastidium* itself was not a 'triumphal' *praetexta* glorifying an individual, but one celebrating the *uirtus* of the Roman people in a time of national crisis (the Second Punic War) and likely to have been performed at the annual *ludi scaenici* organised by the magistrates.[59] Other contexts for *Romulus* might include games accompanying the dedication of a restored Temple of Quirinus. Livy (28.11.4) gives the date of 206 BCE as one of the occasions when that temple was damaged by lightning. Cicero (*Sen.* 50) reports that Naevius' *Bellum Poenicum* was composed in old age, i.e. during (and in response to the pressure of) the Hannibalic war. It seems likely that both *praetextae*, which reveal the same impulse to politicise, belong to the same period.

Two words and possibly the following fragments survive from two (or three) plays.

Clastidium

This *praetexta* dealt with the victory in 222 BCE of the consul Marcus Claudius Marcellus over the Insubres of Cisalpine Gaul at Clastidium (modern Casteggio) in northern Italy. In the battle Marcellus won the *spolia opima*, awarded to a Roman general who kills his enemy counterpart in single combat.

Frag. 1

uitulantis

exulting

Perhaps used of the jubilant Roman soldiers routing the enemy or at the moment of victory.[60] The word appears also in *Lucurgus* frag. 8.

Frag. 2

uita insepulta laetus in patriam redux

With life unburied, joyfully returned to fatherland

This iambic dialogue line is generally taken to refer to Marcellus at the moment of his triumphant return to Rome.[61] *Vita insepulta* is an unusual phrase, which would achieve metatheatrical force if the production date was after the death of Marcellus. Marcellus is 'buried', but his life, here dramatised, remains as a model for aspiration. The line would then, in part, be a statement about the generative and prescriptive power of theatre.

Frag. 3 (?)

fato Metelli Romae fiunt consules.

Fate makes Metelli consuls at Rome.

A highly speculative and controversial assignment of this famous line, which is an iambic senarius but is not attributed to any specific play. Conventionally assigned to one of Naevius' comedies, it could be argued as more appropriately at home in *Clastidium* (depending on the date of its performance). See the discussion on p. 54.

Romulus or Lupus

Some commentators (e.g. Ribbeck and Klotz) treat the above as the titles of two separate plays. Fragment 1 is attributed to Naevius' *Lupus*, fragments 2 and 3 possibly to *Lupus*. Fragment 1, the textual difficulties of which have occasioned much emendation,[62] clearly indicates that the subject of *Lupus* was (at least the early part of) the story of Romulus. Fragments 2 and 3 are quoted by Cicero in *De Senectute* (6.60), and fragment 1 may well be cannibalised by him in the same work (*Sen.* 10).[63] Contrary to what is sometimes asserted,[64] Accius' *Brutus* was not the only early *praetexta* known and read in Cicero's time – and occasionally mined for *exempla* and the articulation of traditional values (e.g. *comitas* in frag. 1).

Frag. 1

rex Veiens regem salutat Vibe Albanum Amulium
comiter senem sapientem. contra redhostis?
    min salus?

Veii's king, Vibe, kindly wishes the old, wise Amulius,
Alba's king, well. Do you return my wishes?
    Me – wish well?

A dialogue in trochaic septenarii (i.e. accompanied by music) between the king of Veii and the king of Alba Longa, Amulius. Amulius had usurped the throne and persecuted Ilia (in the account of Naevius and Ennius, the daughter of Aeneas), exposing her sons Romulus and Remus.[65]

Frags 2 and 3

cedo qui uestram rem publicam tantam amisistis tam cito?

Tell me how you lost your great commonwealth so quickly?

proueniebant oratores noui, stulti adulescentuli.

New orators came forward, stupid juveniles.

These two fragments belong to the same scene, in which fragment 3 is one of the answers to the question asked at fragment 2. The source of the fragments is Cicero (*Sen.* 6.60), who however assigns them to an otherwise unknown Naevian play, *Ludus*, a title emended by several commentators to *Lupus*. Both lines come from speeches which would have been delivered to music (the metre of frag. 2 is iambic octonarius, of frag. 3 trochaic septenarius).

The *fabula praetexta*, whether 'triumphal' or 'national', was a highly political dramatic form, and represents a politicisation of Roman drama similar to Naevius' politicisation of Roman epic. Naevius, it seems, whatever his lowly status as a migrant from Campania, was deeply involved in the political life of late third-century republican Rome. His writing of *Clastidium* indexes him as a client of the Marcelli, one of the most powerful Roman families at the end of the third century whose head, Marcus Claudius Marcellus, was celebrated not only as the victor of Clastidium but as the conqueror of Syracuse (213–12 BCE), and had held the consulship some five times by the time of his death in 208 BCE.[66] The Marcelli were bitter rivals and opponents of the faction associated with the Metelli and the Scipios. Indeed it was a Scipio (Gnaeus Scipio) who was fellow consul and military commander with Marcellus at Clastidium and was outshone by Marcellus' military success and remarkable winning of the *spolia opima*.[67] Various anecdotes deriving from the first century BCE report Naevius as the victim of punishment (including incarceration) inflicted by the chief men of the state (*principes ciuitatis, nobiles*) for his verbal attacks upon them (Gell. 3.15). Some identify the *nobiles* concerned as the Scipios and the Metelli.[68] The reference to the imprisoned 'foreign poet' (*poeta barbarus*) by Plautus at *Miles Gloriosus* 211–12 shows that poets were imprisoned for unbridled speech at this time and commentators have not been slow to identify Plautus' *poeta barbarus* with Naevius.[69]

What survives of the Naevian insults is itself controversial: a fragment, presumably from a comedy, drawing attention to the sexual predilections of an anonymous 'great man', identified by later Romans as Publius Cornelius Scipio, the later Africanus (Gell. 8.5–6); and the following famous line, attacking the Metelli, which received an equally famous response:[70]

Naevius
> fato Metelli Romae fiunt consules.

> Fate makes Metelli consuls at Rome.

Metelli
> dabunt malum Metelli Naeuio poetae.

> Metelli will give poet Naevius grief.

We have no context for either line. The response of the Metelli was regarded by the sources for the line as a Saturnian, and knowledge of it seems to have been so widespread in the early first century BCE as to be assumed by Cicero in his first *Verrine* (*Verr*. 1.29 – 70 BCE). Its context may have been inscriptional,[71] for which Saturnians were regularly used in the third century as in the ancient *elogia* of the Scipios. The Naevian line is, however, an iambic senarius (complete with third-foot caesura), the standard dialogue line of Roman drama. And in his comedies, *Tarentilla* (frag. i Ribbeck) and *Incerta* (frag. v Ribbeck above), Naevius explicitly raises the issue of the greater liberty of the stage over the political and social reality beyond it.

Nevertheless, commentators are right in finding it difficult to assign the *fato Metelli* line to a comedy.[72] There is no difficulty in assigning it to a *praetexta* like *Clastidium*.[73] *Clastidium* may have been performed at the temple games of 205 BCE, the year after the consulship of the pro-Scipionic Quintus Caecilius Metellus and the year of the first consulship of Publius Cornelius Scipio, who was to hold *imperium* as either consul or proconsul until he brought the war with Hannibal to triumphant conclusion in 201 BCE. Slanderous verse was regarded by the socially sensitive Romans of the previous century as so heinous that it was listed in the *Twelve Tables* as one of the few crimes meriting the death penalty (Cic. *Rep*. 4.12, Aug. *Ciu*. 2.9).[74] Prosecutions, however, seem to have been rare; so too – at this time – public insults of Roman aristocrats by low-born clients of their enemies. The notorious iambics are usually dated to the year of

Caecilius Metellus' consulship, i.e. 206 BCE, but there is no necessity to do so.[75] They could have appeared in a 205 performance of *Clastidium*. If so, they would have been topical, topically offensive and, given the public nature of the offence and the overtness of its political provenance, impossible to ignore. All the stories concerning Naevius' troubles with the Metelli and Scipios in the last years of the third century, including imprisonment (and possibly exile),[76] would fit into place. Indeed action taken against Naevius may itself have helped the young Marcellus into his tribunate.

This is (rational) speculation. What is not speculation is that Naevius, who had experienced politics personally as a soldier in the First Punic War, made the implicit imbrication of politics and drama overt. Indeed he made politics and poetry – both dramatic and epic – one. And Romans of later generations believed that he paid for it. The pun attributed by Cicero to Scipio Africanus (*De Orat*. 2.249) – *quid hoc Naeuio ignauius?* – 'What greater knave exists than this Naevius?' – shows that the migrant Campanian's high-born targets were believed to have felt some pain, too.

3

THE SECOND WAVE

Generic confidence

Roman tragedy was not confined to Roman tragedians. The theatrical standing and popular impact of early republican tragedy are reflected in its penetration of the main competitor for dramatic attention: comedy. In the middle of Plautus' *Amphitruo*, a self-described *tragicomoedia* (*Amph.* 59, 63), Alcumena concludes a polymetric *canticum* or aria which could have come straight from a tragedy by one of the playwright's contemporaries:

> uirtus praemium est optumum,
> uirtus omnibus rebus anteit profecto;
> libertas, salus, uita, res et parentes, patria et prognati
> tutantur, seruantur;
> uirtus omnia in sese habet, omnia adsunt
> bona quem penest uirtus.[1]
>
> (*Amphitruo* 648–53)

> *Virtus* is the finest prize,
> *Virtus* is prior to all things assuredly;
> Liberty, security, life, property and parents, fatherland and
> progeny
> Are guarded, are preserved;
> *Virtus* contains all things, all good things attend
> The man possessed of *Virtus*.

Plautus is an important figure in the history of early republican tragedy, since his dramatic career (*c.* 215–*c.* 184 BCE) coincides with the final years of Naevius and the early and middle years of Ennius, and attests not only to the predictable rivalries of the Roman theatre but also to the generic mixture evident in Roman play-writing from the start. The influence of tragic language and style is clear in many of Plautus' plays, which use them sometimes for the purpose of comic burlesque (e.g., *Poen.* 1ff., *Pseud.* 702ff., *Men.* 831ff., *Mer.* 842ff., *Persa* 712, *Bacch.* 932ff., *Cas.* 621ff.),[2] but also deploy them for tonal variety and modulation. Plautus revels in intense emotional scenes, which borrow from the repertoire of tragedy, even its gnomic predilections, to secure an appropriate tone (e.g., *Rudens* 185–289; *Persa* 341ff.).[3] In part Plautus is following the Greek tradition from Aristophanes to Menander of the comic deployment and parody of tragic language and episodes.[4] In part he signals the greater generic mixture and fluidity to be found in the Roman theatre, where most dramatists wrote both comedies and tragedies and where linguistic and metrical differences were less defined. But what he also signals is the theatrical sophistication of the Roman audience, whom Plautus clearly expects to respond to his tragic parodies – and often at the level of some considerable detail. References to Greek tragedies and the parodies which follow need to be 'decoded' by a Plautine audience as references to the versions of rival Roman playwrights and parodies of their style.[5]

But, of course, Plautus wrote only 'comedies', and his attempts at the tragic style were among other things an attempt to display his own skills in an area which he otherwise never tackled – and which was growing more distinct. Although our evidence is too scanty to admit of firm conclusions, Roman tragedy itself, in the second century BCE, started to pursue a more self-conscious and more self-consciously 'high' tragic style, but one which yet admitted of far greater verbal and tonal diversity than is usually acknowledged. Sharp dialogue and generic mixture were not restricted to comedy. The first major figure in this second wave of tragic writing was a poet destined to become a literary giant of Roman literature, Quintus Ennius.

Quintus Ennius

Ennius tria corda habere sese dicebat quod loqui
Graece et Osce et Latine sciret.
(Aulus Gellius 17.17.1)

Ennius would say he had three hearts because he
could speak Greek and Oscan and Latin.

The most famous Roman poet before Virgil, Quintus Ennius, was another south Italian immigrant for whom Latin was at best a second language. Described by Suetonius as, like his predecessor

Livius Andronicus, 'half-Greek' (*semigraecus*, *Gram.* 1.2), Ennius also came from the Greek-dominated Calabrian region of southern Italy, where in 239 BCE he was born (probably into an Oscan family) at the town of Rudiae. His Greek was learned presumably at the nearby city of Tarentum. In the latter part of the Second Punic War he was serving in Sardinia as a ranking officer of one of the south Italian auxiliary units (see Sil. It. 12.393–5), when he seems to have come to the attention of the Roman aristocrat and questor, Marcus Porcius Cato, who may have stopped in Sardinia on his return home from Africa (204 BCE), and who brought Ennius to Rome with him in the following year.[6]

What attracted Cato to Ennius is unrecorded, but it was presumably more to do with his intellectual and thus political potential (probably his evident skill as poet), than with his military accomplishments. In Rome Ennius set up house on the Aventine and began to make a living as a teacher, a *grammaticus* (Suet. *Gram.* 1.2). In Cicero's *De Senectute* (10) Ennius is represented as an intimate (*familiaris*) of Cato, and Suetonius claims that he taught Cato Greek (Suet. *Vir. Ill.* 47.1). But Cato was not the only aristocrat of whom Ennius became what the Romans called an *amicus* – a 'friend', a term applicable to 'intimates' even of lower social status.[7] His aristocratic connections included Sulpicius Galba (younger or elder), Scipio Nasica (younger or elder), and perhaps even the conqueror of Hannibal, Scipio Africanus, whom the poet praised in his work, *Scipio*, just as (apparently) he had praised Cato (Cic. *Arch.* 21).[8] Eventually Ennius' main patron, however, was Marcus Fulvius Nobilior, who (much to Cato's annoyance: Cic. *Tusc.* 1.3) took the poet with him on his military campaign in Ambracia in 189 BCE. Five years later (184 BCE) he seems to have received Roman citizenship (Cic. *Brut.* 79).

Ennius' period as a dramatic writer apparently began about 203 BCE and continued until his death in 169 BCE or slightly later (Cic. *Brut.* 78). Livius Andronicus was probably dead when the south Italian arrived in Rome and there is no evidence that he met Naevius. He is, however, said to have been an intimate or *contubernalis* of the comic playwright Caecilius Statius (whom Sedigitus placed first in his canonic list), and he must have known Plautus, with whom he was in competition as a comic dramatist and who seems to allude to specific Ennian tragedies.[9] For, like Andronicus and Naevius, Ennius wrote both tragedies and comedies. His literary productivity impresses. Some twenty or twenty-one tragedies are attributed to him: *Achilles, Aiax, Alcmeo,*

Alexander, Andromacha, Andromeda, Athamas, Cresphontes, Erectheus, Eumenides, Hectoris Lytra ('Ransom of Hector'), *Hecuba, Iphigenia, Medea, Medea Exul* ('Medea Exiled'),[10] *Melanippa, Nemea, Phoenix, Telamo, Telephus, Thyestes.* Attention to the Trojan cycle is not the only thing notable. To the tragedies should be added two *praetextae, Ambracia* and *Sabinae* ('Sabine Women'), and three attested comedies. Ennius also wrote a plethora of other poems, including *Scipio, Epicharmus,* four books of 'Satires' (*saturae*), several other separately titled pieces, and epigrams.[11]

Like his predecessors Ennius wrote an epic, in fact *the* Roman epic of the republican period, *Annales,* and, although Ennius must have dominated the tragic stage for the first three decades of the second century (twenty or so new tragedies and two *praetextae* in the period 203–169, not to mention reperformances of the more popular plays), it was primarily as poet of *Annales* that later Roman writers celebrated him. In *Annales* Ennius combined Naevius' Roman subject and Livius' Homerising thinking to fuse Greek poetic practice with Roman historical matter in an eighteen-book narrative of Roman history from the foundation of the city to the most recent wars in Greece. Originally the poem had been designed as a fifteen-book work, climaxing in the capture of Ambracia in Epirus by his patron, Fulvius Nobilior, in 189 BCE and (perhaps) in his subsequent dedication of the Temple of Hercules Musarum in Rome shortly after his censorship of 179 BCE (Eumenius *Paneg. Lat.* 9.73). Fulvius' temple united the Italian Camenae with the Muses of Greece, as in a sense did Ennius' epic, which was the first poem to introduce the Homeric hexameter into Roman epic practice.[12] Though predictably criticised by some Augustan poets as primitive,[13] *Annales* boasts of its originality, its modernism, its revolutionary departures from its predecessors, and reveals, as the tragic fragments do, a poet highly self-conscious about his own poetic style (*dicti studiosus, Annales* 7, frag. 209 Skutsch). That style was itself a fusion of drama and epic, deriving much of its vocabulary, linguistic structures and characterisation from the tragic repertoire.[14] It was the first Latin history of Rome. Composed sometime after Fabius Pictor's prose history of Rome in Greek, the poem was 'completed' perhaps a decade or so before the appearance of the first prose history of Rome in Latin.[15] *Annales'* cultural impact would be difficult to overstate. Written by a south Italian immigrant, Ennius' epic yet played a constitutive part in defining for the Roman elite of the next 150 years what it was to be Roman.

For what it was to be Roman became, in the second century, a matter of some dispute. The pressures for social and cultural change in the decades which followed the Hannibalic wars were intense and unremitting. Rome's historians were later to regard the period as one of moral crisis for the city, as the 'traditional' values of frugality, austerity, simplicity, service to the *respublica*, which allegedly defined the city's governing class, became threatened by the onset of *luxuria* ('self-indulgence', 'luxury', 'extravagance').[16] As Rome's generals began to conquer the East, the East sent slaves, art, wealth, ideas, even philosophers and historians, to Rome. The city's population grew and grew more diverse, as dispossessed farmers, the unemployed poor, the increasingly wealthy and competitive elite, the spoils of their conquests, their slaves, their gangs and minions, jostled for attention. Even as the physical body of the city began to be adorned with new monuments in an attempt both to reinforce the 'natural' hegemony of Rome's leaders and to rival the great urban splendours of the East, class anxiety was evident – and manifested itself in politically conservative and repressive acts.[17]

It made itself felt, too, in Rome's theatre, which became a primary site for competitive display. Our knowledge of changes in the decoration of, for example, the facade of the stage-building, the *scaenae frons*, in the early second century is not extensive. But it seems very likely that the developing interest in Hellenistic painting led to the use of painting for the stage-facade, as returning *triumphatores* and others sought to outshine their rivals and predecessors.[18] An important development also occurred in the provision of seating for the audience. As noted above, in 194 BCE at the *Ludi Romani* the curule aediles set aside in the orchestra, between the stage and the wooden tiers of seats, special seating restricted to members of the senate. Since the aediles' instructions came from the censors at the instigation of Scipio Africanus, their divisive action must have reflected Scipio's and the senate's awareness of the theatre as political and societal space. The displeasure of the *plebs*, accustomed to *ludi scaenici* where there was no regard for social status, was expected and profound.[19]

But class anxiety was also often internal, manifesting itself in hostility on the part of Rome's elite towards those of its members who sought to distinguish themselves from the collective body. Predictable and particularly ferocious was the resistance of the senate to the 'overweening' demands and 'dangerous' popularity of returning generals. Ennius' patron, Marcus Fulvius Nobilior, had to struggle to be awarded his triumph, as did the undisputed first man in Rome in 167 BCE, Lucius Aemilius Paullus. Late plays of Plautus such as *Casina* and *Bacchides* and all the comedies of Terence (166–160 BCE) reflect many of the ideological tensions accompanying Rome's rapid social change.

Tragedy and epic were necessarily culturally bound. Even more than his predecessors, perhaps, Ennius was situated at the heart of the Roman political establishment, and his highly sophisticated epic is conscious of its place in both the literary and the political worlds. The (increasingly accepted) story of the placing of Ennius' statue with those of Lucius and Publius Scipio before the tomb of the Scipios on the Appian Way indexes more than literary success.[20] Similarly Ennius' highly operatic tragedies (70 per cent of the surviving lines of which would have been sung or recited to music)[21] allude not only to literary texts. Certainly the creative deployment of the Attic tragedians, especially of Euripides, is patent; so, too, a dynamic interplay with the very figures from whom Ennius tries to distinguish himself, his predecessors in Latin drama. But Roman theatre was necessarily political; the circumstances of a play's production and the elite's control of the *ludi* and of the city's theatrical spaces entailed this. In *fabulae praetextae* and such Plautine comedies as *Poenulus* ('Little Carthaginian') and *Casina* political and social meaning is to the fore. In Ennian tragedy there is always the sense, as in Roman comedy and Ennius' own *Annales*, that we are being treated to reflections on the Roman (elite) self and other, and to a shadow play of contemporary political and moral issues.[22]

Roman aristocratic values pervade the tragedies: *pietas* and *pudor*, 'piety/family duty' and 'shame' (*Telam.* frag. cxxxvii Jocelyn), *imperium* and *fides*, 'power' and 'loyalty' (*Hec. Lyt.*, *Inc.* frags lxxv, clxxxiv Jocelyn), *gloria*, *nomen*, 'glory', 'name/status', and their antitheses *fama*, 'infamy' (*Ach.*, *Hec. Lyt.* frags ix, lxxvi Jocelyn), and *ignobilitas* (*Hec.* frag. lxxxiv Jocelyn), *fortitudo*, *uirtus*, *ius*, 'bravery', 'manliness/virtue', 'justice' (*Eum.*, *Hec. Lyt.*, *Pho.* frags lxvi, lxxi, cxxvi, cxxxii Jocelyn), *otium* and *negotium*, 'leisure' and 'work' (*Iph.* frag. xcix Jocelyn), *amicitia*, 'friendship' (*Inc.* frag. clxxxv Jocelyn), *honestas*, 'honour' (*Inc.* frag. ccxv Jocelyn), *libertas*, 'freedom' (*Erec.*, *Pho.* frags lxi, cxxvi Jocelyn), *pax, concordia, societas*, 'peace', 'concord', 'partnership' (*Inc.* frags clxii, clxix Jocelyn), *gens* and *genus*, 'family' and 'ancestry' (*Telam.*, *Thy.* frags cxxxvi, cxlix Jocelyn), and the ambiguous value of *sapientia* (*Eum.*, *Med.*, *Inc.* frags lxv, cv, clxxi Jocelyn). Tirades against astrologers and soothsayers are notable (*Iph.*, *Telam.* frags xcv, cxxxiv Jocelyn). Occasionally a homiletic fragment is precise in its advocacy of Roman aristocratic ideology. The first 'homily' became a *sententia* taught to schoolboys in Augustan Rome (Phaedrus 3. Epil. 34).

> palam muttire plebeio piaculum est.[23]
>> (*Telephus* frag. cxlii Jocelyn)

For a plebeian to blurt in public is profane.

> licet
> lacrumare plebi, regi honeste non licet.
>> (*Incerta* frag. ccxv Jocelyn)

> The plebs
> May weep, the ruler may not – with honour.

> amicus certus in re incerta cernitur.
>> (*Incerta* frag. clxxxv Jocelyn)

A sure friend is seen when things are unsure.

> philosophandum est paucis; nam omnino haud placet.
>> (*Andromacha* frag. xxviii Jocelyn)

One should philosophise in few things – in all things it's unpleasing.

> sed uirum uera uirtute uiuere animatum addecet[24]
> fortiterque innoxium stare aduersum aduersarios.
> ea libertas est qui pectus purum et firmum gestitat;
> aliae res obnoxiosae nocte in obscura latent.
>> (*Phoenix* frag. cxxvi Jocelyn)

It behoves a man to live quickened by true *uirtus*
And to face his enemies bravely without guilt.
This is liberty: to display a heart pure and steadfast.
But subservience lies hidden in dark night.

In four lines the speaker of the last homily (who may well be Phoenix – possibly replying to his enraged father Amyntor) rings the changes on man, manliness/virtue (*uirtus*), courage (*fortitudo*), innocence, openness, liberty, subservience, purity, steadfastness – and what is proper, *addecet*. The keynote phrase, *uera uirtus*, was already, as its use in Plautus shows (*Cas.* 88, *Cist.* 198: see further Jocelyn *ad loc.*), a platitude of Roman public life. Even the form of this fragment is ideological. As in all the tragic fragments, diction, structure and rhetorical artifice promote precisely the primacy of formal discourse which lay at the heart of the Roman elite's performative hegemony and its displays and assignments of social status. The various figures and structures which mark Ennian tragic style – alliteration, assonance, homeoteleuton, polyptoton, tricolon, anaphora, *uersus quadratus*, antithesis, synonyms, epigram, puns, *figura etymologica* – realise and exhibit aspects of the 'cultural capital' (to use Bourdieu's much-used term) distinguishing the governing from the governed.

Such figures realise and exhibit theatrical purposes too.

> mater grauida parere se ardentem facem
> uisa est in somnis Hecuba. quo facto pater
> rex ipse Priamus somnio mentis metu
> perculsus curis sumptus suspirantibus
> exsacrificabat hostiis balantibus.
> tum coniecturam postulat pacem petens,
> ut se edoceret obsecrans Apollinem
> quo sese uertant tantae sortes somnium.
> ibi ex oraclo uoce diuina edidit
> Apollo puerum primus Priamo qui foret
> postilla natus temperaret tollere;
> eum esse exitium Troiae, pestem Pergamo.
> (*Alexander* frag. xviii Jocelyn)

> Mother Hecuba, when pregnant,
> Dreamt she produced a blazing torch. At which
> The king, father Priam himself, his mind rocked
> By fear of the dream, seized by sighing cares,
> Began sacrificing with bleating victims.
> In pursuit of peace he pleads for a reading
> And beseeches Apollo to instruct him
> How to translate such mighty dream-omens.
> Then from his oracle with divine voice
> Apollo told Priam to forbear to lift
> The first child born to him after this;
> He was Troy's holocaust, Pergamum's plague.

The iambic lines above are assigned by most scholars to the prologue of Ennius' *Alexander*. The play dealt with the recognition of the adult Alexander (= Paris of Troy), who had been exposed at birth, as King Priam's son (Apollodorus 3.12.5.2ff.; Hyginus *Fab.* 91). The recognition was the subject of tragedies by both Sophocles and Euripides, and it is on the latter that Ennius' tragedy seems to have been based (see Varro *LL* 7.82). Note the particular 'tragic' style adopted in this prologue. The mode is 'portentous', but at the same time steady, paced out, simple. The Roman tragedian has taken care to have his narrative details understood. Repetition, prosaic precision, even tautology, make the meaning clear. Prominent alliteration, assonance, periphrastic syntax, polysyllabic language, rhetorical structures, blend tragic tonality with theatrical comprehensibility and power.

The prologue's speaker has been variously named, the prime candidates being Cassandra, Venus and Victoria (=Venus). Certainly Victoria seems to have featured in some tragic prologue, if Plautus' Mercury is telling the truth at *Amphitruo* 41ff., when he tells of tragic prologues delivered by gods such as Neptune, Virtus, Victoria, Mars and Bellona, detailing the benefits they have conferred on the Roman people. Some have attributed divine prologues of this kind to Ennius, nominating Neptune as the speaker of the prologue of his *Andromacha* and Victoria as the speaker of *Alexander*, even speculating that the prologues may have featured praise of prominent political figures, Scipio Africanus, for example, or Cato.[25] No fragments, however, survive testifying to this. But, constituent of a 'divine' prologue or not, *Alexander*'s opening rhetoricity achieves an exact dramatic effect.

Alexander's 'prologue' is but one kind of Ennian style, which is more complex, diverse and nuanced than Lucilius and his modern successors would have one believe – and which functions theatrically in correspondingly manifold ways. Ennian language and structures run down the register from self-consciously high metatragic diction through stately simplicity to informal dialogue and the kind of vocabulary (*muttire, fabulari, aucupare*) more frequently found in comedy. *Quid in castris strepitist,* 'What's the racket in the camp', cries Agamemnon or Achilles in *Hectoris Lytra* (frag. lxxvii Jocelyn). *Quid lasciuis, stolide?,* 'What's this game of yours, blockhead?', quotes the Messenger in *Alexander* (frag. xxii Jocelyn). With stately simplicity Hecuba requests her death: *date ferrum qui me anima priuem,* 'Give me steel to take my life' (*Hecuba* frag. xci Jocelyn).

Different in rhetoricity and theatrical impact is the following fragment from *Alexander*, in which the speaker (Cassandra) moves from meditative, if excited, staccato discourse, filled with self-loathing, to deranged, prophetic trance and climactic vision. All the lines would have been accompanied by music and the central vision (in dactylic tetrameters) sung.

mater, optumatum multo mulier melior mulierum,
missa sum superstitiosis hariolationibus;
neque me Apollo fatis fandis dementem inuitam ciet.
uirgines uereor aequalis, patris mei meum factum pudet,
optumi uiri. mea mater, tui me miseret, mei piget.
optumam progeniem Priamo peperisti extra me. hoc dolet:
men obesse, illos prodesse, me obstare, illos obsequi...
adest adest fax obuoluta sanguine atque incendio.
multos annos latuit. ciues ferte opem et restinguite...
iamque mari magno classis cita
texitur. exitium examen rapit.
adueniet. fera ueliuolantibus
nauibus compleuit manus litora...
eheu uidete:
iudicauit inclitum iudicium inter deas tris aliquis,
quo iudicio Lacedaemonia mulier Furiarum una adueniet.
(Alexander frag. xvii Jocelyn)

Mother, better woman by far than the best of women,
I am impelled by superstitious prophesyings.
Nor does Apollo madden me unwillingly with fate-
     foretellings.
I shun virgin friends, my father shudders at my actions –
That best of men. My mother, I pity you; I disgust myself.
You gave to Priam the best of children apart from me.
This pains: I obstruct, they help, I oppose, they obey ...
It's here, it's here, the torch wreathed with blood and fire.
It hid for many years. Citizens, bring help and quench it ...
And now on the spreading sea a fast fleet
Weaves. It clutches a crowd of deaths.
It will come. A wild band has filled
The shores with sail-flying ships ...
... Ah, see:
Someone judged a judgement between three goddesses,
From which judgement will come a Spartan woman, a Fury.

In a sense this kind of writing is metatragic, highly self-conscious, self-signalling tragic speech: heavy alliteration, assonance, repetition, jabbing sense-units, weighty polysyllables, *uersus quadratus*, *figura etymologica*, vigorous symbolism and metaphor (*texitur*, 'weaves', is especially apposite for the movement of the fleet), dramatic pace, impetus, energy – all employed to connote and put on display 'high' tragic utterance. Roman tragedy was always metatragedy;[26] its rhetoric and arias, verbal and metrical artifice, masks, costuming, music, props and sets always advertised their status as defining constituents of tragic theatre. Ennian language, however, here, as elsewhere, is not simply in business to display its own theatrical register; it provides dramatic enactment of emotional abandon and articulates a fragmented but syncopated vision of Troy's calamitous fate. Notice how the vision ends on the brute historicity of Paris' judgement and its consequences in a precise, almost prosaic final couplet.

Many of the dramatic features apparent in the passages from *Alexander* cited above are evident elsewhere in the tragic fragments. Incisive, emotive language abounds. Battle-descriptions, as in *Annales*, elicit the soldier-poet's fondness for terse, concrete images:

> arma arrigunt, horrescunt tela.
> >   (*Erectheus* frag. lxii Jocelyn)

> They air arms, spears bristle.

> aes sonit, franguntur hastae, terra sudit sanguine.
> >   (*Hectoris Lytra* frag. lxxviii Jocelyn)

> Bronze clatters, spears snap, earth sweats with blood.[27]

Sometimes there is a linguistic enhancement of a Greek 'source-text':

> uide hunc meae in quem lacrumae guttatim cadunt.
> >   (*Hecuba* frag. lxxxv Jocelyn (trans. Eur. *Hec.* 760))

> See the man on whom my tears fall drop by drop.

Sometimes, too, the language displays no debt to predecessors:

> Acherontem obibo, ubi Mortis thesauri obiacent.
> >   (*Iphigenia* frag. xcvii Jocelyn)

> I shall face Acheron, where Death's treasure-vaults lie.

The sacrifice of the young for the old, children for parents, individuals for the collective citizenry, for country, is debated elsewhere in Ennian tragedy (see, e.g., frag. ccxxii Jocelyn). Roman aristocratic ideology had always glorified death for the sake of country, making of *deuotio* a pre-Christian and pre-Islamic form of martyrdom. In the fragment above Iphigenia conveys the richness of her dying for country's sake by transforming death itself into a house of riches.[28] 'Eye hath not seen, nor ear heard ...' A different kind of feeling is expressed and produced by the similarly striking language in which Hecuba articulates her disgust after Ulysses removes her daughter, Polyxena, for sacrifice:

> heu me miseram. interii. pergunt lauere sanguen sanguine.
> (*Hecuba* frag. lxxxix Jocelyn)

> Ah, wretched me. I am dead. They go to cleanse blood with blood.

There is nothing similar in Euripides' Greek.[29] This inversion of 'normal' heroic practice (viz. the washing off of the blood from battle with a stream's clear water) aptly indexes the moral perversion of Greek behaviour.

Terence (*And.* 16–19) cites Ennius as one of his comic predecessors in the practice of *contaminatio*. The practice clearly extended to the tragedies, too: *Aiax*, *Andromacha*, *Hectoris Lytra*, *Iphigenia* are among the plays where *contaminatio* is argued.[30] As the *Hecuba* fragment indicates, Ennius was a creative adaptor of 'source-texts' in other ways, too, and a master of irony. From the same play we witness Hecuba's brilliant parody of Roman triumphal language:[31]

> Iuppiter tibi summe tandem male re gesta gratulor.
> (*Hecuba* frag. lxxxvi Jocelyn)

> Most high Jupiter, I thank you at last for a thing ill done.

Some suggest that Hecuba utters this remark on the completion of vengeance against Polymestor.[32] It is more likely to have been uttered either, as Jocelyn argues,[33] after Hecuba's discovery of the body of her slain son, Polydorus, or after she has received the news of Polyxena's death. But whatever the location of the fragment the originality, the Romanness, the irony and the dramatic power remain. Certainly Ennius was not shy in his adaptation of Greek texts. It is clear from his replacement of Euripides' chorus of Euboean women with one of disgruntled Greek warriors in *Iphigenia* (frag. xcix Jocelyn) that, if he saw significant gains in large-scale alteration, he did not hesitate to act. The placing of the army centre-stage in his adaptation of Euripides' play ensured a dramatic, thematic and cultural transformation of its action. It indexed the different social reality of the Calabrian soldier-poet.

What *Hecuba* and the fragments of *Alexander* cited above show, too, is Ennius' penchant for the dramatisation of high emotional moments, which he transformed into moving recitative and (often) *cantica*. Ennius' rendering of the madness of Alcmaeon (*Alc.* frag. xv Jocelyn) clearly stirred Cicero (*Acad.* 2.52, 88–9), as did Andromache's *canticum* detailing her tragic loss. Deft manipulation of a variety of lyric metres (cretics, trochaics and anapaests) underscores the emotional chaos:

> quid petam praesidi aut exequar, quoue nunc
> auxilio exili aut fugae freta sim?
> arce et urbe orba sum. quo accedam, quo applicem,
> cui nec arae patriae domi stant, fractae et disiectae iacent,
> fana flamma deflagrata, tosti alti stant parietes
> deformati atque abiete crispa ...
> o pater, o patria, o Priami domus,
> saeptum altisono cardine templum,
> uidi ego te, adstante ope barbarica,
> tectis caelatis laqueatis
> auro ebore instructam regifice.
> haec omnia uidi inflammari,
> Priamo ui uitam euitari,
> Iouis aram sanguine turpari.
>
> (Andromacha frag. xxvii Jocelyn)

What fortress can I seek or find, what help
Now rely on for escape or flight?
I am orphaned of citadel and city. Where to kneel, where
    appeal,
When my home's ancestral altars stand no more, lie broken,
    smashed,
The temples consumed by flame, the soaring walls stand
    scorched,
Misshapen, and the firwood crinkled ...
O father, o fatherland, o house of Priam,
Shrine enclosed by high-creaking doors,
I have gazed on you attended by barbaric wealth,
Ceilings fretted and chiselled
Adorned with gold and ivory – regally.
All this I saw in flames,
Priam's life unlifed with force,
Jove's altar blood-befouled.

Cicero, who quotes these lines at *Tusculan Disputations* 3.44, provides testimony to how this kind of dramatic writing affected some members of a first century BCE Roman theatre audience:

> praeclarum carmen. est enim et rebus et uerbis et modis lugubre.

A brilliant monody. For it is mournful in subject and diction and rhythm.

The lines affected Virgil, too, who 'imitated' them on more than one occasion in his *Aeneid*.[34]

A similar focus on psychological interiority and conflict marks several dramatic moments in Ennian tragedy. It clearly worked theatrically. We owe to Cicero a fragment of Alcmaeon's (probable) soliloquy of imprisoning depression and terror. It would have been recited to music.

> multis sum modis circumuentus, morbo exilio atque inopia.
> tum pauor sapientiam omnem exanimato expectorat.
> animus terribilem minatur uitae cruciatum et necem;[35]
> quae nemo est tam firmo ingenio et tanta confidentia
> quin refugiat timido sanguen atque exalbescat metu.
> (*Alcmeo* frag. xiv Jocelyn)

I am much besieged – by sickness, banishment and want.
Fear stifles me and drives all reason from my breast.
My mind threatens my life with dire torture and butchery;
Such that there is no one, however strong and self-possessed,
Whose blood would not flee in terror and blanch with fear.

Seneca much later capitalised on Roman drama's predilection for soliloquies to produce an exceptionally interior drama. That interiority was there in Ennius.

Though he was ranked lowly as a comic dramatist by Sedigitus and mocked as a tragedian by Lucilius (Bk 29, frags 845–9 Krenkel), Ennius' tragic style was clearly admired at least by some in the next century, including Cicero, Catullus and Virgil,[36] and his plays became part of late-republican intellectual life, rhetorical literature and the tragic repertoire. His thematic range is noteworthy. Livian and Naevian tragedy was dominated by the Trojan theme and its aetiological signals. Ennius took that predilection, devoted about half his plays to it, and dedicated the rest of his energies to dramatising for the first time on the Roman stage some of the other great tragic narratives of the Attic tradition: those of Alcmaeon, Athamas, Andromeda, Medea and Thyestes, for example, sagas which would themselves be rewritten by Ennius' later rivals and successors. In doing so, he enlarged and transformed the genre in a way analogous (although not identical) to that in which he enlarged and transformed epic. A concern with cultural origins and identity is still evident in the substantial number of 'Trojan' plays – a concern which would have played well with all Roman citizens, not simply with the Roman elite – but it exists alongside an ambition to put on stage the full range of tragic themes explored by his Greek predecessors, especially by Euripides: madness, betrayal, matricide, puericide, incest, love, revenge, justice, courage, sacrifice, freedom, slavery, pity, cruelty, death, suffering, fortune, power, treachery, tyranny, relations between man and god, *impietas*.

Some critics have maintained that, despite his fascination with Euripides and the 'Euripidean themes of recognition, deception and revenge', Ennius lacks Euripides' penchant for social critique.[37] The patronal world of early-second-century Rome was not that of democratic Athens. But to suggest that Ennius' tragedies, performed at public religious festivals financed by both the state and the Roman elite and (after 194 BCE) before a hierarchical image of Roman social and political power, were not firmly rooted in contemporary political and social debates beggars belief. At the very least they presented to the Roman people dramatic studies in the nature and evils of monarchy or, more generally, of the 'Roman Other', as the 'Greek' figures of the plays were likely to have been received as such by some members of Ennius' audience. And in the case of plays like *Medea Exul*, which explores problems of alterity and marginalisation within a hostile urban community, it is difficult to believe that no one saw the play's relevance to an increasing and increasingly diverse and anxious Roman urban mass. Both *Thyestes* and *Sabinae*, as discussed below, were noticeably directed to the audience's political reality; so, too, clearly was *Athamas*, the sole fragment of which deals with an account of a Bacchic 'orgy' surprisingly involving male as well as female participants (frag. lii Jocelyn). In the years surrounding the prohibition of Bacchic worship by the senate (186 BCE) *Athamas* must have had immediate and central cultural relevance; as must the following proclamation attributed by Nonius to Ennius' *Hectoris Lytra*, whose forceful challenge to contemporary elite values is unaffected by recent attempts to restrict the meaning of *uirtus* to 'martial valour':[38]

> melius est uirtute ius. nam saepe uirtutem mali
> nanciscuntur. ius atque aecum se a malis spernit procul.
> (*Hectoris Lytra* frag. lxxi Jocelyn)

Justice is better than *uirtus*. For the wicked often acquire

Virtus. Justice and fairness keep well away from the wicked.

Cicero, a century or so later, had no problem in reading second-century Roman comedy (*Rosc.Am.* 46–7) and tragedy as a mirror of his Roman world. When the orator writes to a friend in exile (*Fam.* 7.6), he quotes from Ennius' *Medea*; when he appeals to his jury's knowledge of the behaviour of kings, his examples derive from tragedy, most probably from Ennius himself (*Rab. Post.* 29). Ennian tragedy's highly emotional colouring, elaborate diction and structures, its musical force, direct an energy which is as social and ideological as it is literary. Ennian rhetoric has 'political weight'.[39]

The surviving fragments of *Medea Exul*, *Thyestes* and Ennius' two *praetextae*, *Ambracia* and *Sabinae*, follow. The reader should be aware that my arrangement of the fragments of *Medea Exul* and *Thyestes* differs considerably from the order in Jocelyn (frags ciii–cxvi, cxlix–clx).

Medea Exul

Jocelyn (342ff.) argues persuasively that Ennius wrote two tragedies, *Medea Exul*, an adaptation of Euripides' *Medea* set in Corinth, and *Medea*, which was set in Athens. The fragments below can plausibly be attributed to the former play which, like its Euripidean model, dealt with Jason's abandonment of the Colchian princess Medea in Corinth, his marriage to the daughter of King Creon of Corinth, and Medea's killing of Jason's bride (and Creon) and her own and Jason's children in revenge. Ennius seems to have been the first Roman dramatist to tackle the subject of Medea. The play's theme of cultural and personal isolation in a foreign city would have hit home to every member of Ennius' audience, slave-owner and slave, whether a political, economic or intellectual immigrant (like Ennius) or a member of Rome's established elite. The date of the play's first production is not known. But, whatever its date, political and cultural resonance would presumably have emanated from the setting of the action in Corinth, a city which played an important and contradictory role in Rome's post-Hannibalic foreign policy down to the sack of the city in 146 BCE.[40]

The play was clearly one of Ennius' best known and part of the tragic repertoire of the late republican stage.[41] It had many successors in the Roman tradition: Accius, Ovid, Seneca and Lucan wrote a *Medea*, and Ennius' nephew, Pacuvius, wrote a sequel to the entire Medea legend, *Medus*. The play had a strong impact on Poem 64 of

Catullus ('Peleus and Thetis') and on Virgil's presentation of Dido. Citations from Ennius' *Medea Exul* in *Rhetorica ad Herennium* (2.34) and Quintilian's *Institutio Oratoria* (5.10.83–4) indicate the play's position as a source of rhetorical *exempla*.[42]

Frag. 1

utinam ne in nemore Pelio securibus
caesa accidisset abiegna ad terram trabes,
neue inde nauis inchoandi exordium
cepisset, quae nunc nominatur nomine
Argo, quia Argiui in ea delecti uiri
uecti petebant pellem inauratam arietis
Colchis, imperio regis Peliae, per dolum.
nam numquam era errans mea domo efferret pedem
Medea animo aegro amore saeuo saucia.

I wish that beams of fir had not been felled
By those axes in a Pelian grove,
So no point of origin could arise
For the ship which is now named with the name
Argo, because in it an 'Argive' elite
Travelled to get by trickery a ram's
Gold fleece in Cochis, ordered by King Pelias.
Never would my mistress have strayed from home,
Soul-sick Medea, wounded by savage love.

The above iambics open the play. They are delivered by Medea's Nurse. Comparison with the opening of Euripides' *Medea* reveal that Ennius has reversed his model's rhetorical sequence (sailing – tree-felling) and has adopted a less metaphoric, but more alliterative, heavy, periphrastic style. He has also Romanised several details: pine is replaced by the Roman shipbuilding material, fir; the aristocratic Argive 'elite' are made to travel on the *Argo* rather than to row it.[43] The Latin poet revels in etymological punning, employing a *figura etymologica* (line 4) before the etymological exegesis itself. The etymology is innovative and functional. It changes the 'Argonauts' into 'Argives', the resonances of which during decades of collapsing Rome–Greece treaties may have been less than positive. Note Ennius' focus (also not in the Euripidean 'original') on 'trickery', *dolus*, not only a non-heroic way to achieve a goal, but the very opposite of the Roman ideal of *uirtus*, 'manliness', 'courage'.[44] Although, as in Euripides, this is the perspective of Medea's

Nurse, the transformation of Euripides' heroic Argonauts into Argive tricksters initially pushes the audience's sympathy in the direction of the Colchian princess, whose status as displaced exile is underscored by a reference to Medea's 'home' (*domo*), absent from the source-text, and by a brilliant pun: *era errans* (lit. 'mistress missing her way'), Medea's status as victim alliteratively inscribed.

Frag. 2

antiqua erilis fida custos corporis,
quid sic te extra aedis exanimatam eliminat?

Ancient, loyal protector of your mistress' person,
What extrudes you expiring from the palace like this?

The Tutor to Medea's children enters and questions the Nurse (see Eur. *Med.* 49–51). Notice her role as *custos*, 'protector', of Medea,[45] which Ennius has added to Euripides to emphasise again the Colchian princess' vulnerable isolation in Corinth: her status as Medea *exul*. Notice, too, the Greecising, self-consciously 'tragic' language, especially the tragic coinage, *eliminat* (literally 'unthresholds', translated 'extrudes'), which drew the attention of the grammarians for its 'unnaturalness',[46] and the Aeschylean quality of *erilis corporis* ('mistress' person'), imitated perhaps from Naevius.[47] Alliteration, assonance and the visual pointedness of *exanimatam* ('breathless', 'expiring') ornament an inquiry of some thematic point.

Frag. 3

cupido cepit miseram nunc me proloqui
caelo atque terrae Medeai miserias.

Desire has drawn miserable me to declare
To sky and earth the miseries of Medea.

The Nurse speaks to the Tutor (see Eur. *Med.* 57–8). Alliteration and assonance make for an immensely speakable line.

Frag. 4

... fructus uerborum aures aucupant.

... Ears catch the fruits of words.

Context obscure. Possibly the lines come from the opening dialogue between the Nurse and Tutor, during which in Euripides' play (*Med.* 67–72) the Tutor describes a moment when he overheard the news of Creon's edict of exile against Medea. Others take the words to be a translation of Euripides' *Medea* 131 or 772–3.[48] The line, though castigated by some as 'bombastic', would have been at home in comedy.[49] Ennian tragedy is by no means 'generically' pure.

Frags 5 and 6

quae Corinthum arcem altam habetis, matronae opulentae
    optumates,
ne mihi uitio uos uortatis [exul a patria quod absum].[50]
multi suam rem bene gessere et publicam patria procul;
multi qui domi aetatem agerent propterea sunt improbati.

Wealthy, well-born ladies, who possess the soaring city of
    Corinth,
Find no fault with me [because I am an exile away from my
    fatherland].
Many have performed private and state business well, far from
    the fatherland;
Many who passed their days at home have been despised for
    this.

    nam ter sub armis malim uitam cernere
quam semel modo parire.[51]

    For I'd rather risk my life thrice in arms
Than give birth but once.

In fragments 5 and 6 Medea addresses the chorus of Corinthian women. Notice the highly sententious, anaphoric and alliterative style of fragment 5 (see Eur. *Med.* 214–18), and the assonance and verbal jingle of fragment 6. If the Euripidean model was adhered to, fragment 6 would have been towards the end of the speech begun in fragment 5 (see Eur. *Med.* 250–1). The metre is trochaic and the speech would have been accompanied by music. This may well have been part of Medea's entrance speech, and its operatic nature contrasts sharply with the Euripidean iambic dialogue which it 'translates'. There is a contrast of character, too. The deceptively ingratiating figure of Euripides' play has been replaced by a Medea with apparent self-assurance, unafraid to confront her foreign hosts with an implied critique of their behaviour. (Wives who keep their husbands at home do not serve the state well.) Note how Medea's address to the Corinthian women in fragment 5, which highlights their rootedness in their city and settled social position (in Euripides they are simply addressed as 'Corinthian women', *Med.* 214), implicitly signals Medea's exilic status, which is then (possibly) overtly stated and (certainly) brilliantly transformed through association with the praiseworthy category of service to the *respublica* abroad. Note, too, the particularly Roman character of Medea's contrast, in lines 3 and 4 of fragment 5, between home and abroad (which replaces the Euripidean contrast of private and public), especially Medea's defence of (Roman) public service abroad, which, as the city's imperial commitments grew, was being demanded more frequently of Rome's elite. Such demands conflicted with traditional Roman disapproval of prolonged absence from family and the *domus*. It is difficult, too, not to see some self-reflection here by the poet from Rudiae who spent most of his creative life 'abroad' at Rome, eventually receiving Roman citizenship in 184 BCE.[52] Behind Medea's recitative can be detected Ennian isolation and a contemporary moral and social Roman debate.[53]

Frag. 7

qui ipse sibi sapiens prodesse non quit nequiquam sapit.

The sage who cannot help himself is sage in vain.

Attributed by Cicero to Ennius' *Medea* and probably also to its protagonist (*Fam.* 7.6.2), this trochaic line seems to be a version of a Euripidean line from another play (fr. 905 Nauck: see Cic. *Fam.* 13.15.2), which may have been present in Ennius' text of *Medea*. Its context could be anywhere, including Medea's opening speech (frags 5 and 6, also in trochaics), but it would also obviously suit the Creon–Medea scene, in which Medea traditionally feigns compliance with Creon's edicts. Whatever the context, Medea's apparent denigration of herself as *sapiens* plays into the Roman elite's distrust and marginalisation of (Greek) intellectuals, who were banned several times from Rome as injurious to the collective well-being of the citizens.

Frag. 8

si te secundo lumine hic offendero,
moriere.

If I catch you here at dawn tomorrow,
You shall die.

Controversial fragment disputed by Jocelyn (349). Possibly to be assigned to Creon as he gives Medea one last day before her exile (see Eur. *Med.* 352–4) – in clear, paced-out language to allow no ambiguity. The fragment comes from a speech by Cicero (*Rab. Post.* 29), who uses it to show the threatening imperiousness of kings and, in doing so, reveals the power of Roman tragedy to inform political perception.

Frag. 9

nequaquam istuc istac ibit. magna inest certatio.
nam ut ego illi supplicarem tanta blandiloquentia
ni ob rem? qui uolt quod uolt, ita dat se res ut operam dabit.
ille trauersa mente mi hodie tradidit repagula
quibus ego iram omnem recludam atque illi perniciem dabo,
mihi maerores, illi luctum, exitium illi, exilium mihi.[54]

Things will never go that way. A great fight is on.
Would I grovel to him with such honeyed words without
Purpose? When you want what you want, strategy gives
     results.
That crooked-minded man has handed me this day
Keys to unlock all my wrath and create ruin for him,
Sorrows for me, grief for him, death for him, exile for me.

All spoken by Medea after Creon has left the stage, having given her the fatal last day to provide for her children and her exile (see Eur. *Med.* 364–75). Here Medea takes pride in her deceptions and in her power to achieve her revenge. The 'purpose' (*rem*) of line 3 is the achievement of Medea's will. Again Ennius' sententious, antithetical manner – and fondness for *uersus quadratus* (line 6) – is in evidence. Note the strong imagery: *repagula … recludam*, 'Keys to unlock'.

Frag. 10

quo nunc me uortam? quod iter incipiam ingredi?
domum paternamne? anne ad Peliae filias?

Where now am I to turn? What journey to embark on?

To my father's house? Or to Pelias' daughters?

These lines form part of Medea's verbal onslaught on Jason in the central scene of the play. See Eur. *Med.* 502–3. Their iambic form is surprising for a scene of such high emotion; Jocelyn even suggests that they may have been treated as lyric.[55] The dramatic intelligibility of Medea's mental turmoil is a function of the clarity of Ennius' language and a simple rhetorical figure (the dilemma).

Frag. 11

tu me amoris magis quam honoris seruauisti gratia.

You saved me for love more than honour.

Jason replies to Medea in the central conflict scene, employing sharp antithesis, rhyming emphasis, and the Roman concept of social status or *honor*, rather than the Greek concept of *charis*, 'favour', employed by Euripides (*Med.* 508, 526). The rhyme, *amoris … honoris*, far from being chosen simply 'for the sake of a jingle',[56] underscores Ennius' Romanisation of the *Eros/charis* contrast of the Greek play.

Frag. 12

saluete, optima corpora.
cette manus uestras measque accipite.

Greetings, treasured creatures.
Come give me your hands and take mine.

Probably an address by Medea to her children – either before or after they deliver the poisoned dress and crown to Jason's bride (see Eur. *Med.* 1069–80).[57] Chiastic structure and alliteration tighten the form of this contextually charged address, in which Medea requests to touch and embrace the children whom she will shortly kill.

Frag. 13

Iuppiter tuque adeo summe Sol qui res omnis inspicis
quique tuo lumine mare terram caelum contines

inspice hoc facinus prius quam fit. prohibessis scelus.

Jupiter and you, most high Sun, who behold all things
And enfold with your light the sea, the earth, the sky,
Behold this deed before it is done. Prevent the crime.

Delivered by the chorus after Medea has left the stage to murder her children (see Eur. *Med.* 1251–60). The perfect subjunctive of line 3 mimics the archaic formulae of Roman prayers.[58]

Frag. 14

sol qui candentem in caelo sublimat facem ...

Sol whose shining torch soars in the sky ...

Context obscure. Sol, the Sun god, is Medea's grandfather, and sends his chariot for her escape at the end of the play.

Frag. 15

utinam ne umquam, Medea Colchis,[59] cupido corde pedem
    extulisses.

I wish, Colchian Medea, you and your lusting heart had never
    left.

Context uncertain, but possibly from Jason's acrimonious outburst in the final scene of the play when he is confronted with his murdered children.

Thyestes

The feud between Atreus and Thyestes, the sons of Pelops, over the throne of Mycenae (or Argos) dramatised by Sophocles and others, was well known. Banished for seducing Atreus' wife, Aerope, Thyestes was recalled to Mycenae by his brother only to be given a banquet there of his murdered sons. The plot of Ennius' final play, *Thyestes*, produced at the *Ludi Apollinares* of 169 BCE just before his death, seems to have focused on events subsequent to the famous cannibalistic feast. Jocelyn, 412–19, argues plausibly for a dramatic setting in Epirus at the court of Thesprotus, where Thyestes' daughter Pelopia was being reared by the king. Hyginus (*Fab.* 88) relates that Thyestes journeyed to Epirus, where he raped his daughter. The latter was subsequently given in marriage to Atreus, who had gone to Epirus to effect his brother's return in response to an oracle of Apollo. The oracle had stated that only Thyestes' return to Mycenae would end a drought afflicting the kingdom. Jocelyn suggests that Ennius' play focused on the rape of Pelopia by her unknowing father and her subsequent marriage to Atreus. Pelopia will later give birth to Aegisthus, who will avenge his father's treatment at the hands of Atreus by seducing the wife of Atreus' son Agamemnon and killing him. Hyginus (*Fab.* 88.30) adds that Aegisthus also killed Atreus, but it is unclear that any of the many dramatic treatments of this myth used that variant (Seneca's *Agamemnon* certainly did not). Possible influences on Ennius' play include: Sophocles' *Atreus* and two or three *Thyestes* plays, including a *Thyestes in Sicyon*; Euripides' *Thyestes*, *Plisthenes* and *Cressae*; several other plays with the title of *Thyestes* or *Aerope*, which are recorded for Agathon, Chaeremon, Carcinus, Cleophon, Diogenes of Sinope and Apollodorus of Tarsus.[60] It had many successors: Accius, Cassius of Parma, Varius Rufus, Sempronius Gracchus, Aemilius Scaurus, Pomponius Secundus, Seneca, Curiatius Maternus and the obscure Rubrenus Lappa are all credited with an *Atreus* or *Thyestes*. Performances of Ennius' play in the late republic are attested by Cicero (*Pis.* 43; *Orat.* 184).

Both the date and the context of the play's first performance merit attention. The date (July 169 BCE) renders it inevitable that political resonances were intended by the setting of this play in Epirus. The third Macedonian war between Rome and Perseus, the king of Macedon, aided by Epirus, had begun two years earlier (171 BCE), and would reach its military climax at the Battle of Pydna in June of the following year (168 BCE). Atreus and Thyestes may well have exemplified to Ennius' audience the corruption, deviousness and decadence of Rome's Greek enemies. The performance context, the *Ludi Apollinares* in honour of the god Apollo, before whose temple *Thyestes* was probably acted, gives local piquancy to the role of Apollo's oracles in driving the events of the play (see frag. 11 on p. 82). It is difficult to believe that Ennius was unaware of the dramatic potential of this context.

Frag. 1

ibi quid agat secum cogitat parat putat.

There he reflects, plans, ponders what to do.

The subject of this iambic senarius is probably Thyestes or Atreus. If it comes from the play's prologue and that prologue was delivered by Thyestes, the subject would be Atreus. However, as Jocelyn remarks, 'the context of this fragment is obscure'[61] – but not the fragment's asyndetic clarity.

Frag. 2

> nolite hospites ad me adire. ilico istic.
> ne contagio mea bonis umbraue obsit.
> tanta uis sceleris in corpore haeret.

> Don't approach me, strangers. There, over there –
> Lest my touch or shadow harm good men.
> Such force of sin sits fast in my body.

Probably to be attributed to Thyestes, perhaps near the beginning of the play when he would have recently arrived at the court of Thesprotus. The lines (bacchiacs and cretic-trochaic) – and fragments 3 and 4 – seem to have been part of a lyric exchange between the 'polluted' Thyestes and the chorus (*hospites*, 'strangers'), to whom the injunction above is addressed. Again verbal clarity and syntactic compactness mark an Ennian dramatic exchange.

Frags 3 and 4

> quidnam est obsecro quod te adiri abnutas?

> Why, I ask, do you refuse to be approached?

> quemnam te esse dicam qui tarda in senectute –

> Whom shall I say you are who in sluggish age –

Questions addressed by the chorus-leader in song (the lines are in bacchiacs) to the foreigner, Thyestes, who has recoiled from the approach of the chorus.

Frag. 5

> Tantalo prognatus Pelope natus qui quondam a socru
> Oenomao rege Hippodameam raptis nanctus nuptiis.

> Tantalus' grandson, son of Pelops, who once got Hippodamia
> By bride-rape from her father king Oenomaus.

Perhaps a reply by Thyestes to the question of fragment 4. The lines are trochaic septenarii.

Frag. 6

ipse summis saxis fixus asperis, euisceratus,
latere pendens, saxa spargens tabo sanie et sanguine atro.
neque sepulcrum quo recipiat habeat, portum corporis,
ubi remissa humana uita corpus requiescat malis.

Transfixed on steep crags, disembowelled, hanging
From his side, dappling the rocks with gore, filth, black blood
– No tomb to hide in, no haven for his body,
Where the body may rest from pain as life dissolves.

A curse on Atreus by Thyestes. This seems to have been spoken by Thyestes to another party, perhaps (so Jocelyn: 415) when he knew that Atreus was on his way to Epirus. The lines (trochaic octonarii and septenarii) pile image on image. There would have been musical accompaniment.

Frag. 7

aspice hoc sublime candens quem uocant omnes Iouem.

See this glowing firmament which all men call Jove.

The context of this line is obscure. Any reference to the firmament or sun in a play on Atreus and Thyestes would always be likely to trigger the audience's memory of the sun's eclipse and the blackening of the firmament attendant on the cannibalistic feast.

Frags 8 and 9

eheu mea fortuna ut omnia in me conglomeras mala.

Ah, my fortune, how you roll all ills on me.

quam mihi maxime hic hodie contigerit malum.

How massively misfortune hit me here today.

Both these lines perhaps belong to a lament by Thyestes after discovering that he had raped his own daughter.[62]

Frag. 10

sed sonitus auris meas pedum pulsu increpat.

But the sound of feet strikes upon my ears.

Context obscure. In a line which (again) could have come from comedy, a character, perhaps the chorus-leader, announces the entrance of another character, perhaps Atreus. Or perhaps ...

Frag. 11

set me Apollo ipse delectat ductat Delphicus.

But Delphic Apollo himself charms, draws me.

This lyric line (combination of cretics and trochaics) is attributed by Jocelyn (413–14) either (a) to Thyestes with reference to the oracle which proclaimed that he would father a child on his own daughter and that the child would avenge him, or (b) to Atreus with reference to the oracle which dictated that the drought afflicting Mycenae would end only when Thyestes returned. I favour the latter attribution.

Frag. 12

eho tu: di quibus est potestas motus superum atque inferum,
pacem inter sese conciliant, conferunt concordiam.

See you: the gods, who own the power and movement of things
Above and below, make peace among themselves, create
    concord.

A disputed fragment, placed among the *Incerta* by Jocelyn (frag. clxii) but assigned by Warmington (1.357) to Thesprotus, king of Epirus and foster father of Pelopia, after Atreus has arrived at his court. Thesprotus is presumably suggesting the possibility of a reconciliation between the brothers. Note the portentous phraseology, pronounced alliteration and assonance, chiastic structure – 'high' language for 'high' diplomacy.

Frag. 13

impetrem facile ab animo ut cernat uitalem brabium.[63]

May I easily get him to judge the vital prize.

Again context obscure. One possibility would be that the 'vital prize' is Pelopia and the reference is to securing Atreus' consent to marrying her. But it is a complete guess, and 'vital prize' is based on a change of the ms. reading.

Frag. 14

sin flaccebunt condiciones repudiato et reddito.

But, if the contract wilts, reject and return her.

The contract mentioned above may be that of marriage between Pelopia and Atreus. If so, the words would have been spoken by Thesprotus, betrothing the latter to the Mycenaean king. Notice the archaic, 'legal' imperatives and the appositely sexual metaphor for the contract's failure.

Ambracia

The subject of this *praetexta* was the capture of Ambracia in 189 BCE by Ennius' patron, Marcus Fulvius Nobilior. The date of its performance is unknown. Fulvius experienced difficulty in securing the triumph he thought he deserved and received it, a year later than might have been expected, in 187 BCE. It is possible that *Ambracia* was performed in 188 BCE as part of the campaign to secure Fulvius' triumph or at the *ludi* acccompanying Fulvius' triumph in 187 BCE. A more likely context, however, would have presented itself a decade or so after Fulvius' victory at the dedication of the Temple of Hercules Musarum, financed apparently by money made available during Fulvius' censorship of 179 BCE (Eumenius *Paneg. Lat*. 9.7.3). The temple housed Rome's first inscribed *fasti*, i.e., calendar (Macr. *Sat*. 1.12.16), in the annotation of which Ennius probably assisted,[64] and some of the spoils of Fulvius' Ambracian victory, viz. statues of the nine Muses probably carved by Zeuxis, which Fulvius had shipped from Ambracia to Rome.[65] The temple also contained a bronze shrine of the Camenae (Italian Muses), thought to have been created in the time of Numa and previously located in the Temple of Honos et Virtus just outside the Porta Capena. Greek and Italian Muses were thus united in this shrine to brute force (Hercules) and high culture.[66]

A performance of Ennius' *Ambracia* would have fittingly accompanied the dedication of Fulvius' temple,[67] which probably became the headquarters of the Collegium Poetarum formed at some time during the second century BCE. But, whatever the date or context of its performance, it seems clear that both it and the account of the Ambracian campaign in Ennius' *Annales* were concerned to enhance Fulvius' status in the competitive hierarchy of the Roman social elite – and clearly succeeded. Hence the elder Cato's censure of Fulvius for taking poets with him to his province (Cic. *Tusc.* 1.3). I have reversed the order of fragments 2 and 3 in Klotz. Fragments 1–3 are recitative (trochaic septenarii).

Frag. 1

esse per gentes cluebat omnium miserrimus.

The world titled him the most wretched of all men.

Frag. 2

... agros audaces depopulant serui dominorum domi.[68]

... wanton house-slaves ravage their masters' fields.

Frag. 3

bene mones; tute ipse cunctato. o uide fortem uirum![69]

You advise well; but hold back. O view the brave man!

Frag. 4

... et aequora salsa ueges ingentibus uentis.

... and you stir the salt seas with mighty winds.

The context of the four surviving fragments of *Ambracia* cannot be ascertained. The account of the Ambracian campaign in *Annales* 15 dealt with the siege of the town and the attendant fighting. Warmington (1.359–61) suggests that fragment 1 refers to an Aetolian (note the ironic use of the honorific term, *cluebat*, 'titled'), fragment 2 refers to the 'lawless character of the Aetolians', fragment 3 is addressed to someone during the campaign, and fragment 4 to the 'dangers of the Adriatic'. Fragment 2 could come from a messenger's speech describing the chaos following the Roman victory. Fragment 3 refers to a third person as the 'brave man', apparently announcing his arrival on stage; this may or may not be Fulvius. The addressee of fragment 4 seems to be a deity (Neptune?), and the line may come from a prayer to effect a safe return.[70] All this is conjecture. Further speculation might extend to a symbolic display of some of the extraordinary quantity of Ambracian spoils (including allegedly over a thousand statues: Livy 39.5.14–16) which Fulvius brought back to Rome.

Sabinae

Like the siege and capture of Ambracia, the rape of the Sabine women by Romulus and his womanless Romans was a subject treated by Ennius in his *Annales*. Indeed the rape of the *Sabinae* occurred in the first book of *Annales* and the Ambracian victory in what was originally the epic's final book (Book 15). How Ennius dealt with the Sabine rape is unknown. But it is worth noting that Rome's treatment of its women was a major political issue in both the final years of the Second Punic War and the first half of the second century BCE. The Oppian Law of 215 BCE had sought to restrict women in terms of their dress, transport and possession of gold, but it had been repealed in 195 BCE (despite Cato's protests against *luxuria muliebris*, 'female luxury') after Rome's women had picketed the forum in protest (Livy 34.1–8). And the Voconian Law of 169 BCE (the year of Ennius' death) had sought to restrict women in matters of inheritance. A play showing perhaps the political importance of Roman women – in traditional accounts they prevent 'civil' war between Romans and Sabines (see Livy 1.13.1–5; Ovid *Fas*. 3.177–228) – would have constituted a prominent intervention in contemporary social issues. It is perhaps relevant to note that in Livy's account (34.5.8) of the debate attending the repeal of the Oppian Law Lucius Valerius, who proposed the repeal, cites – as an example of action by Rome's women for the public good – the role of the Sabine women, now Roman *matronae*, in stopping the Roman–Sabine war. That role would have been dramatically emphasised by (presumably) having the Sabine women form the chorus of this play.

What needs to be noted, too, and is perhaps more obvious, is the play's relevance to the theme of the recurring internal discord of the Roman state. At the beginning of the Second Punic War a new temple to Concordia was set up on the Capitol (vowed in 218, begun in 217: Livy 22.33.7; 23.21.7). Even as it reinforced the imperatives of the existing temple or shrine to the goddess at the head of the Via Sacra, it underscored the civic fragility which the goddess was there to protect. It seems likely that this fragility and its associated dangers underlay Ennius' dramatisation of the stopping of a conflict which was later regularly interpreted as a paradigm of civil war (see Livy 1.13.1–4; Ovid *Fas.* 3.199–232).[71]

Frag. 1

> cum spolia generis detraxeritis,
> quam inscriptionem dabitis?

> When you have wrested spoils from your sons-in-law,
> How will you inscribe them?

Notably the single fragment from *Sabinae* underscores the moral paradox of civil war, the value without value of victory over one's kin. 'Spoils' and 'inscriptions' are the honorific, status-conferring symbols of military conquest. If they come from the defeat of one's kin, what improved social standing, what glory, what *honour*, can result? The scene is the battlefield of the Roman–Sabine war, i.e. the valley which will be the Roman Forum – although it is difficult to believe that the whole play was located there. The speaker is presumably Hersilia, formerly a Sabine, now wife of Romulus, addressing the Sabine leaders, including the king, Titus Tatius. If the Roman audience caught the line's allusion to Jocasta's speech to Polynices at Euripides *Phoenissae* 571–6,[72] the *impietas* of civil war would be further underscored.

Clearly it was not only in his *praetextae* that Ennius alluded to contemporary debates. The intertextual relations of Ennius *tragicus* embraced both the political and the literary worlds. When discussing Ennius' *Medea* Cicero had voiced the oft-quoted judgement that the Latin author had translated 'word for word from the Greek' (*ad uerbum e Graecis expressas, Fin.* 1.4). A cursory glance at the Euripidean text on which some of the above fragments are based demonstrates otherwise. Cicero was much nearer the mark when he claimed that Roman tragedians expressed the 'force' of the plays, their *uis*, 'not the words', *non uerba* (*Acad.* 1.10). Many changes are apparent even to the most casual of critics: musical, metrical, verbal and ideological. Dramatic form and dramatic meaning are altered, and altered precisely for thematic or ideological purposes, through the inclusion, for example, of terms central to the Roman elite's political and moral image and the social status that image sustained, or through the focus on issues of contemporary cultural concern. How could any performance of *Medea* not raise issues at the heart of the Roman social hierarchy and its defining institutions in the post-Hannibalic world? In the *praetextae* we see unfettered the dynamic interplay between Ennian drama and the Roman social and political context. But throughout all the plays that Roman world is there, and the interplay, if less patent, is no less potent than in the *praetextae* themselves.[73]

Marcus Pacuvius

> Tragoediae scriptores ueterum Accius atque Pacuuius clarissimi grauitate sententiarum, uerborum pondere, auctoritate personarum. ceterum nitor et summa in excolendis operibus manus magis uideri potest temporibus quam ipsis defuisse. uirium tamen Accio plus tribuitur; Pacuuium uideri doctiorem qui esse docti adfectant uolunt.
>
> (Quintilian *Institutio Oratoria* 10.1.97)

> Among the ancients the writers of tragedy, Accius and Pacuvius, were the most distinguished for the seriousness of their reflections, the weight of their words, the authority of their dramatic characters. But the lack of polish and final touch in the completion of their works can be seen as a property of the times rather than of themselves. But Accius is accredited with more potency; those who affect learning want Pacuvius seen as the more learned.

Equally embroiled in the contemporary world of the first half of the second century BCE was Ennius' younger rival and nephew – and Cicero's most esteemed tragedian[74] – Marcus Pacuvius. Born at the Magna Graecia port of Brundisium in 220 BCE (and, like his uncle, probably into an Oscan family),[75] Pacuvius was considered to be the first Latin playwright to confine himself to tragedy. The titles of (at least) thirteen tragedies and one *praetexta* survive – *Antiopa*, *Armorum Iudicium* ('Judgment of Arms'), *Atalanta*, *Chryses*, *Dulorestes* ('Slave Orestes'), *Hermiona*, *Iliona*, *Medus*, *Niptra* ('Foot Washing'), *Orestes*, *Pentheus* (or *Bacchae*), *Periboea*, *Teucer*, and the *praetexta*, *Paulus*.[76] Pacuvius is said to have lived to the age of 90 (i.e. until 130 BCE) and was writing at least until the age of 80, producing one of his plays in 140 BCE at the same *ludi* as Accius (Cic. *Brut.* 229), who in the later 130s visited his elder rival during the latter's retirement to Tarentum (Gell. 13.2.1–4). Pacuvius seems to have enjoyed great success as a dramatist,[77] and may even have extended his literary activity to the writing of *saturae* in the Ennian manner.[78] But he seems to have been dependent for a living neither on his literary activity nor on the theatre. He was an accomplished painter; indeed, according to Pliny (*HN* 35.19), the most famous painter of his generation in Rome, whose painting in the Temple of Hercules in the Forum Boarium was the second-most celebrated Roman painting in the city. Pliny also implies that Pacuvius was a 'person of status' (*honestus*), which suggests that he was not only a Roman citizen but a member of the equestrian class. Cicero (*Amic.* 24) represents him as an *amicus*, 'friend',[79] of Gaius Laelius, the consul of 140 BCE and intimate of Scipio Aemilianus. Some kind of association between Scipio Aemilianus and Pacuvius may be assumed from the fact that the latter's sole *praetexta* honoured Scipio's father (see further on p. 106).

Pacuvius' financial independence resulted in turn in theatrical independence and some striking new departures. Not one of his tragedies bears the same title as any of his uncle's plays. In so far as they relate to his uncle's tragic *oeuvre*, that relationship seems at times one of (often recondite) sequel to, or competitive variant on, his uncle's canon.[80] Pacuvius is clearly drawn to the mythological cycles already treated in Attic and Ennian tragedy: those of the Argonauts and Thebes, for example, or, most especially, the Trojan cycle – here Pacuvius mirrors the preference of his Roman tragic predecessors. But Pacuvius' choice of myths within those cycles reveals a penchant for the obscure, the exotic, the novel. *Dulorestes*, for example, deals with the myth (otherwise unknown in ancient literature)[81] of Orestes' disguise as a slave and of Clytemnestra's attempt to marry Electra to Oeax, and cannot be traced to a Greek original. Neither can *Medus*, concerned with Medea's son by Aegeus and his avenging of the death of his grandfather, Aeetes, nor *Iliona*, with its extraordinary switch of Polydorus, Iliona's brother, and Deipylus, Iliona's son, and the resulting murder of the latter by his own father, Polymestor. The former is a sequel to, and the latter a variant on, famous tragedies by Euripides and Ennius (*Medea* and *Hecuba*), but their independence seems marked.[82]

Of course, postclassical Greek tragedy, which has not survived, would have had an influence, even a substantial one, on Pacuvius' plays

– in addition to the influence of Pacuvius' Roman predecessors. But the fragments make it clear that Pacuvius' plays are in no sense slavishly dependent either on those Latin pre-texts or on Greek 'originals'.[83] Even where indebtedness is manifest, the changes are profound. On occasion such changes derive in part from *contaminatio*. *Armorum Iudicium*, for example, takes from Aeschylus and Sophocles, even as it obviously functions as a prequel to Ennius' *Ajax*. *Niptra* enacts a 'fusion of two Sophoclean tragedies',[84] but much of its interest may have lain in a non-Sophoclean focus on Odysseus' putative genealogical connections to Italy and thus on his suffering as Roman paradigm (see Cic. *Tusc.* 2.48).[85] Although his *Chryses* may be indebted to Sophocles' play of the same name (some deny this),[86] it certainly involves material from two Euripidean plays. The plot of *Chryses* seems to be a sequel to Euripides' *Iphigenia in Tauris*, and one particular fragment shows that space was opened up for a meditation on the aether and earth, derived from Euripides' *Chrysippus* (frag. 836N)[87] and accompanied by the flute (the metre is trochaic septenarius):

> hoc uide circum supraque quod complexu continet
> terram ...
> solisque exortu capessit candorem, occasu nigret,
> id quod nostri caelum memorant, Grai perhibent aethera:
> quidquid est hoc, omnia animat format alit auget creat
> sepelit recipitque in sese omnia, omniumque idem est pater,
> indidemque eadem aeque oriuntur de integro atque eodem
>   occidunt ...
> mater est terra. ea parit corpus, animam aeter adiugat.
>   (*Chryses* frags vi–vii Klotz)[88]

> Behold this around and above which holds in its clasp
> The earth ...
> And at sunrise catches a candescence, at sunset blackens,
> That which our people name 'sky', the Greeks call 'aether':
> Whatever this is, it quickens, shapes, feeds, increases, creates,
>   buries
> All things and receives all things into itself, and is father of all
> And from the same place the same rise afresh and in the same
>   place die ...
> The mother is earth. She births the body, ether adds life's
>   breath.

Although Cicero (*ND* 2.91) claims in respect of line 4 of the above fragment that the playwright seems to have forgotten that the character speaking the lines is supposed to be Greek, Pacuvius' distinction between the speaker (Thoas?) and the Greeks may have had thematic purpose.

Not all of Pacuvius' changes can be traced to Attic tragedy. Sometimes another variant of a myth is incorporated,[89] at other times the changes seem to be original. Witness the following passage, which is again recitative in trochaic septenarii, is probably delivered by a chorus, and is variously attributed to *Chryses*, *Dulorestes* and *Hermiona*. The text, as so often with these fragments, is occasionally uncertain.

> Fortunam insanam esse et caecam et brutam perhibent
>   philosophi,
> saxoque instare in globoso praedicant uolubili.
> id quo saxum inpulerit fors, eo cadere Fortunam autumant.
> insanam autem aiunt, quia atrox incerta instabilisque sit;
> caecam ob eam rem esse iterant, quia nihil cernat quo sese
>   adplicet;
> brutam, quia dignum atque indignum nequeat internoscere.
> sunt autem alii philosophi, qui contra Fortunam negant
> ullam miseram in rebus esse, temeritatem esse autumant.
> id magis ueri simile esse usus reapse experiundo edocet:
> uelut Orestes modo fuit rex, factust mendicus modo
> naufragio. nempe ergo id fluctu, hau Forte aut Fortuna obtigit.
>   (*Incerta* frag. xiv Klotz)[90]

> Fortune, philosophers contend, is demented and blind and
>   insensate,
> And stands, they maintain, upon a rolling ball of stone.
> Where chance drives the stone, there falls Fortune, they
>   declare.
> She is demented, they say, because she is cruel, fickle and feckless;
> She is blind, they repeat, because she cannot see where to steer;
> Insensate, because she cannot tell the deserving from the
>   unworthy.
> But there are other philosophers who deny that wretched Fortune
> Exists anywhere in the world, but affirm the existence of chance.
> That this is more like the truth experience and events teach;
> As Orestes was once a king, and just now made a beggar
> Through shipwreck. Surely a wave did this, not Fors or Fortune.

The rhetoric of this passage is Pacuvian: alliteration, assonance, homeoteleuton, repetition, parallelism, inversion, sign-posting structure the speech.[91] Nor is the rhetoric alone Pacuvian. It is unlikely that there was any Greek original behind or beneath this text.[92]

What both the above passages display, too, is Pacuvius' penchant for the dramatisation of ideas. Regarded by the ancient critics as the most learned (*doctus*) of the Roman tragedians (Hor. *Ep.* 2.1.55, Quint. *Inst.* 10.1.98), he seems to have quite self-consciously intellectualised the genre, making it respond to the flood of ideas, philosophies and ideologies now entering Rome from the East. Victories in Greece resulted not only in the importation of Greek slaves and artefacts to Rome – paintings, sculpture, plaques, gold, silver, ivory, bronze[93] – but Greek books, ideas and idea-makers. The historian Polybius was himself an imported detainee; and Roman aristocrats like Lucius Aemilius Paullus filled their households with Greek rhetoricians, Greek teachers and Greek books for their sons.[94] In the 160s and the decades following, many Greek philosophers made their way to Rome, including the Stoics, Crates of Mallos and Panaetius of Rhodes, and the leader of the Athenian Academy, the Sceptic Carneades, who in 155 BCE engaged in a famous debate at Rome with his Athenian rivals, the Peripatetic Critolaus and the Stoic Diogenes. Carneades was regarded by Cato as profoundly 'unRoman' in his 'verbal pyrotechnics' and ratiocinative elevation of words over deeds, reality and truth.[95] The traditional schism between the philhellenism of various elements of the Roman elite, including the so-called 'Scipionic Circle', and the antihellenism of other sectors, including Cato, is now recognised as overly simplistic. But it is clear that opposition to the new Graecism was real and manifested itself in attempts to expel Greek intellectuals from the city.[96] It is equally clear that Pacuvius' own self-conscious intellectualism embraces the new thinking and the new value of the word and the idea.

The passages quoted above show Pacuvius' interest in weaving Greek natural philosophy and Stoic and Epicurean ideas into the dramatic texture of his plays – into their musical texture, too, since both the above passages were recitative. *Antiopa* even featured a celebrated disputation on the respective value of the active and contemplative lives (*Ad Her.* 2.43; Hor. *Ep.* 1.18.41–4) and quasi-philosophical observations on the operation of the sun (frag. viii Klotz); while the main focus of *Armorum Iudicium* seems to have been the debate between Ajax and Ulysses on their respective worthiness to receive Achilles' armour. That four of Pacuvius' small output of plays (*Chryses*, *Dulorestes*, *Hermiona*, *Orestes*) featured the 'just matricide' Orestes indexes not only the dramatist's interest in aetiological history (Orestes was credited with the foundation of Diana's cult at Aricia,[97] and his ashes were later listed as one of the guarantors of Roman *imperium*: Serv. *ad Aen.* 7.188), but in complex moral dilemmas and their intellectual and rhetorical possibilities.[98] As late republican commentators show, Pacuvius' philosophical interests struck a thoroughly Roman cord and aided the successful reception of his *oeuvre*.

Pacuvius' fascination with ideas is also a fascination with language, with words, where a philosophical and a painterly interest fuse. The result, as the surviving fragments attest, is not only a predilection on Pacuvius' part for picturesque description and for constructing lines and scenes that openly play with language (sophistic debates, for example, discussions of ambiguity and hermeneutics,[99] or dramatised riddles, as in the *testudo* fragment of *Antiopa*),[100] but a passion for linguistic experimentation. The fragments, of course, often chosen as they were for their linguistic idiosyncrasies, perhaps overly represent this aspect of Pacuvius' dramatic writing. Certainly they abound in bold neologisms, stunning coinages, archaic and archaising forms, suggestive of an attempt to rival the richness and diversity of Attic tragic diction and to create an appropriate Roman tragic language, even as Pacuvius' contemporary Terence was working at creating an appropriate language for comedy. Ennius' attested stylistic self-consciousness was mentioned above. We do not have his nephew's thoughts on dramatic language. But the prologues of Terence's comedies clearly suggest a heated debate in dramatic circles of the 160s BCE about language, dialogue, diction, tone and style, all of which seem embraced by the Terentian notions of *oratio*, *stilus* and *scriptura*.[101]

The linguistic audacity and rhetorical syntax of the Pacuvian fragments themselves constitute a response to that debate – a response clearly in part metadramatic, advertising the notorious linguistic forms and structures as generically 'tragic', but also more complex, nuanced and 'dramatic' than is often represented. Medea offers to avert disaster from Perses in *Medus*:

> possum ego istam capite cladem auerruncassere.
>
> > (*Medus* frag. xvii Klotz)

> I can averticate that disaster from your head.

The unusual word, *auerruncassere*, was already archaic in Pacuvius' day, reserved for religious ritual as Cato's use of it in *De Agricultura* (141.2) illustrates.[102] Pacuvius' use of the word was mocked by Lucilius (Bk. 26, frag. 616 Krenkel), but it both elevates the diction and moves it to a register familiar to his audience. The famous neologisms quoted by Quintilian (1.5.67) show linguistic experimentation at its most extreme. The line perhaps comes from the storm narrative of *Teucer* (fragment 9 on p. 102):

Nerei repandirostrum incuruiceruicum pecus

Nereus' flattened-snouted, incurved-necked herd

The colourist at work, creating linguistic (adjective–noun) compounds where none existed before, and hitting the top of any conceivable tragic register. The line exemplifies early Roman tragedy's predilection for what Horace called *sesquipedalia uerba*, 'words one-and-a-half feet long' (*Ars* 97).The result may strike the modern reader as bizarre, but it should be noted that the line is designed to echo and vanquish Livius' famous description of dolphins in *Aegistus* (frag. 2 on p. 31) and is made to work sonally through deft alliteration and assonance.

Pacuvius' theatrical fame and success were no accident. His sense of what would work dramatically is not confined, as has sometimes been suggested, to routine stage-directions of the kind found scattered over Roman comedy (the *ecce* sign of entering actors, the creaking of stage-doors, etc.),[103] but it manifests itself also in audacious language audaciously structured to seize an audience's attention. Thus alliteration, asyndeton, homeoteleuton:

inluuie corporis
et coma prolixa impexa conglomerata atque horrida
(Antiopa frag. xv Klotz)

Body's filth
And hair wild, matted, compacted and stiff

hic sollicita studio obstupida suspenso animo ciuitas[104]
(Atalanta frag. viii Klotz)

Then the city tense with fervour, dazed, minds uncertain

Alliteration, asyndeton, the rarest of metaphors (*clupeat*, *lapit*),[105] and (in the second example) triple chiasmus:

currum liquit, clamide contorta astu clupeat bracchium.
(Hermiona frag. xxi Klotz)

He left the chariot, with twisted cloak cleverly shields his arm.

lapit cor cura, aerumna corpus conficit.
(Periboea frag. iii Klotz)

Anxiety stones the heart, hardship consumes the body.

Sometimes, too, a radical metaphor encapsulates the moral paradoxes of the action. Thus Orestes (or Electra):

> utinam nunc matrescam ingenio ut meum patrem ulcisci queam.
> (*Dulorestes* frag. xviii Klotz)

O to motherify my nature to avenge my father.

The ability of language at times to constitute the world and to impact the soul –

> o flexanima atque omnium regina rerum oratio
> (*Hermiona* frag. xiv Klotz)

O bender of minds and queen of the universe, eloquence

– was integral to Pacuvius' tragic vision and its dramatic force.

What the fragments also reveal is Pacuvius' taste for the sensational, the visually and emotionally arresting, the dramatic. Most obviously this can be seen in Pacuvius' fondness for exotic stage-settings, but it manifests itself, too, in spectacular stage-action. *Antiopa* may have concluded with the appearance of Mercury as *deus ex machina* (Hyg. *Fab.* 8); *Medus* (frag. xi and *Inc.* xxxvi Klotz) seems to have featured an appearance by Medea in her airborne chariot drawn by winged snakes (Cic. *Rep.* 3.14). *Orestes* (or *Hermiona*) may have contained a stage pursuit of its hero not only by the Furies but also by his murdered mother, and Furies may have figured, too, in Pentheus' manic vision scene in *Pentheus*.[106] Perhaps the most famous Pacuvian spectacle is the ghost-scene in *Iliona*, when the *umbra*, 'shade', of Deipylus rises from the earth to address his mother as she sleeps:[107]

> mater, te appello, tu, quae curam somno suspensam leuas
> neque te mei miseret, surge et sepeli natum ...
>   ... prius quam ferae
> uolucresque ...
> neu reliquias semesas sireis denudatis ossibus
> per terram sanie delibutas foede diuexarier.
> (*Iliona* frag. iv Klotz)

Mother, I call on you. You suspend anxiety in soothing sleep
And have no pity for me – rise and bury your son ...
    ... before wild beasts

And birds ...
Do not let my remains, half-eaten, the bones all stripped,
Fetid with blood, be dragged foully over the land.

Strong imagery and situational pathos join with theatrical spectacle and music to make the scene especially effective and affective. Cicero (*Tusc.* 1.106) comments on the emotional power of the scene, as the above recitative, chanted to subdued and tearful melodies (*pressis et flebilibus modis*), 'would induce sorrow in whole theatres'. What the Ciceronian record also attests is something all but irrecoverable: Pacuvius' use of music, which would have enhanced and dramatically empowered the majority of his scenes and been a constitutive and affective part of the theatrical spectacle. Pacuvius' painterly style seemed regularly drawn to the macabre and its possibilities for evocative imagery – to the depiction of dreams, portents, shipwrecks, imprisonment, squalid neglect, violent revenge, emotional recognitions and self-sacrifice – and most of these descriptions would have been sonically charged and modulated through music. Such was the interconnection between Pacuvian tragedy and its music that Cicero could claim that expert members of a theatre audience in the late republic could recognise Pacuvius' *Antiopa* by the flautist's first note (*Acad.* 2.20).

Of course, much of the emotional force of a Pacuvian scene derived from the human situations and interactions dramatised. Noticeably, many of the most powerful of such scenes are constructed out of issues of identity. Cicero twice (*Amic.* 24, *Fin* 5.63) refers to the audience's clamorous reaction to the scene (in either *Chryses* or *Dulorestes*) where Pylades pretends to be Orestes to save his friend (*Incert.* frag. xiiib Klotz). Lost and false identities leading to startling recognitions seem to have been something of a *forte* for Pacuvius, whose *Antiopa*, for example, seems to have climaxed in the reunion of the persecuted and abused Antiopa with her long-lost sons:

saluete gemini, mea propages sanguinis!
(*Antiopa* frag. xiii Klotz)

Hail twins, my prolongation of blood.

Lost and false identities were a prominent concern of Euripidean tragedy (see, e.g., *Ion* and *Iphigenia in Tauris*) and a regular motif of Greek 'New Comedy' and of Roman comedy, which clearly influenced Pacuvius greatly. The famous swapping of identities between master and slave in Plautus' *Captiui* bears some theatrical relationship to the scene in Pacuvius' *Chryses* or *Dulorestes* noted above. But it is the mother–son recognition scene which figures most strongly in the fragments.

Another such scene occurs at the climax of Pacuvius' *Atalanta* where Parthenopaeus' birth-ring reveals the truth of his parentage (frags xiii–xvi Klotz). The emotions of the scene are dwelt upon by the dramatist, whose Atalanta is ashamed to tell the story of her son's birth:

> mi gnate, ut uerear eloqui, porcet pudor.
> > (*Atalanta* frag. xvii Klotz)

My son, shame prevents me, so I fear to speak.

Indeed in *Atalanta* Pacuvius seems to have doubled the mother–son separation situation by including as Parthenopaeus' companion and 'life-twin' Telephus, in search of his own lost mother.[108] In this doubling he may have been influenced by – or himself have influenced – his younger contemporary playwright, the comedy-dramatist Terence.[109] Mother–son separation/recognition situations were something of an obsession of Pacuvius, whose *Medus* uses the Medea–Medus separation to play with the falsification of false identities and whose *Iliona* uses the Iliona–Polydorus reconciliation (frag. xii Klotz) to create a most compelling murder-confrontation scene between the son-no-son, Polydorus, and the father-no-father, Polymestor (frag. xiv Klotz).

Sometimes identity comes at the cost of paradoxical realities. Thus Chryses, son of Chryseis the controversial Trojan captive of *Iliad* I, who has just realised that he is the son of Agamemnon and half-brother of Orestes, declares:

> atque, ut promeruit, pater mihi patriam populauit meam.
> > (*Chryses* frag. iii Klotz)

And, as it deserved, my father ravaged my fatherland.

Potent emotional scene, potent alliteration (a stammering array of 'p's and 'm's), potent and morally paradoxical language reinforced by homoeoteleutic focus (on *meam*) and political transferability. Pacuvius articulates the quintessential contradiction of the colonised or conquered who is now part of the imperial power.[110] Whether delivered with ironic tone or not, the line would have shocked: think of Polybius praising Rome's devastation of Greece. Pacuvian moral paradoxes were not confined to the stage. The following line of Ajax from *Armorum Iudicium* was sung at the funeral of Julius Caesar:

men seruasse ut essent qui me perderent?
                    (*Armorum Iudicium* frag. xv Klotz)

Did I save them to be my assassins?

Suetonius, who is the source of this information (*Iul.* 84), reports that the words were sung with the intention of eliciting pity (*miseratio*) for, and resentment (*inuidia*) at, the dictator's assassination – just as (the implication is) these words on the Roman stage had elicited from audiences of the late republic pity and resentment at Ajax' treatment in the Pacuvian play. Roman values and the reception of *Armorum Iudicium* are illuminated through the reification of a Pacuvian paradox as history.

It is unsurprising that Pacuvius' plays were used in the world of political theatre. As was observed on p. 3, Roman political life was innately theatrical. And its public institutions were operated through a form of speaking governed by the same principles of rhetoric informing the discourse of tragedy. During the second century BCE much Roman public speaking became influenced by the full-blown, self-consciously 'grand' Asianic style, emanating primarily from Pergamum. It was to have a huge impact on the evolution of Roman oratory, reaching its apex in the style of Cicero. Opposed to the spare, so-called 'Attic' style, it was a form of verbal structure which rejoiced in the details of language itself and in the theatrical possibilities that language offered. Varro (Gell. 6.14.6) cited Pacuvius as a fine example of this 'grand' style, the defining property of which he nominated as *ubertas*, 'richness', 'fertility', 'abundance', and certainly one of the hallmarks of Pacuvian tragedy is clearly its rhetorical pleasure and power, its deliberate construction of affective declamatory moments (see, for example, Telemon's denunciation of Teucer in *Teucer*, frag. 19 on pp. 104–5). But stylistic antitheses are always simplistic. And Pacuvian tragic language is as capable of dramatic spareness and simplicity as it is of *ubertas*, as the extant fragments attest.

The connection between the Pacuvian 'grand' style and contemporary oratory needs stressing not simply for stylistic or cultural purposes but to underscore the former's contemporary accessibility and force. The nephew of Ennius was as concerned as any orator to direct his words and themes to the larger social and political world in which they were exhibited. Hence political power, its use and abuse, is a prominent theme of several plays, and issues of justice, injustice, vengeance and punishment are debated, dramatised – even theologised:

di me etsi perdunt, tamen esse adiutam expetunt
quom prius quam intereo spatium ulciscendi danunt.
(Iliona frag. ix Klotz.)

Though the gods destroy me, they seek to help
By providing time for vengeance before I die.

Thus (probably) Iliona plotting revenge on her husband and would-be
slayer of her brother, the tyrannical Polymestor, in a more theological
mode than the vengeance-seeking Orestes (or Electra) cited above.
Tyrants are not restricted to *Iliona* (Polymestor) and *Dulorestes*
(Aegisthus and Clytemnestra). They may also be found in *Antiopa*
(Dirce), *Chryses* (Thoas), *Medus* (Perses), *Pentheus* (Pentheus), *Periboea*
(Agrius) and *Teucer* (Telamon). Tyranny, tyrannicide, revenge, punishment, family blood-feuds are at the heart of the tragic genre, but
Pacuvius seems – and ought – to have had little doubt about their
contemporary resonance. Whether his *Dulorestes* had any relationship
to the Sicilian slave revolts of the 130s BCE, as some have argued,[111] is
clearly unknowable. But his *Pentheus*, like Naevius' *Lucurgus*
(discussed on pp. 47–9), could not but have impacted on Roman
thinking about the social and religious issues involved in the prohibition of the Bacchants and in attitudes to foreign cults.[112]

Similarly Pacuvius' exploration of identity confusions, relationships between fathers/mothers and sons, between brother and
brother, brother and sister, friend and friend, his focus on courage,
loyalty, friendship, justice, *uirtus*, *pietas*, *fides*, *pudor*, *patria*, exile,
prodigies, augury, oracles, the gods, ambition, pleasure, fortune,
chance, death, philosophical reason, the exchange of favours,
benefacta, moral reciprocity, the citizen body, the *populus* – and on the
quintessentially Roman theme of *orbitas*, the lack of a child or parent
(imagined or real) – are unsatisfactorily reduced to theatrical varia-
tions on the inherited tragic *corpus*. All have a bearing on the social,
moral and political problems and changes of the second century BCE
at Rome.[113] The words with which Orestes thanks his supporters in
Dulorestes could have come from any member of Rome's second
century elite:

... ista si ita sunt promerita uestra, aequiperare ut queam
uereor, nisi numquam fatiscar facere quod quibo boni.
(Dulorestes frag. xxviii Klotz)

... if such are your merits, I fear that I cannot reciprocate
Except by never failing to perform what good service I can.

As could this revealing language on the imperatives of 'loss of face':

> patior facile iniuriam si est uacua a contumelia.
> (Periboea frag. v Klotz)

I endure injury easily if it is free from insult.

Or the laudation of oratory quoted above (*Hermione* frag. xiv Klotz). Roman political and religious language can be seen to interlace the dramatic action itself: *inimicitia*, 'enmity', *redamptruare*, 'ritual dancing', *antiqui amici maiorum meum*, 'ancient friends of my ancestors', *augurare* 'perform augury', *lingua auium*, 'bird language' (from *Chryses*).[114] Cicero's comments (*Tusc.* 2.48) on Ulysses in Pacuvius' *Niptra* show how carefully the dramatist restructured inherited tragic material to accord with Roman social practice and ideals. Remarks on the *grauitas* of Ulysses (so Cicero above) or on the *auctoritas* of Pacuvian characters (so Quintilian, *Inst.* 10.1.97) acknowledge and underscore cultural and social reformations.

But, although the dramatic world of Roman tragedy is almost as public and open as that of a political assembly, it is not entirely so. And in Pacuvius we encounter the first extant undeniable soliloquy of Roman tragedy (there are, of course, 'probable' soliloquies in Ennius), with some of the hallmarks of its development to Seneca already in place, especially the address to the mind or soul. Thus Diomedes in *Periboea*, using the standard iambic dialogue line (senarius) to exhort himself:

> consternare, anime, ex pectore aude ecuoluere[115]
> consilium subito, mens, quod enatumst modo,
> qui pacto inimicis mortem et huic uitam offeras.
> (Periboea frag. viii Klotz)

Be stirred, soul, dare to unroll from the heart
Suddenly, mind, the plan just now born,
How to bring my foes death, and this man life.

The soliloquy, like the aside, although common in Hellenistic drama, was foreign to the more public world of Attic tragedy;[116] it functions as an index of the greater focus in Roman tragedy, especially later in Seneca, on psychological interiority, on the detailed dramatisation of the workings of human thought and emotion prior to action. Silence, too, merits words:

miseret me, lacrimis lingua debiliter stupet.

(*Incerta* frag. vi Klotz)

I pity, tears unnerve, benumb my tongue.

Pacuvius' interest in language was also an interest in human psychology, in constructing character, emotion, passion on stage from language and its delivery. Cicero's comments on *Teucer* fragment 19, reported on p. 105, show how effective such constructions could be.

The surviving fragments of *Teucer*, one of Pacuvius' most famous and most popular plays, and of his *fabula praetexta*, *Paulus*, follow.

Teucer

The play is a sequel to Pacuvius' *Armorum Iudicium* ('Judgement of Arms'), in which the Greek warrior Ajax of Salamis competes for but is not awarded the arms of the dead Achilles at Troy, and commits suicide. It is, however, possible that *Teucer* was written first, followed by *Armorum Iudicium* as a prequel. The plot of *Teucer* deals with the aftermath of Ajax' death and centres upon the return to Salamis of his half-brother, Teucer. Teucer was famed as an archer and had fought alongside his half-brother at Troy. When he returns home without his brother, he is banished by his father Telamon. He is reputed then to have founded the city of Salamis on the island of Cyprus. Teucer was the son of Telamon by his slave-mistress, the Trojan princess Hesiona; Ajax was Telamon's legitimate son and heir by his wife. Probable source-texts for the play were Aeschylus' *Salaminiae*, Sophocles' *Teucer* and Ennius' *Telamo*. The subject was also popular with other tragedians, including Ion of Chios, Euaretus and Nicomachus.[117] It is also possible that Livius Andronicus wrote a *Teucer*. There would have been an obvious and special rivalry between Pacuvius' play and the *Telamo* of his uncle. Pacuvius' *Teucer* was part of the tragic repertoire of the late republican theatre and performed more than once.[118] For a notorious performance (probably of this play) in 51 BCE, at which the famous orator Hortensius was hissed, see Cicero's letters (*Fam.* 8.2.1). The order of the fragments below is extremely uncertain.[119]

Frags 1–4

quae desiderio alumnum, paenitudine,

squale scabreque, inculta uastitudine

Who aching for her nurselings, with penitude,
Drab and dirty, dishevelled, in her solitude

flexanima tamquam lymphata aut Bacchi sacris
commota, in tumulis Teucrum commemorans suum

Her mind turned, like one maddened or stirred by rites
Of Bacchus, calling aloud her Teucer among the tombs

postquam defessus perrogitando aduenas
omnis de gnatis, neque quemquam inuenit scium

After he grew tired of asking every stranger
About his sons, and found not one who knew

neque perpetrare precibus imperio quiit

And his prayers, his power can produce nothing.

These iambic dialogue lines, perhaps from the prologue, apparently describe the desolation of Telamon's concubine, Hesiona, as she longs for her 'nurselings' (*alumnum*), Ajax and Teucer, away at the Trojan war, and the anxiety of Telamon, as he seeks news of them. In fragment 1 Pacuvius' painterly style is in evidence, with language which draws attention to itself, laid on like colours from a palette. Notice the homoeoteleuton, resulting in end rhyme. In fragments 2–4 notice how, contrary to his reputation of maintaining a 'grand' style, Pacuvius adopts clear, well-paced utterance for the communication of essential information to his audience. The alliterative pattern of fragment 4 gives verve to the line. If these lines are from the prologue, it was clearly not the kind of 'contorted Pacuvian prologue' (*contorto aliquo ex Pacuuiano exordio*) satirised by Lucilius (Bk. 29, frag. 844 Krenkel). Fragment 2 is placed in the *Incerta* (= frag. 1) by Klotz. Fragment 4 is regarded as obscure and unlocatable by D'Anna (1967), 232.

Frag. 5

nihilne a Troia adportat fando?

Does he bring no report from Troy?

Someone has just arrived from Troy (Teucer?) and an inquiry is made of him.[120]

Frag. 6

quam te post multis tueor tempestatibus!

How many seasons since I looked on you!

Teucer addresses Telamon, Hesiona or his native land (it is not likely to be an address by Telamon to Teucer before learning of Ajax' death).[121] Notice again the comparative simplicity of the writing, as in fragments 2–5, patterned as in fragment 4 by alliteration but with a heavy final word.

Frag. 7

periere Danai, plera pars pessum datast.

The Danai perished, the prime part sunk deep.

Teucer (or a messenger) tells of the disastrous Greek shipwreck, with alliterative, asyndetic, patterned precision.

Frags 8–13

mihi classem imperat
Thessalum nostramque in altum ut properiter deducerem.

He orders me to hurry
And take to sea Thessaly's fleet and our own.

Nerei repandirostrum incuruiceruicum pecus

Nereus' flattened-snouted, incurved-necked herd

... profectione laeti piscium lasciuiam
intuemur nec tuendi capere satietas potest.[122]
interea prope iam occidente sole inhorrescit mare,
tenebrae conduplicantur, noctisque et nimbum obcaecat
     nigror,
flamma inter nubes coruscat, caelum tonitru contremit,
grando mixta imbri largifico subita praecipitans cadit,
undique omnes uenti erumpunt, saeui existunt turbines,
feruit aestu pelagus.

... Joyful in departure we gaze upon the dancing
Of the fish, and the gazing admits of no satiety.
Meanwhile, as sunset now nears, the sea bristles,

Darkness doubles, black night and storm-clouds blind us;
Flame flickers amid the clouds, sky trembles with thunder,
Hail mixed with drenching rain suddenly crashes down,
On all sides every wind explodes, fierce twisters rise,
The sea's surge boils.

rapide retro citroque percito aestu praecipitem ratem
reciprocare undaeque e gremiis subiectare adfligere.[123]

Quickly back and forth with heaving swell waves toss the ship
Headlong from both sides, smash it down, dash it from their
    bosom.

... armamentum stridor, flictus nauium,
strepitus, fremitus, clamor tonitruum et rudentum sibilus [124]

... creaking of tackle, colliding of ships,
Noise, roar, the clash of thunder and whistle of ropes

ubi poetae pro sua parte falsa conficta canunt,[125]
qui causam humilem dictis amplant

When poets for their part sing the false, the fictive,
Amplifying a trivial theme with their words

Accompanied by the flute (the lines are trochaic septenarii), Teucer
narrates the departure from Troy and describes the storm which
attacked the fleet. Normally one would expect such a description
to emanate from a messenger, and some have suggested a
messenger as speaker here.[126] But fragment 8 (in which the 'he' of
'he orders' must be Agamemnon and 'me' must refer to a fleet
commander) makes that very difficult. Several scholars place these
fragments after Telamon's famous outburst in fragment 18.[127]
Fragments 9 and 10 (= Klotz *Incerta* frags xliv and xlv) are not
specifically attributed to this play but may well belong here.
Fragment 9 is discussed on p. 93. Fragment 10, the storm-scene (a
topos of ancient tragedy and epic), gives Pacuvius full space for the
realisation of his descriptive talents in an explosion of violent
imagery and verbal pyrotechnics: 'Latin poetry's first and finest
description of a voyage and sea-storm'; its influence on later poets,
including Virgil, is notable.[128] Fragments 10–12 display Pacuvian
ubertas, the 'grand' style, used with dramatic appropriateness and
alliterative and assonantal force.[129] Chiasmus, asyndeton,
homoeoteleuton, clause variety and parallelism structure and
empower the speech. The second line of fragment 12 was imitated

(parodied?) by Lucilius (frag. 1309 Krenkel), and is quoted by Caelius Rufus in a letter to Cicero (*Fam.* 8.2.1) to describe the unfavourable reception which the advocate Hortensius received on entering Curio's theatre in June 51 BCE. Caelius' letter shows the degree to which the language of republican tragedy penetrated Roman social discourse – despite Lucilius' attempts to stop it. Fragment 13 may well belong elsewhere; most commentators refuse to place it.

Frags 14 and 15

nos illum interea proliciendo propitiaturos facul[130]
remur.

We think that in the meanwhile we'll placate him easily
With enticements.

nam Teucrum regi sapsa res restibiliet.

For the truth itself will restore Teucer to the King.

These two fragments seem to deal with an attempt (by the chorus? – notice 'we', *nos*, in frag. 14)[131] to reconcile Teucer with his father Telamon. Nothing too 'grand' about the style once more, but calculated alliteration gives each line structure and vocal force. Fragment 14 (iambic octonarius) was recited to the flute.

Frags 16–21

haud sinam quidquam profari prius quam accepso quod peto.

I'll not let you say anything before I get what I seek.

    nisi coerceo
proteruitatem atque hostio ferociam

    unless I check
Your insolence and repay your boldness

facessite omnes hinc: parumper tu mane!

All of you go; but you – stay for awhile.

segregare abs te ausus aut sine illo Salaminem ingredi
neque paternum aspectum es ueritus quom aetate exacta indigem
liberum lacerasti orbasti extinxti, neque fratris necis

neque eius gnati parui, qui tibi in tutelam est traditus ...?

You dared to separate and come to Salamis without him,
And did not fear your father's sight, his years spent, childless,
Torn, bereaved, destroyed by you, careless of a brother's death
And his tiny son, who was entrusted to your care ...?

quamquam annisque et aetate hoc corpus putret

Although this body rots with years and age

te repudio nec recipio; naturam abdico. facesse!

You – I reject and spurn; I renounce nature. Away with you.

The fragments above seem to have been delivered by Telamon to
Teucer in anger at his failure to return with his half-brother, Ajax,
and Ajax' son, Eurysaces, the 'tiny son' (*gnati parui*) of fragment 19.
The order of the fragments is again uncertain. Fragment 16 has a
staccato alliterative pattern that would facilitate the dramatic
speakability of the lines. Fragment 18 seems to indicate that in
Pacuvian tragedy, as later in Seneca, the chorus could leave the stage
during the dramatic action. Fragment 19 (*segregare* ..., 'You dared
...') is famous for the impression it made on Cicero as he watched a
performance of the play in late-republican Rome. Cicero's
comments (*De Or..* 2.193) on the theatrical power of the lines
describe the eyes of the actor burning from out of the mask (*ex
persona ... ardere*), such was his apparent anger and grief for Ajax as
he spoke the words to the accompaniment of the flute. At *quom
aetate* ... ('his years spent ...') the actor modulated his voice to a
pitiful tone (*ad miserabilem sonum*), sobbing and grieving as he
spoke.[132] A triple asyndetic homoeoteleuton (*lacerasti orbasti
extinxti*) structures the anger and the grief.

Frags 22 and 23

aut me occide, illinc si usquam probitam gradum.

Or kill me, if I ever step from here.

... ut ego, si quisquam me tagit

... as I, if anyone touches me

Fragment 22 seems to have been spoken by Teucer. Fragment 23 is
obscure.

Frag. 24

profusus gemitu, murmure 'occisti' antruat.[133]

Sprawled, he rejoins with a groan, a murmur: 'You have killed me'.

The text of this fragment is fraught with difficulties. Its subject is likely to be Telamon.

Frag. 25

patria est ubicumque est bene.

The fatherland is wherever it is well.

This Latin rendering of a famous line at Aristophanes *Plutus* 1151 is attributed by Cicero (*Tusc.* 5.108) to Teucer, and so perhaps belongs to this play. If so, it would most suit a finale, as Teucer leaves for exile and a new *patria* in Cyprus. The sentiment was/became proverbial.[134] The line is omitted by Klotz.

Paulus

The subject of Pacuvius' sole known *praetexta* was Lucius Aemilius Paullus, consul of 168 BCE, censor of 164 BCE, most famous for his ending of the Third Macedonian War through the defeat of the Macedonian king, Perseus, at Pydna on the north-east coast of Greece in 168 BCE. The main focus of the play seems to have been the battle of Pydna itself. A scholiast to Boethius (*Cons.* 2.2) indicates that the play contained a scene in which Paullus shed 'pious tears' (*pias impendisse lacrimas*) for the calamity suffered by Perseus and the unreliability of human fortune.[135] Occasions when the *praetexta* may have been performed include *ludi* associated with Paullus' dedication of Phidias' statue of Minerva in the Temple of Fortuna Huiusce Diei at Rome in 167 BCE (Pliny *HN* 34.54) or with his triumph of the same year, or the *ludi* organised at his funeral in 160 BCE.[136] If the play was performed prior to Paullus' triumph, it could certainly be regarded as designed among other things to combat the considerable resistance to the triumph which Paullus faced (Livy 45.35–9; Plut. *Paul.* 30.4–32.1).

The funeral *ludi*, however, are the only ones for which there is evidence, and it is known that they featured *ludi scaenici*, which included the first performance of Terence's *Adelphoe* and the second (failed) performance of his *Hecyra*. From the production notices (*didascaliae*) accompanying the plays we learn that the funeral games, hence *Adelphoe* and *Hecyra*, were financed by Lucius' surviving sons (both adopted into other families), Quintus Fabius Maximus and Publius Cornelius Scipio Aemilianus. Since the central issue of *Adelphoe* is natural and adoptive filiation, it is clear that these sons of Paulus were interested in drama with a strong bearing on their own political and social world. Perhaps they commissioned Pacuvius' *Paulus* for the same occasion. They already had an actor (*mimetes*) on hand for the funeral procession, trained to impersonate Paullus (Diod. Sic. 31.25.2). Accounts of the battle of Pydna may be found in Polybius (29.14–21), Livy (44.36–43), and Plutarch (*Paul.* 16–23). For the order of the fragments I have followed Warmington (2.302–5).

Frag. 1

qua uix caprigeno generi gradilis gressio est.

Where is scarce a foothold for the goat-born brood.

Context obscure. Warmington 2.302, who follows Plutarch's *Aemilius Paullus*, places this iambic senarius first, construing it as part of a description of the Roman assault on Mt Olympus by Scipio Nasica (*Paul.* 15–16). Possible locations are at the beginning of the play (perhaps part of a prologue) before the main action, which seems to have centred on the battle of Pydna, or later in the play as part of a messenger's report. Klotz places this fragment last of the four. Again alliterative effects are to the fore, and an etymological pun: *caprigeno generi*.

Frag. 2

pater supreme, nostrae progenii patris

Father most high, of our whole line's father

Perhaps an appeal to Jupiter as divine ancestor of the Aemilii,[137] made by Lucius Aemilius Paullus, probably on the day of battle just before the fighting commenced. Plutarch (*Paul.* 17.5–6) represents him as sacrificing before battle. Note the careful, alliterative structure of the line: *pater … pr … tr … pr … patris*. Perhaps the next line began with *progenitor*.[138]

Frag. 3

niuit sagittis, plumbo et saxis grandinat.

It snows with arrows, with lead and stones it hails.

A description of the battle of Pydna (by a messenger?), in which Pacuvius trumps Uncle Ennius by developing the simile of spears 'like rain' (*uelut imber*) used by the latter in his depiction of Nobilior's siege of Ambracia (*Annales* 15, frag. 391 Skutsch) and transforming it into a powerful double metaphor, expressed through a neat chiasmus, playfully weighted (dissyllabic verb and trisyllabic noun, followed by two dissyllabic nouns and trisyllabic verb).

Frag. 4

nunc te obtestor, celere sancto subueni censorio.[139]

Now I beg you – quickly – help a venerable man of censorial rank.

The reference to 'censorial rank' means that this trochaic line was delivered (with emotion, accompanied by the flute) by an actor playing (or, perhaps more likely, an actor/messenger reporting the words of) Marcus Porcius Cato Licinianus,[140] who lost his sword in the battle (Plut. *Paul.* 21.1) and who is here represented as appealing for help, using his father's former status as censor (184 BCE) to do so. The panic of the moment still allows for a precise, alliterative chiasmus: *c ... s ... s ... c.*

Cicero nominates Pacuvius as the finest tragedian of the republic (*Opt. Gen.* 2), although the republican satirist Lucilius and his imperial followers, Persius and Martial, found his language inflated and not to their taste.[141] Certainly his plays were popular in the century after his death. As was observed above, lines from the *Armorum Iudicium* were chosen for their evident appropriateness to be sung at Julius Caesar's funeral. *Iliona, Medus, Antiopa* were each performed in the late republic and clearly on more than one occasion,[142] as was *Teucer*, which seems to have been something of a favourite of Cicero's – perhaps because it dealt with the issues of ingratitude and unjust exile.[143] Even one of Cicero's own correspondents quotes from *Teucer* (*Fam.* 8.2.1) – he knew the allusion would be well received. Horace (*Ep.* 2.1.55–62) indicates – with less than total approval – that Pacuvius' plays, like those of Accius, Plautus and Terence, still packed Rome's theatres in mid-Augustan Rome.

4

TRAGIC APEX

Poetic form and political crisis

In 151 BCE a stone theatre being built on the Palatine Hill near the Lupercal was demolished by order of the senate. It had been commissioned by the censors three years earlier (Vell. Pat. 1.15.3), and was the culmination of several attempts to erect a permanent theatre in Rome. All had failed. This time the chief instigator of the theatrical interdiction was Publius Scipio Nasica, former consul and censor, who argued that a permanent theatre served no function (*inutile*) and would be damaging to public morality (*nociturum publicis moribus*: Livy *Epit.* 48). In furtherance of the last claim, a prohibition was declared on the provision of public seating at games held within the city.[1] Whatever the pretexts, the senate was determined to maintain its control of the *ludi scaenici*. In 151 Pacuvius was nearly 70 years old and approaching his final years of tragic composition. Lucius Accius was nineteen and (presumably) had yet to write.

Lucius Accius

in Accio circaque eum Romana tragoedia est.
(Vell. Pat. 1.17.1)

Roman tragedy exists in Accius and around him.

Though Marcus Pacuvius and Lucius Accius knew each other and even had plays performed on one occasion at the same *ludi*, these two tragedians inhabited different worlds. Pacuvius' world was one of social and moral turmoil; but the second half of the second century BCE, Accius' prime creative period, witnessed that turmoil turn into revolutionary violence and political crisis. Lucius Accius wrote just before, during and after the start of the bloody process which Ronald Syme was to call 'The Roman Revolution',[2] viz. the civil conflicts whereby Rome was transformed from a 'republic' ruled by a senatorial oligarchy (and the people) to an 'empire' governed by one man. Seven years after one of Accius' early plays was performed at the *ludi* of 140 BCE the tribune Tiberius Gracchus was assassinated, as was his brother Gaius some eleven years later. Accius lived through the resisted attempts of populist politicians to resolve the agrarian crisis in Italy, improve the conditions of the Roman people and its allies, and diminish the power and wealth of the senate. He witnessed, too, Rome's destruction of Carthage and Corinth and annexation of north Africa, Greece and much of Asia Minor; Scipio Aemilianus' ruthless siege of Numantia in Spain; the rise of Gaius Marius through the war with Jugurtha in Numidia and with the Cimbri and Teutones in north Italy; Marius' radical reforms of the army and monopolisation of the consulship; perhaps the start of the civil war between Marius and Sulla and of Rome's war in the east with Mithridates of Pontus. He almost certainly experienced at least part of the Social War of 91–89 BCE between Rome and its Italian allies – a war which not only revealed the vast problems at the heart of the Roman empire but could well have destroyed that empire from its centre. If he lived into the Marian proscriptions of 87–6 BCE, he would almost certainly have seen the head of his dramatic rival Julius Caesar Strabo impaled on the rostra of the Roman Forum (Cic. *Brut.* 307, *De Or.* 3.10). Lucius Accius was the tragedian of the beginnings of 'The Roman Revolution'. His immense tragic output merits examination not only for its literary and dramatic properties but for its relationship to the political crises of his time.

The major figure of republican tragedy was a Roman citizen and, like his immediate predecessor Pacuvius, long-lived. But unlike the other tragic dramatists, Lucius Accius came from the north – from Umbria, the birthplace of Plautus. Born at Pisaurum probably in 170 BCE and perhaps into a family of freedman status (Jerome *Chron.* ad Ol. 160.2),[3] Accius lived at least to his mid- or late eighties, if Cicero's claim to have had literary discussions with him is to be believed (*Brut.* 107). Accius used his long life productively. In addition to almost 50 attested tragedies and two *praetextae*, he wrote works on stage-history and stage-practice (*Didascalica* and *Pragmatica*), the fragments of which reveal a predictable interest in props, costumes, masks (*miriones*),[4] genre and choruses (he criticises Euripides for carelessness in this area: *Didasc.* 11–12 Warmington), and a less predictable interest in audience reception and misunderstanding (*Prag.* 5–6 Warmington). He also attempted several kinds of non-dramatic poetry including an *Annales* on Roman festivals, *Parerga* perhaps on agriculture, *Praxidica* on practical advice, (possibly) amatory poems, and *Sotadici* (although these are perhaps to be identified with the amatory poems). Accius was both poet and scholar, and his interest in writing extended to orthography, in which he advocated a number of radical changes. It is as a philologist that he features as the addressee of Varro's early work, *De Antiquitate Litterarum.*

From Accius' long career little biographical information survives. In 140 BCE he and Pacuvius produced plays for the same *ludi* (Cic. *Brut.* 229). About 135 or 133 BCE, on a journey to Asia Minor, he visited the retired Pacuvius in Tarentum, to whom he read his *Atreus* only to have its writing criticised for its harsh and acerbic qualities (Gell. 13.2.1–4).[5] Possibly about 120 BCE Accius became the head of the Collegium Poetarum.[6] Shortly after this, in 115 BCE there was another repressive move against the theatre, resulting in censorial expulsion of some theatrical personnel from the city (Cassiodorus *Chron.* 450). At some time unspecified in the sources Accius successfully sued a mime actor for mentioning his name on the stage (*Rhet. ad Her.* 1.24, 2.19). In 104 BCE Accius' *Tereus* was first produced (Cic. *Phil.* 1.36). About 90 BCE in the headquarters of the Collegium Poetarum (probably the Temple of Hercules Musarum in the Circus Flaminius) he refused to stand up when the patrician playwright Julius Caesar Strabo entered, conscious of his own superiority as a dramatist (Val. Max. 3.7.11).[7] In that very same temple, too, perhaps forty years earlier (about 130 BCE) the rather short Accius had had erected a very tall statue of himself, which inevitably occasioned comment (Pliny *HN* 34.19). Lucilius, ever the enemy of the republican tragedians, remarked that Accius' statue was in inverse proportion to his pride and intransigence (frag. 747 Krenkel). Cicero, however, thought highly of this 'most eloquent' (*disertissimus*, *Sest.* 120), 'grave and brilliant poet' (*grauis et ingeniosus poeta*, *Planc.* 59), whose plays remained popular through to Augustan Rome (Hor. *Ep.* 2.1.55–62).

Cicero also clearly knew the Accian *oeuvre* well, and Accius himself, and should therefore command belief for the substance of another and most important piece of biographical information (*Arch.* 27): the existence of a relationship of some closeness between Accius and the consul of 138 BCE, Decimus Junius Brutus Callaicus, the conqueror of the Lusitanians and Callaici. Brutus allegedly adorned the vestibules of the monuments financed by his war-spoils with verses by Accius. Amongst such monuments was the temple to Mars in the Circus Flaminius, which he dedicated probably shortly after 133 BCE, inscribing its entrance with Accian Saturnians.[8] Cicero may have exaggerated the closeness between the poet and the aristocrat (it was in the interest of his client, the poet Archias, for him to have done so), but the fact of the existence of the relationship seems beyond doubt.[9] Indeed Cicero provides evidence (*Brut.* 107) that Accius may have also been on close terms with a number of aristocrats, including Quintus Fabius Maximus Allobrogicus, conqueror of the Gallic Allobroges, who in 121 BCE erected on the Sacra Via at the east end of the Roman Forum the Fornix Fabianus, a triumphal arch celebrating his victories and his ancestors.

Accius' nearly 50 tragedies (forty-six titles can be ascribed to him)[10] show a catholic range of subject matter combined with an eclectic use of sources. His plays tackle the main sagas of the house of Atreus, of the Trojan war and its aftermath, of the Theban cycle, of the Argonautic expedition, as well as myths of Bacchus, Hercules, Theseus, Perseus, Prometheus, Meleager, Io and others. Six of his tragedies are named after the chorus.[11] There is much use of the great Attic triad of tragedians, (presumably) of Hellenistic tragedy, and of Accius' own Roman predecessors, Livius, Naevius, Ennius (most especially) and Pacuvius[12] – as well as of Homer, Hesiod, the poems of the Trojan Cycle and Apollonius of Rhodes. The fragments suggest that, although from among the Greek tragedians he seems to favour Aeschylus and Sophocles over Euripides, his use of all his predecessors was eclectic, 'contaminatory', and creative (*Philocteta* is a prime example).[13] And not a few of Accius' tragedies pursue fairly unusual aspects of the inherited mythic material and may well be 'original' dramatisations, taking their subject matter directly from Homer and other non-dramatic poetry and indebted to no previous Greek or Roman tragic versions. Plays such as *Agamemnonidae, Astyanax, Deiphobus, Diomedes, Epinausimache* ('Battle of the Ships'), *Melanippus, Persidae* or *Persis* have no extant dramatic precedent and may have been première dramatisations by the scholar-poet of existing mythic narratives. Where a dramatic precedent exists, as with pseudo-Euripides' *Rhesus*, an important intertext for *Nyctegresia* ('Night-Sortie'), a substantially different dramatisation may result;[14] even a play with a famous title, such as *Medea*, may have been an essentially original dramatisation.

The fragments suggest, too, that Accius was interested in tracing the mythic sagas in detail through several generations, while focusing on some of the more obscure offshoots of the main myth. Most of the plays can be arranged within one of three large, elaborated cycles: the Pelopides, Thebes, the Trojan War.[15] It has been suggested (controversially) that Accius may have presented the plays cyclically, i.e. according to their position within the cycle, but, even if, as is most likely, this was not the case, a concern with the historical evolution and perhaps interconnectedness of familial calamities and of national calamities (e.g., of Argos and Thebes)[16] – a mark of Accius' originality and generic alterity according to some[17] – would have manifested itself over the course of the tragedian's career and have accorded with an apparent focus on family genealogy and history in the two *praetextae*.[18]

Of the style of Accian tragedy one adjective is used more than any other: Asianic. The plays explode with and through the highly ornate rhetoric of the school of Pergamum, a city Accius is likely to have visited on his celebrated trip to 'Asia' in the 130s (Gell. 13.2.2). Critics have indeed argued for an influence on the style of Accius not only of Pergamene rhetoricians but of such baroque sculptural masterpieces as the Pergamene Altar of Zeus. It is difficult to imagine that this most extraordinary sculptural display, now housed in the Pergamonmuseum in Berlin, would not have had a profound impact on the tragedian, had he viewed it.[19] But it is clear that from well before the date of Accius' possible Pergamum visit, in fact from about 150 BCE onwards, the style of Roman oratory was itself already moving towards the grand, the emotional, the ornamented and ornamental. The consul of 144 BCE, Servius Sulpicius Galba, and, more famously, Gaius Gracchus, the revolutionary tribune assassinated in 122 BCE, were themselves practitioners of the ornate, portentous, 'Asianic' style geared towards the manipulation of the emotions of an audience and the generation of conviction through spectacle and pathos.[20]

Whatever the merits of the label 'Asianic', the extant fragments of Accius' tragedies reveal a consistent concern with verbal muscle and display, with sheer rhetorical force or *uires*, to use Quintilian's term (*Inst.* 10.1.97). Thus in *Diomedes* grandiose, metaphorical diction (*exanclauimus*) and sonic echo (*execrabile*) elevate a statement of suffering:

> fere exanclauimus
> tyranni saeuum ingenium atque execrabile.
> > (*Diomedes* frag. i Klotz)

> We have almost dreg-drained
> The tyrant's savage and execrable nature.

In *Eurysaces* a messenger rings the changes on Telamon's state of mind with a quadruple asyndeton:

persuasit maeror anxitudo error dolor.
>   (*Eurysaces* frag. x Klotz)

Grief, anxiety, wandering, pain persuaded.

Neoptolemus offers a six-fold asyndeton, although its context is unclear. The four elisions all but turn the line into an extraordinary compound noun.

uim ferociam animum atrocitatem iram acrimoniam
>   (*Neoptolemus* frag. iv Klotz)

Violence, ferocity, will, cruelty, wrath, spite

In *Astyanax* the paradoxical ethics of violence are encased in a wall of alliteration:

ferum feroci contundendum imperiost, saeuum saeuiter.
>   (*Astyanax* frag. vi Klotz)

Brutality brutally must be crushed, savagery savagely.

In *Armorum Iudicium* ('Judgement of Arms') Ajax expresses deep feeling through anaphora, alliteration, assonance, high diction (*anxitudo*) and a tricolon of increasing colonic length:

ibi cura est, ibi anxitudo acerba, ibi cuncta consiliorum
ratio et fortuna haesit.
>   (*Armorum Iudicium* frag. viii Klotz)[21]

There distress lies, there clings acid anxiety, there all
Calculated counsel and fortune.

Elsewhere in the same play a neat chiasmus informs Ajax' cutting homily to his son, Eurysaces:[22]

uirtuti sis par, dispar fortunis patris.
>   (*Armorum Iudicium* frag. x Klotz)
In virtue be like your father, unlike him in fortune.

Cantica, too, are composed with the same attention to alliterative sound and rhetorical structure. Thus in *Phinidae* Jason or perhaps a chorus of Argonauts evoke (probably early in the play) a scene of natural beauty in an orchestrated alliterative mosaic:

hac ubi curuo litore latratu
unda sub undis labunda sonit ...
simul et circum stagna tonantibus
excita saxis saeua sonando
crepitu clangente cachinnant.

(Phinidae frs. i and ii Klotz)[23]

Here where on the arcing beach
Waves under waves roll and roar ...
All around, thundering rocks
Stir pools to savage sounds.
Crashing, clapping, cackling.

In *Philocteta* Philoctetes lyricises his pain in an anapaestic aria, concluding the quatrain below not with a cry of agony but a neat chiasmus:

heu! quis salsis fluctibus mandet
me ex sublimo uertice saxi?
iam iam absumor: conficit animam
uis uolneris ulceris aestus.

(Philocteta frag. xix Klotz)

Ah, who might send me to the salt waves
From the soaring summit of the cliff?
Now, now I'm consumed. Life finished by
Virulence of wound, ulcer's fire.

Accius developed such a reputation for oratorical skills that the anecdote is preserved by Quintilian (*Inst.* 5.13.43) that, on being asked why he eschewed a career as a court lawyer, he replied that he would not then be able to control what his adversaries said. Further examples of Accius' rhetorical fire may be found in the fragments of *Atreus*, *Tereus* and *Decius* presented later in the chapter. But already it will be apparent that Accius 'of the spirited tongue', as Ovid calls him (*animosi ... oris*, *Am.* 1.15.19),[24] directed his famed rhetorical power to dramatic purposes. Criticisms by modern literary historians of Accius' 'overheated' style, full of 'bombast' and 'hyperbole', are parochially prejudicial, and mislead.[25] As later in Seneca, rhetorical patterning gives speakability and force to lines; bombast has dramatic function and dramatic effect.

Here are the three longest speeches preserved in the fragments.[26] The first is from the prologue to Accius' *Medea* or *Argonautae*; the speaker is a shepherd, who, as Cicero reports (*ND* 2.89), has never seen a ship.

> tanta moles labitur
> fremibunda ex alto ingenti sonitu et spiritu;
> prae se undas uoluit, uortices ui suscitat;
> ruit prolapsa, pelagus respergit, reflat.
> ita dum interruptum credas nimbum uoluier,
> dum quod sublime uentis expulsum rapi
> saxum aut procellis, uel globosos turbines
> existere ictos undis concursantibus;
> nisi quas terrestres pontus strages conciet;
> aut forte Triton, fuscina euertens specus
> subter radices penitus, undanti in freto
> molem ex profundo saxeam ad caelum eruit.
> sicut citati atque alacres rostris perfremunt
> delphini ...
>   Siluani melo
> consimilem ad aures cantum et auditum refert.
>   (*Medea* frags i-iii Klotz)

> So immense a mass slides
> Roaring from the deep with mighty howl and hiss;
> It swirls waves before it, forces whirls in its wake.
> It sinks in collapse, it sputters, it spews the sea.
> You would think a shattered thundercloud rolled at you,
> That a boulder was caught and hurled by the winds
> Or storm-clouds, or that round-balled tornadoes
> Sprang up from the shock of colliding winds –
> Unless the ocean stirs some havoc of the land
> Or perhaps Triton with his staff heaves some cavern
> From deep beneath its roots and flings a mass of rock
> In the billowing ocean from its depths to the sky.
> Like swift and sprightly dolphins humming
> Through their beaks ...
>   it sends music
> Like Silvanus' song to my ears and hearing.

A showpiece of a speech, certainly; a metatragic one,[27] in which dramatic language draws attention to itself and parades its own artifice, as Accius' verbal virtues (*uerborum uirtutes*, Vitr. 9. Pref. 16) are manifested in baroque description, heavy and mannered alliteration, elaborate, shifting similes, polysyllabic diction, asynedic structures, a translingual pun (behind *perfremunt*, 'humming', lies the Greek *bremein*, used of both speech and music)[28] – the shepherd's helpless astonishment reflected in astonished and astonishing language. Linguistic spectacle anticipates, in part constitutes, dramatic spectacle – and introduces a nature/culture opposition ironically reflected and dissolved in the unsophisticate's verbal and rhetorical sophistication.

The second and third speeches are from the *praetexta*, *Brutus*. The speaker of the second speech (in iambic senarii) is the last king of Rome, Tarquinius Superbus, describing a dream in which he foresees his own expulsion at the hands of his nephew Brutus, whose brother he had killed. The speaker of the third speech (in recitative, trochaic septenarii) is a seer or priest interpreting Tarquin's dream, perhaps (although this is not certain) in immediate response to Tarquin's speech.

> quoniam quieti corpus nocturno impetu
> dedi sopore placans artus languidos,
> uisus est in somnis pastor ad me adpellere
> pecus lanigerum eximia pulchritudine,
> duos consanguineos arietes inde eligi
> praeclarioremque alterum immolare me;
> deinde eius germanum cornibus conitier
> in me arietare eoque ictu me ad casum dari;
> exin prostratum terra, grauiter saucium,
> resupinum in caelo contueri maxumum ac
> mirificum facinus: dextrorsum orbem flammeum
> radiatum solis liquier cursu nouo.
>
> (*Brutus* frag. i Klotz)[29]

When I gave my body to rest as night came on,
Soothing with slumber my languishing limbs,
I dreamt I saw a shepherd driving towards me
A woolly flock of amazing beauty;
Two rams of the same blood were then chosen
And I sacrificed the more splendid of the two.
Then its brother butted me with its horns,
Rammed at me, and the blow caused me to fall.
Prostrate on the ground and gravely wounded,
I saw in the sky, as I lay there, a great and
Marvellous thing: the sun's flaming orb and rays
Melted away to the right on a new course.

rex, quae in uita usurpant homines, cogitant curant uident
quaeque agunt uigilantes agitantque, ea si cui in somno
　　accidunt
minus mirandum est. sed di in re tanta haut temere improuiso
　　offerunt.
proin uide ne quem tu esse hebetem deputes aeque ac pecus,
is sapientia munitum pectus egregie gerat
teque regno expellat; nam id quod de sole ostentum est tibi,
populo commutationem rerum portendit fore
perpropinquam. haec bene uerruncent populo. nam quod ad
　　dexteram
cepit cursum ab laeua signum praepotens, pulcherrume
auguratum est rem Romanam publicam summam fore.

(Brutus frag. ii Klotz)

My king, that what men do in life, ponder, fret over, observe,
That what they practice and plan in their waking hours befall
　　them in sleep
Astonishes little. But the gods surprise you in this prime
　　matter with point.
So be careful lest the man you hold to be as obtuse as a sheep
Wears a heart egregiously armoured with wisdom
And expels you from the kingdom. For what was shown to you
　　by the sun
Portends that for the people a revolution of the state is
Imminent. May this turn out well for the people. For the fact
That the prince of stars moved from left to right favourably
Foretold that the Roman commonwealth would be supreme.

Neither 'bombast' nor 'hyperbole' is an appropriate term here. Alliteration, asyndeton, the piling up of synonyms, inversion, assonance, anaphora, etymological puns (*egregie*, lit. 'out of the flock') – all subject initially to a relatively subdued tone and steady pace appropriate to the accents of meditative dialogue. The dream narrative itself is sharp, spare, compressed in an affective succession of images. The recitative of the seer is no frenzied outburst, but a predominantly calm presentation of complex interpretative thinking, involving a 'new', indeed psychologically precocious theory of dreams.[30] It is a formal presentation, too, using occasional 'grand' language (*commutationem*, *perpropinquam*) and the diction of Roman ritual, *uerruncent* ('turn out'). The latter is used as the seer inverts his point of view to side with the people, not the king, and either exclaims his subversive wish and prophecy or speaks the subversive lines in an aside, *sotto voce*. *Verruncent* occurs elsewhere in Accius in a similar context in *Aeneadae* or *Decius* (see frag. 6 on p. 139), and may possibly be part of a (predictable) strategy to emphasise Roman institutions, ritual and practice in the *praetextae*.[31] This is language on display, capable of winning the praises of a Vitruvius; but its effect is not simply or primarily linguistic. There are complex theatrical issues involved. As at the opening of *Phoenissae* (Jocasta is speaking) –

> sol qui micantem candido curru atque equis
> flammam citatis feruido ardore explicas,
> quianam tam aduerso augurio et inimico omine
> Thebis radiatum lumen ostentas tuum.
>
> > (*Phoenissae* frag. i Klotz)[32]

> Sun, whose gleaming chariot and hurtling horses
> Unfurls darting fire with fervid heat,
> Why with such adverse augury and hostile signs
> Do you show your radiant light to Thebes?

– Accius' self-displaying language creates and performs a dramatic world.

That dramatic world was as visual as it was aural. Horace in his remarks on Roman theatre comments on how the mind is more affected by the eyes than the ears (*AP* 180–2). Accius' dominance of the Roman tragic stage in the last decades of the second century BCE reveals his full awareness of that fact. Even from the fragments it is clear that he was fond of structuring the dramatic action around moments of high spectacle. *Phoenissae* opens with the spectacle of Jocasta's prayer to the Sun, *Medea* with the bombastic bewilderment of the ignorant shepherd (see p. 116). *Andromeda* features the famous 'voyeuristic' scene of the maiden chained to a rock awaiting the onset of the sea-monster (frags viii–x Klotz). *Decius* (frags 10–11 on pp. 140–1) climaxes in ritual self-sacrifice, *Atreus* (frag. 14 on p. 132) in the gruesome revelation in which Thyestes learns of his cannibalistic feast. *Pelopidae* may well have climaxed in Aegisthus' discovery, when about to slay Thyestes, of his own incestuous birth (frag. iv Klotz).[33] *Philocteta* exploits, throughout, the spectacle and visuality of pain. In *Epigoni* Accius has Alcmaeon confront the spectacle of his mother, Eriphyle, wearing the necklace and robe (of Harmonia) with which she had been bribed to send her husband, Amphiaraus, and (later) Alcmaeon himself off to war and (in Amphiaraus' case) death. She appeals to her son, who grabs her on stage before killing her (on stage or otherwise).

In *Eriphyla* visual attention seems drawn to the Harmonia necklace as prop by quite extraordinary language:

> Pallas bicorpor anguium spiras trahit.
>
> > (*Eriphyla* frag. Klotz)

> Bicorporeal Pallas drags serpents' coils.

The monstrous, serpentine necklace binding Eriphyle's throat receives its appropriate monstrous, serpentine description. If the necklace is in full view, as the present tense may suggest, language is used to direct the audience to visual details of a spectacular prop. Just as in *Andromeda* language (alliterative, assonant and imagistic) points to the stage and the set itself.

> immani tabe templum obuallatum ossibus
>
> > (*Andromeda* frag. x Klotz)

> A shrine of monstrous decay, walled with bones

In plays where we can observe that Accius has changed a source-text, it is sometimes clear that the Roman playwright's changes are directed precisely to achieving greater visual impact on stage. Thus in *Antigona* the heroine's capture by Creon's soldiers, only reported in Sophocles, is enacted on stage in Accius' version. High spectacle would almost always be accompanied by music, but that there were also on occasion other, more 'special' sound-effects seems clear. So in *Troades*, perhaps of a messenger witnessing the appearance of Achilles' ghost (cf. Sen. *Tro.* 168–80):

> sed utrum terraene motus sonitusne inferum
> peruasit auris inter tonitra et turbines?
>
> > (*Troades* frag. ii Klotz)

> Did earthquakes or the howling of the dead
> Penetrate my ears amid thunder and tornadoes?

Often, too, spectacle joins with pathos as Accius aims directly at the audience's emotions, presenting scene after scene of unbearable suffering. The cannibalistic climax of *Atreus* (see frags 14–16 on p. 132) is a most famous instance of this fusion of spectacle and pathos. But it is clearly an Accian trait, as a glance at the passages already cited indicates. It is worth adding to them the focus in several plays on the spectacle of female suffering. In *Andromeda* that suffering is centre-stage.

misera obualla saxo sento, paedore alguque et fame[34]
(Andromeda frag. viii Klotz)

Piteous, walled in by craggy rock, by filth and cold and hunger

The above line may have been spoken by Andromeda herself. In *Astyanax* it is clear that a character on stage is affected by the sight of female pain (of Andromache or Hecuba), to the impressive spectacle of which the audience's attention is drawn:

abducite intro, nam mihi miseritudine
commouit animum excelsa aspecti dignitas.
(Astyanax frag. xiii Klotz)

Take her inside, for the soaring nobility
Of her look has stirred my heart to pity.

Strong, complex and suffering women, sometimes displaying specifically Roman virtues (here *dignitas*), pervade Accian tragedy,[35] and are often at the centre of its dramatic focus. Seneca was to learn much from Accius in this matter (see, e.g., *Tro.* 736–813).

Accius' dramatic world appealed to the minds and moral sensibilities of his audience as well as to their emotions and physical senses. Accius' plays are filled with the social and moral language of the Roman elite and the traditions they promoted and sustained.[36] And, like all Roman tragedies, they contain their proportion of homiletic, sometimes contradictory wisdoms, which were to reach their teleological destiny in Senecan *sententiae*.

multi iniquo, mulier, animo sibi mala auxere in malis
quibus natura praua magis quam fors aut fortuna obfuit.
(Andromeda frag. vii Klotz)

Many men of malice, woman, have made evil for themselves,
Blighted by their crooked nature rather than chance or fortune.

fors dominatur neque uita ulli
propria in uita est.
(Medea frag. xvii Klotz)

Chance is the master; no one's life
In life is his own.

erat istuc uirile, ferre aduorsam fortunam facul.
(Meleager frag. xvi Klotz)[37]

It was a manly thing to face bad fortune finely.

nam is demum miser est, cuius nobilitas miserias
nobilitat.

(Telephus frag. vii Klotz)

He alone is wretched, whose fame makes wretchedness
Famed.

As these examples show, such 'wisdoms' are often quickened by
verbal play.

At times Accian lines have a political and social, not simply
moral edge.

> neque fera hominum pectora
> fragescunt, donec uim persensere imperi.
> (Aegisthus frag. iv Klotz)

> Nor do the wild hearts of men
> Break till they have felt the force of power.

nihil credo auguribus, qui auris uerbis deiuitant
alienas, suas ut auro locupletent domos.

(Astyanax frag. iv Klotz)

I do not trust augurs, who enrich other ears
With words to fill their own houses with gold.

non genus uirum ornat, generi uir fortis loco.
(Diomedes frag. iii Klotz)[38]

Birth does not adorn a man, courage adorns his birth.

satin ut, quemcumque tribuit fortuna ordinem,
numquam ulla humilitas ingenium infirmat bonum?
(Persidae or Persis frag. Klotz)[39]

Suffices it that, whatever rank fortune has given,
Low estate never weakens a good nature?

probis probatum potius quam multis fore
(Epinausimache frag. v Klotz)

Better to be honoured by the honourable than the many

tua honestitudo Danaos decepit diu.
(Myrmidones frag. vi Klotz)

Your high status has long duped the Danai.

It seems clear that, contrary to some modern commentators,[40] Accius' plays cannot but have participated in contemporary moral and social questions. Literature and politics were never far apart in Roman culture. In the late republic and early empire, tragic tags were frequently used by political figures at decisive self-dramatising moments in their own life-theatre. But even in 146 BCE we find Scipio Aemilianus quoting Homer's *Iliad* 6.448–49 at the destruction of Carthage (Diod. 32.24; Appian *RH* 8.132),[41] and in 133 BCE, on receiving the news of Tiberius Gracchus' death, we find him quoting *Odyssey* 1.47 (Diod. 34/35.7.3; Plut. *Tib. Gracch.* 21.7). Scipio Aemilianus was perhaps the most famous second-century case of a major political and military figure gathering around him a philhellenic circle of intellectuals. Cicero called Scipio's 'circle' a *grex*, 'flock' (*Amic.* 69), using the word which also means 'theatre company'; it included philosophers (Panaetius), historians (Polybius) and satirists (Lucilius). Other prominent members of the Roman elite had their own *greges*.[42] These *greges* included playwrights, as both the word suggests and as Terence's association with Scipio Aemilianus indicates. Terence was in the forefront of the communication of the new Hellenic ideals and in promoting politicised drama. But when Cicero mentions the political use of the theatre in the second century BCE the period he cites is that of the Gracchi and Saturninus (*Sest.* 105) – the precise period when and through which Accius wrote. The relationship between Accius and the political world must be addressed.

Accius' connection with Brutus Callaicus was mentioned above. It seems to many (but not all)[43] a reasonable assumption that Accius wrote the *praetexta*, *Brutus*, at least in part to glorify by association his own patron, who may have had it performed at his triumphal games celebrating his Spanish victories (about 133 BCE) or at the dedication of one of his manubial monuments, perhaps that of the temple to Mars in the Circus Flaminius shortly after the triumph. Its two main fragments are quoted above. The remaining two (certain)[44] one-line fragments appear to come from the end of the play, from speeches by Brutus or other opponents of Tarquin at the time of the latter's expulsion.

> Tullius qui libertatem ciuibus stabiliuerat
> > (*Brutus* frag. iv Klotz)

> Tullius who had made civil liberty firm

> ... qui recte consulat consul cluat
> > (*Brutus* frag. iii Klotz)[45]

... That the man of right counsel be titled consul

Note the term, *cluat* ('be titled'), denoting honorific naming and thus appropriate 'high' diction, used ironically in Ennius' *Ambracia* (frag. 1 on p. 84) and often used by Plautus in parodic passages to derail the values of tragedy or the self-important.

There is more at issue in these two fragments than a *praetexta's* expected celebration of Roman institutions. What stands out here is the validation of the consulship itself and the representation of it as the successor to good kingship in its protection of *libertas*, civil freedoms, which the usurper Tarquin through the murder of King Servius Tullius had destroyed and which the consuls and Rome's new constitution restore and guarantee. At a time of severe questioning of the political hegemony of the consuls and Rome's senate Accius' play seems to promote a self-consciously conservative position. While obviously praising by association Brutus Callaicus, its political position is wide-ranging in import. If Livy's 'theatrical' narrative used Accius' play (and it is difficult to imagine that he could have ignored such a popular drama),[46] the climactic scene of *Brutus* may well have been the drawing of the sword from Lucretia's body and the oath to avenge her death and restore *libertas*. The scene is in both Livy (1.59.1) and Ovid (*Fas.* 2.837–46), where it functions in part as literary mimesis of the great statue of Brutus on the Capitoline, sword in raised hand (Plut. *Brut.* 1.1).[47] If Accius' *Brutus* featured such a scene, its dynamic with one of Rome's great monuments would only have increased its support of the senatorial status quo. A production of the play during or shortly after 133 BCE may well have targeted the tyranny of Tiberius Gracchus, whose death his opponents justified on the grounds that he was aiming at 'the crown', *regnum*.[48]

Brutus' colleague in the consulship of 138 BCE was Publius Scipio Nasica, son of the man responsible for the theatrical interdiction of 151 BCE and himself responsible for the assassination of Tiberius Gracchus in 133 BCE five years after his own consulship. In Cicero's *Brutus* (121) Scipio Nasica is himself described as a Brutus-like figure, as the one who 'without public office rescued Roman liberty from the tyranny of Tiberius Gracchus'. In the face of the ensuing popular uproar, however, he had to be sent on a senatorial mission to Asia Minor, the very place where our sources tell us that Accius was at about this time. This is speculation, but there is a chance that Accius was a member of the retinue of Scipio Nasica in Asia Minor.[49] Certainly, as the ancient sources and Accius' two *praetextae* indicate (for *Decius* see pp. 137–42), the playwright seems to have been strongly associated with the senatorial aristocracy throughout this turbulent period. Other plays, too, such as *Atreus*, and, if dated to this period, *Antenoridae* and *Eurysaces*, it has been argued,[50] sought to advance the causes of individual conservative aristocrats and the actions and policies of the anti-Gracchans.

It is true that some Accian fragments maintain that noble birth is not everything; it has to be 'adorned', for example, by 'courage' (see p. 122). But the precise context of such utterances is unknown; and, even if uttered by a dramatically sympathetic figure, they accord with patrician ideology. Accius' concern with genealogy is well known; it is allied with his admiration of the ancient Greek genealogical poet, Hesiod, to whom the first book of Accius' *Didascalica* gave chronological priority over Homer (Gell. 3.11.4). What the tragedies seem especially and pervasively to show is a preoccupation with bad genealogy, with polluted birth, with genealogical miasma and multi-generational evil: the whole unhappy saga of the house of Atreus in all its multiple ramifications and evolutions is traced to its origins in the oriental exile Pelops and his blood-stained marriage to Hippodamia, daughter of Oenomaus, son of the Titan, Atlas.[51] In an ominous pointer to the possibility of bad blood within Rome's own history, the same genealogical disquisition traces the line of Evander, the early Arcadian settler on Rome's Palatine, to Oenomaus' sister Maia (Serv. Auct. *ad Aen.* 8.130).

In a sense Accian tragedy confirms the genealogical pride of the Roman nobility by presenting in extensive and evolving detail its negative mirror-image, sagas of inherited evil blood. The procession of the ancestral *imagines* and the genealogical laudations which accompanied the funeral of a Roman aristocrat (and some of Accius' tragedies must have been performed at the *ludi funebres* attached to such funerals) are in Accian tragedy given their inverted realisation. Similarly the tragedies' preoccupation with political and personal conflict, monstrous killing, rape, mutilation, revenge, punishment, injustice, betrayal, exile, flight, conspiracy, intrigue, the triumph of sophistry over virtue, the criminal struggle for and usurpation of power – and most especially the corrupt and corrupting nature of tyranny, monarchy and the east (with which even Rome's final, tyrannical king, Tarquinius Superbus, is associated)[52] – not only reflect the attitudes of the Roman elite to the bloody familial feuds and 'decadent barbarism' of the Seleucid, Ptolemaic and Mithridatic courts (Accius' *Medea* has been argued to be a commentary on the fratricidal Mithridates),[53] but have an obvious bearing on the whole Roman social and political world of the late second century BCE. As noted in the previous chapter, the East was associated in the minds or at least the speeches of many of Rome's leaders with the moral decadence known as *luxuria* ('self-indulgence', 'luxury', 'extravagance') – a vice those same Roman leaders attempted to eradicate on at least four occasions during Accius' lifetime through the passing of sumptuary laws designed to curb the growth of Eastern excess.[54]

Not that the tragedies' view of the East is without its complexities. Certainly in plays like *Bacchae* and *Stasiastae* or *Tropaeum Liberi* ('The Rebels' or 'Liber's Trophy'), which dealt with the downfall of Pentheus and Lycurgus as a result of their hostility towards Bacchus/Liber, the very action of the tragedies must have provided a warning, as in Naevius' play *Lucurgus*, against blanket opposition to religions from the east.[55] The Bacchanal affair of 186 BCE would still have been in the cultural memory, reinforced by more recent interdictions of Eastern practices. In 139 BCE, for example, Chaldaean astrologers were banished from Rome and Italy (Livy *Per.* 54; Val. Max. 1.3.3). The distrust of 'augurs', quoted from *Astyanax* on p. 122, where the reference must have been to the Greek seer Calchas, probably mirrored a widespread view of (not only) Eastern prophets and priests.

The tragedies clearly, systematically and repeatedly present the dire consequences of autocracy and of the overthrow of legitimate rule. The Gracchi may have appeared to some as great revolutionaries, but their opponents were concerned to portray them as demagogic tyrants trying to destroy the political status quo and the legitimate rule of the Roman senate. Such was clearly the intended message of another late-second-century text: the Temple of Concord, dedicated in the Roman Forum by Lucius Opimius in 121 BCE following the killing of Gaius Gracchus, and directed to promoting the *concordia* of Rome under senatorial government, i.e. the political status quo.[56] A case can certainly be made that both the form of Accian tragedy and its subject matter are inherently conservative, in that the former reinforces the hegemonic language and oratorical practices of the Roman elite, their cultural capital,[57] and the latter presents warning after warning of the political, social and moral collapse that attends the overthrow of legitimate government. It seems less a literary accident, more a historical index, that Accius seems to have been the first Roman tragedian to dramatise the paradigmatic tragic myth of civil war – the conflict of the sons of Oedipus over the throne of Thebes.[58] From that dramatisation, *Phoenissae*, comes the following admonition against civil discord:

ne eorum diuidiae discordiae dissipent
et disturbent tantas et tam opimas ciuium
diuitias.

(Phoenissae frag. iv Klotz)

Let not their divisions, discords dissipate
And disturb the wealth so great and so large
Of citizens.

The lack of a single complete tragedy or anything like a substantial proportion of one makes all this speculative. Of the losses of Latin literature that suffered by Accian tragedy is one of the most severe and most lamentable. The fragments of two tragedies and of one *praetexta* follow.

Atreus

This celebrated and relatively early play (already produced by 133 BCE, possibly by 135) dramatised the traditional struggle over the throne of Argos/Mycenae between the two sons of Pelops, Atreus and Thyestes, focusing on Atreus' revenge for Thyestes' earlier seduction of his wife, Aerope, and subsequent theft of the golden-fleeced ram/lamb on which the throne depended. Atreus' vengeance consisted in killing and cooking Thyestes' sons and serving them to him in the infamous cannibalistic meal, which caused the sun to flee in horror and plunged the world in darkness. The prologue of the play seems to have dealt fairly fully with the genealogy of Atreus, starting from Sterope and Atlas, one of whose children, Oenomaus, fathered Hippodamia, by whom Pelops fathered Atreus and Thyestes. So Servius Auctus on *Aeneid* 8.130, where it is also noted that the genealogical passage included a detailed account (*plenius*) of the descent of Evander, the pre-Roman settler on the Palatine, from Oenomaus' sister, Maia, via Mercury and the Arcadians. Accius, like Livius and Naevius with Danae, seems to have been concerned to implicate Greek tragic myth in the history of Rome. And, although Evander was heralded as an important culture hero by early Roman historians such as Fabius Pictor, Cincius Alimentus and Cato,[59] and was to become a positive and seminal figure in Augustan poetry, his surprising presence in a genealogy which connects him to Atreus does more than set up a contrasting model of good kingship to Atreus' evil tyranny; it links the saga of Atreus to Rome. It would have served to alert Accius' audience to the play's ramifications for their world.

127

That world at the time of this play's production was a turbulent one. One prominent contemporary Roman may have been especially important for the play: Tiberius Gracchus, whose land commission and judicial authority were represented by his opponents as tyranny (see p. 124), and who has been argued to underlie the portrait of Atreus. Accius' subject is, of course, an old one. It goes back to the Attic tragedians of the fifth century BCE: to Aeschylus, who recounts the main items of the myth at *Agamemnon* 1583–603, and to Sophocles and Euripides, who, as noted above (p. 79), wrote several plays on the saga. Some counterpoint with Ennius' *Thyestes* can be assumed. For other influences, see the introductory comments on Ennius' *Thyestes*. Like the Ennian play, Accius' *Atreus* was popular in the tragic theatre of the late republic; its title role was a favourite of the great tragic actor, Aesopus.[60]

Frag. 1

simul et Pisaea praemia erepta a socru possedit suo

As soon as he possessed Pisa's prize torn from his bride's father

This is generally regarded as belonging to the genealogical prologue (see above); it would have been recited to an accompanying flute (the metre is iambic octonarius).[61] As with the other early dramatists, alliteration is used to structure the line and give it oral power. The reference is to Pelops' victory over Oenomaus in a chariot race at Pisa and his ensuing marriage to Oenomaus' daughter, Hippodamia. Pelops won the race through bribing Oenomaus' servant to make his master's chariot collapse. The use of *erepta*, 'torn', underscores the violence of the event, part perhaps of a negative evaluation of Atreus' genealogy.

Frags 2–6

iterum Thyestes Atreum adtrectatum aduenit.
iterum iam adgreditur me et quietum suscitat.
maior mihi moles, maius miscendumst malum
qui illius acerbum cor contundam et comprimam.

Once more Thyestes comes to fight with Atreus.
Once more he approaches and shakes my peace.
Greater grief, greater groans must I grind out
To crush and crunch that bitter heart of his.

oderint dum metuant.

Let them hate, provided they fear.

qui non sat habuit coniugem inlexe in stuprum

who was not satisfied with defiling my wife

> quod re in summa summum esse arbitror
> periclum: matres conquinari regias,
> contaminari stirpem, admisceri genus.

> What I think at the highest level
> Is highest danger: the violation of queens,
> The stock's pollution, confusion of the line.

addo huc quod mihi portento caelestum pater
prodigium misit, regni stabilimen mei,
agnum inter pecudes aurea clarum coma,
quem clam Thyestem clepere ausum esse e regia,
qua in re adiutricem coniugem cepit sibi.

I add the fact that the father of gods sent me
A portent and prodigy, my realm's surety,
A lamb whose golden fleece shone in the flock,
Which Thyestes dared to steal from the court,
Helped in this by an accomplice, my wife.

The five fragments above are iambic dialogue lines and, if the second act of Seneca's *Thyestes* is any guide (*Thy.* 176–335), seem to come from a scene featuring Atreus and an intimate/minister in which Atreus plots Thyestes' downfall and justifies his vengeance. The speaker of all five fragments seems to be Atreus. The implication of fragment 2 is that Thyestes is returning of his own accord as in Aeschylus (*Ag.* 1587–8), rather than after being invited by Atreus as in Seneca (*Thy.* 296–9). Fragment 2 does, however, anticipate several motifs in Seneca's own presentation of Atreus (including the *quies* and *maius* motifs, see *Thy.* 202, 254, 267, 274f.). The order of the fragments here mirrors the order of the corresponding sentiments in Seneca's second act except for fragments 5 and 6 which preserve the Ciceronian order (see Sen. *Thy.* 192–204, 207–12, 222, 239–40, 223–35, and Cic. *ND* 3.68). Rhetorical patterning, repetitions and alliterative effects (sometimes heavy-handed: see frag. 2, lines 3–4) are used to convey Atreus' manic energy. Fragment 3, which owes something to his predecessor Ennius (see frag. clxxxii Jocelyn), was justly famous,[62] and later (allegedly) bandied about by Rome's own Atreus,

Caligula (Suet. *Gai.* 30.1; see also *Tib.* 59.2). It was clearly the ancestor of the arresting apothegm of Seneca's Atreus: *quod nolunt uelint*, 'Let them choose what they do not choose' (*Thy.* 212). Fragments 4–6 are quoted by Cicero as ingredients of a negative evaluation of the Accian Thyestes, whom he describes as acting rationally but 'with extreme wickedness' (*summa improbitate, ND* 3.68–9). To Cicero, at least, the Accian Thyestes is no innocent victim; Atreus' complaints struck home.

Frags 7 and 8

uigilandum est semper, multae insidiae sunt bonis.

Be vigilant always; noble men face many traps.

id quod multi inuideant multique expetant inscitia est postulare, nisi laborem summa cum cura ecferas.

What many envy and many desire it is folly
To demand, unless you work at it with utmost care.

Spoken by either Thyestes or Atreus to their sons. If Thyestes is the speaker, the occasion may have been as he and his sons approach Atreus' court. In the third act of Seneca's *Thyestes* (423–89) Thyestes delivers a series of homilies to his sons on the dangers of the false glitter of power and wealth and the need for constant vigilance, as they draw near to the palace. The opposing view of the two fragments has them addressed by Atreus to Agamemnon and Menelaus.[63] *Boni*, 'noble men', in fragment 7, may have had a contemporary political resonance; the *boni* were the senatorial party, opposed to the reforms of the Gracchi.[64] Fragment 7 is in the standard dialogue metre (iambic senarius); fragment 8 (trochaic septenarii) would have been accompanied by music.

Frags 9 and 10

ne cum tyranno quisquam epulandi gratia
accumbat mensam aut eandem uescatur dapem.

Let none lie down at the table with the king
To feast or consume the same banquet.

ego incipio, conata exequar.

I begin, I shall complete my plan.

These two fragments may have been spoken by Atreus during the preparation of the impious feast. Fragment 9 would then be an instruction by Atreus to his court not to sit with 'king' Thyestes; fragment 10 either a description of his intentions to an intimate/minister or part of a soliloquy. Fragment 10 may not belong to this scene but to one earlier in the play (e.g. the scene envisaged in frags 2–6 above). Klotz places it much earlier in the play. The interpretation of fragment 9 as spoken by Thyestes after the banquet with reference to the 'tyrant' Atreus is possible, but unlikely.[65] Also possible is the attribution of fragment 9 to a messenger (see frags 11 and 12), when it would then be a general, moralising prohibition ('Let none lie down at the table with a king …').

Frags 11 and 12

epularum fictor, scelerum fratris delitor

The banquet's creator, blotter of brother's sins

    concoquit
partem uapore flammae, ueribus in foco
lacerta tribuit.

    He boils
A part in the flame's heat, he puts the arms
On spits in the hearth.

These dialogue lines seem to be a description by someone (a messenger?) of Atreus' gruesome preparation of the banquet, the boiling and the roasting of the bodies of Thyestes' sons. The effect of attention to detail in the cooking may have been, as it was later in Seneca's analogous account, to present the act as perverted religious ritual.

Frag. 13

sed quid tonitru turbida toruo
concussa repente aequora caeli
sensimus sonere?

But what is this raging thunder
Rocking heaven's stormy plains
Ringing in our ears?

These anapaestic lyric lines seem clearly to be a response to the cosmic upheaval caused by the infamous banquet, most famously the disappearance of the sun. They belong perhaps to one of the play's final choral odes, even its last, if the 'Star-Chorus' of Seneca's *Thyestes* (789–884) is a guide.

Frags 14–20

(Atr) natis sepulcro ipse es parens.

(Atr) You, father, are your children's tomb.

(Thy) fregistin fidem?
(Atr) neque dedi neque do infideli cuiquam.

(Thy) You broke your oath?
(Atr) I neither made nor make one to a perjurer.

(Thy) ipsus hortatur me frater ut meos malis miser
    manderem natos.

(Thy) My brother encourages me to chew in misery
    On my children.

(Thy) egone Argiuum imperium adtingam aut Pelopis digner
    domo?
quoi me ostendam? quod templum adeam? quem ore funesto
    alloquar?

(Thy) Could I rule Argos or be reckoned worthy of Pelops' house?
    Where could I show myself? What shrine approach? Whom
    address with my death-mouth?

(Atr) probae etsi in segetem sunt deteriorem datae
    fruges, tamen ipsae suapte natura enitent.

(Atr) Good grain, though planted in a poorer field,
    Will shine forth because of its own nature.

(Thy) numquam istam imminuam curam infitiando tibi.

(Thy) Never will I lessen your anxiety by denying it.

(Atr) ecquis hoc animaduortet? uincite.

(Atr) Is anyone listening? Chain him.

These remaining fragments seem to belong to the play's final act. They feature Atreus' revelation to Thyestes of the latter's consumption of his own children (frag. 14), part of Thyestes' response and Atreus' reply (frag. 15), two fragments (frags 16 and 17) from Thyestes' recitative describing his inexpressible misery, and (possibly) a closural injunction from Atreus (frag. 20). Fragments 18 and 19 could come from almost anywhere in the play. I place them here as part of a climactic exchange between Atreus and Thyestes, since one of the most plausible contexts is precisely right at the end of the play when (at least in Seneca's *Thyestes*) Atreus seeks assurance that his children (Agamemnon and Menelaus) were not fathered by Thyestes (see Atreus' anxiety on this matter at frag. 5 above). Fragments 16 and 20 are quoted by Cicero to exemplify the vocal dimensions of anger. Fragment 17 may well be recalled in a quotation attributed to Gaius Gracchus by Cicero (*De Orat.* 3.214).[66] To assist the reader I have prefaced each fragment with an indication of the speaker, although this is not always certain. It hardly needs saying that the relative position of these fragments is highly conjectural. Fragment 14's dramatic deployment of the belly-as-tomb *topos* recalls Ennius (frag. cl Jocelyn) and was redeployed by Seneca (*Thy.* 1030f.). The *topos* always had an especial charge in a culture which invested so much value in the dead and their burial.

Tereus

This late play – first produced in 104 or 103 BCE (Cic. *Phil.* 1.36) and the latest known of Accius – dramatises the renowned tale of rape, mutilation and filicide associated with the house of Tereus, king of Thrace. Tereus had married Procne, one of the daughters of Pandion, king of Athens, and had fathered a son, Itys, by her. While escorting a second daughter, Philomela, to see her sister, Tereus had violated and imprisoned her, and had cut out her tongue to silence her. Philomela, however, wove the tale of her rape and mutilation into a tapestry, which she sent to Procne. The two sisters enacted their revenge by killing and cooking Itys and giving him to Tereus to eat. The sisters fled, pursued by Tereus, but all three were turned into birds: Procne into a nightingale, Philomela into a swallow, Tereus into a hoopoe. A major intertext of this play was Sophocles' *Tereus* (see Sutton 1984: 127–32); also (and necessarily) the *Tereus* of Livius Andronicus, which would have received its first performance in Rome over 100 years earlier. For further details of the myth, see Ovid's lengthy narrative at *Metamorphoses* 6.424–674, which is most likely to have been influenced by the Accian play and by its representation of Tereus as a tyrant figure (see Ovid *Met.* 6.436, 549, 581). The setting of the play seems to have been Tereus' palace in Thrace.

A late-republican performance of this play – together with precise political resonance and an overtly 'political' reception – is attested for the *Ludi Apollinares*, July 6, 44 BCE.[67] The play's critical presentation of foreign tyranny and depravity (its antityrannical sentiments are as clear from the fragments as they were to the audience of 44 BCE) would have had an equally clear, but different and more wide-ranging, political and cultural relevance to the Rome of 104 BCE. Its implications would have stretched further than the Mithridatic court or the recently defeated Numidian king, Jugurtha. Despite the play's presentation of Tereus as the antithesis of Roman values, Accius' own *Brutus* had presumably already shown that tyrants could be made at Rome. The city's audiences did not have to wait until 44 BCE or until Ovid's *Fasti* (2.851–6) to see the parallels between the two sagas – or to identify a modern Tereus/Tarquin in their midst. Nor have some modern commentators been reluctant to posit contemporary names.[68]

Frag. 1

Tereus indomito more atque animo barbaro
conspexit in eam. amore uecors flammeo,
depositus facinus pessimum ex dementia
confingit.

Uncontrolled and with a barbarous heart
Tereus gazed at her. Senseless with flaming love,
Crushed, he manufactures the foulest crime
From madness.

A narrative of earlier events in iambics, reminiscent of the prologues of Euripides. Hence perhaps from the prologue of *Tereus*. The speaker is unknown. The lines describe Tereus' lust for and rape/mutilation of Philomela, Procne's sister. The depiction of the Thracian king's unrestrained appetites, his madness and inability to control his own passions, signals his status as archetypical 'barbarian' and tyrant.[69] He functions as a clear paradigm of the Roman 'other', presented to the audience before the events of the play unfold. Note in respect of the style of the lines a more restrained and nuanced use of alliteration and assonance. For Ovid's account of Tereus' gaze and ensuing *furor*, see *Metamorphoses* 6.478–82.

Frag. 2

atque id ego semper sic mecum agito et comparo
quo pacto magnam molem minuam miseriae.

I mull this over constantly in my mind, and work
To diminish the mighty mass of misery.

This iambic fragment seems to be a statement by Procne, beginning to plan her course of action: either the rescue of Philomela from her imprisonment or the final horrific revenge itself. The lines perhaps come from a dialogue between Procne and an intimate, possibly her old nurse.

Frag. 3

uideo ego te, mulier, more multarum utier,
ut uim contendas tuam ad maiestatem uiri.

I see that you, woman, act like many women
In violently fighting a husband's sovereignty.

Someone, perhaps the chorus leader or a confidante of Procne (her nurse?), addresses Procne on her burgeoning plans. The situation is the conventional warning against a woman's breach of the social imperatives of subservience. *Maiestas* is a Roman term, used of the 'sovereignty' of magistrates and the state. The iambic lines may have belonged to the same dialogue as those of fragment 2.

Frag. 4

deum Cadmogena natum Semela adfare et famulanter pete.

Address the god born of Cadmus' child, Semele, and beg like a servant.

In this recitative line (trochaic septenarius or iambic octonarius) someone is instructed to call upon the god Bacchus, perhaps at the festival of Bacchus, which in Ovid's *Metamorphoses* provides the setting for Procne's rescue of Philomela from the hut in which she was imprisoned (*Met.* 6.587–600). Given the controversial nature of Bacchus and Bacchanals in Roman culture, the association of the sisters with Bacchic worship problematises them. It also foreshadows their violence.

Frag. 5

suauem linguae sonitum! o dulcitas
conspirantum animae!

tongue's honeyed sound! O the sweetness
Of breath of those in unison.

A difficult fragment to place. Possibilities include a speech by
Procne lamenting the loss of the sweet sound of her sister's tongue,
which she contrasts with the sweet 'breath' of the conspiring sisters,
or a speech in which Procne is responding to a honeyed plea from
Itys, which she contrasts with the sweet breath of their conspiracy
(see Ovid *Met.* 6.632–3).

Frag. 6

alia hic sanctitudo est, aliud nomen et numen Iouis.

Here sanctity is different, Jove's name and will different.

A trochaic line, perhaps delivered by Procne justifying her revenge
in a context – or indeed in a country ('here', *hic*, could refer to
Thrace) – where normal moral values are in abeyance. It is a
powerful, shocking line, in which the stable Roman world of
sanctitudo and the gods is replaced with a moral vacuum. In addition to the anaphora and the portentous moral language, note the
play with *nomen* and *numen*, which gives the line intellectual bite. If
Procne is the speaker, Accius went to some lengths to make her a
complex, terrifying tragic figure. Compare Ovid's Procne: *scelus est
pietas in coniuge Tereo* ('Faithfulness – with Tereus for husband – is a
sin', *Met.* 6.635).

Frags 7 and 8

struunt sorores Atticae dirum nefas.

The Attic sisters plot dreadful evil.

sed nisi clam regem auferre ab regina occupo
puerum

But unless without the king's knowledge I first remove
The boy from the queen

Both of the above iambic fragments would have been spoken by characters other than Tereus or the sisters: perhaps a nurse or the chorus leader. Frag. 7 (= *Trag. Inc.* frag. cxli Klotz) is not assigned to this play or even to Accius in the sources, but may perhaps belong here. Both fragments show awareness and disapproval on someone's part of the sisters' designs. Frag. 8 even expresses an intention to rescue 'the boy', Itys.

Frag. 9

noua aduena, animo audaci, in medium proripit sese ferox.[70]

A stranger, just arrived, thrusts boldly into the fray – ferocious.

This recitative line, perhaps from a messenger's speech, seems to describe the part of Philomela, the stranger to the palace, in the revenge. See Ovid *Met.* 6.657–60, where Philomela springs forward and throws the bloody head of Itys at Tereus.

Frag. 10

famae enim nobilitas lata ex stirpe praeclara euagat.[71]

Fame's renown spreads far from an illustrious line.

A trochaic line, potentially from anywhere in the play, perhaps early, perhaps late as part of a moralising conclusion, perhaps part of a messenger's speech with fragment 9.

Aeneadae or Decius

This play dealt with the *deuotio* or self-sacrifice of the consul, Publius Decius Mus, at the Battle of Sentinum in 295 BCE during the third Samnite war. The battle was one of the great turning-points of Roman history. Rome faced an extraordinary coalition of Samnites, Gauls, Etruscans and Umbrians, defeat by whom would have severely checked (and may have ended) Rome's ambitions in the Italian peninsula.[72] Sentinum is situated in Umbria not far from Accius' birthplace, Pisaurum. Decius' ritual self-sacrifice for the sake of victory was modelled on that of his father in 340 BCE at the Battle of Mt Vesuvius during the conflict with the Latins. At Sentinum the right wing of the Roman army was commanded by Quintus Fabius Maximus Rullianus, Decius' fellow consul, who drove the Samnites back. Decius' left wing was overrun by the Gauls, but his ensuing self-sacrifice rallied the army and led to a victorious outcome. Livy's account (10.24–9) may well have used Accius as a source. The action of the play may have been set in the Roman camp. There seems to have been a chorus, probably of Roman soldiers (see frag. 2 below). The order of the fragments is conjectural. Livy's narrative has been consulted for conjectured contexts (see also Polybius 2.19.5–6). The fragments evidence several textual problems.

Frag. 1

nihil neque pericli neque tumulti est quod sciam.

There is no danger or commotion I'm aware of.

This iambic line seems to come from an early part of the play prior to any awareness of an imminent encounter between Romans and Samnites/Gauls. Warmington 2.553 postulates a scout as speaker; but it could be anyone, even Fabius, who at Livy 10.26.1–3 counters the exaggerations of the praetor Appius Claudius concerning the dangers of the possible war.

Frag. 2

Caleti uoce canora
fremitu peragrant minitabiliter.[73]

The Caleti roaring
In concert cross menacingly.

This anapaestic lyric fragment, sung either by one of the main characters or (perhaps more probably) by a chorus (of Roman soldiers? Less likely, of Gauls),[74] describes the threatening onset of the Gallic troops, the 'Caleti', allied with the Samnites.

Frag. 3

quod periti sumus in uita atque usu callemus magis.

Because we are skilled in life and practice makes us wiser.

A trochaic line attributable to any speaker almost anywhere in the play. A possible context might be Fabius' justification of his receiving the major military command without any drawing of lots – much to the chagrin of Decius (Livy 24.5–7). He was by far the more experienced of the two consuls. At any rate the fragment is likely to have come from a discussion between the two.

Frag. 4

fateor. sed saepe ignauauit fortem in spe expectatio.

I admit it. But hope's deferment often debased the brave.

A trochaic line expressing a rather complex thought that the deferment of hope's realisation (lit. 'expectation in hope') can turn courage into cowardice. The thought suits the belief of Livy's Fabius that the Samnites and Gauls fight well at the start of a battle but are 'less than women' at the end of a lengthy struggle (Livy 28.3–4).

Frag. 5

uim Gallicam obduc contra in acie exercitum.
lue patrium hostili fuso sanguen sanguine.[75]

Lead the army in formation against the Gallic force.
Atone ancestral blood with the spilt blood of foes.

The text of these iambic lines is most uncertain. The context may be Fabius' instructions to Decius to command the left wing of the Roman army against the Gauls.[76] If so, there may be a reference here to the earlier *deuotio* of Decius' father some forty-five years earlier, and *patrium sanguen* would be better translated 'your father's blood' – as against 'our fathers' blood'. *Patrius* recurs at frag. 11 on p. 140, where it clearly seems to signify 'father's'. 'Ancestral blood' keeps the ambiguity here.

Frags 6 and 7

te sancte uenerans precibus, inuicte, inuoco,
portenta ut populo patriae uerruncent bene.

You, holy, unvanquished, I invoke in veneration
That the portents work well for people, for patria.

et nunc quo deorum segnitas? ardet focus.

And why are the gods slow now? The hearth blazes.

Two separate iambic fragments, perhaps from the same scene. Warmington 2.555 places fragment 6 early in the play, suggesting that Marcus Livius, a priest of the Roman army, is the speaker and that 'portents' may refer to the omen of the wolf and the hind described in Livy's narrative just before the start of the battle (10.27.8–9). 'Portents' clearly suggest some unusual occurrences which an appropriate priest (Livius) or magistrate (Fabius?) seeks to turn to Rome's advantage by an expiatory sacrifice. Notice, as in *Brutus* (see pp. 118–9), the ritual word *uerruncent*, the cluster of other religious terms, and the alliterative patterning and formulaic structure of the prayer.[77] Perhaps, as suggested on p. 119, such focus on Roman ritual was a feature of early *praetextae*, underscoring the relationship between Roman religious and cultural practice and military success, and giving the plays themselves a distinctly sacral quality.

Frag. 8

clamore et gemitu templum resonit caelitum.

With cries and groans the sky-gods' precinct echoes.

A description of the fighting attributable to anyone (a messenger?) and locatable almost anywhere in the main body of the play.

Frag. 9

dice, summa ubi perduellum est? quorsum aut quibus a partibus gliscunt?[78]

Tell me, where is the main fighting? To what point or from where Are they massing?

The text of this fragment is problematic. Its context may be an enquiry by Fabius after the Gallic rout of the Decian wing of the army. Others place the fragment earlier in the play during Fabius' questioning of deserters from Clusium (see Livy 10.27.4).[79]

Frags 10 and 11

quibus rem summam et patriam nostram quondam adauctauit
    pater.

With which my father once increased the commonwealth and
our *patria*.

patrio exemplo et me dicabo atque animam deuoro hostibus.

On my father's model I'll dedicate myself and vow the foe my
life.

These two fragments seem to have been part of the (climactic?) scene
of *deuotio* (the 'Höhepunkt des Stücks'),[80] in which Decius ritually
vows his life to the enemy (and to the spirits of the dead) in exchange
for his army's victory. In comparison with statements of self-sacrifice
in Attic tragedy,[81] Decius' religious piety is evident. The words of
Decius could of course have been reported by a messenger. The
trochaic lines would have been accompanied by the flute.

Frag. 12

castra haec uestra est. optume est is meritus a nobis.[82]

The camp is yours. He has deserved the best from us.

Trochaics delivered perhaps by the victorious Fabius to the Roman
army after they have overrun the Samnite camp. 'He' (*is*) presumably
refers to the dead Decius. The line may have been delivered at Decius'
funeral, which Livy describes as conducted 'with every honour and
deserved eulogies' (*omni honore laudibusque meritis*, 10.29.20).

Accius' *Decius*, although it furnishes us with less lines than his
Brutus, provides more discrete fragments than any other republican
praetexta. What they reveal is of the utmost importance. It is clear
from the fragments (as we can also infer from the remains of Accius'
Brutus and the comments of later grammarians, and actually see in
the later *Octavia*)[83] that *fabulae praetextae* were no mere triumphal or
historical tableaux but dramas with a plot and narrative structure.
The full range of tragic devices seems to have been employed,
including: the oscillation between lyric, recitative and iambic
dialogue; vigorous (political, strategic, moral) debate; scenes of
anxiety, questioning, action and spectacle; climactic scenes (possibly
reported) of high drama; moral endings. Although there may be
reason to think that *praetextae* sometimes (perhaps regularly)
employed changes of scene (such would accord with their relationship to triumphal tableaux), all the fragments of this play can
plausibly be located to a single location: the Roman commander's

camp.[84] The fragments reveal, too, a marked interest in promoting the values of the Roman elite: the importance of birth, inheritance, genealogical imperatives and paradigms; self-sacrifice for the good of the *patria* and the state; the close connection between Roman military success and Roman religious practice; the experience, wisdom and courage justifying the hegemony of Rome's elite – especially that of great families such as the Fabii, who supplied the victor at Sentinum (Rullianus) and whose contemporary descendant, a possible patron or *amicus* of Accius (Allobrogicus), triumphed over the Gauls.[85]

The play also, and most decisively, dramatises the hegemony of Rome. For perhaps the most notable feature of this *praetexta* is its relationship to a major social problem of the second half of the second century BCE – the dissatisfaction of the Italian allies (*socii*), long barred from an equal share in Rome's increasing wealth and excluded from power, but imperiously called upon to supply armed contingents for Rome's wars. This dissatisfaction was used by populist politicians from Gaius Gracchus in the 120s BCE to Drusus in the late 90s, and eventually resulted in the so-called Social War of 91–89. The subject matter of this play – the crushing of Italian enemies (now Roman 'allies') and others in the Third Samnite War, at a battle far bloodier than any Rome had fought before[86] – carried with it a clear statement of Rome's superior military power and the personal values, courage, patriotism and self-sacrifice which underlay that superiority. Ironically the Samnites were to be at the heart of the rebellion of the *socii* in the Social War itself.[87] It may also be the case that the alternative title *Aeneadae* ('Descendants of Aeneas') for this play points not to a claimed descent of the Decii or the Fabii from Aeneas,[88] but to the Trojan origins of the whole Roman people, marking them as ethnically and culturally different from the native Italians and 'justifying' their superiority. The play seems to have featured a chorus of Roman soldiers (see frag. 2 on p. 138), to whom the alternative title may have referred. *Aeneadae* or *Decius* may even have begun with a genealogical prologue.[89] The play's intervention in contemporary political issues was a conservative one. It may have provoked. Not all *spectatores* at the *ludi* would have been Roman citizens.

5

CANONISATION AND TURMOIL

The end of the republic

etenim tribus locis significari maxime de re publica
populi Romani iudicium ac uoluntas potest:
contione, comitiis, ludorum gladiatorumque cons-
essu.

(Cicero *Pro Sestio* 106)

The judgement and will of the Roman people in
public affairs can be made most manifest in three
places: at a political meeting, in the assemblies, at a
gathering for plays or gladiators.

Roman tragedy was a prestige business at the end of the republic.
Accius' refusal to stand in deference to the aristocratic playwright
Julius Caesar Strabo, when he entered the Temple of Hercules
Musarum, is itself testimony to the tragic poet's increased social
status (Val. Max. 3.7.11). The Collegium Poetarum or 'Guild of
Poets', which met in the temple, seems, unlike the earlier 'Guild of
Writers and Actors', to have been reserved only for poets to the
exclusion of actors and other theatrical personel. As the case of
Strabo, the aedile of 90 BCE, shows, such poets included members of
Rome's elite. Indeed writers of tragedies in the late republic
included not only Strabo, among whose plays were an *Adrastus*, a
Tecmessa and a *Teuthras*, but such important figures as Asinius Pollio,
who in addition to tragedies praised by Virgil (*Ecl.* 8.9–10) and
Horace (*Odes* 2.1.11–12) wrote at least one *praetexta* (43 BCE),[1]
Cassius of Parma, one of Caesar's assassins and author of an *Orestea*, a
Thyestes and (perhaps and most intriguingly) a *Brutus*, and the
quaestor Cornelius Balbus, who presided over a performance of
(probably)[2] his own *praetexta*, *Iter* ('Journey'), in 43 BCE at Gades
(Cic. *Fam.* 10.32.3). *Iter*, set in northern Greece just before the
Battle of Pharsalus (48 BCE), dramatised Balbus' 'journey' to the

Pompeian camp at Dyrrhacium and his failed attempt to win over the proconsul, Cornelius Lentulus Crus, from Pompey's side. The chief instrument of persuasion noted by Cicero, i.e. bribery (Cic. *Att.* 8.11.5), was presumably omitted from the play.

Other names of 'tragedians' appearing in the sources are Gaius Titius (a contemporary of Accius), Pompilius, Santra, who wrote a *Nuptiae Bacchi* ('Bacchus' Nuptials'),[3] Pupius and Atilius, the last-mentioned being the author of an *Electra* which was performed in 44 BCE at Julius Caesar's funeral games. Written (but certainly unperformed) tragedies are also attributed to Cicero, his brother Quintus, to Julius Caesar and Octavian (see p. 145). The title of an unattributed *praetexta* has also survived: *Nonae Caprotinae*, an aetiological drama on the annual sacrifice by Roman women to Juno Caprotina on the Nones of July, which may – or may not – have been written by one of the above. According to Varro,[4] this *praetexta* was performed at some time during the late republic at the *Ludi Apollinares* (presumably on the Nones of July). The *praetexta* on Claudia Quinta, mentioned in Ovid's *Fasti* (4.326),[5] may also belong to this period.

Even if some of the aforementioned dramatists were Augustan rather than republican, we have – in addition to Accius – a substantial number of attested writers of tragedy and/or *praetextae* 'practising' in the late republic, several of whom were members of Rome's social and political elite. As to the dramatic quality of the writing of these poets, little can be ascertained, since from this entire body of work some ten or so lines survive.[6] Here, for example, are all the extant lines of Strabo. They reveal an unsurprising fondness for alliterative effects and a taste for redundant language.

> cum capita uiridi lauro uelare imperant
> prophetae, sancta ita caste qui purant sacra
> > (*Adrastus* frag. Klotz)

> When priests prescribe heads veiled with verdant laurel,
> Thus making the holy rites pure and clean

> flammeam per aethram late feruidam ferri facem
> > (*Teuthras* frag. Klotz)

> Through flaming sky the fiery torch flies far

> corpusque suaui telino unguimus.
> > (*Incerta* frag. Klotz)

> And we smear the body with fragrant balm.

Many of the *ludi scaenici*, of course, featured replays of the old masters, especially of Ennius, Pacuvius and the most recent 'old master', Accius. Cicero attests performances of over twenty separate plays by the early triad, whose works clearly dominated the late-republican tragic stage.[7] Some plays (e.g. Ennius' *Andromacha*, Pacuvius' *Teucer*, Accius' *Atreus*)[8] were performed several times. A reasonable assumption is that most of the attested late-republican tragedians mentioned above also had their plays performed at the annual festivals. But there was also a new phenomenon: the writing by members of Rome's elite (sometimes at the summit of that elite) of tragedies not for performance, but for recitation or private reading. Julius Caesar is credited with an *Oedipus*, Octavian/Augustus with an *Ajax*, although the latter may be later (Suet. *Iul.* 56.7; *Aug.* 85.2); neither was performed. Cicero and his brother Quintus seemed to have regarded tragic composition as a literary divertissement. The orator was responsible for a translation of Aeschylus' *Prometheus Vinctus* and his brother for the writing (not for the stage) of four tragedies in sixteen days (Cic. *Q.Fr.* 3.5.7). Asinius Pollio certainly gave recitations of his writings (*scripta sua*) to an invited audience (Sen. *Con.* 4 pref. 2–6), but whether this included his plays and, if so, whether it was additional to actual performance is not known. In the 30s BCE there may well even have been dramatic poetry competitions in the Temple of Hercules Musarum itself.[9]

Acting, too, though in itself always socially disreputable, became a path to wealth, fame and some kind of social place. Relatively few names of actors have come down to us; Rupilius, Diphilus, Antiphon and Cimber are among the tragic actors mentioned in the sources. The most famous actors of the late republic – and cultural icons of their age – were Quintus Roscius Gallus (born *c.* 125 BCE), who occasionally acted in tragedy (*De Or.* 3.102) but specialised in comedy, and the great tragic actor and Roscius' younger contemporary, Clodius Aesopus. Aesopus was most famous for the power of his voice and the 'gravity' (*grauitas*) of his performances.[10] Horace (*Ep.* 2.1.82) calls Aesopus 'heavy', 'weighty' (*grauis*), Roscius 'masterful' (*doctus*); Quintilian (*Inst.* 11.3.111) similarly calls Aesopus 'weighty' (*grauior*), but changes Roscius' defining characteristic to 'animated' (*citatior*). The epithets refer to modes of delivery, which were often modelled on those of the orators, for whom delivery (*actio*, *pronuntiatio*) included not only tonality of voice (*uox*), but expression, movement and gesture (*uultus*, *motus*, *gestus*). Rhetorical treatises of the late republic underscore the importance of delivery in the orator's art (*Rhet. Her.* 3.19, Cic. *Or.* 55).[11] Any treatise on acting that had survived – we know of at least one by Roscius himself[12] – would have displayed the same emphasis. This was a 'period of virtuoso acting'[13] on the speaker's platform or the stage in which gesture, movement, 'voice' (and the changes thereof: *mutationes*, Cic. *Or.* 55) were major constituents of successful performance. Rigorous vocal training, including daily singing (Cic. *De Or.* 3.86) – for the actor's 'voice' had to display itself powerfully and with nuance across the three registers of aria, recitative and dialogue – was only part of what defined the stage professional.

Some sense of the 'reality' of Roman acting in the late republic may be gleaned from Cicero's 'eye-witness' description of an actor playing Telamon in Pacuvius' *Teucer*:

> quid potest esse tam fictum quam uersus, quam scaena, quam fabulae? tamen in hoc genere saepe ipse uidi ut ex persona mihi ardere oculi hominis histrionis uiderentur spondaulia illa dicentis:
>
>> segregare abs te ausus aut sine illo Salaminem ingredi
>> neque paternum aspectum es ueritus
>
> numquam illum aspectum dicebat quin mihi Telamo iratus furere luctu filii uideretur. at idem inflexa ad miserabilem sonum uoce –
>
>> quom aetate exacta indigem
>> liberum lacerasti orbasti extinxti, neque fratris necis
>> neque eius gnati parui, qui tibi in tutelam est traditus …?
>
> – flens ac lugens dicere uidebatur.
>
> (*De Oratore* 2.193)

What can be as unreal as verse, as the stage, as plays? Yet in this area I have often witnessed how the eyes of the man, of the actor, seemed to me to burn from out of the mask as he delivered these lines to the flute:

> You dared to separate and come to Salamis without him,
> And did not fear your father's sight

He would never deliver that word 'sight' without my believing that it was the angry Telamon raging with grief for his son. But the same man modulated his voice to a pitiful pitch –

his years spent, childless,
Torn, bereaved, destroyed by you, careless of your brother's
   death
And his tiny son, who was entrusted to your care ...?

– apparently sobbing and grieving as he spoke.

Clearly tragic actors in the late republic wore masks. There is some evidence to suggest that in the latter years of the second century BCE they did not.[14] Their introduction or (more likely) re-introduction would have thrown even greater emphasis on non-facial bodily gesture, movement and vocal tonality and power. The tragic mask, with its towering forehead (the *onkos*), and large, gaping mouth, was its own dramatic spectacle. The description quoted above could have been of Aesopus, except one might expect Cicero to have said so. Aesopus was renowned for his ability to be so immersed in his acting that it was as if some force (*uis quaedam*) had taken control of him (Cic. *Div.* 1.80).[15] Famous for his role as the maniacal Atreus in Accius' great play (Cic. *Tusc.* 4.55), he clearly commanded an extensive repertoire which ranged from the grief-stricken Andromache of Ennius (Cic. *De Or.* 3.103), through the compassionate and courageous Teucer in Accius' *Eurysaces*, into (probably) the historically resolute Brutus of the same playwright's famous *praetexta* (Cic. *Sest.* 120–3).

According to Valerius Maximus (8.10.2), Aesopus, like Roscius, studied the rhetorical performances and gestures of the Roman orator, Hortensius. In turn – or so Plutarch reports (*Cic.* 5.3–4) – Aesopus' delivery was studied by Cicero in the theatre itself. Acting and oratory were both forms of *actio* or performance,[16] and, as Roscius' own treatise confirms, were clearly seen by their most accomplished practitioners as allied arts of communication performed before the same audiences, often in the same venue (Roman Forum), with the same ends (to stir the emotions)[17] and employing similar means: rhetoricised and rhythmic language, visual props and often identical gestures.[18] This common vocabulary of gesture made for greater visual comprehensibility in the *contio* (political meeting), the courts and the theatre, but the affinity of the two arts was not unproblematic for the status-conscious orator. Indeed Hortensius seems to have been criticised for being too like an actor (Gell. 1.15). But, although the two arts still conferred on their respective practitioners 'officially' a very different public status, and orators strove hard to distinguish their practice from that of the theatre,[19] the lines of social demarcation were occasionally blurred. Aesopus could boast of friendship with Cicero (*Div.* 1.80, *QFr* 1.2.14), just as Roscius could with the aristocrat Lutatius Catulus (Cic. *ND* 1.79) and the dictator Sulla (Plut. *Sulla* 36.1) – as well as with Cicero, who defended him on a fraud charge. In 81 BCE Sulla even elevated Roscius to the equestrian order, after which he performed without a fee (Macr. *Sat.* 3.14.13; Cic. *Rosc. Com.* 23). In the late republic, drama – especially tragic drama – permeated Roman social and cultural life profoundly.

As index of this, note the transformation of the Roman civic and religious year to embrace even more days given over to the performance of plays. Precise calculations vary, but it seems that the number of days allowed for *ludi scaenici* increased from about eleven in Plautus' day to about 55 in the late 40s BCE, not including any extra days allowed for *instauratio*, i.e. the repetition of spoiled *ludi*.[20] Indeed the theatre was becoming a common metaphor not only for oratory (Cic. *Brut.* 290), but for the normal performance of public life:

> sic obtinui quaesturam in Sicilia prouinicia ut omnium oculos in me unum coniectos esse arbitrarer, ut me quaesturamque meam quasi in aliquo terrarum orbis theatro uersari existimarem.
>
> (Cicero *In Verrem* 2.5.35)

I conducted the quaestorship in the province of Sicily in such a manner that I considered the eyes of all to be focused on me alone, that I regarded myself and my quaestorship on display as in some global theatre.

> theatrum totius Asiae uirtutibus tuis est datum.
> (Cicero *Ad Quintum Fratrem* 1.142)

The theatre of all Asia has been presented to your virtues.

Similar thoughts may be found elsewhere in Cicero,[21] whose works, both private and public, are filled with quotations from, and analogies with, Roman drama, most especially with citations from the Roman tragedians, the language of whose plays had clearly embedded itself in the minds of Rome's elite and of the poets who wrote for that elite and borrowed allusively from their tragic predecessors.[22] Like Cicero, Catullus, Lucretius and (later) Virgil testify to the informing power and cultural centrality of Roman tragedy, as did Rome's public spaces, now occasionally adorned with tragic subjects. Inside the Temple of Venus Genetrix in Caesar's Forum were the famous paintings of Ajax and of Medea by Timomachus of Byzantium (Pliny *HN* 35.136). The occasional production of a *fabula praetexta* (Accius' *Brutus*, for example) with its overt dramatisation of Roman history would have played its part in the increasing theatricalisation of public life.[23]

Changes took place in the physical theatre itself. Even as public life was representing itself as theatrical, the physical theatre transformed itself into a closer representation of Roman life by structuring itself into a tripartite social image of Rome. The famous Roscian law of 67 BCE (*lex Roscia theatralis*), introduced by the Tribune of the People, Lucius Roscius Otho, assigned the first fourteen rows of seats at the theatre to members of the equestrian order. Since the orchestra had already been given over to seating for the senators, the Roman theatre from 67 BCE onwards presented an image of Roman society's tripartite social structure; it became a mirror of graded political, social and economic power. The division rankled with the *plebs*, who, four years later in 63 BCE when Otho was praetor, hissed the instigator of the Roscian law at the theatre and threatened him with violence – until the consul Cicero calmed them (Plut. *Cic.* 13.2–4; Pliny *HN* 7.117). The theatre became an image of the Roman private world, too. The increasingly sophisticated aesthetics of the Roman theatre – its *scaenae frons*, scene painting, elaborate masks – were taken up and used in the motifs of second-style Romano-Campanian wall-painting to colour and shape the private spaces of the (affluent) Roman house.[24]

The theatres themselves became more elaborate and – eventually – less temporary. In 99 BCE the multicoloured stage facade of Appius Claudius was adorned with such realistic architectural painting that crows were alleged to have tried to land on its painted roof tiles (Pliny *HN* 35.23). In 63 BCE a roofed theatre made its appearance (Pliny *HN* 36.102).[25] At the *Ludi Apollinares* of 60 BCE 'awnings', *uela*, which had been used nine years earlier at Lutatius Catulus' rededication of the Capitol, were introduced to Roman theatres by the urban praetor, Cornelius Lentulus Spinther, who had them stretched across the *cauea* or auditorium to protect the audience from the sun (Val. Max. 2.4.6; Pliny *HN* 19.23).[26] With their intense colours and constant motion, the awnings brought a new aesthetic and kinetic dimension to the watching of the *ludi*.[27] In the 60s and 50s stage decoration became a site for competitive display:

silver, gold and ivory were used in their turn to embellish and transform the stage (Val. Max. 2.4.6).

There was also clearly – as Rome's population continued to grow (reaching perhaps a million by 30 BCE) – a pressing demand for larger theatres. The Theatre of Scaurus, though a temporary structure built in 58 BCE by the curule aedile Aemilius Scaurus, had the largest capacity of any theatre known to Rome. Pliny (*HN* 36.113–15 – see also *HN* 34.36), who thought that Scaurus' theatre 'undermined Roman morals' (*prostrauerit mores*), exaggerates when he nominates its capacity as eighty thousand, but it was perhaps not far from twenty-five thousand.[28] Its main attraction was its *scaenae frons* with its 360 columns in triple tier (the lowest of marble, the second of glass, the highest of gilded wood) and its 3,000 bronze statues positioned between the columns.[29] The columns of the lowest storey were thirty-eight feet in height.

The location of the Theatre of Scaurus was presumably in the Campus Martius, where five years later, in 53 BCE, Rome received another extraordinary temporary playing space: the Theatre of Gaius Scribonius Curio. Curio devised a double theatre in which to hold the funeral *ludi* of his father. Constructed of wood, the theatre was essentially an amphitheatre cut into two revolving halves, which could be positioned back to back for the performance of plays and conjoined for the holding of gladiatorial games (Pliny *HN* 36.117–20). Unlike the Theatre of Scaurus the theatre was not demolished after the performance of its *ludi*, but was still in existence and actively being used at least two years later (Cic. *Fam.* 8.2.1). For between the Theatre of Scaurus and that of Curio the notion of Rome's theatrical spaces as temporary had been overturned by perhaps the most momentous event in the city's theatrical history: the completion of its first stone and permanent theatre.

In 55 BCE the Theatre of Pompey was dedicated in the year of Pompey's second consulship (Plut. *Pomp.* 52.4), built by him as a victory monument following his triumph of 61 BCE. A revolutionary concrete, tufa and marble structure, in which stage-building, semicircular orchestra and tiered concave auditorium were united in a closed, holistic space, the Theatre of Pompey became instantly Rome's most dazzling recreational monument and the model for the theatres of the capital and the empire to come.[30] The auditorium or *cauea* had 17,580 *loca* according to the Regionary Catalogues, for perhaps 11,000 *spectatores*.[31] Its exterior, which was between 150 and 160 metres in diameter, consisted of three arcaded tiers of peperino, possibly with engaged columns of red granite (although these may have been added in a later restoration), rising from forty-four giant vaulted arches at ground level. Bronze and marble statuary abounded (Pliny *HN* 7.34). The *spectatores* seem from the beginning to have been sheltered from the sun by massive linen awnings, stretching over the auditorium, and cooled by water flowing down the aisles (Val. Max. 2.4.6). To increase their sensuous delight, Cilician saffron was frequently sprinkled on the stage.[32] The *scaenae frons* was initially perhaps of wood, and probably soared to the height of the triple-storeyed *cauea* opposite it. Decorated with sculpture and fantastic paintings (Pliny *HN* 7.34), it contained three (probably columnated) doorways which opened on to the high, very wide stage (of 1.5 metres in height, about 95 metres in width).[33] Perspective, architectural painting – of the kind common in second-style wall-painting – may well have adorned the facade.[34] The stage may also have featured the revolving painted scenery stands (*periaktoi*) and the (moveable) sets mentioned by Vitruvius (5.6.8–9), and various other theatrical devices including trapdoors, the stage-machine known as the *exostra*, and special curtains (*siparia*) for concealing the *scaenae frons*.[35] The main stage curtain (*aulaeum*), though undoubtedly lavishly decorated,[36] would have been of the traditional kind: lowered into slots in the stage floor at the beginning of a performance and raised at the end.

To overcome the opposition of conservative moralists (and the envious) and to underscore its triumphalist purpose, Pompey constructed the theatre's *cauea* as a stairway to a temple to Venus Victrix, 'Venus Victorious' (Tert. *Spec.* 10), placing the goddess' shrine at the centre of a group of five shrines at the top of the *cauea*, and dedicating the temple three years later during his third consulship (52 BCE: Gell. 10.1.7). Pompey was also fully aware that the theatre was still regarded as a religious context,[37] but took care to ensure that each of the four shrines at the top of the *cauea* flanking that to Venus Victrix similarly honoured a deity suggestive of Pompey's military glory: *Honos* ('Honour'), *Virtus* ('Courage'), *Felicitas* ('Success'), *Victoria* ('Victory').[38] He also recognised that the theatre's location in the Campus Martius and thus outside the *pomerium* meant that even active military commanders (e.g., Caesar), who were forbidden from entering the city while holding *imperium* (their right to command), could attend.[39]

Attached to the theatre was a large, rectangular, colonnaded precinct known as the Portico of Pompey, some of the functions of which were connected directly with the theatre,[40] while others were either political (the sustenance of Pompey's *dignitas* and hegemony) or social. The portico's open areas, adorned with plane trees, fountains and sculptures, its extensive collection of paintings (including ones by Polygnotus, Antiphilus and Nicias: Pliny *HN* 35.59, 114, 132), its long colonnades, clothed with *aulaea* or tapestries and resplendent, too, with sculptures, made it an ideal place for strolling and for social interaction.[41] Predictably this expensive complex did not win the approval of Cicero (*Off.* 2.60), despite the orator's public laudations (*Pis.* 65); there is a different evaluation from the later Horace, for whom the theatre served as the *locus* of a treasured personal memory (*Odes* 1.20.3–8, 2.17.26–7). Four hundred years after its dedication the whole building complex was still heralded as one of the outstanding monuments of Rome (Amm. Marc. 16.10.14).

Pompey had not only followed Scaurus' example in transforming the smaller, even at times almost intimate, playing area of Rome's early theatre (consider, for example, the narrow area in front of the Temple of Magna Mater) into a vast spectatorial and acting space, which demanded and received spectacular productions; he had transformed Rome's temporary theatrical spaces into a permanent political space for the glorification of himself. All performances in that theatre necessarily hymned his praises. But, of course, only in part. For neither the plays nor the semiotics of performance were so controllable. In the turmoil of the late republic the politicisation of tragic (and comic)[42] performances was becoming increasingly overt and pointed, and was more in the control of the players than the payers. Cicero in *Pro Sestio* (120–4) gives a (prejudicial) account of a performance by Aesopus at the *Ludi Apollinares* of 57 BCE, in which Aesopus emphasised, transposed and interpolated lines to under-score his appeal for Cicero's recall from exile. The plays being performed were Accius' *Eurysaces* and *Brutus*, and (possibly) Ennius' *Andromacha*. Lines from *Eurysaces* (frag. xiii Klotz) such as –

> qui rem publicam certo animo adiuuerit
> statuerit, steterit cum Achiuis

> Who with unwavering mind aided, stabilized
> The state, stood alongside the Achaeans

and

> re dubia
> haut dubitarit uitam offerre nec capiti pepercerit

> In doubtful fortune
> Did not doubt to offer his life, did not spare his own head

and

> exsulare sinitis, sistis pelli, pulsum patimini.

> You allow his exile, allowed his expulsion, suffer his banishment.

– were deliberately made to refer to the absent Cicero, receiving much applause from the audience.

Aesopus even added lines, and transferred lines from Ennius' *Andromacha* into the Accian play to praise Cicero as *pater patriae* and garner sympathy for the burning of his house.

But the most extraordinary political catechresis was the use of a line from Accius' *Brutus* –

> Tullius, qui libertatem ciuibus stabiliuerat
> > (*Brutus* frag. iv Klotz)

> Tullius, who had made civil liberty firm

– in which Accius' description of Servius Tullius, the sixth king of Rome, was metamorphosed into a eulogy of the present 'Tullius', Marcus Tullius Cicero. The line, according to Cicero, was echoed by the audience *miliens*, literally 'a thousand times' (often = 'very many'). Aesopus was not alone. At the *Ludi Apollinares* two years earlier (59 BCE) Pompey had had his 'Greatness' turned against him by the tragic actor Diphilus, who attacked him in performance with the line (Cic. *Att.* 2.19.3):

> nostra miseria tu es Magnus.

> To our misfortune you are Great.

After repeating the line 'countless times' (*miliens* again), he followed with:

> eandem uirtutem istam ueniet tempus cum grauiter gemes.

> Time will come when you will mightily moan your manliness.

The whole theatre erupted. And all this, it should be remembered, took place within a socio-legal context in which the defamation of someone through *carmen* ('song', 'poetry', 'drama') was still technically a capital offence.[43]

What the politics of Aesopus' and Diphilus' performances reveal is the semiotic contract which had developed between actors and audience, as the two parties came together to generate new meaning. The contract does not surprise. Roman audiences had always been actively involved in the creation of the play and its playing. The *ludi*, after all, were not simply a context for the enhancement of the social or political status of the organising magistrate. They were the Roman people's due, and had to be of a quality to meet the people's own sense of *dignitas* or worth (Cic. *Leg. Agr.* 2.71). Audiences were intensely involved in the playmaking, in the quality both of the acting and of the play, responding fully to its dramatic highspots. Cicero describes weeping by an audience at the opening speech of Pacuvius' *Iliona* (*Tusc.* 1.106), applause after the *oderint dum metuant* line of Accius' *Atreus* (*Off.* 1.97), standing ovations for the Orestes–Pylades scene of *Chryses* (*Amic.* 24), and hissing by an audience in the case of actor or chorus errors, even in technical matters of metrical pattern or bodily movement (*De Or.* 1.259, 3.196; *Or.* 173). The Roman audience of the late republic was large, discerning, participatory, demanding and critical:

> in qua [scaena] cum omnes in oris et uocis et motus moderatione elaborent, quis ignorat quam pauci sint fuerintque quos animo aequo spectare possimus?
>
> (Cicero *De Oratore* 1.18)

> On the stage, although all of them work at modulating expression and voice and movement, who is unaware how few there are and have been whom we can comfortably watch?

Audience expertise was such that some members of an audience could recognise Ennius' *Andromacha* or Pacuvius' *Antiopa* or an aria from them with the flute-player's first note (*Acad.* 2.20, 2.86).[44] Lines of canonic plays were not only known by heart but were occasionally bellowed by an audience at the actors themselves.[45]

Famously, too, in the late republic, audience emotion, critical response and collective involvement were frequently directed towards and against political figures in the theatre itself. Thus while a popular consul or tribune might be applauded on entering the theatre, an unpopular consul or tribune might be abused (Cic. *Sest.* 117; Suet. *Iul.* 80.3), and even the great orator/lawyer Hortensius or even greater Pompey might be hissed (Cic. *Fam.* 8.2.1, *Att.* 2.19). It was a politically dynamic context in which actors could rely on audience expectation and participation to create

a contemporary political discourse out of the inherited tragic repertoire. Ironically certain actions on the part of the city's elite may
have contributed to this increased theatrical politicisation. A ban
(between 64 and 58 BCE) on the *Ludi Compitalicii*, which were held
away from the city centre in a Saturnalian atmosphere where
subversive sentiment was perhaps not uncommon, may simply have
channelled frustrated political energies into the main theatres.[46]
Although in a strict sense the audience in the theatre was not truly
representative of the Roman citizen body (it included slaves,
women, and non-Romans, seating was limited, and, although
tickets were free, access to the non-senatorial and non-equestrian
seats was initially in the hands of the organiser of the *ludi* and
others),[47] in the final decades of the republic the Roman theatre was
not far from being what Cicero describes in the epigraph to this
chapter: the assembly and court of the people. It was – more than
the more easily manipulated political meetings (*contiones*) and
assemblies (*comitia*) – the people's parliament:

> populi sensus maxime theatro et spectaculis perspectus est.
> (Cicero *Ad Atticum* 2.19.3)

The will of the people is most clearly seen in the theatre
and at the shows.

Just over two years after the Aesopus performance of 57 BCE, the
celebrated actor was recalled to participate in the most momentous
theatrical event in Rome's history, the opening of the Theatre of
Pompey in August/September 55 BCE.[48] Aesopus disappointed,[49]
but the whole show itself (despite Cicero's claimed boredom: *Fam.*
7.1.2) did not. In an effort to recapture and transcend the
triumphalist display of six years previously, Pompey had arranged
the most lavish spectacle. Among those whom Pompey must have
consulted was his *amicus*, Varro, the greatest of Rome's scholars and
an authority on the *ludi scaenici*, to which he devoted Book 10 of his
monumental *Antiquitates Rerum Diuinarum*. The organiser of these
special *ludi* was Spurius Maecius Tarpa (Cic. *Fam.* 7.1.1), who
superintended not only Roman plays, but Greek and Oscan dramas,
and athletic competitions, gladiatorial fights, and beast hunts in the
Circus Maximus.[50]

According to Cicero, the Greek and Oscan plays were apparently
ill-attended, but not the Roman plays, which were produced in the
most grandiose fashion and replayed the triumphalist semiotics of

the theatre itself. Two famous 'old' Roman tragedies formed the main billing, Accius' *Clytaemestra* and (probably Naevius') *Equos Troianus*, 'Trojan Horse', accompanied by what Cicero contemptuously describes as 'Diverse armed infantry and cavalry in some battle' (*uaria armatura peditatus et equitatus in aliqua pugna*, Cic. *Fam.* 7.1.2). The production values of the performances – even in a theatrical context now used to large casts and lavish display[51] – were extraordinary. When Agamemnon entered in Accius' tragedy, he was preceded by 600 mules; and the *Equos Troianus*, which dealt with the sack of Troy, featured 3,000 bronze bowls as booty. These production values were those of the triumphal display, in which Agamemnon's entrance dramatically mirrored Pompey's triumphal procession of 61 BCE and the 3,000 bronze bowls the many counted items of booty paraded in the earlier triumph. Focus on number seems to have been a feature of that triumph.[52] It is possible that the third spectacle referred to by Cicero ('Diverse armed infantry …') was a *fabula praetexta*, written for this occasion to glorify Pompey's battles.[53] If so, the three plays (if the last was a play) succinctly replayed the battles, the city-sacking, and the triumphal procession of Pompeius Magnus, 'Pompey the Great', the latter's proclaimed conquest of the East emblematised in Agamemnon's conquest of Troy.[54]

The triumphalism of the plays was reinforced by the theatre itself. Around the exterior of the *cauea* (probably 'against the piers of the exterior arcade')[55] were the fourteen statues sculpted by Coponius representing the tribes/nations conquered by Pompey (Pliny *HN* 36.41; Suet. *Nero* 46.1), the names of which had adorned Pompey's lavish two-day triumph some six years earlier (Plut. *Pomp.* 45.2). Pompey had succeeded in creating out of Rome's theatre, and especially its tragic theatre, a permanent monument to his own unsurpassed glory.

This was not Pompey's first appropriation of the theatrical. His triumph of 61 BCE was a blatant piece of theatre. Apparently not content simply to play Jupiter in the triumphal procession itself, Pompey had donned the cloak of Alexander the Great (Appian *Mithr.* 117), his military icon whose conquests his own now rivalled. A fourth-century painting of Alexander by Nicias later adorned the portico of the theatre (Pliny *HN* 35.132). Such associations were always necessarily problematic. Alexander died an early death, and the 55 BCE association with Agamemnon was fraught with uncontrollable ambiguities. Pompey, who seems to have seen himself as an 'Agamemnon' well before the performance of this play

(Suet. *Iul.* 50.1), may have wanted the association in Accius' tragedy to end after Agamemnon's great triumphal entry; but meaning is not so malleable. And the betrayal and murder of Agamemnon which followed that entry would inevitably have reflected on Pompey himself, who, seven years later, as it transpired, was betrayed and murdered. Indeed even before Pompey's death the association with Agamemnon shadowed him. Among the criticisms of Pompey reported by Plutarch as contributing to making his name despised was that of Domitius Ahenobarbus, who had called the great general 'Agamemnon' and 'King of Kings' (*Pomp.* 67.3).[56] Rome's tragic repertoire was not something to be played – or played with – lightly.

The confusion of play and reality, of tragic drama and 'tragic' event, was not confined to Rome. Plutarch reports a horrific instance of this confusion in the anti-Rome, Parthia. A scar on Rome's honour was the Parthian annihilation of Crassus' three legions at the Battle of Carrhae in Syria in 53 BCE. One extraordinary aspect of this, if Plutarch is to be believed (*Crassus* 3.3), was a performance of Euripides' *Bacchae* before the Parthians with Crassus' head employed as the head of Pentheus. At least Pompey's head awaited Caesar on his arrival in Egypt in 48 BCE as a gift, not as a stage prop. Caesar, however, learnt from Pompey's use of the theatre. As aedile in 65 BCE Caesar had conducted the games under his control, the *Ludi Megalenses* and *Ludi Romani*, in sumptuous style, and had privately commissioned gladiatorial games in commemoration of his father, also named Gaius Julius Caesar, a praetor of 91 BCE who had died in 85 (Suet. *Iul.* 10.1–2). These *ludi* achieved their political goal most effectively, but were completely overshadowed by the triumphal games of Pompey in 61 BCE. Hence in 46 BCE Caesar celebrated his victory in the civil war and the dedication of the Temple of Venus Genetrix in his new forum with the most lavish games yet, the *Ludi Veneris Genetricis*,[57] held in the Roman Forum, the Circus Maximus and in a naumachia newly constructed in the Campus Martius. The games were clearly intended to outshine both Pompey's triumphal games and those held at the opening of his theatre (Dio 43.22–23).

Caesar planned his own permanent theatre, too, 'of the greatest size' (*summae magnitudinis*) on the slopes of the Tarpeian rock (Suet. *Iul.* 44.1). The plans were to reach fruition under Augustus as the Theatre of Marcellus, located by the Tiber near the Circus Flaminius. Before that happened two other theatrical events took place: the killing of Caesar at the foot of the statue of Pompey in

Pompey's own theatre,[58] and Caesar's funeral, an impressive and impressively stage-managed event,[59] at which performances of Atilius' *Electra* (a play chosen presumably because it would feature mourning and revenge for an unjustly slain conqueror) and of Pacuvius' *Armorum Iudicium*, 'Judgement of Arms', seem to have been held,[60] in which lines were specifically emphasised 'to arouse pity and resentment at his murder' (*ad miserationem et inuidiam caedis eius*, Suet. *Iul.* 84.2).[61] Pacuvius' play was proleptic. What followed Caesar's funeral was another fight over arms or armies, those of Caesar himself.

Shortly after Caesar's death his enemies decided to make use of tragedy's political power. At the *Ludi Apollinares* later in the year, the urban praetor, Marcus Junius Brutus, one of Caesar's chief assassins, tried *in absentia* to have Accius' *Brutus* performed, and instructed Gaius Antonius (Mark Antony's brother) to arrange it.[62] The intention was clearly to represent the modern Brutus as a 'regicide' (and Caesar as the 'last king', *rex*, of Rome).[63] If Cicero's account of Caesar's assassination is close to the truth (*Phil.* 2.28), Marcus Brutus may already have played his putative ancestor by raising his bloody dagger on high in imitation of the famous statue on the Capitoline – and perhaps also in self-conscious reenactment of the Brutus of Accius' play.[64] In the event Gaius Antonius substituted Accius' *Tereus* for his *Brutus*, but this affected little the political semiotics of the occasion. *Tereus* dealt with vengeance successfully enacted against a tyrant whose attempts to mute his raped victim had catastrophically failed. It would have taken little imagination in that fervid political context to have seen the essential point: Rome's liberation from Caesar, whose muting of the city through tyranny would have been heard and seen in Accius' mythic play. Cicero observes that the audience thundered its applause for the absent liberator 'as one verse followed another' (*in singulis uersibus, Phil.* 10.8). For the cerebrally slow, there seem to have been hired claques in the audience to advance Brutus' cause (Appian: *BC* 3.24).

A *Brutus* may have been performed prior or subsequent to this political *Tereus*, perhaps in the cataclysmic decade of the 40s, although we have no precise notice of its date: the *Brutus* of Cassius of Parma, another of Caesar's assassins, who also seems to have been the author of plays on other paradigm sagas of tyranny, *Thyestes* and *Orestea*.[65] One line survives from Cassius' *Brutus*, cited by Varro (*LL* 6.7, 7.72), although this is sometimes attributed to Accius.[66] Lucretia is speaking of Sextus Tarquinius:

nocte intempesta nostram deuenit domum.

At dead of night he came to our house.

All we know of the play was that it clearly dealt with the rape of Lucretia. But we can guess that its preoccupation was with the removal of a tyrant and that its allusions were to the contemporary tyrant, Caesar. After all, one of Cassius' other plays was a *Thyestes*, the anti-tyrannical sentiments of which are likely to have been aimed at either Caesar or his heir, the latter of whom Cassius is said to have attacked in political pamphlets (Suet. *Aug.* 4.2).[67] Cicero, too, uses the paradigm of Atreus to castigate that other tyrannical 'heir' to Caesar, Mark Antony (*Phil.* 1.33–34). In the dying years of the Roman republic it seems to have been virtually impossible to write, produce or even cite a tragic drama without contemporary political meaning. Cicero was murdered in the proscriptions of 43 BCE; his severed head and hands were brought to his 'Atreus' and then displayed on the Forum's rostra, the 'stage' of the Roman republic (Livy frag. 50). We are but fourteen years before yet another *Thyestes* makes its appearance: in 29 BCE, at the triumphal games of Octavian, conqueror of Cleopatra, Antony and the east.

6

ROMA THEATRUM

The early empire

supremo die identidem exquirens an iam de se
tumultus foris esset, petito speculo capillum sibi
comi ac malas labantes corrigi praecepit et admissos
amicos percontatus ecquid iis uideretur mimum
uitae commode transegisse, adiecit et clausulam:
ἐπεὶ δὲ πάνυ καλῶς πέπαισται, δότε κρότον
καὶ πάντες ἡμᾶς μετὰ χαρᾶς προπέμψατε.

(Suetonius *Diuus Augustus* 99.1)

On his final day repeatedly asking whether there was
any uproar outside on his account, he asked for a
mirror and ordered his hair to be combed and his
slipping jaws to be straightened. And, after admit-
ting his friends, he asked them whether they
thought that he had played life's mime well, adding
the tag:

> Since the part has been played to perfection,
> All clap and send me off with applause.

Augustan tragedy

As Suetonius implies, the life and career of Rome's first emperor,
Augustus, had always been a performance. In this they differed only
in degree from those of his political and military predecessors.
Through playing his part well as the son of the god, the divine
Julius Caesar, and the champion of Italy and the west, he had
achieved by 30 BCE sole dominion of the Roman world.
Appropriately his rule began with spectacle and with theatre.
Returning to Rome from his victories over Cleopatra and Antony in

Egypt, he celebrated in August 29 BCE a great triple triumph, for his successes in Illyricum, at Actium and at Alexandria (Dio 51.21.5–9). The triumph lasted three days, and the *ludi* which accompanied it featured a new Roman tragedy, *Thyestes*, specially commissioned for this occasion at an unprecedented cost (a million sesterces is reported).

Thyestes had been written, according to the scholiasts, 'with great care' (*magna cura*)[1] by the epic poet and friend of Virgil, Lucius Varius Rufus. Still appreciated a century or so later, when it was praised by both Tacitus (*Dial.* 12.6) and Quintilian (*Inst.* 10.1.98) – the latter claimed that Varius' play equalled those of the Greeks[2] – this extraordinarily important tragedy perished, apart from the following tantalizing six-word fragment, attributed by Quintilian (*Inst.* 3.8.45) to Varius' Atreus:

> iam fero infandissima,
> iam facere cogor.
>
> > *(Thyestes* frag. Klotz)

> Now I endure the ineffable,
> Now I am forced to enact it.

These are well written lines, which show a forceful use of anaphora and of alliterative effects. They are also seminal lines, which allow one to conjecture that the setting of the play was Mycenae or Argos (rather than Epirus as in Ennius' version) and that the action dealt with Atreus' enactment of vengeance on Thyestes (for his adultery with the former's wife, Aerope) at the cannibalistic feast. More than this can hardly be said about the contents of Varius' play.[3]

More can be said about the choice of *this* tragic myth for a spectacle centred upon Augustus.[4] Theoretically a tragedy dealing with fraternal hatred and revenge, rife with potential for anti-tyrannical criticism of the victorious brother – and that Varius' play dealt with tyranny was clear to Ovid (*Pont.* 4.16.31)[5] – would have seemed a most inappropriate subject for a drama at Augustus' triumphal games. Indeed there may already have been an anti-Augustan or anti-Caesarian *Thyestes*, written by Cassius of Parma a few years earlier, and perhaps another anti-tyrannical *Thyestes* by Sempronius Gracchus, which, however, is more likely to have been written in the aftermath of Varius' play.[6] What Augustus seems to have decided to do, whether prompted by Cassius' play[7] or not, was to subsume this potentially most damning critique of tyranny within a triumph to glorify himself and thereby appropriate its ideology, making of the play a negative paradigm which his own hegemony disavowed. The play shows the evils of a monarch, a tyrant, a *rex*. Augustus the triumphant consul was to restore the republic. Previous association in political literature, especially in Cicero's *Philippics*,[8] of Atreus or of tyrannical atrocities and an appetite for blood with Mark Antony may have assisted a pro-Augustan reading. Nothing, however, could have prevented anti-Augustan reverberations. The 'meaning' of a *Thyestes* play can never end with its final words. The staging of this play was a huge risk for the prospective emperor.

It was a risk he must have known. Augustus had always realised the semiotic and political power of spectacle. He had reached his political maturity quickly in the mid-forties when the Roman theatre and the games were openly politicised. Right at the start of his climb to greatness, in the middle of 44 BCE, he had used the *ludi* to bolster his uncertain status in Rome by following Brutus' eight-day *Ludi Apollinares* almost immediately with the eleven-day *Ludi Victoriae Caesaris*; and eleven years later in 33 BCE, just prior to the showdown with Antony, he had consolidated his position in the city by having his lieutenant, Agrippa, hold, as aedile, sumptuous and prolonged games in which gifts were literally showered on the people (Dio 49.43.2–4). For Augustus spectacle, authority, power were imbricated realities. When his own political supremacy was assured, he set about turning the whole of Rome into a spectacle in honour of himself.

The city Augustus inherited was a multivalent urban complex, dotted with a plethora of uncoordinated monuments glorifying a host of diverse *triumphatores* and preventing the citizen from reading the city as the celebration of a single figure.[9] After 29 BCE things changed. Augustus asked for help in the restoration of temples from the descendants of their original founders (Dio 53.2.4) and in the repair of roads (and other practical and less prestigious projects) from recent *triumphatores* (Suet. Aug. 30.1, Dio 53.22.1), but, after Augustus' return to the city, there was little public building that was not an Augustan icon.[10] The unprecedented, almost frenetic building programme in Rome of 29–17 BCE reshaped the Roman Forum, the Palatine, the Capitoline and the Campus Martius with such buildings as the Temple of the Divine Julius (29 BCE), the Curia Julia (29 BCE), the Temple of Apollo (28 BCE), the Basilica Julia, two triumphal arches (29 and 19 BCE), the Julian Mausoleum

(28–23 BCE), the first Pantheon (27–25 BCE), the Saepta Iulia (26 BCE), the Basilica of Neptune (25 BCE), the Baths of Agrippa (25–19 BCE), the Temple of Jupiter Tonans (22 BCE), and culminated in the new Rome celebrated by the *Ludi Saeculares* of 17 BCE. This was followed by three decades of personal and dynastic architectural consolidation,[11] in which overtly ideological constructions such as the Theatre of Marcellus (11 BCE), the Horologium Augusti (10 BCE), the Ara Pacis Augustae (9 BCE) and the Forum Augustum (2 BCE) were supplemented by monuments built or restored by his (eventually) named successor, Tiberius, his sister, Octavia, and his wife, Livia. The general style of all this building bore little relationship to the surreal architectural designs favoured by contemporary (i.e. 'third style') wall-painters. Augustan architectural forms – classicising, conservative, majestic, and suggestive of authority, power, history, tradition, unity, permanence – masked the revolutionary appropriation of Rome which was taking place, its transformation into a marmoreal *scaenae frons* which not only provided the backdrop to the emperor's contemporary performances but reconfigured Rome's past and cultural memory to validate his hegemony.

In this vast programme of public works Augustus did not neglect the theatre. In 32 BCE he had completed restoration work on Pompey's Theatre, possibly adding to it a new Portico of Nations.[12] He also constructed by the banks of the Tiber a new theatre, the Theatre of Marcellus.

> Capitolium et Pompeium theatrum utrumque opus impensa grandi refeci sine ulla inscriptione nominis mei ... theatrum ad aedem Apollinis in solo magna ex parte a priuatis empto feci, quod sub nomine M. Marcelli generi mei esset.
>
> (Augustus *Res Gestae* 20–1)

> I rebuilt the Capitol and the Theatre of Pompey, both works at immense expense, without any inscription of my name ... I built the theatre by the Temple of Apollo on ground purchased for the most part from private owners – the one which was to carry the name of Marcus Marcellus my son-in-law.

There was also a third theatre constructed in Rome, the last public building of record to be built in the city by someone other than a member of the imperial family or the senate until the fourth century CE: the Theatre of Balbus.[13] Situated just north of the Theatre of Marcellus, it was dedicated in 13 BCE and was the smallest of Rome's three permanent theatres (with a capacity of about 7,700 spectators).[14]

It was the Theatre of Marcellus, however, which became the new great theatre of Rome. The second stone theatre to be started in the city (although its dedication date may be later than that of the Theatre of Balbus, it was sufficiently complete to be used in the *Ludi Saeculares* of 17 BCE: *CIL* 6.32323.157), it was originally the idea of Julius Caesar, who cleared the area in the southern Campus Martius for its construction and laid the foundations. Augustus completed the project and dedicated it as a memorial to his deceased nephew and son-in-law, Marcellus, in either 13 or 11 BCE.[15] Its status as a family memorial was underlined by Augustus' order that 'a golden image' of Marcellus, 'a golden crown and a curule chair' should be carried into the theatre at the *Ludi Romani* and set in the middle of the officials in charge of the games (Dio 53.30.6). The theatre's *scaenae frons* seems to have reused four huge marble columns of Scaurus' earlier temporary theatre, probably to flank the central door of the facade, the *porta regia*.[16] The building's remarkable fusion of social functionality, engineering necessity, political semiotics and powerful aesthetics (especially successful in this regard were the exterior facade's brilliant travertine, arcuated rhythm and layered use of the Greek orders), made it one of the most impressive Augustan monuments. It was the largest of Rome's three theatres (the 20,500 *loca* of the Regionary Catalogues convert conservatively to '13,000 spectators'),[17] and quickly became the most important one, commanding a prime position at the east end of the Circus Flaminius. The division of the *cauea* or seating section of the theatre into *cunei* or wedge-shaped areas separated by stair-cases and into three vertical zones enabled the social segregations of the *lex Iulia theatralis* (Suet. *Aug.* 44.1–2) to be implemented with ease. At a glance one could view the social hierarchy of Rome – slaves, freedmen, women, boys, married men, soldiers, imperial servants, equestrians, Vestals, senators, major magistrates and priests (in addition to visiting foreign dignitaries and other 'aliens') – in discrete, controlled display.[18] Rome's male social elite, members of the senatorial and equestrian classes, sat at the front in the orchestra and in the first fourteen rows. High up and furthest from the stage, where they would not distract the men, sat Rome's women – respectable *matronae*, freedwomen, prostitutes, the myopic of whom saw little.

What this carefully structured audience looked upon became increasingly sophisticated and dramatically diverse. As far as the adornments of the stage and its facade are concerned, both contemporary wall-paintings and writings suggest that the tendency towards more use of painted sets, scenery stands and the like continued and became more elaborate and spectacular. Complex collapsible structures and flying devices are also attested, used both in the theatre and elsewhere for scenic effect (Strabo 6.2.6; Phaedrus 5.7). Probably, too, the stage curtains, lowered at the start of a performance and raised at the end (Hor. *Ep.* 2.1.189), became more intricate in their design (see Virgil *Geo.* 3.25; Ovid *Met.* 3.111–14). Livy writes in the early Augustan period, before either of the two Augustan stone theatres had been built, of 'how from sane beginnings the theatre has reached an insanity which can hardly be supported by opulent monarchies' (*quam ab sano initio res in hanc uix opulentis regnis tolerabilem insaniam uenerit,* 7.2.13). Horace (*Ep.* 2.1.194–207), as noted on p. 20, comments brilliantly on the theatrical audience's susceptibility to spectacle, even the spectacle of an actor's costume, a violet-dyed cloak (*laena Tarentino uiolas imitata ueneno, Ep.* 2.1.207).

Theatres were big business architecturally, and Vitruvius, the Augustan architectural writer and theorist, devoted most of the fifth book of his *De Architectura* to theatre design and related topics. He provides important information on stage scenery and stage-entrances/exits:

> The stage facade itself is so laid out that the middle doors are designed like a royal palace, those on the left and right lead to the guest quarters. Adjacent are spaces prepared for scenery (*ornatus*), which are termed *periaktoi* in Greek from the location there of machines with rotating triangles corresponding to the three types of scenery (*ornatio*).[19] When changes in the plays, or arrivals of the gods with sudden thunders, are about to occur they are turned and change the type of scene facing the audience. Next to these are the angles which run out and create the entrances onto the stage, one from the forum, one from abroad. There are three types of stage-sets (*scaenae*): one is called tragic, the second comic, the third satyric. The scenery of each of these differs and has a different rationale. Stage-sets for tragedy (*tragicae*) are designed with columns and gables and statues and the other trappings of royalty; comic sets (*comicae*) have the look of private buildings and balconies and projections

with views from[20] windows arranged to imitate the manner
of regular buildings; satyric sets (*satyricae*) are decorated
with trees, caves, hills and the other rustic features, like a
designed landscape.

(Vitruvius *De Architectura* 5.6.8–9)

Note Vitruvius' tripartion: tragedy, comedy, satyric drama. It is clear
that satyric drama, as Horace's *Ars Poetica* itself implies, was, like
tragedy and comedy, a regular feature of the Augustan theatrical
programme; like them, it was allocated its own distinct stage-set. All
stage-sets must have been (easily?) changeable to accommodate
different kinds of play in the same theatres. One attested way of
doing this during the late-republican and Augustan periods, at least
in temporary theatres (i.e. not in the stone theatres with a permanent
scaenae frons discussed by Vitruvius), was the employment of *scaenae
ductiles*, 'drawn scenery', i.e. sliding painted scenery panels partly
visible behind a wooden stage facade, interchangeable and able to be
concealed by special curtains (*siparia*) during the change-over.
Another way (suggested by the second-century CE author, Pollux) was
through the employment of *katablemata*, decorated panels or curtains
which were 'let down'. Other methods, too, have been postulated.[21]

This Augustan theatrical energy was not restricted to a recycling
of the inherited repertoire. Recycling did take place. Horace himself
lists Pacuvius, Accius, Afranius, Plautus, Caecilius and Terence as
playwrights whom 'mighty Rome learns by heart and watches,
crowded in the narrow theatre' (*ediscit et hos arto stipata theatro/ spectat
Roma potens, Ep.* 2.1.60–1).[22] But new plays were written in the
Augustan period, including new tragedies, even if, as Horace deri-
sively implies (*Ep.* 2.1.50–89), the modern taste was for premodern
works. Tragic writers included two of the finest poets of the era:
Varius, who has already been mentioned, and Ovid. Other names to
survive are those of Lynceus (perhaps a fictive name), Turranius, and
Sempronius Gracchus, who achieved notoriety as one of the adul-
terous lovers of Augustus' daughter Julia, a crime for which he was
banished to Cercina. He was later (14 CE) executed by Tiberius (Tac.
Ann. 1.53.3–6). To Gracchus are attributed an *Atalanta*, *Peliades* and
Thyestes. The plays of Santra and Pupius, too, may belong to this
period. There are also references in Augustan sources to dramas
whose authors we do not know: such as the *praetexta* on the third-
century historical figure, Claudia Quinta (see Ovid *Fas.* 4.326).[23]
Augustus himself seems also to have begun to write a tragedy, *Ajax*,
which he is then alleged to have destroyed (Suet. *Aug.* 85.2).

That very few lines survive from these Augustan tragedians should not be taken as testimony to their dramatic achievement. They are plausibly credited with a 'classical refinement'[24] of subject-matter and form. The extant titles suggest a possible restriction of Augustan tragedy to subjects tackled by the great Attic triad, and the surviving fragments indicate a reshaping of the loose iambic dialogue line, the *senarius*, into something approaching the metrical discipline of the Greek trimeter – at least if Horace's strictures are anything to go by (*AP* 251–74). There is also evidence of self-conscious use of the early republican tragedians (Tac. *Dial.* 21.7). Later Quintilian selects Varius as the only Roman tragedian to compare with the Greeks, and nominates Ovid's play as (one of) the finest of his works:

> iam Varii Thyestes cuilibet Graecarum comparari potest. Ouidii Medea uidetur mihi ostendere quantum ille uir praestare potuerit, si ingenio suo imperare quam indulgere maluisset.
>
> (Quintilian *Institutio Oratoria* 10.1.98)

> Now Varius' *Thyestes* can be compared to any Greek tragedy. Ovid's *Medea* seems to me to reveal what that man could have achieved if he had preferred controlling his talent to indulging it.

At least in the case of Varius' *Thyestes* the production date is known. We do not even possess that information for the Ovidian *Medea*, which is generally dated to Ovid's early period and may well have been written in conjunction with, and inspired by, the opening of two new stone theatres in Rome in the period 13–11 BCE. Possibly relevant here is *Amores* 3.1, which depicts a playful competition between sexy Elegy and buskined, sceptre-wielding Tragedy for Ovid's poetic services, and which certainly belongs to the period 20–2 BCE. The play must have been influenced by the versions of Ennius and Accius (especially the former, which was in the blood of the Roman poetic tradition – it had influenced the poetry of Catullus and – probably – Virgil)[25] and in turn helped to shape the great tragedy of Seneca to follow. Ovid's masterwork, *Metamorphoses*, provides potent testimony to his dramatic abilities both in the area of tragic structure (the stories of Phaethon, Tereus and of Myrrha are but three obvious illustrations) and in the composition of dramatic monologues prior to tragic action. Ovid clearly cannibalised much from the early republican tragedians,[26] and Seneca cannibalised in turn from

Ovid, especially from the presentation of psychological conflict in *Metamorphoses* and in the monologic epistles of the earlier *Heroides*.[27] Few have surpassed Ovid in the verbal enactment of the transgressive female mind.

But all that survive from Ovid's single play are two lines, one dialogue, one lyric:

> seruare potui. perdere an possim rogas?
>
> > (*Medea* frag. i Klotz)

I could save. You ask if I can destroy?

> feror huc illuc ut plena deo.
>
> > (*Medea* frag. ii Klotz)

I'm tossed here, there, like a woman filled with god.

Both lines were clearly delivered by Medea. The iambic dialogue line (technically a 'trimeter' because of its correspondence to Greek practice) was presumably spoken by Medea to Jason or (less likely) to a nurse or other intimate. In Seneca's play, Medea's saving of the Argonautic crew is an important motif in the scene with Creon, but the menacing tone of Ovid's line makes a confrontation with Jason or a riposte to a doubting intimate a more likely context. Note the rhythmic alliteration of 'p's and nuanced repetition of 'r's, making it a forceful and speakable line reflective of Medea's contempt and strength of will. Quintilian (*Inst.* 8.5.6) cites the line for its force, *uis*, which he attributes to its particularity. The second line is anapaestic and must have been part of a *canticum* sung by Medea. The most probable context would have been a deliberative aria just before she kills her children.[28] The Elder Seneca (*Suas.* 3.7) quotes the line to illustrate Ovid's 'open borrowings' from Virgil. In his sole tragedy, as in his poetic work at large, Ovid self-consciously displayed his place in the literary tradition.

From the few surviving fragments of Augustan tragedy nothing can be gleaned about its dramaturgical practice. Horace provides some insight:

> neue minor neu sit quinto productior actu
> fabula quae posci uolt et spectata reponi.
> nec deus intersit, nisi dignus uindice nodus
> inciderit, nec quarta loqui persona laboret.
>
> > (*Ars Poetica* 189–92)

Let no play be less or longer than a fifth act
If it wants to be called for and restaged.
Let no god intervene, unless there's a knot fit
For a liberator; let no fourth actor try to speak.

Thus we have the five-act rule, the three-actor rule, the *deus ex machina* (but only in appropriate circumstances) – and, immediately following this (*AP* 193–201), recommendations for the chorus to play the role of an actor (*actoris partes*), assist with the movement of the plot and action, and act as a symbol of moral rectitude and fine counsel throughout. Elsewhere there are clear prescriptions for a lofty but varied and nuanced tragic style (always following the law of decorum: *AP* 90–98), for diction suited to the emotional state, age, sex and social status of the character (*AP* 99–118), for traditional or (in the case of invented material) consistent characterisation (*AP* 119–27), for a replication of the *mores*, 'manners', of the several ages of man (*AP* 153–78); and there is a forceful interdiction against the display of tragic violence on the stage (*AP* 179–88). Horace's view (*AP* 333–46) about the aim of dramatic poetry is especially interesting: it is the fusion of utility (*utile*) and pleasure (*dulce*). Only such can succeed on the stage:

centuriae seniorum agitant expertia frugis;
celsi praetereunt austera poemata Ramnes.

(*Ars Poetica* 341–2)

Rows of greybeards drive the profitless from the stage;
Arrogant young bloods reject pleasureless poems.

How far such prescriptions were adhered to by playwrights such as Varius and Ovid is unknowable. Several of the Horatian 'rules' were not strictly adhered to by Seneca. But if Senecan practice is anything to go by, probably already in Roman tragedy the following dramaturgical features (foreign to fifth-century Attic tragedy, but common in Hellenistic drama, especially New Comedy) are evident: the five-act structure, the use of extended asides, including entrance monologue-asides, choral exit and re-entry (in fifth-century Attic tragedy the chorus enters after the prologue and remains on stage throughout the play), and such items of stage-business as withdrawing to plot future action or surveying the stage for eavesdroppers. Probably, too, a chorus smaller than that of Attic tragedy was common (to make choral exit and re-entry easier); and the chorus would have delivered all its odes from the stage, to which it was now restricted, since the orchestra was used for senatorial seating (Vitr. 5.6.2).

But if the Augustan period (30 BCE–14 CE) was one of 'classical refinement' and generic consolidation for tragedy and one which witnessed an expansion both in theatrical venues and in the production values of performance, it was also a period of increased political control. In many senses the senatorial elite lost control of the theatre in the final years of the republic, just as they lost control of the republic itself. Augustus gradually took back control of the *ludi* and the theatre – to and for himself. In 23 BCE lavish games had been held by the last aedile to do so: Marcellus, Augustus' nephew and son-in-law, who died later in that year (Dio 53.31.2–3; Vell. Pat. 2.93). In 22 BCE Augustus over-hauled the whole administration of the *ludi* by giving nominal control of them to the praetors (whose 'election' he would have approved), severely restricting the cost to the magistrates involved, and dictating the size and frequency of gladiatorial games (Dio 54.2.3–4). The days of competitive display were over. There was now only one person who was allowed to impress – without limits – by means of spectacle, which he did, 'surpassing all predecessors in the frequency, variety and splendour of his shows, his *spectacula*' (Suet. *Aug.* 43.1).

Four years or so after the administrative changes of 22 BCE Augustus brought in new controls on the theatre audience, too, introducing legislation, the *lex Iulia theatralis*, designed to regulate seating in the theatre and the circus:[29]

> militem secreuit a populo. maritis e plebe proprios ordines assignauit, praetextatis cuneum suum et proximum paeda-gogis, sanxitque ne quis pullatorum media cauea sederet. feminis ne gladiatores quidem, quos promiscue spectari sollemne olim erat, nisi ex superiore loco spectare concessit. solis uirginibus uestalibus locum in theatro separatim et contra praetoris tribunal dedit.
>
> (Suetonius *Diuus Augustus* 44.2–3)

> He separated the military from the people. He assigned married plebeian men their own seats, boys their own section and their slave-tutors one next to it, and decreed that no one in a dark toga sit in the central rows. He would not permit women to view even the gladiators except from the upper deck, although it had long been customary for them to be viewed by men and women together. He gave only the Vestal virgins a place on their own, opposite the praetor's tribunal.

A perfect image of Rome's social and political structure for the emperor's controlling gaze. As noted on p. 164, the wedge-shaped sections of the *caueae* of the stone theatres enabled such social segregation to be realised easily. Augustus tried to extend social segregation to the circus, which certainly reserved special seats for senators and knights (at least from 5 CE: Dio 55.24.4) and places for each of the thirty Roman *curiae* or wards. But contemporary witness, most especially the poetry of Ovid (*Am.* 3.2, *Ars* 1.135–63), makes it clear that the circus did not maintain the severe sexual segregation of the theatre. In the circus (possibly until the time of Hadrian: Dio 69.8.2) men and women could and did sit together.[30] Augustus himself usually watched the games in the Circus Maximus from the Palatine itself, either from the houses of friends or from the specially constructed 'imperial box', *puluinar* (Suet. *Aug.* 45.1).

Augustus' control of the theatre was further extended by his implementation of the *infamia* law and the underscoring of the theatre's traditional association with such standard Roman vices as *luxuria*, *licentia* and *immodestia*.[31] Although he seems to have restricted the power of magistrates to flog actors to 'the games and the stage' (*ludi et scaena*), that power was realised on several occasions, even by himself (Suet. *Aug.* 45.3–4). He also reaffirmed in 22 BCE the ban on senators and their sons appearing on stage, and enlarged the ban to include the grandsons of senators, if they were members of the equestrian class (Dio 54.2.5). The punishment for such conduct remained disfranchisement (Dio 56.25.7–8).[32] There were also other legal penalties.[33] Such penalties and their attendant grounds had political goals. Reminders of the social and moral baseness of actors and acting ensured a context in which no Aesopus or Roscius might emerge with the authority to politicise a play or exploit a historical moment.

Further control was achieved through diversifying, trivialising and spectacularising the dramatic repertoire and marginalising tragedy itself. For the expansion in theatrical venues did not result in an increased number of tragic or comic (or 'satyric') performances but in a substantial change in the Roman theatrical experience. During the Augustan period the 'low culture' dramatic forms of mime and Atellan farce started to take over the Roman theatres[34] – accompanied by a new Augustan form, the pantomime. Introduced at Rome in 22 BCE, this highly expressive 'ballet' featured a masked, silent performer who, accompanied by instrumental music and/or a chorus and/or a solo singer, interpreted through dance and gesture a theme (generally) from Greek mythology in a comic or tragic mode. Its leading dancers,

Pylades and Bathyllus (Athenaeus *Deipn.* 1.20d–e: Pylades also wrote a treatise on dancing), were freedmen respectively of Augustus and his friend Maecenas. Pantomime was a demanding art form, in which the dancer had to represent character, feeling and plot through bodily movement and a complex code of gestures.[35] It became immensely popular and received imperial support, projecting its main practitioners to 'stardom'; in the process, although it may have used excerpts from the dramatic repertoire as libretti for the accompanying singers, it marginalized the more discursive (and potentially political) forms of tragedy and comedy.

Pantomime's popularity led to occasional outbreaks of violence between the dancers' rival supporters. But that this scenic entertainment had a politically quietist function was, according to Dio, recognised by the dancers themselves.[36] There is evidence to indicate that mime, too, which in the republic was also used politically, was actively depoliticised.[37] Tragedies and comedies seem to have been regularly performed, as the 'literary epistles' of Horace clearly suggest;[38] and occasionally a tragic performance might work its emotional effect like a magician (*ut magus*), transporting the audience to Thebes or Athens (*Ep.* 2.1.210–13). But the position of tragedy (and comedy) within the Roman theatrical experience was becoming less central and increasingly prone to the spectacular production values of the Roman theatre, in which the appeal, even to the wealthier, more educated members of the audience, was less to the ear (or mind) than to the eye:

> uerum equitis quoque iam migrauit ab aure uoluptas
> omnis ad incertos oculos et gaudia uana.
> quattuor aut pluris aulaea premuntur in horas,
> dum fugiunt equitum turmae peditumque cateruae.
> mox trahitur manibus regum fortuna retortis,
> esseda festinant, pilenta, petorrita, naues,
> captiuum portatur ebur, captiua Corinthus.
> (Horace *Epistles* 2.1.187–92)

But now the whole pleasure even of a knight has migrated
From the ear to wandering eyes and vain delights.
For four hours or more the curtain remains lowered,
While cavalry squadrons and throngs of infantry flee.
Then they drag in the destiny of kings with hands tied,
Chariots rush by, coaches, wagons, ships;
Captured ivory is trundled in, captured Corinth.

Horace's description is clearly of tragedies (compare the production of Accius' *Clytaemestra* and Naevius' *Equos Troianus* at the opening of Pompey's Theatre) and/or *praetextae* – their discursive potential muted, if not removed. But that such discursive, even critical, political potential did not expire overnight is revealed by a rare anecdote recorded by Suetonius. During a dramatic festival a line describing a eunuch priest of Cybele –

> uidesne ut cinaedus orbem digito temperat?
> <div align="right">(Suetonius <i>Diuus Augustus</i> 68)</div>

Do you see how a catamite beats the drum with a finger?

– was reinterpreted by the theatre audience as 'Do you see how a catamite controls the world with his finger?' Amidst loud applause it was applied to Augustus himself. As always, the exception proved the political rules.

Augustus' frequent presence at the games was in itself an appropriation of them, although the ancient evidence suggests that Augustus discouraged the kind of acclamation with which his appearance (as the neophyte Octavian) at the *Ludi Victoriae Caesaris* in 44 BCE was greeted.[39] Appropriation was also achieved simply through the holding of special *ludi* to celebrate 'Augustan' events: the triumphal games of 29 BCE, for example, and the games to celebrate the dedication of the Temple of Divus Julius shortly afterwards; the *ludi* of 28 BCE to celebrate the dedication of the Temple of Apollo on the Palatine; the games of 13 or 11 BCE associated with the dedication of the Temple of Marcellus (Dio 51.21.5–9, 22.4–9; 54.26.1) ... and so on.

> On three occasions I gave a gladiatorial show (*munus gladiatorium*) in my own name and on five occasions in the name of my sons or grandsons; at these shows about ten thousand men fought in combat. Twice in my own name I presented to the people the spectacle (*spectaculum*) of athletes called from everywhere and on a third occasion in the name of my grandson. I produced shows (*ludi*) four times in my own name, and twenty-three times in place of other magistrates. On behalf of the College of Fifteen (*quindecimuiri*), as its master (*magister*), with Marcus Agrippa as colleague, I produced the Centennial Games (*Ludi Saeculares*) in the consulship of Gaius Furnius and Gaius Silanus (17 BCE). In my thirteenth consulship (2 BCE) I first produced the

Games of Mars (*Ludi Martiales*), which the consuls produced thereafter in succeeding years by a decree of the senate and by law. I gave to the people hunts (*uenationes*) of African beasts in my own name or that of my sons and grandsons in the circus or in the forum or in the amphitheatres on twenty-six occasions, at which about three thousand and five hundred beasts were killed. I gave to the people the spectacle (*spectaculum*) of a naval battle across the Tiber at the place where the Grove of the Caesars is now located, excavating a site eighteen hundred feet long and twelve hundred feet wide, in which thirty beaked triremes or biremes and several smaller ships joined in battle. In these fleets there fought, apart from the rowers, about three thousand men.

(Augustus Res Gestae 22–3)

Augustus enhanced these occasional appropriations by appropriating the Roman calendar itself both through an increase in state festivals, celebrating the achievements of Augustus and his family, and an increase in non-festival days memorialising a Julian or Augustan anniversary.[40] Some anniversaries fell within the period of already established *ludi*, thereby Augustanising the ancient festival.[41] Other anniversaries became the occasion for new, regular, honorific *ludi*. The annual *ludi* begun in 46 BCE to celebrate Caesar's Victory, *Ludi Victoriae Caesaris*, alone occupied eleven days of the high summer (July 20–30),[42] but other regular, sometimes annual, honorific *ludi* were added to these in 28, 13 and 11 BCE.[43] On a handful of recorded occasions exceptional *ludi* were celebrated by someone other than a member of the imperial family, but these were generally subtly appropriated by Augustus.[44] In 7 BCE Augustus transformed even the suburban *ludi* into ostensibly loyalist performances. A major reorganisation of Rome into 265 districts or *uici* resulted in the placement at the centre of each of them, the *compita* or crossroads, a statue of Augustus' Genius flanked by two statues of the Lares, the crossroads' protecting gods. The result was that the *Ludi Compitalicii* (January 3–5), which had proven sufficiently troublesome in the late republic to be banned for several years,[45] now had a different political focus: the celebration of the Augustan hegemony.

On several occasions, too, Augustan spectacle was unpredicted, but more politically and theatrically potent because of that. The emperor's attempts to create a dynasty were baulked by fate, as heirs or stepsons perished and were interred in the great Julian mausoleum in the Campus Martius. The state funerals of Marcellus (23 BCE), Agrippa (12 BCE), Drusus (9 BCE), Lucius (2 CE) and Gaius (4 CE), were not only lavish pieces of theatre, but occasions for promoting overtly the glories of the imperial house. On two notable occasions Augustus held quite extraordinary *ludi*, designed to stamp an age and to mythologize the regime. The *Ludi Saeculares*, the 'Centennial Games', allegedly held every century and previously held in 249 and 146 BCE, were celebrated over three nights and three days in 17 BCE, and aimed through a series of elaborate religious rituals to proclaim as divinely sanctioned the rule of Augustus and his house, and to index that rule as the dawn of a new age.[46] The *Ludi* themselves featured dramatic performances and were followed by seven days of additional dramatic performances in Latin and Greek and other entertainments, including a beast hunt. No details are provided of these plays and shows, but like Varius' *Thyestes* – and even more so – they would have been subsumed in an expressly ideological spectacle.

Fifteen years later in 2 BCE, when Augustus dedicated the Temple to Mars Ultor in a completed new Forum Augustum, the iconosphere of which presented the *princeps* as the culmination of Roman religion, myth and history, the celebratory games seem to have featured no theatrical performances. Ovid even takes pains to underscore the 'unsuitability' of drama for (after 2 BCE) these annual *Ludi Martiales*.

> sollemnes ludos Circo celebrate, Quirites.
> non uisa est fortem scaena decere deum.
>
> (*Fasti* 5.597–8)

> Hold the festival games in the Circus, Quirites:
> The stage seems not to suit the manly god.

Augustus' aim in the celebrations which accompanied the dedication of the Temple of Mars in his great forum was to make the whole event unforgettable (Vell. Pat. 2.100.2). This 'unforgettability', however, involved no Varian *Thyestes*, but spectacle of the most crowd-pleasing kind. According to Dio (55.10.6–8), 260 lions were slaughtered in the Circus Maximus and thirty-six crocodiles in the Circus Flaminius, gladiatorial fights took place in the Saepta Iulia, the Battle of Salamis was re-enacted (with possible allusions to the Battle of Actium)[47] in a *naumachia* built for this purpose, and the 'Troy Game', *Lusus Troiae*, was held, featuring Agrippa Postumus,

Augustus' grandson. The great moments of the theatrical *ludi* of the republic – the political performance of a *Clytaemestra*, a *Brutus*, *Tereus* or *Atreus* – were a thing of the past. As for the future, shortly after Augustus' death the senate expanded the annual games in honour of Augustus, now Divus Augustus, the *Ludi Augustales*, into an eight-day festival (October 5–12).[48] The death and deification of the emperor only served to make Roman spectacle more imperial.

Tiberius to Nero

The extension of the *Ludi Augustales* did not herald a new golden age for theatre under Tiberius. Tiberius' disdain for the *ludi* had been apparent during Augustus' reign, when he absented himself even from those which he had sponsored (Suet. *Tib.* 7.1). Tiberius' aversion to popular spectacles continued during his principate (14–37 CE), and was such a marked feature of his personality that Tacitus even speculates on its psychological basis (*Ann.* 1.76). More importantly, during Tiberius' principate itself there were political and social reasons for this aversion. Perhaps as a result of the extinguished power of the popular assemblies, the political function of the *ludi* increased, since it provided the opportunity for a meeting between the Roman people and their emperor, which not only increased the former's self-esteem but the sense of its own power. In such an open venue a crowd could make demands of the *princeps* which would be impossible in any other context.

Tiberius' fear of such demands clearly made him reluctant to attend the theatre (Suet. *Tib.* 47; Dio 57.11.6),[49] which now also became the site of frequent popular disturbances, stemming from (among other sources) clashes between rival groups of pantomime supporters. Tiberius initially reacted to the problem of *theatralis licentia* with legislation designed to curb the influence of the pantomimes (Tac. *Ann.* 1.77; Dio 57.14.10), and eventually, in 23 CE, with decrees of banishment against not only pantomimes but 'actors', *histriones*, including actors of the Atellan farce, and the leaders of the rival claques (Tac. *Ann.* 4.14.3; Suet. *Tib.* 37.2; Dio 57.21.3). Actors were not recalled to Rome until 37 CE, the first year of Caligula's principate (Dio 59.2.5). Four years before the banishment of *histriones* a new senatorial decree had also reimposed and strengthened the ban (apparently relaxed in 11 CE) on senators or equestrians appearing on stage or in the arena.[50]

Tiberian Rome was not a fertile context for theatrical production or innovation, although clearly some courageous individuals inserted barely concealed Tiberian insults into their plays (Suet. *Tib.* 45). The dangers of doing so were clear from the fate of the anonymous playwright who was charged with 'having insulted Agamemnon in a tragedy' (Suet. *Tib.* 61.3) and executed. Criticisms of mythological tyrants were clearly taken as treasonable insults against the emperor himself, as the example of the tragedian Mamercus Aemilius Scaurus, author of an *Atreus*, attests.[51] So Dio (58.24.3–5) writes of the year 34 CE:

> Mamercus Aemilius Scaurus, who had neither governed a province nor received bribes, was convicted because of a tragedy, and fell to a fate more terrible than what he described. His play was *Atreus*, and he advised (on the model of Euripides) one of that man's subjects to endure the ruler's folly. Upon learning this, Tiberius stated that the line had been said in reference to himself, claiming that he was Atreus because of his bloodthirstiness, and, adding 'I will make him Ajax', forced him to commit suicide. This, however, was not the accusation, but rather that of having committed adultery with Livilla.

Tacitus (*Ann.* 6.29.4–7) adds that it was the enmity of Tiberius' praetorian prefect and head of the secret police, Macro, which caused his downfall, and that it was Macro who informed against him to Tiberius. In the poisonous atmosphere of late Tiberian Rome it is surprising that any tragedies were created, let alone one on the subject of Atreus, which, as Seneca's later misreading of Accius' famous tragedy shows (he thought it was a critique of Sullan Rome: *Ira* 1.20.4), was always already political. Unsurprisingly Scaurus' *Atreus* and the *Agamemnon* (?) of the anonymous tragedian are the only tragedies (of which we know) created during the principate of Augustus' successor.

In 37 CE the actors returned to Rome (Dio 59.2.5). The new emperor, Gaius, better known as Caligula, was a passionate devotee of the 'theatrical arts of singing and dancing' (*scaenicas saltandi canendique artes*, Suet. *Gai.* 11). All the accounts of the period underscore Caligula's 'obsessive theatricality'[52] and penchant for self-dramatisation and (often costumed) role-play. The young *princeps* was especially fond of 'playing' gods and women, with all the appropriate dramatic props, even on occasion accompanied by a chorus.[53] Philo's 'eyewitness' account of Caligula's reception of the Jewish embassy of 40 CE compares the emperor to 'an actor wearing many masks' (*Leg.* 111). According to Dio (59.5.5), Caligula's performances eventually included 'driving chariots, gladiatorial fighting, dancing and acting tragedy'. These 'performances', however, seem to have been in private, controlled venues such as the imperial palace or Caligula's own circus in the Vatican valley, and not on the public stage; they were among other things an expression of imperial power aimed at the humiliation of the Roman elite. The emperor's love of the theatre seems, however, to have been genuine. Suetonius remarks that 'even at public shows he could not refrain from singing along with the tragic actor (*tragoedus*) as he delivered his lines and from openly imitating the actor's gestures (*histrionis gestus*) as if in praise or criticism' (*Gaius* 54.1). Clearly being a tragic actor in Caligulan Rome was not for the faint of heart. Indeed the most famous tragic actor of the day, Apelles, was an intimate of Caligula's, but this did not prevent the emperor from having him flogged.[54] The pantomime, Mnester, was another of Caligula's favourites; but in his case Caligula chose to flog any spectator who made a sound during one of his performances (Suet. *Gaius* 36.1; 55.1).

Such performances were many, for the emperor both increased the number of days for *ludi scaenici* and varied their location, even using the great roofed hall known as the Diribitorium, attached to the Saepta Iulia, instead of the city's theatres when the weather was hot (Dio 59.7.8). Sometimes he held dramatic festivals at night (Suet. *Gaius* 18.1–2). To encourage attendance at the theatre he relaxed some of the formal procedures and dress requirements, and not only attended the theatre himself but assigned seats to his own sisters among those allocated to the Vestal Virgins (Dio 59.3.4; 7.6–8). The tendency for the public spectacles to be the sites for political display increased during Caligula's reign, and both the emperor and the people used them for political ends. The latter's aim was to show displeasure with (or approval of) imperial behaviour, to demand the surrender of informers, or to protest new taxes and the like.[55] The emperor's main purpose seems again to have been the humiliation of the upper class, and this he achieved in a variety of ways, sometimes forcing equestrians into the arena (Dio 59.10.1–4), sometimes simply giving seats in the equestrian section of the theatre to the lower class (Suet. *Gaius* 26.4). Nor were members of the lower orders exempt from the possibility of being suddenly thrust into the arena with wild beasts, arrested after leaving the theatre, or executed on the spot in the Circus Maximus.[56]

In this volatile and dangerous atmosphere it is unlikely that any tragedies were written. Certainly there is no evidence that any were.

Not only was the example of Scaurus still recent, but, if the anecdote concerning Caligula's execution of the author of an Atellan farce is true, there was ample evidence of the perils of the written word:

> Atellanae poetam ob ambigui ioci uersiculum media amphitheatri harena igni cremauit.
>
> (Suetonius *Gaius* 27.4)

> He burned alive in the middle of the amphitheatre's arena a writer of an Atellan farce because of a line with an ambiguous joke.

Indeed, although performances of tragedies abounded, the only new tragedies of which we have evidence were the real-life ones imposed by Caligula on various members of the Roman elite. From the way he allegedly bandied about the famous line from Accius' *Atreus* (Suet. *Gai.* 30.1; see also *Tib.* 59) – *oderint dum metuant*, 'Let them hate, provided they fear' – it seems that Caligula viewed his entire reign as a self-scripted tragedy. On 22 January, 41 CE, he was preparing 'to dance and to act a tragedy' (Dio 59.29.6), but this time the drama was a tyrannicide scripted by others.

With Claudius (41–54 CE) and Nero (54–68 CE), imperial support for the *ludi*, including theatrical *ludi,* continued, even increased. Claudius made sure that he appeared frequently at the games but avoided the oppressive theatrical control and behaviour of Caligula. Apart from obvious pieces of political theatre he played the role of imperial observer of spectacle and observed imperial observer. Major spectacles during his reign included: *ludi scaenici* at the rededication of the Theatre of Pompey (41 CE); triumphal games for victories in Britain (44 CE), which featured *ludi scaenici* held simultaneously in the Theatre of Pompey and the Theatre of Marcellus; *ludi saeculares* (47 CE), which again contained theatrical performances; and an extraordinary *naumachia* on the Fucine Lake (52 CE), involving 19,000 sailors and soldiers (Suet. *Claud.* 21.1–2, 21.6; Dio 60.6.8, 60.23.4–6). There was also active support of actors, including a confirmation and extension of the rights granted by Augustus to the itinerant 'Artists of Dionysus'. Indeed, as an adjunct to Claudius' 'British Games', the theatrical profession (strictly 'artisans of the stage', Dio 60.23.6) organised its own festival in honour of the emperor.

One anecdote also suggests that it was possible once again to turn lines in a theatrical script into criticism of a politically powerful figure present in the audience – and even for that figure to respond with a gibe against the emperor.[57] The play being performed was a comedy of Menander; the political figure in the audience was the freedman head of one of Claudius' administrative departments, Polybius – the year 47 CE:

> Once when an actor in the theatre spoke the much bandied line, 'A successful scoundrel is unbearable', and the whole people turned their gaze towards the emperor's freedman Polybius, he shouted out that yet the same poet said, 'Former goatherds now are kings'. But the emperor took no action against him.
>
> (Dio 60.29.3)

Other anecdotes suggest that Claudius was also capable of bloody retribution if a piece of stage machinery did not work in the arena (Suet. *Claud.* 34.2).

Under Nero (54–68 CE), the last and the most 'artistic' of the Julio–Claudian emperors, Rome itself became a theatrical spectacle – if the ancient accounts are to be believed. In Tacitus' narrative of Nero's reign (*Ann.* 13–16) and its immediate aftermath 'acting' is elevated into the emblematic metaphor of the age. The distinction between play and public reality disappears. The play literally is the thing. The young emperor's initial 'mimicries of sorrow' (*tristiae imitamenta*, *Ann.* 13.4) at the funeral of his stepfather Claudius lead into insistent attention not only to Nero's appearances on the stage but to the political and social imperatives of role-playing in the theatricalised world of imperial Rome, where citizens mourn what they welcome, applaud what they grieve, offer thanksgivings for monstrous murder, and celebrate triumphs for national humiliation or horrendous and impious sin.[58] Tacitus' account of the mass executions attending the Pisonian conspiracy of 65 CE culminates in the ugly theatre of Roman servility:

> sed compleri interim urbs funeribus, Capitolium uictimis; alius filio, fratre alius aut propinquo aut amico interfectis, agere grates deis, ornare lauru domum, genua ipsius aduolui et dextram osculis fatigare.
>
> (*Annales* 15.71)

> Funerals abounded in the city, thank-offerings on the Capitol. Men who had lost a son or brother or relative or friend gave thanks to the gods, bedecked their houses with laurel and fell at the feet of Nero, kissing his hand incessantly.

Equally theatricalised is the historian's description of the people's reaction to Otho's conspiracy four years later, 69 CE –

> uniuersa iam plebs Palatium implebat, mixtis seruitiis et dissono clamore caedem Othonis et coniuratorum exitium poscentium ut si in circo aut theatro ludicrum aliquod postularent. neque illis iudicium aut ueritas, quippe eodem die diuersa pari certamine postulaturis, sed tradito more quemcumque principem adulandi licentia adclamationum et studiis inanibus.
>
> (*Historiae* 1.32)

> The whole populace together with slaves now filled the palace, demanding with raucous cries the death of Otho and the destruction of the conspirators as if they were calling for some show in the circus or theatre. They had neither sense nor sincerity (for on the same day they would clamour for the opposite with equal passion), but followed the convention of flattering whoever was emperor with unlimited applause and empty enthusiasm.

– and of the 'spectatorial' response of the same people to the bloody fighting between the Vitellian and Flavian forces at the end of that year (Tac. *Hist.* 3.83). Tacitus' narrative of Nero's notorious matricide, the murder of his mother, Agrippina (*Ann.* 14.1–13), emphasises not only role-play and sets, but props, dialogue, stage-directions and tragic structure. The theatrics are overt and highly allusive. Agrippina's 'final words', when she receives the sword-thrust from the centurion-executioner, even draw Seneca's Jocasta into the text – *protendens uterum 'uentrem feri' exclamauit,* 'Thrusting her womb forward, she shouted "Strike the belly"' (*Ann.* 14.8.4; cf. Sen. *Oed.* 1038f., *Pho.* 447) – as Nero's mother reveals herself as the theatrical, incestuous figure she had always been. The chorus' account of Agrippina's death in the anonymous *praetexta, Octavia* (369–72), embeds the same analogy.

Seneca's prose works offer contemporary testimony to this theatrical world. Cato is paraded as a moral 'spectacle', *spectaculum* (*Prov.* 2.9ff.), Lucilius is exhorted to do everything 'as if before a spectator (*tamquam spectet aliquis*)' (*Ep.* 25.5; cf. *Ep* 11.8ff.), and 'human life' is declared 'a mime-drama, which assigns parts for us to play badly' (*hic humanae uitae mimus, qui nobis partes quas male agamus adsignat, Ep.* 80.7). Though the Stoic goal is the single part, 'we continually change our mask (*personam*) and put on one the very opposite of that we have discarded' (*Ep.* 120.22). In life, as in a play (*quomodo fabula, sic uita*), what matters is not the length of the acting but its quality (*Ep.* 77.20). Stoicism as a philosophy abounds in theatrical tropes, as both Greek Stoic writings and Seneca's own *Epistles to Lucilius* testify,[59] demanding from its heroes a capacity for dramatic display and exemplary performance. And Stoicism was the philosophy of prime choice for the Neronian Roman elite.

But it was not only philosophy which turned Roman men into actors. Few educated Romans would have found either theatrical self-display or a multiplicity of *personae* difficult. On the contrary, rhetorical training in declamation (*declamatio*), most especially mastery of the 'persuasion-speech' *suasoria,* which required diverse and sustained role-playing, gave to contemporary Romans not only the ability to enter into the psychic structure of another, i.e. 'psychic mobility' or 'empathy',[60] but the improvisational skills required to create a *persona* at will. As works such as Petronius' *Satyricon* exhibit, the cultural and educative system had generated a world of actors. So, too, the political system. The younger Pliny's depiction of Nero as 'stage-emperor', *scaenicus imperator* (*Pan.* 46.4), catches only one aspect of the theatricality of the times. Nero's public appearances on stage made not only himself but the audience actors, equal objects of spectatorial attention.[61] Upper-class members of that audience were well fitted for the required role of approving *spectator*, as for many others. Even their private iconospheres – at least so the evidence from Herculaneum and Pompeii and from Nero's own Domus Aurea suggests – were theatrical. The walls of the houses of the elite seemed regularly to have been adorned with theatrical paintings, especially of subjects drawn from tragic myth.

It is arguable that, in early imperial Rome's confounding culture, personal identity began to be constructed from the performance of a plurality of politically and socially determined roles, thus collapsing the distinction between *persona* and person. Certainly the distinction between 'reality' and 'theatre' dissolves conspicuously within the theatre/amphitheatre itself, where buildings burn, actors bleed, spectators are thrust into the arena, human and animal bodies dismembered, and pain, suffering, death become objects of the theatrical gaze and of theatrical pleasure.[62] In the year after Nero's death the emperor Vitellius sought popular support by joining 'the audience at the theatre, supporters at the circus' (*in theatro ut spectator, in circo ut fautor*, Tac. *Hist.* 2.91) only to become later the spectacle itself.

In this theatricalised world the young *princeps* Nero was both a major impresario and a 'star' performer, singing, acting, playing the lyre and driving chariots – at first in private, eventually in the major public venues. For this he was both criticised (by the Roman aristocracy) and loved (by the Roman people: Tac. *Ann.* 16.4.4). Among his most prominent actions were the construction of a new, wooden amphitheatre in the Campus Martius for aquatic and gladiatorial displays and for beast-hunts (Tac. *Ann.* 13.31.1; Suet. *Nero* 12.1),[63] and the addition of new, elaborate festivals, most notably the *Iuvenalia* in 59 CE and the *Neronia* in 60 and 64 CE, each of which featured athletic and musical competitions, including dramatic recitals and performances. The *Iuvenalia* were held in a private area and Nero participated in them as a lyre-player. In the 'public' festival of the *Neronia*, which was modelled overtly and controversially on the agonistic festivals of Greece, Nero did not compete in 60 CE, but seems to have been awarded the prizes anyway for oratory and poetry, and to have also been offered that for lyre-playing.[64] Nero did compete in both the curtailed and the full version of the *Neronia* in 64 CE, appearing for the first time on the stage of the Theatre of Pompey (Pliny *HN* 37.19). Sometimes, too, members of the senatorial and equestrian orders were 'encouraged' to participate in these festivals as gladiators, pantomimes, actors, musicians and charioteers.[65] To his discredit – so Tacitus implies (*Ann.* 15.65.2) – the aristocrat Piso, who fatally aspired to replace Nero, sang tragic arias on the stage. And even the Stoic senator and future 'martyr', Thrasea Paetus, although he refused to participate in the *Iuvenalia* at Rome, sang in tragic costume at the Antenor games of his native Padua (Tac. *Ann.* 16.21.1).

As well as being awarded the appropriate prizes, Nero's performances were followed by rapturous applause and acclamations led, after 59 CE, by his own special claque, the *Augustiani*.[66] Claques had been a factor in Roman theatrical events at least from Plautus' time (*Amph.* 65–85) and were prominent in the late republic (Cic. *Sest.* 54, *Phil.* 1.37) and early empire. As noted on p. 176, the disturbances they caused during the Tiberian principate were sufficient for their leaders to warrant banishment, along with actors, in 23 CE.[67] Civil disturbance and rioting by fans of the different actors, especially pantomimes, became a regular feature of the imperial Roman theatre and resulted during other principates, too, in the occasional banishment of claque leaders and/or pantomimes whom they supported (see, e.g., Tac. *Ann.* 13.25.3). Nero's attempt in 55 CE to see if theatre crowds could behave in an orderly manner without the presence of troops to control them was a dismal failure (Tac. *Ann.* 13.24). But after the formation of Nero's own claque, the *Augustiani*, the emperor's troops regularly served another function. Their presence in the aisles of the theatre led coercive support to the bullying applause of Nero's young, strong, and conspicuous fans. The *Augustiani* and the soldiers watched for deviant behaviour. Nero's audience was observed as much as the emperor on the stage; adverse responses, indifference and absence were noted (Tac. *Ann.* 16.5).

But that Nero's dominance of the theatrical scene stemmed from personal rather than political motives seems indicated by the emperor's relative tolerance of anti-imperial barbs in the theatre itself. The ancient writers record the story of an Atellan farce actor, Datus, who pointedly aimed the opening line of a Greek song, 'farewell father, farewell mother', at the deaths of Claudius and Agrippina by pantomimic gestures of drinking and swimming. He was simply banished (Suet. *Nero* 39.2–3). Indeed, rather than seeking to hide his familial crimes, Nero sought to parade them by playing roles on the stage which mirrored his life. Among the tragic parts which he is reported by Suetonius (*Nero* 21.3) to have played wearing the tragic mask (*personatus*) were 'Canace in Labour' (*Canace Parturiens*), 'Orestes the Matricide' (*Orestes Matricida*), 'Oedipus Blinded' (*Oedipus Excaecatus*), and 'Hercules the Mad' (*Hercules Insanus*). Dio (62.9.4, 22.6) lists, in addition, the roles of Thyestes and Alcmaeon. That the masks he wore were sometimes made to resemble either his own features or those of women with whom he was in love (Suet. *Nero* 21.3; Dio 62.9.5) further confounded the distinction between illusion and reality, between Rome's theatre and Rome's world.[68]

The actual merits of Nero as poet, actor, lyre-player, dancer, continue to be debated. What is clear is that in the heady theatricality of Claudian and Neronian Rome we witness not only the re-performance of such canonic plays as the *fabula togata*, 'The Fire' (*Incendium*) of Lucius Afranius (Suet. *Nero* 11.2ff.), but the emergence of two new tragic dramatists: Publius Pomponius Secundus and Lucius Annaeus Seneca. Seneca *tragicus* will be examined in the next chapter. To Pomponius Secundus are attributed an *Atreus* and an *Aeneas*, the latter presumably a *fabula praetexta*. The 'Lives of the Poets' claim, too, that a tragedy, *Medea*, was written by Seneca's nephew, precocious epicist and close intimate of Nero, Lucan, and a *praetexta* by the satirist Persius.[69]

Pomponius' plays were clearly of more than average competence. Quintilian's Flavian entry on him (*Inst.* 10.1.98) praises him as 'by far the best' (*longe princeps*) of those whom he has seen (presumably an intended slight against Seneca, whom he famously disliked),[70] mentioning both Pomponius' reputation for *eruditio* ('learning') and *nitor* ('brilliance'), and the criticism of him (by the 'old guard', *senes*) as 'insufficiently tragic' (*parum tragicum*). Tacitus' Maternus also testifies to Pomponius' high standing in Flavian Rome (*Dial.* 13.3); and the historian himself comments on the 'glory' of Pomponius' poetic *oeuvre* (*carminum gloria*) in his *Annales* (12.28). In Claudian Rome Pomponius' plays, when performed in the theatre, sometimes received a less than favourable response:

> Claudius ... reproved through severe edicts the misbehaviour in the theatre (*theatralis lasciuia*) shown by the people, because they had hurled insults at the ex-consul Pomponius Secundus – he wrote for the stage (*is carmina scaenae dabat*) – and at women of rank.
>
> (Tacitus *Annales* 11.13.1)

Claudius clearly favoured the consular poet (he awarded him *ornamenta triumphalia*: Tac. *Ann.* 12.28), and something by Pomponius may well have featured as part of the *ludi scaenici* of the Secular Games held by the emperor in 47 CE. His *Aeneas* would have fitted the bill perfectly, as well as according with Claudius' own antiquarian interests.[71] There was clearly some rivalry between Pomponius and the post-exilic Seneca:

> I remember when I was still a young man (*iuuenis admodum*) that Pomponius and Seneca disputed even in their prefaces whether *gradus eliminat* ('unthresholds his steps')[72] ought to be spoken in tragedy.
>
> (Quintilian *Institutio Oratoria* 8.3.31)

'While still a young man, a *iuuenis*' is a tantalizingly opaque phrase. If Quintilian (who was born *c.* 35 CE) is being truthful, the dispute could have taken place at any time in the 50s or early 60s CE, in late Claudian or Neronian Rome.

Little survives from Pomponius' dramatic works: three words from his *Aeneas* (*ex humile rege*, 'from a low-born king': *GL* 1.132.15–16 Keil); a possible line and a half from *Atreus* (see Klotz p. 312), possibly three other words, and two sets of choric lines from uncertain plays, one of which may be *Aeneas*.[73] The following choric lines (in dactylic tetrameters) are not the ones ascribed to *Aeneas*:

pendeat ex umeris dulcis chelys
et numeros edat uarios, quibus
adsonet omne uirens late nemus,
et tortis errans qui flexibus.

(Incerta frag. ii Klotz)

Let the sweet lyre hang from the shoulders
And produce rich melodies for all
The greening grove to echo afar
And the wanderer with twists and turns.

It is clearly impossible to gain any real sense of the politics of Pomponius' works. But the fact that he was imprisoned on a charge of treason for seven years by Tiberius (Tac. 5.8; Dio 59.6.2), and seemed to suffer imprisonment, too, under Caligula (Dio 59.26.4), and the attribution to him of an *Atreus* suggest someone other than an imperial sycophant. Tacitus' praise may have been ideological as well as aesthetic.

But even though Pomponius' plays were sometimes performed in the theatre, this was by no means the only way in which dramatic texts were experienced. Tragedies were published and therefore read. They seem also to have been performed in the imperial palace (perhaps from Augustus' time), and in private houses (*intra domum*: a phenomenon even in Marius' day).[74] Comedies and tragedies, too, were commonly 'recited' (by a single speaker). The recitation took place in a private house or recitation-hall, *auditorium,* both for its own sake and as a preliminary to theatrical performance and/or publication (see Pliny *Ep.* 1.15.2; 3.1.9; 7.17.11). It was perhaps such 'readings' (complete with 'prefaces') prior to performance or publication that Quintilian witnessed. Recitations whether of dramatic or other texts were, like theatrical performances themselves, often lively occasions in which speakers were interrupted with cries of approval or heckling (Hor. *AP* 428–30; Pers. *Sat.* 1). Sometimes the dramatic recitation took place in the theatre itself as a virtuoso recital of a tragic speech or episode or the singing of a tragic aria (*tragoedia cantata*), the latter perhaps in theatrical counterpoint to the popular *tragoedia saltata* ('danced tragedy') of the pantomime. The virtuoso recital or aria might be accompanied (by other speaking actors, or a chorus) or performed solo. The *tragoedia saltata* was itself often accompanied by choric or solo singing (sometimes perhaps of excerpts from an existing tragedy on the appropriate subject). To the category of *tragoedia cantata* probably belong at least some, if not all, of Nero's own performances (Suet.

Nero 21.3) of 'the tragedies of heroes and gods wearing the tragic mask *(personatus)*'. Seneca himself refers to the variety of dramatic performances available simply in the theatre itself:

> in theatrum uoluptatis causa ad delectandas aures oratione uel uoce uel fabulis ducimur.
>
> (Seneca *Epistulae Morales* 108.6)

> We are drawn to the theatre for pleasure – to delight the ear – through a speech or song or plays.

The late Julio-Claudian theatres themselves were technological marvels. Although temporary wooden stages continue to be erected for occasional theatrical performances, stone theatres abounded throughout Italy and the empire. The three in Rome itself provided (conservatively) over 30,000 seats. Their concrete structures, marble revetments, socially stratified seating (beneath a great linen awning), holistic design, deep stages, richly decorated stage curtains, revolving scenery-stands, massive flying devices and collapsible sets, their baroque stage-buildings adorned with statues, scene-paintings, masks and garlands – constituted spectacle informing spectacle. Seneca the tragedian himself draws attention to the Roman theatre's penchant for spectacle, as he comments thus on Posidonius' second category of 'arts', *artes ludicrae*, 'the arts of entertainment/of the theatre'.

> To this category are to be assigned the 'stage technicians' *(machinatores)*, who devise scaffolding *(pegmata)* which rises by itself and platforms which soar silently aloft and other diverse surprises, as when things joined fall apart or things not connected come together automatically or things standing erect collapse into themselves little by little.
>
> (Seneca *Epistulae Morales* 88.22)

Reference has been made in the previous chapter to such theatrical devices of the republican stage as *siparia* and the *exostra*. Other features of the late Julio-Claudian *ludicrae artes* include the 'drop-curtain', raised at the beginning of a performance and lowered at the end, and probably such devices, evident in Greek theatre from the fifth century BCE, as the *ekkyklema* (a moveable platform which could be wheeled out to reveal an interior scene) and the *mechane* (a crane used to transport dramatic figures in mid-air).[75]

Although there is no evidence to this effect, it is likely that the *ekkyklema* and *mechane* were devices of the republican theatre, too. An increasingly sophisticated use of scene-painting may be inferred, perhaps with semi-circular tableaux (*hemikyklia*) positioned 'by the orchestra' and paintings known as 'reveals' (*stropheia*) indicating the aftermath of an event (e.g. an apotheosis).[76] Probably, too, the tragic mask with its towering *onkos* had reached the canonic imperial form represented in Pompeian wall-paintings, and the tragic boot its full height. Other items of the tragic actor's costuming, such as the full-length, belted tunic, padded round the chest and stomach (see Lucian *Salt.* 27), continued the trend towards the elaborate and spectacular evident in Horace's observations at *Epistles* 2.1. 200–7.[77] The emotional focus and gestural force of tragic (and other) acting remained constant (Sen. *Ep. Mor.* 11.7).

Despite the richness and diversity of its acting practices, the sophistication and adulation of its audiences, and the technological sophistication of its theatres, Rome proved too small for Nero's artistic ambitions. His reign climaxed in an extended tour of Greece (October 66 to January 68 CE), where the major four-yearly festivals were rescheduled to occur during this period so that Nero could compete – and win. The triumphal procession held on his return was a provocative parody of one of Rome's most revered institutions. Nero, accompanied by theatrical props, a lyre-player and an army of claques, wearing a crown of olive and carrying the Pythian laurel, ascended not to the Temple of Jupiter on the Capitoline but to that of Palatine Apollo. The procession heralded the last of Nero's theatrical extravaganzas. Five months later the 'stage-emperor' died after uttering an appropriately narcissistic, self-consciously theatrical utterance: *qualis artifex pereo*, 'What an artist dies in me!' (Suet. *Nero* 49.1; Dio 63.29.2). Even at the end the distinction between theatrical and actual death remained dissolved.

7

SENECA'S TRAGIC THEATRE

> I doubt whether there bee any amonge all the
> Catalogue of Heathen wryters, that with more
> grauity of Philosophicall sentences, more waightynes
> of sappy words, or greater authority of sound matter
> beateth down sinne, loose lyfe, dissolute dealinge,
> and unbrydled sensuality; or that more sensibly,
> pithily, and bytingly layeth downe the guerdon of
> filthy lust, cloaked dissimulation and odious
> treachery; which is the dryft, whereunto he leueleth
> the whole yssue of ech one of his Tragedies.
>
> (Thomas Newton *Seneca His Tenne Tragedies* (1581))

Seneca is one of the great tragedians of the European tradition. Ten
extant plays have come down under his name, eight of which are agreed
to have been written by him: *Hercules Furens*, *Troades*, *Medea*, *Phaedra*,
Oedipus, *Agamemnon*, *Thyestes* and *Phoenissae.* Such is the order and (with
one exception) the titles of the plays in the most famous manuscript of
the tragedies, the Codex Etruscus.[1] Only *Phoenissae*, which lacks choral
odes, is (probably) incomplete. Of the remaining two plays, *Hercules
Oetaeus* and the *praetexta*, *Octavia*, the latter is definitely not by Seneca,
and the former unlikely to be so. Both are discussed in the next chapter.
Each of the eight Senecan tragedies is marked by dramatic features
which were to influence Renaissance drama: vivid and powerful verse,
psychological insight, highly effective staging, an intellectually
demanding verbal and conceptual framework, and a precocious preoccupation with theatricality and theatricalisation.

Composed presumably in the second half of Seneca's life, the plays
cannot be dated with certainty. The earliest unambiguous reference to
any of Seneca's plays is the *Agamemnon* graffito from Pompeii, of
uncertain date but obviously before the catastrophe of 79 CE;[2] the
next is by Quintilian (*Inst.* 9.2.8), writing a generation after Seneca's

death. Seneca, although he refers to tragedy and the theatre in his prose works, makes no mention there of his own plays. Many commentators allocate them to the period of exile on Corsica (41–9 CE) during the principate of Claudius; others regard it as more likely that their composition, like that of the prose works, was spread over a considerable period of time. A stylometric study has attempted to break the plays into three chronologically consecutive groups (1. *Agamemnon, Phaedra, Oedipus*; 2. *Hercules Furens, Medea, Troades*; 3. *Thyestes, Phoenissae*),[3] but the groupings and implied chronology are by no means agreed. Most contemporary scholars would perhaps accept that on stylometric, dramatic and other grounds *Thyestes* and the incomplete *Phoenissae* are Seneca's final (extant) tragedies.

Lucius Annaeus Seneca was born in 1 BCE or shortly before in Cordoba (modern Cordova) in Southern Spain, the second of three sons to the cultivated equestrian, Annaeus Seneca (*praenomen* probably also Lucius), author of a lost history of Rome and two surviving (badly mutilated) works on Roman declamation, *Controuersiae* and *Suasoriae*. The youngest son, Mela, was the father of the epic poet, Lucan. Brought to Rome as a young child and given the standard education in rhetoric, Seneca had become by the early years of Tiberius' principate (14–37 CE), while still in adolescence, a devotee of philosophy. The focus of his early passion was an ascetic, locally taught form of Stoic-Pythagoreanism with a strong commitment to vegetarianism. Before long he had been dissuaded from it by his father (*Ep.* 108.17–22). During his youth and throughout his adult life Seneca suffered from a tubercular condition, and was compelled on one occasion to contemplate suicide when he despaired of recovery. He records that only the thought of the suffering which he would have caused his father prevented his death (*Ep.* 78.1f.).

Ill health presumably delayed the start of his political career, as did a substantial period of convalescence in Egypt during the 20s under the care of his maternal aunt. He returned to Rome from Egypt in 31 CE (surviving a shipwreck in which his uncle died), and entered the senate via the quaestorship shortly afterwards, as did Gallio his elder brother. By the beginning of Claudius' principate (41 CE) he had also held the aedileship and the tribunate of the people. In the thirties, too, he married (although whether it was to his wife of later years, Pompeia Paulina, who survived him, is uncertain), and he achieved such fame as a public speaker as to arouse the attention and jealousy of Caligula (Suet. *Gaius* 53.2; Dio 59.19.7f.). By the late 30s Seneca was clearly moving in the circle of princes, among 'that tiny group of men on which there bore down, night and day, the concentric pressure of a monstrous weight, the post-Augustan empire'.[4] His presence in high places was initially short-lived. He survived Caligula's brief principate only to be exiled in the first year of Claudius' reign (41 CE). The charge was adultery with Caligula's sister, Julia Livilla, brought by the new empress, Claudius' young wife, Messalina.

Seneca's exile came at a time of great personal distress (both his father and his son had recently died – *Helv.* 2.4f.), and, despite pleas for imperial clemency (see, esp., *Pol.* 13.2ff.), lasted eight tedious years. In 48 CE Messalina was executed. In the following year Seneca, through the agency of Agrippina, Claudius' niece and new wife, was recalled to Rome and designated praetor for 50 CE. His literary and philosophical reputation was well established (Tac. *Ann.* 12.8.3), and he was appointed tutor to Agrippina's son, Nero. This appointment not only placed Seneca once again at the centre of the Roman world, but brought him immense power and influence, when Agrippina poisoned her emperor husband and Nero succeeded to the throne (54 CE). Throughout the early part of Nero's principate Seneca (suffect consul in 56 CE) and the commander of the praetorian guard, Burrus, acted as the chief ministers and political counsellors of Nero, whom they increasingly became unable to control. Nero's matricide in 59 CE, to which it is probable that neither Seneca nor Burrus was privy, but for which nevertheless Seneca wrote a *post factum* justification (Tac. *Ann.* 14.11), signalled the weakening of their power. When Burrus died in 62 CE (perhaps poisoned – Tac. *Ann.* 14.15.1), Seneca went into semi-retirement. In 65 CE he was accused of involvement in the Pisonian conspiracy against Nero and was ordered to kill himself. This he did, committing suicide before his friends in a self-scripted Socratic performance and bequeathing to them his one remaining possession and his best – 'the image of his life' (Tac. *Ann.* 15.62.1).

Apart from the tragedies, some epigrams, and a prose-verse satire on Claudius (*Apocolocyntosis*, 'Pumpkinification'), Seneca's works were essentially philosophical and in prose. They comprise the *Naturales Quaestiones* ('Natural Questions'), the ten so-called *Dialogi* ('Dialogues'), *De Beneficiis* ('On Benefits'), *De Clementia* ('On Clemency' – addressed to Nero on his accession), and the *Epistulae Morales* ('Moral Epistles'), addressed to the Roman knight Lucilius. These works are infused to a greater or lesser extent with Stoic ideas concerning fate, god, virtue, wisdom, reason, endurance, self-sufficiency and true friendship, and are filled with condemnation of the world of wealth and power (to which Seneca belonged) and contempt for the fear of death. The prose works cover perhaps the whole of Seneca's creative life.[5] Their relationship to the tragedies remains enigmatic. Certainly the latter abound in Stoic moral ideas, and their preoccupation with fate, with emotional pathology and with the destructive consequences of passion, especially anger, is deeply indebted to the Stoic tradition. But such Stoicism is no outer ideological clothing but part of the dramatic texture of the tragedies, in which the world-view is generally unStoic, even a negation of Stoicism,[6] central principles of which are critically exhibited within a different, more disturbing vision.

The issue of the mode of 'performance' for Senecan tragedy continues to be debated. Some scholars believe that Seneca was not much interested either in dramaturgy or in theatrical spectacle, arguing that he wrote his tragedies not for performance in the great theatres of Rome or in a private house or villa, but rather to be read (privately) or recited.[7] The theatrical situation and practice of Seneca's day, described in the previous chapter, were complex; plays admitted differing forms of realisation. It is not recorded and may never be known whether Seneca's tragedies were performed on stage or otherwise during their author's lifetime.[8] But it is certainly the case that they were and are performable: they have been and are performed.[9] The contemporary practice of *recitatio* clearly affected the form of Seneca's plays, which, appropriately edited, could have been used for selective theatrical recital or for a public 'reading' by the author prior to performance. The latter seems to have been Pomponius Secundus' practice, as it was later the (occasional) practice of Corneille.[10] Extracts from the tragedies could also have been used as libretti for *tragoediae cantatae* or for sung accompaniments (by a chorus or soloist) to *tragoediae saltatae*, the pantomimic dance.

But, just as the purpose of the tragedies was clearly not to serve as a collection of arias or pantomimic adjuncts, so there is little possibility that either recitation or (even less) private reading was their intended primary mode of realisation. Not only do the 'reading' and the 'recitation' hypotheses generate more problems than those they seek to address,[11] but they are vitiated by the theatricality of Senecan tragedy, its concern with dramatic structure and effect and with the *minutiae* of stagecraft. Many of Seneca's dramaturgical practices derive from Hellenistic drama but were probably also standard Augustan practice.[12] Recent analyses of Seneca's stage techniques reveal theatrical mastery in the shaping of dramatic action, the structural unfolding of dramatic language and imagery, the blocking of scenes and acts, the disposition of roles, the handling of actors and of the chorus, the interrelationship between choral odes and acts, the use of ghosts, messengers, extras, mutes, the dramatic and thematic use of stage-setting and props, the employment of implicit stage-directions in the text itself (especially entrance and exit cues, random but more substantial than often noted, identification cues, and implicit directions for stage-business) – and in Senecan tragedy's manipulation of pace, movement, violence, spectacle and closure.[13] As Herington demonstrated in his foundational essay of 1966, the 'recitation' hypothesis self-destructs. If Seneca's tragedies were written for recitation *in toto*, they were undeniably written to be delivered by a number of voices playing separate parts – that is to say, for 'dramatic' performance,[14] whether the performance envisaged was in the theatre or in a private house to a coterie audience (or both).[15] Indeed it was partly on the grounds of representational power (*rappresentatione*), i.e. theatrical effectiveness, that Giraldi Cinthio, a practical dramatist who 'never for a moment imagined that Seneca did not write for a stage performance', preferred Seneca to the Greeks.[16] The Elizabethan translators would have concurred.[17] Those who condemn Seneca's dramatic sense out of hand would do well to remember that even T. S. Eliot, whose essays on Seneca have been as injurious as any, thought that they might be regarded as 'practical models for ... broadcasted drama'.[18] Senecan tragedy belongs, if anything does, to the category of Roman performance theatre.

The declamatory style

But, if the performance values of Senecan tragedy have often – inappropriately – been criticised, so, too, has Seneca's rhetoricity. The plays not only flaunt their rhetoricity openly, but use it to structure the action and to articulate some of Seneca's most theatrically powerful moments. Listen to Andromache's entrance speech in *Troades*, in which she reproves her fellow captives with a host of rhetorical techniques, even as she frames her own devastation with hyperbole, paradox and epigram:

quid, maesta Phrygiae turba, laceratis comas
miserumque tunsae pectus effuso genas
fletu rigatis? leuia perpessae sumus
si flenda patimur. Ilium uobis modo,
mihi cecidit olim, cum ferus curru incito
mea membra raperet et graui gemeret sono
Peliacus axis pondere Hectoreo tremens.
tunc obruta atque euersa quodcumque accidit
torpens malis rigensque sine sensu fero.
iam erepta Danais coniugem sequerer meum,
nisi hic teneret. hic meos animos domat
morique prohibet. cogit hic aliquid deos
adhuc rogare. tempus aerumnae addidit.
hic mihi malorum maximum fructum abstulit:
nihil timere. prosperis rebus locus
ereptus omnis, dira qua ueniant habent.
miserrimum est timere, cum speres nihil.

(*Troades* 409–25)

Wailing band of Phrygians, why tear your hair,
Beat sorrowing breasts and drench cheeks with floods
Of sobs? Our sufferings must be trivial
If tears suffice. For you Ilium fell just now,
For me long ago, when that brutal chariot
Ravaged my limbs and Pelian axle
Screamed aloud shuddering beneath Hector's weight.
That day crushed and wasted me. I endure
Events numb and stiff with pain, impervious.
I'd escape the Danai and follow my spouse
Now, if he (*points to Astyanax*) didn't hold me. He tames my
  pride
And prevents my death. He compels me still
To importune the gods. He prolongs my pain.
He's robbed me of suffering's finest fruit:
Fear of nothing. All chance of happiness
Is snatched away, horrors can still reach us.
Fear is its most painful when hope is dead.

Listen to Medea, as she builds upon a conventional interchange with
her Nurse, turning the latter's barrage of commonplaces and sententious epigram into a conceptual and verbal duel, in which the
Nurse's words are thrown back in her face and a rapid, at times

stichomythic, exchange leads to the linguistic annexation of the universe for a redefinition of 'Medea':[19]

> *Nutrix* Sile, obsecro, questusque secreto abditos
>   manda dolori. grauia quisquis uulnera
>   patiente et aequo mutus animo pertulit,
>   referre potuit: ira quae tegitur nocet;
>   professa perdunt odia uindictae locum.
> *Medea* Leuis est dolor qui capere consilium potest
>   et clepere sese: magna non latitant mala.
>   libet ire contra.
> *Nutrix* Siste furialem impetum,
>   alumna: uix te tacita defendit quies.
> *Medea* Fortuna fortes metuit, ignauos premit.
> *Nutrix* Tunc est probanda, si locum uirtus habet.
> *Medea* Numquam potest non esse uirtuti locus.
> *Nutrix* Spes nulla rebus monstrat adflictis uiam.
> *Medea* Qui nil potest sperare, desperet nihil.
> *Nutrix* Abiere Colchi, coniugis nulla est fides
>   nihilque superest opibus e tantis tibi.
> *Medea* Medea superest: hic mare et terras uides
>   ferrumque et ignes et deos et fulmina.
>
> (Medea 150–67)

> *Nurse* Be silent, I beg you; bury complaints
>   In secret pain. Whoever bears grievous blows
>   Quietly with calm, enduring spirit
>   Can repay them. Anger stabs when concealed;
>   Displays of hate destroy the chance for vengeance.
> *Medea* A trivial pain can accept advice
>   And stay concealed: great wrongs do not lie hid.
>   I rejoice to face him.
> *Nurse* Stop this mad impulse,
>   My child; even still silence may not shield you.
> *Medea* Fortune fears the brave and crushes cowards.
> *Nurse* Courage is applauded when the time is right.
> *Medea* Never can the time be wrong for courage.
> *Nurse* No hope shows a way through our calamity.
> *Medea* Who hopes for nothing, despairs of nothing.
> *Nurse* The Colchians are gone; your husband's vows are nothing;
>   Nothing remains of all your wondrous wealth.
> *Medea* Medea remains. Here you see ocean and land,
>   Iron and fire, gods and thunderbolts.

Examine Theseus' declamation of his agony at *Phaedra* 1201–12, a deluge of balanced cadences and clauses, alliterated consonants, sonal and syntactic repetition, violent imagery, portentous diction, uniting with a 'steady rhythmic punch'[20] and an architectural crescendo structure, which climaxes in pith and epigram to overwhelm an audience with verbal power. As Theseus shows, bombast and rhetoric define victim as well as victimiser.[21]

When faced with Senecan bombast it is well to remember Eliot's dictum: 'the art of dramatic language … is as near to oratory as to ordinary speech or to other poetry'.[22] What should also be noted is that rhetoric not only structures and empowers Senecan tragedy, but gives it contemporary accessibility. It accords with a contemporary passion for rhetoric and contemporary fullness of response to rhetoric, to declamation, dialectic, verbal brilliance and ingenuity. Late Julio-Claudian Rome was a highly rhetorical age, in which public declamations by rival professors and declamatory 'debates' between them, epideictic competitions and the quasi-theatrical recitations of verse were a social institution and a regular form of public and imperial entertainment, to which audiences responded noisily with heckling and acclaim.[23] Not only were the members of Rome's elite trained in declamatory techniques and rhetorical role-play (the *Controuersiae* and *Suasoriae* of Seneca's father indicate the training involved), and in responding to the employment of those techniques by other speakers, but the late Julio-Claudian iconosphere itself, its architecture, sculpture and painting, moved towards the rhetorical and the baroque.[24]

Not that Seneca's rhetoric is merely a rhetoric of surface. In an age which revelled in exteriority and display Senecan bombast, paradox, word-play, epigram both parade that display and excavate it to exhibit states of mind and to create tragic character. Thyestes' castigation of the false world of power at *Thyestes* 446–70 affords a window on a mind which will succumb to that world of power almost immediately; the asexual idealisation of the wild by Hippolytus at *Phaedra* 483ff. reveals the self-delusion and psychological pathology which will prove a motor to tragic disaster. The opening speech of Phaedra (*Pha.* 85–128) and the opening soliloquies of Oedipus (see, esp., *Oed.* 28–36) and Helen (*Tro.* 861–71) similarly dramatise minds about to shape dramatic action.[25] Indeed Seneca's predilection for self-presentational soliloquies or monologues, like his frequent use of the aside (a device, as was noted above,[26] foreign to the more public world of Attic tragedy), signals far more than his dramatic *oeuvre*'s debt to the *Metamorphoses* of

Ovid; they index his plays' concern with psychological interiority and with its theatrical and structural potential.

But Seneca's declamatory style is also the style of shock, product of a world which screamed its aesthetic and moral structures, which imaged through hyperbole in the arts, in the arena and in political and social behaviour the vacuum and appetitive excess of aristocratic Roman life. Phaedra's entrance speech is as much a function of this 'style of shock' as the nightmarish images and scenes that to many define Senecan tragedy: the apparition of Laius' ghost in *Oedipus* (619–58), the monstrous bull from the sea in *Phaedra* (1035–49), the preparation, cooking and eating of human flesh in *Thyestes* (759–82), Medea's black mass (*Med.* 740–842). So, too, the often praised 'cosmic imagery' of Seneca, from which the Elizabethans took so much, the capacity of his characters to appropriate the universe in their process of self-dramatisation.

Sometimes this 'cosmic' imagery takes the form of a geographical or astronomic catalogue, in which the immensity of the world is proclaimed even as its itemisation vainly attempts to control it (e.g., *Pha.* 54–72, *Tro.* 814–57, *Thy.* 844–74). At other times it is to be found in the enigmatic proclamations of a Medea. Her climactic riposte to the Nurse (*Med.* 166f.) was noted on p. 195. Worthy of study, too, is her speech prior to the entrance of Jason in Act 3 (*Med.* 397–414), in which once more she purloins the universe for the construction of her self and unleashes that self and its passion in a rhetorical avalanche of turbulence and 'psychic aggression'.[27] Compare it with Hippolytus' linguistic assault on the cosmos in his famous transcendent crescendo of moral rage in response to his stepmother's revelation of lust (*Pha.* 671–9), as a rhetoric of cosmic and psychic violence is again used for self-construction and self-dramatisation – and for theatrical shock.

Form and meaning

The shock has intellectual as well as dramatic function. Seneca had something compelling to say. Among the themes and ideas the eight tragedies dramatise: the determinism of history; the genealogy and competitive cyclicity of evil; the fragility of social and religious forms; the fragility of epistemological forms; the failure of reason; civilisation as moral contradiction; man as appetite, as beast, as existential victim; power, impotence, delusion, self-deception; the futility of compassion; the freedom, desirability, and value-paradox of death; man, god, nature, guilt, unmerited suffering; the certainty of human pain, the terror of experienced evil; the inexorable, paradoxical, amoral – even morally perverse – order of things; the triumph of evil; in one play (*Hercules Furens*), the possibility of human redemption; in all, the gap between language and the world.

As noted on p. 192, Seneca's tragedies, textured though they are with Stoic ideas, exhibit a series of world-views which are neither simply Stoic, nor simple. There are conspicuous ideological differences between play and play. On moral order, for example. In *Agamemnon*, *Hercules Furens*, *Phaedra*, *Medea* crime, *scelus*, is punished; gods, nature, fate, fortune seem in quasi-moral control; prayer (though not necessarily to gods) sometimes seems answered. Electra's prayer to Strophius (*Ag.* 929–31), Amphitryon's to Jupiter and Hercules (*HF* 205ff., 516ff.), the Nurse's to Diana (*Pha.* 406–23), Theseus' to Neptune (*Pha.* 945–58), Medea's to Sol and to Hecate (*Med.* 32–36, 817–42), all appear answered, even if, as in the case of the Nurse in *Phaedra*, in a way that was not foreseen. But neither *Phaedra* nor *Medea* asserts the moral order implied in *Agamemnon* or the redemptive possibilities of *Hercules Furens*; nor is nature's order as presented in *Phaedra*, where all suffer and human impotence seems total, identical with the cosmic order of *Medea*, in which one of the human figures, working with the divine forces of the cosmos, triumphs.

Thyestes differs radically from all four plays. Here nature, the gods are reduced to shocked, impotent observers of human bestiality and sin. There is no life-destroying storm to punish *scelus* as in *Agamemnon* (465ff.); no monster from the sea as in *Phaedra* (1007ff.); no Hecate-generated fire that feeds on its natural antagonist water, as in *Medea* (885ff.). *Scelus* is unpunished and prayers unfulfilled. 'The gods are fled,' cries Thyestes, *fugere superi* (*Thy.* 1021). And he is right; as is Oedipus in asserting the existence of mendacious gods (*Oed.*1042ff.) in a world where those who use reason to escape crime and guilt compound them both. Senecan moral and metaphysical tragedy investigates distinct and distinctive worlds. The world of *Oedipus* is not that of *Thyestes*. Nor is it that of *Troades* or *Medea.*

The theatrically effective realisation of ideas evident in Senecan tragedy is product in part (a substantial part) of dramatic structure. Seneca's plays display painstaking attention to dramatic structure and form, and to density of verbal and ideological texture. The first word of *Medea*, for example, is *di*, 'gods'; the last word (1027) is *deos*, 'gods'. Within this verbal circle prayers, appeals, statements, questions to and concerning gods permeate the play's actions and chorus.[28] Similarly imagery and motifs of birth, law, power, cosmos, sun, fire, sacrifice and serpent dominate the prologue (1–55), texture the play,[29] and climax in the play's finale (esp. 983ff.), when the Colchian princess annexes the powers of the cosmos, gives birth to death, sacrifices her sons, consumes Corinth with fire, removes the final vestige of law from herself, and climbs to freedom in the serpent-drawn chariot of the sun. *Medea*'s finale is the imagery of its prologue realised.

Phaedra and *Troades* are also cyclically structured. The former is textured, too, by recurrent imagery – especially that of the hunt;[30] the latter is pervaded with a whole syntax of polarities which the play itself dissolves.[31] *Thyestes* has one of the richest of Senecan imagistic patterns, especially important and pervasive being the Tantalid images of hunger, thirst, eating, drinking, emptiness, fullness, feast. In *Oedipus* legal imagery and the fate/fortune motif are important;[32] in *Agamemnon* storm, feast, sacrifice and wound,[33] although *Agamemnon* is one of the less well crafted plays in this regard.[34] In *Hercules Furens*, also less well crafted, the most permeating motif is that of the hero's hand, *manus*.[35] All the plays are textured through and through with the Senecan moral vocabulary of *pudor*, *furor*, *scelus* and *nefas*, 'shame', 'passion', 'crime' and 'evil'.

In most plays, too, the dramatic action is textured with and structured by analogies with the past.[36] *Agamemnon* and *Thyestes* even feature ghost-prologues which programmatically announce the very cycle of crime to be realised in the ensuing action. In *Medea* the Argonautic expedition, to which the long central choral odes are dedicated (301–79, 579–669) and which pervades Medea's thoughts,[37] performs an analogous function. It sits like an incubus on the play, encapsulating a series of events which proves model for and cause of the events of the play itself. The unloosing of nature's bonds and breach of nature's covenants (*foedera*, 335, 606) by the crew of the *Argo*, the fear generated (*metus*, 338; *timores*, 341) and the death and destruction which ensued as 'penalty' for the breach (esp. 616ff.), are mirrored in Jason's breach of marital 'faith', *fides* (see esp. 434ff.), in exhibited Corinthian fear,[38] and in the chaos and destruction of the finale, where Medea's past actions on behalf of Jason and his comrades (her breaking of familial bonds, murder of kin and flight into exile)[39] are re-enacted in her dissolution of all familial ties, the murder of her children, and her climactic serpentine flight. The determinant nature of Medea's past is unconcealed. In the final act the appearance of the ghost of Absyrtus (963ff.), the intoxicated reverie on the erasure of the post-Jasonic past (982–4, quoted on p. 216), and Medea's final acerbic question –

> coniugem agnoscis tuam?
> sic fugere soleo.
>
> *(Medea* 1021–2)

> Don't you recognise your wife?
> This is how I always escape.

– underscore the relationship between the play's denouement and its titular figure's earlier history.[40]

Phaedra and *Troades*, too, are studded with analogies with the past, articulating a compelling sense of history and nature's cyclicity, of *semper idem*. *Troades'* concentric structure seems itself to suggest the circles of history, even as its action is structured to re*present* the past. The delay or *mora* of the Greek fleet at Aulis at the beginning of the war, which was ended by the sacrifice of Agamemnon's virgin daughter, Iphigenia, and her alleged 'marriage' to Achilles (see *Ag.* 162ff.), authorised by Calchas and vainly opposed by Agamemnon, is re-enacted in another *mora* for the fleet, ended by the sacrifice of Priam's virgin daughter, Polyxena, and her 'marriage' to Achilles' ghost. The sacrifice is again authorised by Calchas and vainly opposed by Agamemnon (esp. *Tro.* 164ff., 246ff., 287ff., 331, 353ff., 360ff.). Notable also in the play is the way Achilles' wrath and demand for compensation are visited a second time on the Greeks (*Tro.* 193f.), and once again the demand is for a girl-prize; the concluding 'marriage' between Greek and Trojan (Achilles and Polyxena) recalls the earlier 'marriage' between Greek and Trojan (Helen and Paris), heralding once again the departure of a fleet and both Greek and Trojan loss.

In *Phaedra* analogies between Phaedra and her mother, Pasiphae, between Hippolytus and the bull that Pasiphae loved, and between the Minotaur and the bull from the sea,[41] the latter the product of Phaedra's love as the former was the product of her mother's love (note especially the pregnancy imagery of 1016 and 1019f.), and other analogies, too (e.g., between Hippolytus and the Minotaur), seem to assert the imperatives of history, the dispassionate cyclic order of things, the circle of fate, fortune, nature. Time past becomes time present; time present becomes time future. Verbal and ideological patterns signal sameness. The world changes to remain identical:

> constat inferno numerus tyranno.
>
> *(Phaedra* 1153)

> For hell's king the numbers tally.

Always. Even the delusion of human power recycles to stay constant, as the Roman analogies of *Phaedra*'s opening act and *Medea*'s first Argonautic chorus show. To *natura*, fate or history belong the power and the glory.

Intertextual play

Senecan verbal and ideological dynamics are not only within texts. Intertextuality gives flesh to dramatic meaning. *Agamemnon* and *Thyestes* are a paradigm case. The two plays are bound through subject-matter (the Tantalid saga), ghost-prologues, the figure of Thyestes himself, and imagistically and verbally through a whole series of common images and motifs. But they present quite different worlds, whose difference is clarified theatrically through each play's use of the same ideological and verbal repertoire. On the feast-day of *Agamemnon*, the lion, Agamemnon, king of kings, *uictor ferarum* (*Ag.* 738–9), is sacrificed, but the palm of victory goes not to the beast that slays him but to the avenger, Orestes, who will slay that beast and restore, if problematically, 'loyalty', 'duty', 'righteousness', *fides* and *pietas*, to the Argive world (*Ag.* 929–43). On the feast-day of *Thyestes*, the lion, Atreus, *uictor* (*Thy.* 732–3), is not sacrificed but sacrificially slays; he is true beast, god and king of kings. Dissolving the distinctions on which civilisation depends, he receives the true palm, *uera palma* (*Thy.* 1096–7), emblem of his victory and his truth. *Agamemnon*'s ambiguous moral order gives way, if *Agamemnon* is the earlier play, to *Thyestes*' cultural death.

The *Agamemnon* and *Thyestes* intertextuality is not exceptional. Similar intertextuality seems to govern *Agamemnon*'s relationship to *Troades* and *Phoenissae*'s relationship to *Oedipus*;[42] while the entire Senecan dramatic corpus is itself intertexted with recurrent themes, ideas, images and motifs. And this is to leave aside the complex – and generally misunderstood – intertextual relationship between Seneca's dramatic and philosophical works.[43]

There is another kind of intertextuality, too – one which concerns the relationship between Seneca's dramatic texts and the dramatic and poetic tradition which they inherit and rewrite. *Thyestes*, for example, embeds a semiotic interplay, not only with Seneca's *Agamemnon*, but with all the many texts it rewrites, including most overtly Ovid's Tereus–Procne–Philomela narrative of *Metamorphoses* 6 (424–674), which it re-plots.[44] *Hercules Furens*, *Troades* and *Medea* similarly owe much to Ovid as well as to Virgil and to both the Greek and Roman dramatic traditions. *Phaedra* fairly obviously alludes to and rewrites (*inter alios*) Virgil, Ovid and Euripides, most especially the latter two. Ovidian texts are alluded to pervasively, especially *Heroides* 4, which is expressly remodelled in Phaedra's revelation speech at 652ff.[45] *Phaedra*'s rewriting of Euripides' second *Hippolytus* (the one we have) is even more conspicuous.[46]

Observe the following. Euripides separates Aphrodite and Artemis; Seneca fuses Venus and Diana. Hippolytus' outburst of misogyny follows the revelation of Phaedra's love in Euripides (*Hipp.* 616ff.), precedes it in Seneca (*Pha.* 559ff.). Euripides' Theseus curses his bastard son with the first prayer granted him by Poseidon (*Hipp.* 887ff.); Seneca's with the last one (*Pha.* 942ff.), and the son is now an 'assured heir' (*certus heres, Pha.* 1112). Phaedra hangs herself (*Hipp.* 764ff.) and accuses Hippolytus by means of a written tablet (*Hipp.* 856ff.) in the Greek play; in the Roman play she kills herself (*Pha.* 1197f.) with the very sword she had used as proof of Hippolytus' guilt (*Pha.* 896f.), and with which she had asked Hippolytus to enter her (*Pha.* 710ff.). And the accusation itself, plain and unadorned in Euripides (*Hipp.* 885f.), in Seneca is ambiguous and encrusted with irony (*Pha.* 891–3). As for Phaedra's inherited family curse and the determinism of the past made so much of by Seneca,[47] they have virtually no role to play in Euripides' drama, which makes but a single brief reference to Pasiphae and the bull (*Hipp.* 337f.) and none to the Minotaur. Significantly, Hippolytus' mother, unnamed in Euripides, is named (*Pha.* 226ff., 926ff.) and dramatically exploited (see esp. *Pha.* 578f.) in Seneca.

Both dramatists have choruses on sexual desire (*Hipp.* 525ff., *Pha.* 274ff.): Euripides limits its operation to humankind, Seneca, rewriting also Virgil's *Georgics*,[48] extends its operation to the gods and all sentient life, and identifies it crucially with *natura* (*Pha.* 352). The two messenger speeches (*Hipp.* 1173–254, *Pha.* 1000–114) have much in common and much not. Seneca's phantasmagoric monster (*Pha.* 1035ff.) is not in Euripides; nor is the Senecan contrast between the effect of the bull on Hippolytus' companions and the countryside at large and its effect on Hippolytus himself (*Pha.* 1050–6). And Seneca, unlike Euripides (*Hipp.* 1218ff.) and Ovid (*Met.* 15.514ff.), in accord with his own thematic design gives Hippolytus an *aristeia* of controlling power (*Pha.* 1054ff.). He was to be followed in this to some extent by Racine (*Phèdre* 1527–34).[49] It goes without saying perhaps that Seneca's hunting imagery (see especially *Pha.* 1085–7) and the sexualisation of Hippolytus' death (*Pha.* 1098f.) are not in

Euripides. Nor is Seneca's rewriting of Euripides in *Phaedra* limited to Euripides' *Hippolytus*. The final scene, for example, as Theseus attempts to piece together the dismembered limbs of his son's body, conflates Euripides' *Hippolytus* and *Bacchae*.[50]

Intertextuality of this order has complex effects. Some of these are clearly thematic and/or relate to differences in the dramatisation of the main figures of the play. Some are cultural signals. In the final scene of *Phaedra*, even as Euripides' *Hippolytus* and *Bacchae* are almost brought together, Seneca asserts a distinctly Roman world through a spectacular theatricalisation of the Roman ritual of *concinnatio corporis*, the gathering of the body parts and remaking of the body, owed to the dead.[51] The last lines of the play make reference to Athens and derive from Rome.

> patefacite acerbam caede funesta domum.
> Mopsopia claris tota lamentis sonet.
> uos apparate regii flammam rogi;
> at uos per agros corporis partes uagas
> inquirite. istam terra defossam premat,
> grauisque tellus impio capiti incubet.
>
> > (*Phaedra* 1275–80)

> Open the dismal palace sour with death.
> All Attica resound with loud lament.
> You prepare the flames of the royal pyre;
> You search the fields for parts of the body
> Astray. (*Points to Phaedra*) This one – earth press deep upon her,
> And soil lie heavy on her impious head.

Theseus' curse on Phaedra in the play's final line not only employs the social distinctions inherent in Roman funerary practices (aristocratic cremation for his son, ignoble inhumation for his wife), but reformulates the standard grave-formula, *sit tibi terra leuis* ('may earth lie gently on you'), into a command of spite. Differences from Euripides here, as elsewhere, are markers of a different world.

Let one more scene suffice. It was remarked on p. 202 that Phaedra's accusation of Hippolytus is more ambiguous and contextually ironic in Seneca. That ambiguity and irony derive in part from Seneca's Romanising of the interrogation scene through allusion to one of the city's foundational myths, the suicide of Lucretia.[52] Seneca has Phaedra play Lucretia to Theseus' Collatinus. What also needs to be noted in this context is how the accusation itself is preceded in Seneca by a verbal exchange of extraordinary dramatic power which not only (obviously) has no counterpart in Euripides' extant *Hippolytus* but also cannot plausibly be derived from Euripides' other Hippolytan play. It signals a distinctly non-Euripidean world. Towards the end of his interrogation of Phaedra on her intended suicide, Theseus asks:

> quod sit luendum morte delictum indica.
>
> (*Phaedra* 879)

Tell me what sin is to be purged by death.

Phaedra replies:

> quod uiuo.
>
> (*Phaedra* 880)

That I live.

Theseus, of course, ignores Phaedra's reply, construing it, if at all, along the lines of the aristocratic tradition, represented by Lucretia, of death before sexual dishonour. For the audience 'that I live', *quod uiuo,* has other meanings. To Phaedra, who has lost both Hippolytus and honour, life is intolerable, valueless. More importantly, to Phaedra, for whom nature's ordinances and nature's inversion, life and monstrous love, existence and guilt, moral consciousness and the violation of integrity, honour, 'shame', *pudor*, are inextricably interwoven, living is itself a sin, an obscenity, a *delictum.*

> fatale miserae matris agnosco malum.
>
> (*Phaedra* 113)

I recognise poor mother's fateful evil.

> et ipsa nostrae fata cognosco domus:
> fugienda petimus.
>
> (*Phaedra* 698–9)

I, too, recognise the fate of our house:
What we should shun, we seek.

> quod sit luendum morte delictum indica.
> quod uiuo.
>
> (*Phaedra* 879–80)

Tell me what sin is to be purged by death.
That I live.

The timing of *quod uiuo* is dramatically important. Just before Phaedra is forced to accuse Hippolytus, the dramatic focus falls on the profoundly tragic nature of Phaedra's life, and simplistic moral judgements are averted. Her comment has more than theatrical force. The inevitable corollary of Seneca's presentment of life as sin, as obscenity, as *delictum* and *monstrum*, as unbreakable circle of suffering, as entrapment in catastrophic revolutions and reversals (1123ff.), Phaedra's death-wish (see also 710ff., 868ff., 1188ff.), like that of Theseus (1238–42), seems to be mirror of an age.

Roman palimpsests

Phaedra is a palimpsestic text. That is to say, it is like a palimpsest or document written upon more than once, with traces of earlier writing visible beneath. It is not the only palimpsestic Senecan dramatic text. Beneath each Senecan tragedy are a host of subtexts – Greek and Roman, Attic, Hellenistic, republican, Augustan, and early imperial – clarifying and informing their discourse. In *Troades*, for example, almost as a pointer to the play's concern with the recycling of history, Seneca rewrites and recycles many texts: most obviously, Homer's *Iliad*, the cyclic epics, Sophocles' *Polyxena*, Euripides' *Andromache*, *Hecuba*, *Troades* and *Iphigenia at Aulis*, Naevius' *Andromacha*, Ennius' *Iphigenia*, *Hecuba* and *Andromacha*, Accius' *Astyanax*, *Hecuba* and *Troades*, Lucretius' *De Rerum Natura*, Catullus' *Peleus and Thetis*, Horace's *Odes* 3.30, Virgil's *Aeneid*, Ovid's *Metamorphoses*, and (possibly) Seneca's own *Agamemnon*. And *Troades* rewrites and recycles these texts self-consciously. Overt textual allusion and metaliterary language make of *Troades* a self-reflective, multi-referential text, which engages in a constant and pervasive counterpoint with the dramatic and poetic tradition. The play's concept of 'fate', *fatum* (lit. 'what has been said'), seems itself at times to signal this tradition,[53] as the dramatic figures struggle against not only the determinism of history but the determinism of the literary past and of their own literary pedigrees.

The rewriting of Euripides is again instructive. In Euripides the deaths of Astyanax and Polyxena are the dramatic focus of two separate plays (*Troades* and *Hecuba*), and both are announced by the Greek herald Talthybius. Seneca gives the two deaths equal and conjoined dramatic focus in one play, does not have Talthybius announce either, and unlike Euripides connects both deaths with the delay of the Greek fleet. Euripides' plays begin with gods or ghosts, Seneca's play with a paradigm of human suffering, the *mater dolorosa*, Hecuba; it climaxes, unlike either of Euripides' plays, in the wedding-sacrifice of Polyxena. For Euripides Polyxena's death is in essence simply sacrifice.[54] Female conflict and relationships are realised differently by each playwright. Euripides' conflict between Helen and Hecuba is replaced by one between Helen and Andromache, and Hecuba, who demands Helen's death in the Greek *Troades* and is equally hostile in *Hecuba* itself, appears sympathetic towards Helen in Seneca's play, taking upon herself much of the responsibility for Troy's fall. The figure of Ulysses, too, deserves mention. In Euripides' *Troades* it is Ulysses/Odysseus who proposes Astyanax' death; in Seneca it is Calchas, spokesman of fate and index of history's cycle. Seneca's Ulysses plays the more sympathetic role, played by Talthybius in Euripides, of reluctant executor of the army's will. He pointedly does not play the role assigned him in Euripides' *Hecuba*, the removal of Polyxena from her mother. Seneca's inversion of Euripidean figures extends to Polyxena, who speaks at length in *Hecuba* but remains silent in Seneca's play, and most noticeably to Helen, who, far from being the *femme fatale* of Euripides' *Troades*, is reflective, self-critical, compassionate and desirous of the comfort of shared grief.

Other differences – and not only from Euripides – abound. They are differences with point. Seneca's rewriting of earlier texts, including Euripidean ones, is itself a model of one of his play's central themes: the recycling and rewriting of history. Seneca's palimpsestic play differs from all the works it rewrites; its main figures, for example, are more humane, compassion is a more prominent value. But Astyanax and Polyxena are again killed; Ulysses and Helen play against but fulfil their inscribed selves;[55] the Trojan women, enslaved and allotted, head 'once more' (*repetite*, 1178) to the sea; the Greek fleet departs (*classis mouet*, 1179). The pattern of the tragic myth, like the pattern of history, remains constant. Like the past, the myth changes to remain the same. Seneca's *Troades* is not merely palimpsestic; it images a palimpsestic world.

The palimpsestic world imaged is the world of the play. But it is not only the world of the play. Late Julio-Claudian Rome, especially (but not only) the Rome of the last Julio-Claudian emperor, Nero, was itself a palimpsestic world, a world dominated by the forms of its past, political, social, religious, legal, which it attempted to re*present*. According to the Roman historian Suetonius (*Nero* 10.1), Nero at the start of his reign proclaimed his intention to rule *ex Augusti praescripto*, that is, in accordance with the prescription of the founder of the dynasty, the first emperor, Augustus; his professed aim was to realise Augustus' *pre*-text. Ironically he fulfilled this aim in ways he never comprehended. For what Nero succeeded in doing was to recycle the tyranny of his predecessors (including that of Augustus) together with the political, social, religious and legal forms of the Roman world emptied of their substance.

Late Julio-Claudian Rome was a palimpsestic world on the verge of dissolution, and portrayed as such by the great writers of the period, Lucan, Petronius, Seneca, all of whom dissolved themselves through suicide before Nero's reign ended. It was a palimpsestic world on the verge of dissolution, in which death was a source of aesthetic pleasure (Sen. *NQ* 3.18) and the death-wish, *libido moriendi (Sen. Ep.* 24.25), a paradigm emotion, as individuals sought the empowerment they lacked in life through the controlled artistry of death. It was left to Seneca's Phaedra (*Pha.* 880) or Petronius' withered Sibyl to articulate the appropriate response: *apothanein thelo*, 'I want to die' (*Sat.* 48). It was a palimpsestic world on the verge of dissolution, in which the modalities of life had become perversely and irredeemably confused. Nero was a fratricide, matricide, sororicide, uxoricide; most relevantly for *Troades* he was a political murderer of children (Britannicus) and of brides (Octavia). Relevant, too, to *Troades* is the way the social and religious rituals of the state were used by Nero to implement bloody savagery – something the Roman historian Tacitus particularly focuses upon in his account of Nero's reign (*Ann.* 14–16). Indeed Tacitus refers to the same conflation of wedding and funeral in the brutal murder of Nero's wife, Octavia (*Ann.* 14.63), as Seneca does – pervasively – in the dramatisation of Polyxena's death.

What should be recognised, too, is that, though perhaps most appropriately dated to the Neronian principate (its actual date is unknown), *Troades* in no sense depends upon such dating for its relevance to late Julio-Claudian Rome. Nero simply realised in sharp and telling form the palimpsestic dimension and modality confusion of this 'new' imperial world – an imperial world for which the Trojan myth itself furnished an apposite and easily cognisable grammar. The cultural semiotics of the Trojan myth were laid out and played out in political (and artistic) word and fact throughout the whole of Seneca's lifetime. Imperial Rome was Troy rewritten and reborn. After Virgil's *Aeneid*, Ovid's *Metamorphoses* and *Fasti*, and the 'Trojan' imagery of the Augustan monuments (especially the Ara Pacis and Augustan Forum), no writer, reader, *spectator* or emperor could forget it. The Julio-Claudian dynasty, of which Nero was the final member, traced its ancestry back to the Trojan Aeneas and the house of Assaracus blazing in the opening lines of Seneca's play (*Tro.* 17). Virgil's *Aeneid*, a school text in Seneca's day, makes this claimed ancestry the basic datum of the epic and pointedly refers to the connection between the house of Assaracus and the Julian family in Jupiter's great prophecy of Augustus' birth in *Aeneid* 1 (*Aen.* 1.284).[56]

To underscore Rome's Trojan past Augustus had established the 'Troy Game', *Troiae Lusus* (referred to by Andromache at *Tro.* 778), as a regular state event, and the tradition was continued by both Caligula and Claudius.[57] Neronian writers – Calpurnius Siculus (*Ecl.* 1.44f.), Persius (*Sat.* 1.4), Lucan (*BC* 9.961–99), Petronius (*Sat.* 89) – conspicuously exploited the connection with Troy.[58] So, too, did Nero himself. He participated in the Trojan Games of 47 CE (together with Claudius' son, Britannicus: Tac. *Ann.* 11.11) at the age of nine; he delivered an oration on behalf of the contemporary city of Ilium (Tac. *Ann.* 12.58) in 53 CE at the age of sixteen, 'setting out at length', according to Tacitus, 'the origins of the Roman people in Troy, Aeneas the founder of the Julian house'; and during his maturity (if one may call it that) he wrote an epic, *Troica*, from which his detractors claim he sang during the great fire of Rome in 64 CE.[59] *Troades* thus exploits a myth of immediate contemporary import. The death of a civilisation, the dissolution of a culture, dramatised in *Troades*, has patent ramifications for the palimpsestic, dissolving world of late Julio-Claudian Rome. Its ramifications were realised in history. Three years after Seneca killed himself at Nero's command, history's cycle dissolved Nero's world. The Julio-Claudian dynasty came to an end as abrupt as that of the royal house of Troy.

Senecan metatheatre

Some of the ramifications of Seneca's palimpsestic mode are autobiographical. The analogies with the past which structure the majority of Senecan plays underscore Senecan tragedy's relationship to its own past, which it cites and recycles. The 'anxiety of influence' (to use Bloom's terminology)[60] which dominates the behaviour of characters such as Phaedra, Hippolytus, Atreus, Thyestes, Aegisthus, Oedipus, Jocasta, Agamemnon, Helen, Medea mirrors Seneca's own anxiety before the determining literary past and prescriptive parental figures of the Graeco-Roman poetic tradition. Dramatic action and dramatic focus signal properties of the works themselves. It seems no accident, for example, that Theseus' attempt to put together the separated fragments of his dismembered son in the final act of *Phaedra* is the construct of a scene which is itself an attempt by Seneca to put together the separated fragments of the dismembered *oeuvre* of Euripides – as the Roman dramatist endeavours to bring together fragments of Euripides' *Hippolytus* and *Bacchae* into a new, harmonious whole. Appropriate ramifications of Theseus' failure for the poetics of Senecan tragedy are at hand. What seems involved is not only Seneca's sense of the impossibility of recreating the Attic form in a postclassical age, but also his location of discord at the centre of the new style.[61] Seneca's failed re*membering* articulates his theatrical world.

Similarly introspective is Seneca's preoccupation with the death-from-life paradox – what creates destroys, the origin of life *is* the origin of death – a paradox which he pursues dramatically in figures such as Hercules, Thyestes, Theseus and most particularly Medea, and which in *Medea* itself he enlarges into the socio-moral thesis, that what creates civilisation destroys it. Seneca's preoccupation with this paradox reflects critically on his own created work. Literary form gives life; it also gives death. The postclassical declamatory mode, the 'pointed', antithetic, epigrammatic style, which animates Senecan tragedy and gives it moral urgency and life, is the form, too, which at notorious moments in the history of European scholarship and taste killed it.[62]

Importantly the self-reflection of Senecan tragedy extends to its status as theatre.[63] The dithyrambic chorus of *Oedipus* (403–508), unique to Seneca's plays, images the god of drama, Bacchus, as an unpredictable and ambivalent god of fantastic, even grotesque, transformative power. It takes little imagination to see the ode's bearing on Seneca's theatrical craft. But relevant too, and more profoundly so, is the association in the preceding ode of Bacchus and the Theban plague:

> occidis, Cadmi generosa proles,
> urbe cum tota. uiduas colonis
> respicis terras, miseranda Thebe.
> carpitur leto tuus ille, Bacche,
> miles, extremos comes usque ad Indos,
> ausus Eois equitare campis
> figere et mundo tua signa primo.
>
> (Oedipus 110–16)

> You are dying, Cadmus' noble line,
> With all the city. You watch the land
> Widowed of its tillers, pitiable Thebes.
> Death plucks your soldiers, Bacchus,
> Comrades to the farthest Indies,
> Who dared to ride on Eastern plains
> And plant your standards at the world's edge.

Little adjustment is required to see these verses' relevance to imperial Rome. But there is a suggestion, too, that the transformative process of plague itself, its grotesqueries, violence and carnage, its production of the 'dreadful face of novel death, more grievous than death' (*dira noui facies leti, / grauior leto*, *Oed*. 180f.; cf. Andromache at *Tro*. 783), its metamorphosis of human behaviour, are essentially Bacchic and belong to Seneca's ideology of theatre. Nor only to Seneca's:

> L'action du théâtre, comme celle de la peste, est bien-faisante, car poussant les hommes à se voir tels qu'ils sont, elle fait tomber le masque, elle découvre le mensonge, la veulerie, la bassesse, la tartuferie.
>
> (Antonin Artaud *Le Théâtre et la Peste*)[64]

> The action of the theatre, like that of the plague, is redemptive, because it impels us to see ourselves as we are. It makes the mask fall; it uncovers the lie, the apathy, the contemptibility, the two-facedness.

Seneca's plague, however, strips theatre itself, exposing its 'two-facedness', its own masking, unmasking, and spectatorial constructedness. The recurrent dramatisation of role-playing – in which characters become actors before other characters as audience:[65] Phaedra before Theseus (*Pha*. 864ff.), Medea before Jason (*Med*. 551ff.), Clytemnestra before Aegisthus (*Ag*. 239ff.), Atreus before Thyestes (*Thy*. 491ff.) – underscores Senecan tragedy's own conventions and artifice. So, too, the related focus on action as spectacle, on characters as *spectatores*,[66] on human behaviour as self-dramatisation; or the staging in *Medea* and *Thyestes* of a character's own staging as character, actor, dramaturge and internal *spectator* of the climactic evil itself. Such features develop the metatheatrical dimension of all Roman tragedy into a constant preoccupation, a pervasive concern on Seneca's part not only to draw attention to his plays' theatricality but to make of that theatricality one of its most persistent and compelling themes.[67] In Seneca, theatrical form self-consciously structures the presentation of human action. His tragedies point to themselves as verbal and performative constructs of the theatrical imagination and re-presentations of a theatricalised world. They are language theatricalised as mirror of *Roma theatrum*.

Troades and *Thyestes* deserve especial notice in this regard. As does *Medea*. In *Thyestes* the metatheatrical note is struck right from the start of the play, when the Fury instructs the 'transcribed' (13) ghost of Tantalus to 'watch' his descendants' cannibalistic drama:

> liberum dedimus diem
> tuamque ad istas soluimus mensas famem:
> ieiunia exple, mixtus in Bacchum cruor
> spectante te potetur.
>
> (*Thyestes* 63–6)

> Today we made you free
> And have unleashed your hunger for this feast.
> Fill your famine, watch the blood mixed with wine
> Being drunk.

Spectare, 'to watch', is also the term used specifically for theatrical viewing.[68] And what the Fury is commanding at the climax of her opening speech in *Thyestes*' prologue is that Tantalus become audience to the very play or plays whose script(s) she elaborated a few lines earlier (25–51), as soon as his prologue performance has achieved its effect: *actum est abunde*, 'Your part has played itself out' (105). Her injunctions display a preoccupation with action as theatre which is to pervade the play.[69] It manifests itself most obviously throughout Acts 2 and 3 in Atreus' mode or even mannerism of self-dramatisation, which begins at his entry into the play with the rejection of the role of 'Atreus Enraged', *iratus Atreus* (180), and continues into his 'plotting' with his script-adviser/minister and his metadramatic inspiration (esp. 250ff.), and into his role-playing before his deluded brother.

Noticeable is not only how Atreus acts out the ironic role of loving, forgiving brother,[70] but how through soliloquy he creates a status for himself as audience to his brother's misery and joins with the audience of the play to watch Thyestes' downfall.

> aspice ut multo grauis
> squalore uultus obruat maestos coma,
> quam foeda iaceat barba. praestetur fides.
> fratrem iuuat uidere.
>
> (*Thyestes* 505–7)

> See how matted
> Filthy hair overwhelms his gloomy face,
> How foul his drooping beard. Now for a show of faith.
> It's a joy to view my brother.

So Atreus invites the audience to 'view' with him the unfolding torture, and to appreciate the verbal ironies which he cannot resist.

The obvious *coup de théâtre* with which *Thyestes'* central act closes, the coronation of the 'power-resistant' brother with the crown that binds, adds 'dramaturge' and 'director' to Atreus' growing list of credits.

The self-conscious theatricality of Act 3 carries over into the messenger scene which follows, where the adoption of a five-'act' crescendo structure for the narrative of horror (641ff.) signals its dramatic artifice. The play's theatricality reaches both its climax and most overt display in the final act itself, in which Atreus plays again (this time pervasively) character, actor, audience and dramaturge, and controls the most minute details (even the lighting, for the sun has disappeared) of the play's dramatic climax. His main anxiety, when he appears, is that his crime will lack an audience. He has dismissed the gods; it gives him pause:

> utinam quidem tenere fugientes deos
> possem, et coactos trahere, ut ultricem dapem
> omnes uiderent! quod sat est, uideat pater.
>
> *(Thyestes* 893–5)

> O that I could check the fugitive gods
> And drag them all against their will to view
> My vengeance-feast! Enough – if the father view it.

In the stage-managing of the subsequent horror, the abundant ghoulish ironies, the two stages of revelation, Thyestes' absolute humiliation and pain, Atrean theatricality is unconcealed. Atreus' need of Thyestes not simply as victim but as audience, as spectator to his revenge, structures the revelation itself:

> *AT.* Expedi amplexus, pater:
>   uenere. natos ecquid agnoscis tuos?
> *TH.* Agnosco fratrem.
>
> *(Thyestes* 1004–6)

> *AT.* Spread wide your arms, father:
>   They have come. Do you recognise your sons?
> *TH.* I recognise my brother.

Indeed Atreus is so concerned with Thyestes as spectator that the revelation of pedophagy yields initially not to Atreus' satisfaction, but to regret that Thyestes and the children themselves were not knowing audience to Thyestes' 'impious feast':

> omnia haec melius pater
> fecisse potuit, cecidit in cassum dolor.
> scidit ore natos impio, sed nesciens,
> sed nescientes.

(Thyestes 1065–8)

> The father could have done
> All this better; his suffering was pointless.
> He chewed his sons impiously, but he didn't know,
> But they didn't know.

The ensuing *Schreirede* of his brother expresses the most inexpressible pain, and the director, satisfied at last with his theatrical production, awards himself victory's palm. Atreus ends the play by defeating his brother in verbal exchange ('I deliver you to your children's punishment', 1112). He knows the scripts of plays to come. The sadistic pleasure he has derived from the spectacle he created competes with the impotent horror and moral revulsion of Thyestes as a model of audience response. The Fury which inspired this play – and therefore inspired Seneca, too – has produced contradictory spectatorial paradigms neither of which dominates the other.[71]

Troades, too, advertises itself as theatre. It features extensive scenes of role-playing, in which characters play actors before other characters as audience: Andromache before Ulysses (556–691), Ulysses before Andromache (627–704), Helen before the Trojan women (871ff.). Metatheatrical language and motifs – 'viewing', 'recognition', 'myth/drama', 'self-dramatisation', 'playing', 'author', 'unlearning', 'presentation', 'spectator', (audience) 'assembly' and 'response'[72] – project and exhibit the play as dramatic artefact and spectacle. Notably the concept of fate in this play seems to embrace the literary and theatrical as well as mythical past.[73] Even the play's final lines suggest completion of a theatrical circle (*repetite*, 'Once more head …', *Tro.* 1178).

In the final act the metaphor of the amphitheatre and theatre pervades the whole of the Messenger's reported action. The Messenger is not only the narrator, but the 'producer/presenter', the *editor* (1067),[74] of spectacle before a 'spectatorship' of Andromache and Hecuba, whose own complex reactions – grief, pleasure, outrage, despair – model possible audience response. The report itself has its own narrated audience, initially amphitheatrical, as the Messenger describes the gathering and positioning of the crowd to watch the death of Astyanax (1075–87) and that crowd's tear-filled viewing (1097–100). For the death of Polyxena the implied analogy of the amphitheatre is replaced overtly by that of the theatre itself:

> praeceps ut altis cecidit e muris puer
> fleuitque Achiuum turba quod fecit nefas,
> idem ille populus aliud ad facinus redit
> tumulumque Achillis. cuius extremum latus
> Rhoetea leni uerberant fluctu uada;
> aduersa cingit campus et cliuo leui
> erecta medium uallis includens locum
> crescit theatri more. concursus frequens
> impleuit omne litus. hi classis moram
> hac morte solui rentur; hi stirpem hostium
> gaudent recidi. magna pars uulgi leuis
> odit scelus spectatque. nec Troes minus
> suum frequentant funus et pauidi metu
> partem ruentis ultimam Troiae uident.
>
> *(Troades* 1118–31)

> When the boy fell sheer from the lofty walls
> And the Achaean crowd wept their own sin,
> The same people turned to another crime
> And Achilles' tomb. The tomb's far side is lashed
> By the soft waves of Rhoeteum's waters;
> Its near side faces a plain where a high
> Vale's gentle slopes enclose a central space
> And rise like a theatre. The thronging mass
> Filled the whole shore. Some think this death dissolves
> The fleet's delay; others are glad to have
> The foe's seedling pruned. Most of the fickle mob
> Hate the crime and watch it. The Trojans, too,
> Attend their own funeral. Quaking with fear
> They view the final act of Troy's collapse.

Note *theatri more*, 'like a theatre'; *partem ultimam*, the 'final act'; and *spectare* again. The crowd hate the crime, but watch it (*spectat*, 1129). There is nothing in Euripides' *Hecuba* (521ff.) like this. Initial spectatorial revulsion and addiction yield to the prescribed, Aristotelian tragic emotions of fear and pity, and the quintessentially Roman response, the marvelling reception of death's spectacle.[75] Corneille was later to separate admiration from tragic pity.[76] Seneca achieves a more complex, more Roman and a conspicuously self-reflective effect through their conjunction:

stupet omne uulgus et fere cuncti magis
peritura laudant. hos mouet formae decus,
hos mollis aetas, hos uagae rerum uices.
mouet animus omnes fortis et leto obuius.
Pyrrhum antecedit. omnium mentes tremunt,
mirantur ac miserantur.

(Troades 1143–8)

The whole crowd is numbed – mankind admires more
What's doomed. Some respond to beauty's glory,
Some to tender youth, some to life's shifting course.
All respond to a brave heart meeting death.
She walks before Pyrrhus. All souls tremble,
Marvel and pity.

This is almost pure metatheatre. The final act of *Troades* 'presents' (*ede*, 1067) the final act of Troy's collapse, complete with unified audience 'tragic' response (admiration, fear, pity) internal to the narrative and individual audience response outside it (Andromache, Hecuba) – the whole suffused with what Racine called 'cette tristesse majestueuse qui fait tout le plaisir de la tragédie'[77] – as the play draws attention to its status both as theatre and as *imago uitae*, image of life. Hamlet's metatheatrical homily to the acting troupe at Elsinore seems realised:[78]

[The] end, both at the first and now, was and is, to hold, as 'twere, the mirror up to nature; to show virtue her own feature, scorn her own image, and the very age and body of the time his form and pressure.

(Hamlet 3.2.21ff.)

– except that *Troades'* 'mirror' dissolves the gap between itself and the world.

This dissolution defines Senecan tragedy – as *Medea* most particularly attests. Its final act is almost self-indulgently theatrical. Everything is stage-managed by Medea. The Messenger enters, delivers with unique brevity the news of Creusa's and Creon's death and the unstoppable fire in the palace (879–90), but, before he can launch into the predictable Euripidean narrative, Medea's entrance drives him from the stage (891). Instead of a messenger's speech the audience receives the longest soliloquy in Senecan tragedy, as Medea incites herself to slay her children and realise her own dramatic myth (893–977): *Medea nunc sum*, 'Now I am Medea' (910). In the end it is the appearance of the Furies, of Megaera, and most especially of the dismembered Absyrtus, which drives her to filicide, redefined at the moment of execution as sacrifice to her dead brother:[79]

> discedere a me, frater, ultrices deas
> manesque ad imos ire securas iube.
> mihi me relinque et utere hac, frater, manu
> quae strinxit ensem. uictima manes tuos
> placamus ista.
>
> (Medea 967–71)

> Tell the avenging goddesses to leave me,
> Brother, to go in peace to the dead below.
> Leave me to myself and use this hand, brother,
> Its sword drawn. With this victim we placate
> Your spirit.

She slays one child. Requiring an audience ('Your "manliness" [*uirtus*] is not to be squandered in secret', 976f.), she takes the other son and the dead child's body to the roof of the palace, where she revels in the triumph of the moment before the eyes of Jason, who has just entered:

> iam iam recepi sceptra, germanum, patrem,
> spoliumque Colchi pecudis auratae tenent.
> rediere regna, rapta uirginitas redit.
> o placida tandem numina! o festum diem!
> o nuptialem!
>
> (Medea 982–6)

> Now, now I've restored throne, brother, father,
> And Colchians keep the golden fleece's prize.
> Realms return, stolen virginity returns.
> Oh gods at last propitious! Oh festal,
> Wedding day!

The power of Medea's language has dominated the play. The Chorus, Creon, Jason (113f., 189, 530), have all tried to silence her, fearing that language's power. Their fear was justified. Medea's language is used in the play not only to evoke the powers of darkness but to realise Medea's own dramatic myth. As Medea's power in the play has grown, so has her domination of the play's language. Domination of the theatrical world and word are the same. In the linguistic reverie above the power of theatrical language to rewrite reality is openly displayed. Its ability to satisfy, however, is truncated, when Medea realises that her vengeance is incomplete. In Euripides' play both children are dead before Jason arrives (1293). In Seneca one child is left to be slain before the scene's internal audience. To Medea the lack of audience nullifies revenge. Oscillating between shame, remorse and pleasure, Medea is transfixed by desire for Jason as *spectator*:

> derat hoc unum mihi,
> spectator iste. nil adhuc facti reor:
> quidquid sine isto fecimus sceleris perit.
>
> *(Medea* 992–4)

> This one thing was missing,
> Him as audience. Nothing is yet achieved:
> What sin we performed in his absence dies.

In this most 'spectacular' of all Seneca's finales, involving armed crowds, rooftop dialogue, child-slaying, and the arrival/departure of the serpent-drawn chariot of the Sun, Medea plays to and with her audience, Jason, whose son will be given to death while Jason watches (*te uidente*, 1001). She kills the second child both as gladiatorial theatre before her spectator husband – *bene est, peractum est*, 'It's home, it's done' (*Med.* 1019)[80] – and as sacrificial spectacle before her own internal 'hurt' (*dolor*, 1019). Again sadistic pleasure and impotent horror compete as models of audience response. It does not surprise that the poet of Augustan decorum expressly forbade the staging of Medea's filicide (Hor. *AP* 185).

Her second son dead, Medea implements the script which she announced in the prologue, mounting her ancestral chariot to be carried through the air. She feigns surprise at Jason's failure to predict this ending:

> coniugem agnoscis tuam?
> sic fugere soleo.
>
> *(Medea* 1021–2)

> Don't you recognise your wife?
> This is how I always escape.

One sense is that, as Medea has been at pains to rehearse in this play (129ff., 276ff., 471ff.), her flights in the past have been accompanied by social chaos, suffering and the murder of kin. The metatheatrical sense (here irresistible) is that this is how Medea always leaves her play. Failure on her part to repeat what are Medea's self-constituting acts would be to lose her theatrical identity. If 'this Medea has read Euripides',[81] this Jason has not. Nor has he read his Ovid (*Met.* 7.394–9).

Further evidence follows. Euripides' *Medea* concludes with Medea's serpentine flight followed by the Chorus' justification of the ways of gods to men (1415ff.).[82] Jason's atheistic proclamation in the final distich of Seneca's play is not only Eliot's famed *coup de théâtre*,[83] but confirmation of how little he has either understood or read. Neither gods nor previous scripts are on his side. They are all with Medea. Jason rewrites Euripides' ending into a theatrical display of failed reading of both literature and the world. The palimpsestic and the theatricalised world and the world of delusion and failed power become one. In the late Julio-Claudian era that world was Rome, the moral, social and political problems of which are reflected and refracted by the representational and metatheatrical energies of Senecan tragedy.

Part III

THE DEATH OF
TRAGEDY AT ROME

TRAGEDY AND AUTOCRACY

The liberty of silence

omnis Caesareo cedit labor amphitheatro:
unum pro cunctis fama loquetur opus.
(Martial *De Spectaculis* 1.7–8)

All human pains yield to Caesar's amphitheatre:
Fame will proclaim a single work for all.

The death of Seneca preceded by perhaps two to three generations
the death of serious tragedy at Rome. Two Roman tragedies survive
from the period after Seneca's death, most probably from the
Flavian period: *Hercules Oetaeus* and *Octavia*. Each is of unknown
authorship; each is parasitic on Seneca's opus.[1] Their relative dates
are not agreed.[2] *Hercules Oetaeus*, which is the longest extant ancient
tragedy, is a Senecanesque dramatisation of the death and apotheosis
of Hercules on Mount Oeta in northern Greece. As in Sophocles'
Trachiniae and Ovid's *Heroides* 9 and *Metamorphoses* 9, Hercules'
death is brought about by his wearing of a robe, poisoned with the
blood of Nessus, given to him by his jealous wife Deianira as a
magic means to regain her husband's love. Deianira suicides and
Hercules achieves deification.

The play is almost twice as long as Seneca's *Agamemnon*, *Oedipus*
and *Medea* (1996 lines as against 1012, 1061 and 1027 respectively),
and 50 per cent longer than the longest of the 'eight', *Hercules Furens*
(1344). It lacks the tension and tensility of a Senecan play. Its long
acts, repetitive speeches and motifs, flaccid choral odes,[3] lack of
intellectual substance, of psychological focus, and of dramatic logic
and energy join with its *cento*-like, often incoherent assemblage of
Senecan phrases and motifs to indicate an author other than Seneca.[4]
The play's convenient *deus ex machina*, a dramaturgical device avoided
in the 'genuine' eight, points in the same direction. As does the
choric ending, similarly avoided in the 'eight':

numquam Stygias fertur ad umbras
inclita uirtus. uiuite fortes
nec Lethaeos saeua per amnes
        uos fata trahent,
sed cum summas exiget horas
        consumpta dies,
iter ad superos gloria pandet.
sed tu, domitor magne ferarum
orbisque simul pacator, ades.
nunc quoque nostras aspice terras,
et si qua nouo belua uultu
quatiet populos terrore graui,
tu fulminibus frange trisulcis.
fortius ipso genitore tuo
        fulmina mitte.

                    (*Hercules Oetaeus* 1983–96)

Glorious *uirtus* never passes
To Stygian shadows. Live, brave ones;
The cruel fates will not pull you
        Across Lethe's streams,
But when the devoured day exacts
        Its final hours
Glory will open a path to gods.
But you, mighty master of the beasts
And pacifier of the globe, come.
Even now look over our lands,
And if any beast's new face strikes
The people with crushing terror,
Smite it with forked thunderbolts
And fling the bolts more boldly
        Even than your father.

The drama is quintessentially Roman in its greater focus (compared with Sophocles' *Trachiniae*) on the pain of Hercules' dying, which it prolongs (some might think, excessively). The play appears pointlessly padded, most noticeably perhaps in the apparently endless repetition of Hercules' labours;[5] but, despite its length, it has nothing of the rich literary and allusive texture of a Senecan play. The move to turn Iole, Hercules' captive mistress, from a *persona muta* in Sophocles to a suffering victim is a good one, but Iole's lyrical self-depiction (*HO* 173–224) seems little more than a rehearsal of Senecan phrases and motifs and an uninspired tour of mythological precedents. It hardly needs saying that the 'positive' Stoicism of *Hercules Oetaeus* and the bland, triumphant close quoted above ill accord with the tenor and the endings of Senecan tragedy. But the play not only presupposes Senecan tragedy but presupposes an audience favourable to it, and, although undated, is perhaps most likely to have been written shortly after Seneca's death. A political reading of the drama's final lines, which would transform *nouo belua uultu* ('beast's new face', *HO* 1992) into a metaphor for a Neronian tyrant-figure (Hercules begins the play by defining himself as the slayer of *perfidi reges*, 'perfidious kings', and *saeui tyranni*, 'cruel tyrants', *HO* 5–6),[6] accords well with an earlier rather than later Flavian dating.

Octavia

More interesting is *Octavia*, a play which had an immense, informing impact on European tragedy from Albertino Mussato's *Ecerinis* (1315 CE) onwards.[7] It is the only *fabula praetexta* to survive complete from the ancient world and thus, although difficult (perhaps impossible) to assess dramatically, of inestimable generic interest.[8] Its attention to historical detail is marked. There is little in the play at odds with the historical record, and much for which the play is the only source.[9] But *Octavia* is also self-consciously a tragedy; its intertexts are not only the tragedies of Seneca,[10] but those of Sophocles (especially *Electra* and *Antigone*) and Euripides (especially *Iphigenia in Aulis* and *Alcestis*). It fuses the forms of the *praetexta* and of tragedy proper in a manner which has its seeds in earlier plays (Accius' *Decius* or *Brutus*,[11] for example, or a possible tragic *praetexta* on Gaius Gracchus).[12] The play focuses, like Senecan tragedy, on present evil as product of the past, but the past *exempla* framing the play's tragic figure come – in approximately equal measure – from myth (e.g. Alcyone, Philomela, Electra, Antigone, Iphigenia) and Roman history (e.g. Virginia, Lucretia, the Agrippinas, Livilla, Julia, Messalina).[13] If such 'generic' fusion was not already part of the *praetexta* tradition, it may have been a predilection of Flavian drama. Certainly the play's denigration of Roman political figures, here the emperor himself, Poppaea, possibly Seneca, though inverting the ostensibly celebratory tendencies of its early republican predecessors, accords with the anti-imperial proclivities of much post-republican verse.[14] Another post-Neronian dramatist wrote *praetextae* in the same vein.[15]

The play deals with the removal of Nero's stepsister and first wife, Octavia, to Pandateria, where she will be 'executed', and his marriage to his mistress Poppaea. *Octavia*'s spare language and 'jejune style',[16] its aversion to declamatory effects, its relative lack of structural tension and interconnections mark the play as non-Senecan.[17] So, too, the play's visual restraint, its avoidance of violent spectacle (even the death of Octavia is foreshadowed rather than enacted or described). The taut interrelation between chorus and act which defines Senecan drama is also markedly absent, as are two of Seneca's most potent dramatic devices, the aside (e.g. *Pha.* 592–9, *Tro.* 607–18, *Med.* 549–50) and the entrance monologue soliloquy with other characters on stage (e.g. *Ag.* 226–33, *Tro.* 861–71, *Thy.* 404–20, 491–507).

The dramatic 'action' structures itself around a series of separate tableaux or scenes, representing events over a three-day period in the year 62 CE, centred on the wedding-day of Nero and Poppaea. Most of the scenes take place on the day before or the day after the wedding.[18] The first and final acts of the play focus on Octavia's distress and the disasters which have befallen the Claudian house; the four (or five)[19] intervening acts present in turn: Seneca's attempts to restrain Nero; the appearance of the ghost of Agrippina and her prophecy of Nero's death; Octavia's departure from the palace; Poppaea's description of the dream on her wedding night; a messenger's report of popular rioting in support of Octavia; Nero's instructions for Octavia's death. Most of the primary scenes are constructed from contrasting pairs of characters: Octavia and her Nurse; Seneca and Nero; Poppaea and her Nurse; Nero and the Prefect. Noteworthy is the playwright's use of dream narratives and nurse scenes on the first and third days of the action, not only for structural balance but to link and contrast Octavia and Poppaea, and perhaps even to generate sympathy for Poppaea herself. There may be a deliberate allusion here to the famous dream of Tarquinius in Accius' *Brutus* and to Queen Atossa's dream in Aeschylus' *Persae*.[20] From Octavia's opening monody onwards multi-allusivity defines this play.

Octavia's use of interiority is bold, innovative and impressive; it contributes to the play's powerfully claustrophobic atmosphere. Apart from the final scene, the whole action takes place within the imperial palace, and, although this is controversial, some scenes may well have been set in rooms of that palace rather than in its open spaces and courtyards.[21] Certainly one of those rooms, the *thalamus* or bedchamber, is used throughout the play as visual embodiment of the central problematic: imperial marriage and power. Eviction from the *thalamus* and position within it track the political movement of the plot; the cursed nature of the *thalamus* foreshadows history.[22] Similarly bold, though perhaps not innovative in respect of the *praetexta* (some have hypothesised a double chorus for Accius' *Brutus*),[23] is the play's use of two choruses (one pro-Octavia, one pro-Poppaea), each with a strong role in the action of the drama.

The two choruses have been thought by some to bipartition the play around the failed pro-Octavia revolution.[24] But it seems more likely that the pro-Octavia chorus of the Roman people is the dominant one, and that the chorus (perhaps of courtiers)[25] supportive of Poppaea is restricted to two odes (762–79, 806–19) and an intervening scene (780–805) with the Messenger. For a chorus of the Roman people to be the dominant one would not surprise. Some have argued that a chorus constituted of the Roman people may have been a convention of the *fabula praetexta*.[26] What may also not have surprised is the revolutionary role of the chorus in the play's action. It attacks Nero's palace in an attempt to restore Octavia (685–9; described 780–855). Revolutionary acts on the part of the chorus were perhaps already a feature of the genre, and may have informed the plots of Naevius' *Romulus* (insurrection against Amulius) and Accius' *Brutus* (insurrection against Tarquinius).[27] Such degree of choric participation in the dramatic action is not found in extant Senecan tragedy.

The distribution of the play's action over a number of days may also have been a generic feature, since it is clearly a property of such plays as Pacuvius' *Paulus*, Accius' *Brutus* and Balbus' *Iter*, and is likely to have been a property of several others.[28] Powerful in that distribution is the devotion of less than a hundred lines (593–689) to the wedding-day, in which the focus is on the curse of Agrippina's ghost (note the striking use of a ghost scene in the middle of the play – against Senecan practice), on the evicted Octavia's distress, and finally on choric anger and revolution. The wedding itself takes place either on stage as non-scripted spectacle or (more probably) offstage as an absent presence shaping and controlling the shifting fortunes of Octavia and of Rome.[29] In performance an offstage wedding could have been indicated by ironically celebratory music and noise. A further generic feature may be *Octavia*'s tableau manner of dramatisation. Some have seen the play's 'sequence of short, intercut scenes' as contributing towards the sense of an evolving crisis,[30] others as an index of poor dramatic structure. But it is also important to note the connection between *Octavia*'s tableau style of presentation and the *praetexta*'s early connections with the iconic rituals of Roman religion and with the Roman triumphal procession. Whatever its effect on dramatic pace and atmosphere, the play's tableau structure may have worked well with a Roman audience because it satisfied generic expectations. Those expectations may have been more than usually satisfied, if, as has been recently argued,[31] the play's final scene is set in a harbour before the ship which will take Octavia to Pandateria.

Octavia is post-Neronian and probably Flavian – and also probably composed for 'stage' performance, perhaps for performance in a private house or villa.[32] Whatever the precise form or date of its production (Galba's short reign,[33] or the early Vespasianic years,[34] or the middle or late Flavian principate),[35] its political semiotics intrigue. At one level the play is a political reading of Senecan tragedy, the subtextual level of which is unearthed and displayed. Indeed *Octavia* has even been described as 'our earliest commentary on *Thyestes*'.[36] Some have seen the play as (at least in part) a defence of Seneca himself against those who saw him as colluding in, if not instigating, the excesses of the Neronian court. In the play's most famous scene, between Seneca and his emperor (*Oct.* 377–592), the tragedian-statesman is made to use language and ideas from his own plays and philosophical writings to articulate a (tired) view of contemporary moral decline and imminent cosmic cataclysm and to advocate a philosophy of monarchic restraint.[37] With unsubtle dramatic timing 'Seneca' completes his attack upon the present (Neronian) age immediately prior to the entrance of the 'savage' *princeps* himself:

> collecta uitia per tot aetates diu
> in nos redundant. saeculo premimur graui
> quo scelera regnant, saeuit impietas furens,
> turpi libido Venere dominatur potens,
> luxuria uictrix orbis immensas opes
> iam pridem auaris manibus, ut perdat, rapit.
>
> > (*Octavia* 429–34)

> A gathering wave of vices from many years
> Floods over us. We're crushed by a heavy age,
> In which crime reigns, impiety rages madly,
> Potent lust lords it with immoral love,
> Wealth triumphant with greedy hands has long
> Plundered the world's great riches – to squander them.

Not all have seen the presentation of Seneca in his dialogue with Nero as uncritical. Indeed it is now fashionable to regard the portrait of Seneca as of a philosopher-politician out of his depth in the political world, although it has also been argued that Seneca is presented as 'the master of an impressive range of cultural competencies'.[38] But nobody thinks the dramatisation of Nero is anything other than condemnatory. The emperor's first commands are for the killing of two relatives living in exile, Plautus and Sulla, and the bringing of their 'severed heads' (*Oct.* 437–8). That action frames Nero's ensuing colloquy with his minister, in which Nero shapes himself as a 'tyrant', lacking the rage and rant of an Atreus but still haunted by fear, love of power and the desire to exercise it. The philosopher-tragedian attempts to restrain him with appeals (among other things) to the prime 'imperial' virtues of clemency, justice, *uirtus* and *pietas*, to the importance of popular support, and (intriguingly) to the role of *consensus* (of the Senate, of the People?) in legitimising the ruler's power (*Oct.* 460). The attempt fails, in part because Nero is equal to the rhetorical moves of his minister and former teacher. He more than holds his own in this most interesting tussle of words and minds (440–592), displaying at times an Atrean 'wit': 'I'd be stupid to fear gods when it's I who make them' (*stulte uerebor, ipse cum faciam, deos*, *Oct.* 449).[39] The emperor's final riposte is one of firm dismissal of his former tutor:

> desiste tandem, iam grauis nimium mihi,
> instare. liceat facere quod Seneca improbat.
> > (*Octavia* 588–9)

> Enough at last of this too wearisome pressure.
> Let my licence be to do what Seneca condemns.

The scene is modelled on several ruler-counsellor scenes of Senecan tragedy, but most especially on that between Atreus and his *satelles* at *Thyestes* 176–335 – with the important difference that Seneca counsels restraint to the end and, unlike Atreus' *satelles*, does not yield to the 'tyrant' or collude with his plans. The dialogue ends in a technical 'stalemate',[40] in which Seneca, however, loses, since he fails to persuade and the predicted popular disapproval proves ineffective. When Nero appears again in the play it is as a full-blown Atreus figure, commanding blood, punishment and terror (820–43).[41] Then the punishment he demands is of all the rebellious citizens (848–57), and the severed head he requires is Octavia's (861).

The denigration of Nero as a bloody despot, a Roman Atreus, Oedipus, Lycus or Eteocles, and the concomitant laudation of the Claudian family, would have played well to the first two Flavian emperors, who portrayed themselves as the successors to the early Julio-

Claudians. Indeed the legal authority conferring imperial power on Vespasian, the *Lex de Imperio Vespasiani* of December 69 CE,[42] explicitly based it 'on that of Augustus, Tiberius, and Claudius.'[43] If the play were, however, to be dated to the Domitianic era, as a recent commentator suggests,[44] the denigration of Nero may well have been aimed at the new Neronian figure, Domitian himself.[45] But even without such an obvious equation the very transferability of *Octavia*'s thematics of fear, hypocrisy, tyrannical power and control of speech ensures the play's bearing on its own imperial world. Nero's articulation of the psychological motor of the principate, to be dwelt upon later by Tacitus, requires no hermeneutic strategy to expound its Flavian relevance:

> munus deorum est, ipsa quod seruit mihi
> Roma et senatus quodque ab inuitis preces
> humilesque uoces exprimit nostri metus.
>
> > (*Octavia* 492–4)

> It is the gods' gift that Rome and the senate serve me,
> And that prayers and humble tones are choked
> From unwilling subjects by fear of me.

Similarly the representation of the Roman elite as 'forgetful of themselves' (*nostri ... immemores, Oct.* 288) and unable to live up to the 'true Roman manhood of old' (*uera priorum uirtus ... Romana, Oct.* 291–2),[46] together with the dramatisation of the Roman people's failure to enact revolution, points as much to contemporary Rome as it does to the Neronian past.[47] That this was an intention of the unknown playwright of *Octavia*, the play's final lines leave unambiguous. They are delivered by the chorus as in *Hercules Oetaeus* and contrary to Senecan practice:

> urbe est nostra mitior Aulis
> et Taurorum barbara tellus:
> hospitis illic caede litatur
> > numen superum.
> ciuis gaudet Roma cruore.
>
> > > (*Octavia* 977–81)

> Our city is crueller than Aulis
> And the barbaric Tauric land:
> There the killing of strangers
> > Appeases the high gods.
> Rome rejoices in citizen blood.

The bloody Rome of the play's final line does more than invert the protective Rome of Seneca's idealising pleas (*Oct.* 490–1),[48] or replay the opening motif of Lucan's great epic of civil war. It is index of a time.

A final not simply formal point – and one in support of the 'staging' of this play. Putting Nero on stage, with an actor playing the dead emperor with a mask of Nero, would have produced an extraordinary theatrical and metahistorical effect. Nero had himself been an actor and had played on stage sometimes in masks bearing his own features or those of Poppaea (Suet. *Nero* 21.3; Dio 63.9.5). The actor playing Nero and the one playing Poppaea could have been the same. He would have provided the Roman audience with an image of Nero unnervingly identical with the reality, conflating the theatrical and the real in a manner constitutive of Neronian (nor only Neronian) Rome.

Flavian Rome

Hercules Oetaeus and *Octavia* were but two of the many intellectual products of Flavian Rome, which was a time of fertile and carefully articulated poetic and artistic energy. During the almost three decades of Flavian rule (69–96 CE) Rome experienced a poetic and intellectual rejuvenation – but a most complex one, which was as fertile as it was imperially regulated and at times repressed. Greek philosophers and rhetoricians abounded in the city (Epictetus, Musonius, Demetrius, Plutarch, Dio Chrysostom – to cite some of the more famous)[49] and were periodically banished from it. Poets of quality flourished, especially in the later, Domitianic period (81–96) – Martial, Statius, Valerius, Silius. New imperially sponsored artistic competitions institutionalised artistic production. As always, the written and performed word were carefully watched for political nuance and criticism. Martial especially draws attention to the dangers of 'malign interpretation' of one's words and the necessity for pre-emptive self-protection (*Epig.* 1 Pref.). Tacitus echoes this in his *Dialogus de Oratoribus* (3.2), set in Flavian Rome.

A main instrument of self-protection was itself literary. Martial and Statius were brilliant users of the figure of speech known as *emphasis*, described by Quintilian (*Inst.*9.2.64ff.) as layered speech, one that employs concealed or latent meaning, where 'something hidden is dug out from something said' (*ex aliquo dicto latens aliquid eruitur*) and 'as it were has to be found by the hearer' (*auditori quasi inueniendum*). Evaluated by Quintilian as the most popular of figures (*frequentissimum*), *emphasis* is specifically denoted as the form of speech to be employed before a tyrant where 'it is unsafe to speak openly' (*dicere palam parum tutum est, Inst.* 9.2.66).[50] What *emphatic* writing or speaking needed – and here the debt to poets such as Ovid is apparent (e.g. *Tr.* 5.1.1) – was a *studiosus lector*, a knowing, attentive, supportive reader, *auditor* or *spectator*. The writer had to be careful, because Rome's powerful elite numbered among the most sophisticated readers, 'attuned' to figural exploitation.[51] Hence Domitian's execution of the younger Helvidius Priscus and of Hermogenes of Tarsus, the latter precisely 'on account of certain "figures" in his history' (*propter quasdam in historia figuras*, Suet. *Dom.* 10.1).

But for all the concern with the relationship between writing and political power, as Martial's own epigrams make abundantly clear, performance rather than writing itself occupied Flavian Rome's cultural centre – and many of those performances had no written scripts. Theatrics were as central to Flavian Rome's cultural and social life as they were to the emperor's own political image. The provision of odeums (by both Vespasian and Domitian), circuses, temples, baths, forums, a *naumachia*, the restoration of theatres (including the Theatre of Marcellus, Suet. *Vesp.* 19.1), the building of the Colosseum, re-energised the cityscape, its spectacles and its pleasures – and the image of the emperor himself. Domitian was especially extravagant in the provision of games and benefactions (Suet. *Dom.* 4.1, 5).

This increased spectacle was both orchestrated and regulated. Part of Domitian's programme as censor (Suet. *Dom.* 8.3) was to revive the *lex Iulia theatralis*,[52] which ensured the display of Rome's intricate pyramidal structure at the theatrical *ludi*: senators at the front followed by equestrians (to whom the first fourteen rows of theatrical seating were once more restricted), Vestals, freeborn seniors and juniors, *pullati* (the common people), freedmen, *matronae*, prostitutes, gladiators, insolvent debtors, slaves – all arranged before the imperial gaze as for a grand, controlled photo-opportunity of the entire Roman social structure. It would have been a noisy photo-op: claques still proliferated in the Roman theatre, each organised by its gang-leader (*dux* or *signifer*), and the rhythmic cacophony they generated – in support or opposition – would have often drowned all other aural perception. Despite the noise and apparent chaos, there were at least social dangers in attempting to ignore the imperatives of the theatre's hierarchical divisions. Thus Martial on the embarrassment of being removed from the seats reserved for members of the equestrian class or 'knights' (cf. *Epig.* 5.23):

> edictum domini deique nostri,
> quo subsellia certiora fiunt
> et puros eques ordines recepit,
> dum laudat modo Phasis in theatro,
> Phasis purpureis ruber lacernis,
> et iactat tumido superbus ore:
> 'tandem commodius licet sedere,
> nunc est reddita dignitas equestris;
> turba non premimur, nec inquinamur' –
> haec et talia dum refert supinus,
> illas purpureas et arrogantes
> iussit surgere Leitus lacernas.

(*Epigrams* 5.8)

> The edict of our lord and god,
> By which benches were assigned more strictly
> And the knights' rows made pure again,
> Phasis was praising in the theatre just now –
> Red Phasis in his purple cloak –
> And proudly boasted, all puffed up:
> 'At last we can sit more comfortably,
> Knightly dignity is now restored:
> We're not crushed or soiled by the mob' –
> As he repeated this and the like,
> Lolling back, Leitus told that purple
> And arrogant cloak to get up.

Vespasian's restitutive patronage of the theatre has already been noted, but by far his most important intervention in the area of Roman spectacle was the remaking of Nero's private pleasure gardens as the site for the 'People's Palace', the Flavian Amphitheatre, later known as the Colosseum. Apparently inspired by an unrealised Augustan idea (Suet. *Vesp.* 9.1), the Colosseum, as an early architrave inscription attests, was essentially Vespasian's project, financed by spoils of the Jewish war. It was dedicated during the reign of Titus in 80 BCE. Its murderous theatrics are well documented. They included not only gladiator fights, beast hunts and naval battles, but 'fatal charades' in which scenes from tragedies, mime or Roman history were parodically and murderously enacted before an engrossed audience of some 50,000 *spectatores*.[53] Here is Martial's 'witty' description of one such 'charade' from his *De Spectaculis*, written to describe and celebrate the Colosseum's inaugural games (*Spec.* 9 Shackleton Bailey):

> qualiter in Scythica religatus rupe Prometheus
>   assiduam nimio pectore pauit auem,
> nuda Caledonio sic uiscera praebuit urso
>   non falsa pendens in cruce Laureolus.
> uiuebant laceri membris stillantibus artus
>   inque omni nusquam corpore corpus erat.
> denique supplicium <dignus tulit: ille parentis>
>   uel domini iugulum foderat ense nocens,
> templa uel arcano demens spoliauerat auro,
>   subdiderat saeuas uel tibi, Roma, faces.
> uicerat antiquae sceleratus crimina famae,
>   in quo, quae fuerat fabula, poena fuit.

> Like chained Prometheus on a Scythian crag
>   Ever feeding the bird on too much breast,
> Laureolus hung on a non-fictive cross
>   Offering Caledonia's bear naked flesh.
> The torn limbs were alive, their parts dripping,
>   And the body was wholly bodiless.
> Finally he got fit punishment: the villain
>   Had stabbed his father's or master's throat,
> Or, crazily, had robbed a shrine of secret gold,
>   Or had put a cruel torch to you, Rome.
> The criminal had vanquished the crimes of legend
>   By turning a play into punishment.

At other times the subject is taken not from tragedy or mime, but from Roman history, as the spectators witness a kind of *fabula praetexta*, arena style: a 'Mucius Scaevola' plunging his right hand into the flames (Mart. *Epig.* 8.30; 10.25).

From the building's construction onwards, the theatrics of the Colosseum dominated Roman theatrical life. Tragedy survived for a short time, as both *Hercules Oetaeus* and *Octavia* attest; indeed there is some evidence that the *fabula praetexta* experienced something of a renaissance. In Tacitus' *Dialogus* there are two *praetextae* ascribed to its central figure, the Vespasianic poet, Curiatius Maternus: *Domitius* and *Cato*. The latter of these had not only recently been recited, but was much talked about and seems to have offended the emperor himself (*Dial.* 3.2–3) – unsurprisingly, given the opposition to Vespasian expressed by such imitators of Cato Uticensis as the Stoic martyr Helvidius Priscus, executed in 74 CE (Tac. *Hist.* 4.4–9), possibly on the order of Titus.[54] Both Helvidius and his father-in-law, the Neronian Stoic martyr Thrasea Paetus, were the subject of provocative biographies by the Flavian authors Herennius Senecio and Arulenus Rusticus, who perished along with their works in the early 90s.[55] Maternus' 'attacks' on imperial governance may even have begun with Nero, since at *Dialogus* 11.2 Tacitus may well be ascribing to Maternus a third and pre-Flavian *praetexta* specifically entitled *Nero*, which the author recited under Galba to powerful effect.[56] Perhaps *Nero* and *Domitius* are the same play.

Maternus is described in Tacitus' *Dialogus* (3.4) as fusing Roman history with Greek tragedy, and thus, unsurprisingly, has been conjectured to be the author of *Octavia*, which evidences a similar fusion. If Maternus were *Octavia's* author, a Domitianic date for the play would be most likely. Maternus is accredited by Tacitus with two mythological tragedies, *Medea* and *Thyestes*, both written in Vespasianic Rome. *Thyestes* in particular seems to have been designed as an overt imperial critique (*Dial.* 3.3). Whether these plays were performed or even intended for performance is unknown. Maternus is described as having recited his plays, but, as was observed above, recitation sometimes preceded performance, and both the recitation-hall *and* the theatre are mentioned in connection with him (*Dial.* 10.5). Suetonius (*Galba* 13) provides evidence that at least in 69 CE, during the short reign of Galba, the theatre had once again become a viable context for direct criticism of the powerful, even of the emperor himself. The eventual result, however, of Maternus' dramatic audacity may have been the poet's own execution, if Syme's identification of the tragic poet and the sophist executed in 91 CE (Dio 67.12.5) is correct.[57]

Names of other Flavian tragic poets survive – in the pages of the unsympathetic Martial: Varro, Bassus (*Epig.* 5.30, 5.53) and Scaevus Memor, whom Martial heralds as *Romani fama cothurni*, 'glory of Roman tragedy' (*Epig.* 11.9.1). To Scaevus are attributed possibly a *Hercules* and a play featuring Hecuba, to whom (= 'Cisseis') the following anapaests are addressed by a chorus presumably of Trojan women (frag. i. Klotz):

scindimus atras ueteri planctu,
Cissei, genas.

We rip black cheeks, Cisseis,
In ancient lamentation.

The performance context of Scaevus' plays is unknown. The writing and reading of tragedy are satirised by Martial (e.g. *Epig.* 3.20.7; 10.4), but not its performance on stage. When Martial notes Scaevus' success (*Epig.* 11.9.1), it is for victory in the Latin poetry competition of the quinquennial Capitoline games (perhaps of 94 CE). The Capitoline competitions called for improvisation, not pre-written scripts.[58]

Tragic and comic drama clearly constituted only one dimension – and its least popular – of the theatrical life of Flavian Rome, which transformed itself into both the greatest and the most multivalent show on earth. The quinquennial *Capitolia* alone provided a most stirring series of sights, from the imperial parade toward the 'Flavianised' Temple of Iuppiter Optimus Maximus on the Capitol – with Domitian flanked by the *Flamen Dialis* and the *Sodales Flauiales Titiales*, the priests of the Flavian dynasty – to the poetic, oratorical and musical events of the festival itself in Domitian's recently constructed odeum in the Campus Martius. The Domitianic Odeum twinned the one built by Vespasian, and both were massive developments of odeums built else-where in Italy and the empire.[59] Domitian's Odeum was a grandly designed, roofed auditorium capable of seating perhaps 5,000–7,000 people, destined to become one of the most spectacular sites of late antiquity;[60] it was spectacle housing spectacle. Since its capacity was much less than, say, the Theatre of Pompey in which Nero performed, it was also elite spectacle housing elite spectacle. Such spectacle would have included a whole range of performances, including music and oratorical displays, poetic recitations, dancing – and (perhaps) dramatic productions, moved to the protective, elitist context of the odeum away from the spectacular productions of the large open-air theatres and the arena, demanded by the Roman masses.[61]

Imperial Rome's addiction to spectacle cannot be overestimated. The biting comments of two post-Flavian writers reveal a fundamental, if partial, truth of the consequences of the imperial system. Juvenal on (probably) Hadrianic Rome (*c.* 125 CE):

> nam qui dabat olim
> imperium, fasces, legiones, omnia, nunc se
> continet atque duas tantum res anxius optat:
> panem et circenses.

> *(Satire* 10.78–81)

> A people that once bestowed
> Commands, consulships, legions, everything, now
> Pulls back, and only frets with desire for two things:
> Bread and circuses.

Fronto, on the Rome of Marcus Aurelius (165 CE):

> ex summa ciuilis scientiae ratione sumpta uidentur ne histrionum quidem ceterorumque scaenae aut circi aut harenae artificum indiligentem principem fuisse, ut qui sciret populum Romanum duabus praecipue rebus, annona et spectaculeis, teneri.
>
> (*Principia Historiae* 20 (Van den Hout))

> The highest principle of political science seems to have dictated that the emperor did not neglect actors and the rest of the performers of the stage, circus and arena, knowing as he did that the Roman people are gripped by two things above all: the corn dole and spectacles.

Flavian Rome was similarly gripped. Apart from such extraordinary festivals as the hundred-day dedication of the Colosseum (if Dio is to be believed: 66.25.4), the Roman religious year at the time of the Flavians devoted some eighty or so days to games: *ludi circenses* involving chariot races; *ludi scaenici* involving theatrical productions, whether comic, tragic or (much more likely) Atellan, mimic and pantomimic; amphitheatrical games (*munera*), involving gladiatorial fights and/or wild beast hunts (*uenationes*). The 'conventional' Roman stage under the Flavians was dominated by mime and pantomime. The latter seems, at least during Domitian's reign, to have regularly celebrated the emperor himself (Pliny *Paneg.* 54.1), and gave rise to superstars such as Paris who had an affair with Domitian's wife, Domitia, and exercised considerable influence at court.[62] Mime not only regularly burlesqued such central Roman institutions as paternal *auctoritas* and marriage in a sexually explicit manner, but was also capable of producing the kind of political satire which might lead to its author's death. The younger Helvidius Priscus is reported by Suetonius as having been executed by Domitian for a mime on (Trojan) Paris and Oenone, which resonated too closely of (Flavian) Paris and Domitia (*Dom.* 10.3). Paris himself was executed in due course, and received from Martial a gentle epitaph, written in the safety of Nerva's Rome (*Ep.* 11.13). Unsurprisingly, Domitian attempted to curb the theatre and restrict performances to private houses (Suet. *Dom.* 7.1). If *Octavia* is Domitianic, a performance (or recitation) in a private house (almost all scenes involve only one or two speaking characters) would clearly have been the most likely.

The imperial peace

Mime and pantomime survived the strictures of the imperial censorship, and flourished at Rome through the second and third centuries CE. Greek tragedy also continued to be performed – not at Rome, but throughout the Roman world, at the festivals held regularly in the main centres of Greek culture. Lucian indeed refers on several occasions to contemporary Greek tragic actors and, in his work on pantomime (*Salt.* 27–9; cf. Philostr. *Vit. Soph.* 1.25), furnishes a highly rhetorical and prejudicial description of such a one in the mid-second century CE. Roman tragic and comic drama, however, seem to have gradually disappeared from the imperial theatrical scene. Pliny records the activities of a comic dramatist friend of his (*Ep.* 7.17.11), and Juvenal rants in his opening satire against the mania for reciting newly composed tragedies (*Sat.* 1.4–6). The satirist also mentions specific contemporary tragic poets and plays – Paccius' *Alcithoe*, Faustus' *Thebae* and *Tereus*, Rubrenus Lappa's *Atreus* (*Sat.* 7.10–12, 71–3)[63] – but there is no reference in his poems to tragic stage performance.

Clearly the practice of reciting tragedies in an auditorium or rich patron's house continued for some time as a form of elite entertainment, and tragic libretti would have regularly accompanied the *tragoedia saltata* of pantomime. No fragments survive. Indeed the great imperial peace under Gibbon's five 'good emperors' (96–180 CE) seems to have been attended by a noticeable dearth of first-rate Roman poets, dramatic or otherwise. With the exception of the satirist Juvenal the major Roman writers wrote in prose. After the brilliant reflorescence of Roman poetic forms in the period from Nero to Domitian, tragedy and epic gave way as serious literary forms to the reflective, analytical prose of the younger Pliny and of Tacitus, the multi-dimensional biographies of Suetonius, the ludic novel of Apuleius – and all literary forms had to compete with the theatrics of the arena.[64] In 69 CE the theatre still served as a public space for the display of citizen grievances (Tac. *Hist.* 1.72 and Suet. *Galba* 13), but the arena eventually took over most of the theatre's political function, providing at the heart of the city and the empire a permanent site for political exhibition, negotiation, confrontation and control. It thus not only refined 'the technology of spectacle as an element of imperial hegemony',[65] but augmented its importance, restructured its power, tied its valency more securely to the emperor, while providing a fixed and potent context for the display of citizen anger and dissent.

Meanwhile, the political pressures on the written word had their effect. Tacitus bruits the new (Trajanic) times as a period of intellectual, political and scribal freedom:

> quod si uita suppeditet, principatum diui Neruae et imperium Traiani, uberiorem securioremque materiam, senectuti seposui, rara temporum felicitate ubi sentire quae uelis et quae sentias dicere licet.
>
> (*Histories* 1.1)

> But if life allow me, I have reserved for old age the principate of deified Nerva and the rule of Trajan, a more fertile and less dangerous subject, owing to the rare felicity of the times when you can think what you wish and say what you think.

But, despite his reassurance in *Agricola* that Nerva and Trajan did the impossible by uniting the concepts of 'the principate and liberty' (*principatus ac libertas*, *Agr.* 3.1), Tacitus never fulfils his promise to write about these 'times of rare felicity'. In his old age he is silent about Trajan's Rome, but not about the imperial system, on which he offers a devastating critique in the form of an 'Annalistic' history of the Julio-Claudian principate. Similar silence is evident in the epigrams of Martial, whose reissued tenth book says little about the contemporary world of imperial power – a subject with which the poet had been obsessed in the first nine books and with which he continued to be obsessed in his eleventh book, written under Nerva before the reissue of Book 10. The main political event to have taken place between the Nervan Book 11 and the second edition of Book 10 was the accession of Trajan. The paradoxical silence of Martial's great successor Juvenal underscores the problematics of freedom in post-Flavian Rome. Famously the Lucilian invective of this most 'indignant' of Rome's satirists is directed not at contemporary Trajanic, political figures but at the famous dead (*Sat.* 1.170–1).

But even as Rome's poetic and critical energies become transmuted and constrained, Greek intellectual life under Rome, as if in ironic fulfilment of some principle of cultural *isonomia*, quickens and grows. The great imperial peace of the second century BCE brought with it both the Greek renaissance now known as the Second Sophistic and – in Roman poetry and Roman tragedy – the liberty of silence. Greek tragedy flourished during the imperial peace and into (perhaps beyond) the third century,[66] as did the imagery of tragedy, whether masks or tragic scenes, on sarcophagi manufactured for the Roman elite;[67] but despite this imagery and despite some kind of sponsorship of drama from the philhellenic emperor, Hadrian (*HA*, *Hadr.* 19.6, 26.4; cf. Athen. *Deipn.* 3.115a–b), Roman tragedy as creative writing or fully staged/ recited performance died. The latter's prime successor in the empire's capital and that empire's many centres of cultural production was not Greek tragedy nor even 'tragic' pantomime, but the arena, whose 'fatal charades' cruelly mimicked the subjects of tragedy and of the *praetexta*, and whose political pragmatics of spectacle and blood enacted – in a potent but less subtle form – the analysis of power and death central to Roman tragedy throughout its evolution.

NOTES

Chapter 1

1 See Appian's highly theatrical account (*BC* 2.146) of Antonius' oration at the funeral of Julius Caesar in 44 BCE. Also Diod. Sic. 31.25.2 for the funeral of Aemilius Paullus.

2 See North (1983), 170.

3 But included by Appian in his description of the same triumph: *Pun.* 66.

4 For a more detailed account of a Roman triumph, see Plutarch on the three-day triumph of Aemilius Paullus in 167 BCE (*Aem.* 32–4).

5 See Versnel (1970), 94–131: 'The three *pompae* [triumphal, funeral and at the circus] are essentially Etruscan' (100). An Etruscan origin was postulated by the ancients not only for the triumphal procession but for the word, *triumphus* (from Greek *thriambos* via Etruscan mediation: Varro *LL* 6.68; Servius *ad Aen.* 10.775). And although aspects of Rome's triumphal rituals, including perhaps the representation of the *triumphator* as Jupiter, may date from *c.* 300 BCE, the central performative ritual of thanksgiving to the great god and the display of the *triumphator*'s own supremacy are probably at least as old as the Capitoline temple itself. See Ogilvie (1965), 272–3.

6 The contrary thesis – that Rome's first attested drama predates the theatricality of Roman political and social life – is presented by Erasmo (2004): 'Only after the establishment of a theatre can the concept of theatricality be recognized by the audience and applied to the interpretation of offstage events' (18). The thesis (to my mind patently false) permeates Erasmo's exposition.

7 So the elder Cato quoted by Cicero (*Tusc.* 4.3). See Zorzetti (1990) and (1991), and Habinek (1998), 36–8.

8 Cic. *Brut.* 72, *Sen.* 50, *Tusc.* 1.3; Aulus Gellius 17.21.42.

9 On Livy and Varro, see Oakley (1998), 43–7.

10 With it should be compared the similar account of Valerius Maximus (2.4.4), itself mainly derived from Livy, on which see Oakley (1998), 776–8.

11 E.g., Etruscan *ister*, from which, as Livy notes, *histrio* ('actor') is derived, seems derived in turn from Greek *histor* ('skilled'). Similarly *scaena* ('stage-building'), *persona* ('mask', 'character'), *ludius/ludio*

('performer') seem to come from Etruscan translations of *skene, prosopon* and *aulodos* ('piper'). See Szemerényi (1975), 307–19.

12 E.g., Wiseman (1994), 10.

13 The thesis of Wiseman (1994), 10 – refuted by Flower (1995), 173–5.

14 As opposed to other Italian languages and to Greek. On the linguistic politics of this period and the expropriation, see Habinek (1998), 39–45.

15 This 'appropriation' was complex in its semiotics, sometimes as much a statement about Roman cultural inferiority, aspirations and evolving identity as it was a 'triumphalist' demonstration of Rome's power. Comments such as that of Habinek (1998), 34, that 'for the Romans, Greek culture, like the Greek population and Greek material wealth, was a colonial resource to be exploited and expropriated' seem to underplay the ambivalence of Rome's relationship to Greece. During the Roman conquest of Magna Graecia and mainland Greece (the third and second centuries BCE) the appropriation of Greek literary forms and the display of 'Greeks' on the Roman tragic and comic stage had a potent imperialist edge. Equally clearly, not only were some of the dramatised 'Greek' myths concerned with Italian/Roman origins, but the Greek-derived theatrical experience was becoming part of what it was to be Roman.

16 Livy's *saturae*, often translated 'medleys', may well refer to some kind of 'satyric' performance: see Beacham (1992), 12, Oakley (1998), 55–8.

17 The chorus was performing the *sikinnis*, a sexually explicit satyr dance, allegedly witnessed by Dionysius himself (7.72.12) in Augustan funeral processions. See Wiseman (1994), 76, who also interprets the *tityristai* of Appian's account of Scipio's triumphal procession in 201 BCE (*Pun.* 66) as 'satyr-dancers'.

18 The case for Etruscan satyric drama has been strongly argued by Szilágyi (1981), and Varro's reference to 'Etruscan tragedy', *tragoedia Tusca*, in the late first century BCE (*LL* 5.55) suggests an even stronger Etruscan theatrical tradition. It seems unlikely that theatricalised early Rome did not produce a simulacrum of this Etruscan heritage.

19 The elder Cato, *Carmen de Moribus*, quoted in Aulus Gellius 11.2.5. According to Cato those who plied their poetic trade for a fee at aristocratic banquets were *grassatores*, 'muggers'.

20 See the references cited by Jocelyn (2000), 341–2, n.131, covering the period 217–199 BCE.

21 The extent to which the comedies of Livius Andronicus were indebted to Greek New Comedy is difficult to evaluate from the surviving fragments and play titles. The latter – *Gladiolus*, 'Little Sword', *Ludius*, 'Player/Dancer', *Virgo*, 'Virgin', or *Verpus*, 'Circumcised' – suggest bawdy, musical farce appropriate to an audience used to the *fabula Atellana*.

22 See Horace *Ep.* 2.1.139–55, where the term is applied to ribald exchanges at harvest-festivals.

23 For the influence of the Roman mid-winter festival of the *Saturnalia* and its inversion of social norms on the development of Roman comedy, see Segal (1968).

24 On some of these local influences, see Beacham (1992), 3–9.

25 Cf. Brooks (1981), 171: 'like the Greek actor-interpolators, the Roman poets kept the great part of the original play, but also cut, expanded and altered many scenes of the play'. For the 'texts' used by early Roman playwrights, see Gentili (1979), 18, Slater (1992), 89. Gentili even argues that contamination was not an innovation of Gnaeus Naevius but 'one of the forms in which Hellenistic theatre developed' (35).

26 The stereotypes included an 'Old Man' (*Pappus*), a 'Buffoon' (*Maccus*), a 'Braggart' (*Bucco*) and a 'Trickster' (*Dossenus*). There was sometimes an ogre (*Manducus*) with huge snapping jaws. Among the titles of Atellan farces surviving: *Maccus the Virgin, Pappus' Bride*.

27 The male children of Rome's nobility wore the *toga praetexta* until their assumption of the *toga uirilis* at the age of sixteen: Isidore 19.24;16.

28 Horace remarks especially on the celebratory function of *praetextae*, seeing a common purpose here with *togatae* to 'celebrate domestic deeds' (*celebrare domestica facta*) as opposed to those of Greece (*Ars* 285–8). However, to reduce all republican *praetextae* to 'theatrical reflections on Rome's rescue from (real or imagined) crisis', as Habinek (2000) 293 does, following Zorzetti 1980, seems misguided.

29 See p. 49.

30 On the similarity of the *praetexta* to tragedy, see, for example, the fourth century CE grammarian Diomedes *Ars Grammatica* 3 (Keil 1. 489). The *praetexta*'s relationship to tragedy has been denied by some modern commentators, who wrongly posit 'panegyric' as a defining feature of the genre. Tacitus, among others, had different ideas; at *Dial.* 2, 3.4, 11.2, he refers to both the *praetextae* and the mythological *tragoediae* of the Vespasianic dramatist Curiatius Maternus as *tragoediae*. For further citations, see Kragelund (2002), 7, n.7, who argues (16–17) that throughout its evolution 'the genre seems to have retained its links to tragedy proper'.

31 A useful analogy may be drawn with Shakespeare's 'history' plays: some are clearly 'tragic' (*Richard II*), others are not (*Henry V*).

32 Or, to use Diomedes' term, *tabernaria*. For Diomedes *Ars Grammatica* 3 (Keil 1. 489), *togata* is an inclusive term, embracing both *praetextae* and *tabernariae*; see also Varro *LL* 6.18, Sen. *Ep.* 8.8. Horace (*Ars Poet.* 288), however, distinguishes firmly between *praetextae* and *togatae*.

33 See Frasinnetti (1953), 45.

34 Leigh (2004), 9–12.

35 For example, *contaminatio* – the purloining and blending of episodes from different previous plays and playwrights, nor only from Greek ones – seems to have been prominent in the *fabula togata*. Afranius defends this practice in the prologue to his *Compitalia* (frags. 27–32 Daviault), where he mentions 'taking' things from both Greek and Latin plays. The Greek borrowings would have to have been 'Italianised'. Among the accusations levelled at him was that he was like Terence.

36 See Wiseman (1994), 68–85, and (1998), 62.

37 See Cic. *Fin.* 2.23.

38 On the theatrical tradition of the *Liberalia* see Wiseman (1998), 35–51, who also cites the Naevius fragment. The amalgamation of

previously separate *ludi* in honour of Liber with those of Ceres is noted by Ovid, *Fas.* 3.783–6.

39 Greek plays were performed at the *Ludi Apollinares* of 44 BCE organised by the absent tyrannicide Brutus as urban praetor (see Cic. *Att.* 16.5.1) and at the opening of Pompey's Theatre in 55 BCE (Cic. *Fam.* 7.1.3). Some evidence suggests, too, the performance of Greek plays by Greek actors at various *ludi uotiui* in the second century BCE. In 186 BCE the *ludi uotiui* of both Marcus Fulvius Nobilior and Lucius Scipio involved Greek *artifices*, who may have been actors, i.e. the Dionysiac *technitai*: Livy 39.22.2, 8–10 (for a sceptical analysis see Gruen, 1992, 195). For plays in Oscan and (possibly) Volscian, see Habinek (1998), 41.

40 For sententiousness, see Sen. *Ep.* 8.8–10 and Gell. *NA* 17.14 on the late republican mimes of Publilius Syrus; for political edge, see the citations on Laberius at n. 57 below.

41 The rites of Cybele (Magna Mater) were notoriously 'alien', and, although the cult of Apollo was an old one in Rome (his temple was dedicated in 431 BCE), the rites of his *ludi* were to be strictly performed in the 'Greek manner' (Livy 25.1–16). See Leigh (2004), 2–3.

42 See Hanson (1959), 85.

43 Gruen (1992), 187, notes that 'such *instaurationes* took place with particular frequency in the late third and early second centuries [BCE]'. The years 200 and 189 BCE are particularly noteworthy: the former witnessed the repetition of one of the performance days of the *Ludi Romani* and a triple repetition of the entire *Ludi Plebeii*; the latter a triple repetition of the *Ludi Romani* and a quintuple repetition of the *Ludi Plebeii,* each in their entirety: Livy 31.50.2–3, 38.35.6. Cicero (*Har. Resp.* 23) elaborates on the grounds for an *instauratio*, which included interruption in the performance, error in the ritual, and (rarely) violent civil commotion.

44 Seventeen is the figure of Hunter (1985), 14; Gratwick (1982), 81, opts for fourteen days, as do Csapo and Slater (1995), 209. The number of days devoted to *ludi scaenici* increased substantially during the empire. It had reached a hundred by 325 CE. See Csapo and Slater (1995), 209; Bieber (1961), 227.

45 See Flower (1995), 181–2.

46 In 65 BCE Julius Caesar presented *munera* in honour of his father, who died in 85 BCE.

47 The first recorded gladiatorial show was that organised by the ex-consul Decimus Iunius Brutus and his brother in 264 BCE in the Forum Boarium to honour their dead father: Livy *Periochae* 16, Valerius Maximus 2.4.7. The show seems to have consisted of three pairs: Ausonius *Griphus* 36–7. Julius Caesar's *munera* in 65 BCE, which featured 320 pairs (Pliny *HN* 33.53, Plut. *Caes.* 5), reveal how the shows increased massively in scale. From 42 BCE onwards gladiatorial shows were included in the official *ludi*: Dio 47.40.

48 The magistrates involved in the organisation of the *ludi* were several and varied. Initially the curule and plebeian aediles, the urban praetor and (rarely) the consuls were involved; later (after 22 BCE) just the praetors. The inaugural *Ludi Florales* are reported to have been organised by the two plebeian aediles (Ovid *Fas.* 5.287), but in 173 BCE, when they were made annual, they were 'discharged' (*persoluere*) by the

consuls Laenas and Postumius (Ovid *Fas.* 5.329–30). Prior to 22 BCE the usual assignment of responsibilities for the other five major *ludi* were: *Ludi Romani* and *Megalenses* to the curule aediles; *Ludi Plebeii* and *Ceriales* to the plebeian aediles; *Ludi Apollinares* to the urban praetor. But it is clear that these assignments were not as rigid as is sometimes maintained. See, for example, Cicero's anticipation (as curule aedile elect) of the honour of organising the various *ludi* for which he would be responsible: *Verr.* 2.5.36. The aediles and other magistrates seem to have kept records (*commentarii*) of the festivals they administered and deposited them with the priestly colleges. Although it is unclear which details would have been recorded, such archives must have been an important source of information for the later writers of the history of the Roman stage. See Jocelyn (1969), 32.

49 Cicero certainly believed in a causal but not necessary relationship between the production of great spectacles as aedile and later political success: *Off.* 2.58–9. See also Cic. *Mur.* 38–40; Val. Max. 2.4.6; Pliny *HN* 36.113–15; Plut. *Sulla* 5.1–2. Even the sceptical Gruen (1992), 190, admits a 'correlation' between the aedileship and the subsequent acquisition of the praetorship.

50 See Cic. *Leg. Agr.* 2.71 on the Roman people's 'due'.

51 E.g., the Senatus Consulta of 187 and 179 BCE (Livy 39.5.7–10; 40.44.8–12). In 22 BCE Augustus not only handed control of the *ludi* to the praetors but severely restricted the cost to the magistrates involved (Dio 54.2.3–4).

52 Festus (436L) also preserves the testimony of the Augustan scholar, Verrius Flaccus, as to the existence of *parasiti Apollinis* ('parasites of Apollo'), a group, even guild of actors, during the Hannibalic war. See further n. 60 below.

53 The movement of the Roman playwrights towards greater social status was a gradual one. Accius was clearly a pivotal figure (see pp. 111–2). But I do not join Jocelyn (1967a), 5–6, in thinking that rare references by Plautus to Latin versions of Greek tragedies by the name of the 'original' Greek author rather than that of the Roman 'translator' (e.g., the *Achilles* of Aristarchus at Plautus *Poen.* 1 is Ennius' version) show that the names of Roman playwrights carried little 'weight' in the minds of the early Roman audience. All such a practice reveals (apart from professional playfulness on the part of Plautus, who shows that he knows Ennius' tragedies well) is that the play's status as a version of a Greek play was known to that audience, who were clearly familiar with the names, if not the works, of a range of Greek dramatists (see, e.g., *Most.* 1149).

54 On this see Horsfall (1976), and further p. 143.

55 See, e.g., Cic. *Rep.* 4.10, which mentions that actors were not only deprived of the rights of other citizens (*honos ciuium reliquorum*) but removed by the censors from the tribal lists. The Ciceronian passage occurs in a fictive conversation of 129 BCE, which itself refers to the prohibition as in the past, clearly indicating that Romans of the late republic thought that the prohibitions on actors were in force from the early days of the Roman theatre. See also Csapo and Slater (1995), 276–7, and 288, which features the Senatus Consultum from Larinum (19 CE), discovered in 1978 and discussed in detail by Levick (1983).

56 For the detailed organisation of these Guilds, which seem to have originated at the beginning of the third century BCE, see Lightfoot (2002),
and also Jory (1970), who, however, probably exaggerates the influence
of the Dionysiac Guilds on the formation of *collegia* at Rome. See the
criticisms of Jory by Brown (2002), 227.

57 The most notorious case was that of Decimus Laberius, the writer of
mimes, in which he was compelled by Julius Caesar to perform, losing
as a consequence his equestrian status. Caesar later restored him to
equestrian rank. See Macr. *Sat.* 2.7.1–8; Sen. *Con.* 7.3.9; Suet. *Iul.*
39.2. That some members of the senatorial and equestrian classes were
keen to appear on the stage seems indicated by explicit senatorial
decrees banning their appearance (in 38 BCE, 22 BCE and 19 CE). The
decrees seem to have proved less than totally effective, being breached
even by Augustus (Suet. *Aug.* 43.3). See Levick (1983).

58 See Suet. *Aug.* 45.3, where Augustus restricts this power of the magistrates to the 'games' (*ludi*) and 'theatre' (*scaena*).

59 The issue of the legal rights and restrictions of the acting profession is a
complex one, not helped by the initial legal imprecision of the concept
of *infamia*. See Levick (1983), 108–10, Edwards (1993), 123–6. Some
(e.g. Frank 1931, 19, Jory 1970, 230–3) have argued that the social
position of actors in the Rome of Naevius and Plautus was somewhat
better than in the late republic and that actors were not so much barred
from military service as exempt from it on the model of the members of
Dionysiac Guilds. Such a theory encounters many difficulties, not the
least of which is the fact that most actors (slaves, foreigners, non-Roman
citizens) would not have been eligible for military service (unlike the
Greek citizens of the Dionysiac Guilds). It seems overwhelmingly likely
(and this accords with Livy's tone and with the later stigmatisation)
that the ban on actors *per se* was a way of sending a powerful message to
any Roman citizen contemplating acting on the stage. Perhaps, as
Brown (2002), 228, notes, the reason why actors in Atellan plays were
not obliged to remove their masks at the end of a performance (Festus
217 M) was precisely because no check was necessary in that context on
whether any of the actors were Roman citizens.

60 On these several 'guilds', ranging from the *collegium* of *scribae* and
histriones, 'Guild of Writers and Actors', and the *collegium poetarum*,
'Guild of Poets', to the *collegium tibicinum Romanorum*, 'Guild of Roman
Flautists', and the *collegium fidicinum Romanorum*, 'Guild of Roman
Lyre-Players', see Jory (1970), who also (237–42) discusses the organisation known as the 'Parasites of Apollo' (*parasiti Apollinis*). This
last-mentioned association was of mimes. Perhaps modelled on the
collegium of *scribae* and *histriones*, and possibly dating from the second
century BCE, the association was initially of very low social standing,
but seems to have increased in prestige during the imperial period
when mime and pantomime began to dominate theatrical entertainment. On the *collegium* of *scribae* and *histriones* and the *collegium
poetarum*, see further p. 35.

61 See Hunter (1985), 15.

62 The evidence for the retention of the Greek chorus in early Roman
tragedy is clear, despite occasional doubt on the matter expressed by
some commentators. See the discussion of Jocelyn (1967a), 19–20.

63 See Jocelyn (1967a), 46–7.

64 E.g., Beacham (1992), 184–5. If Beacham is right, then they seem to have disappeared in the late second century BCE to be reintroduced in the first. See Chapter 5 n. 14. Accius in his *Didascalica* discusses the distorted masks known as *miriones* (Varro *LL* 7.64), but the implications of that discussion for the use of masks in tragedy or comedy in the third and second centuries remains obscure.

65 This difficult question is discussed by Beare (1964), 267–74.

66 Brown (2002), 229.

67 For *spectatores*, see also Hor. *Ep.* 2.178, 215, etc.

68 In 179 BCE a stage and auditorium were constructed near the Temple of Apollo (Livy 40.51.3), presumably for the *Ludi Apollinares*. For the *ludi scaenici* of the *Ludi Megalenses* held in the narrow playing space in front of the Temple of Magna Mater on the Palatine, see Cic. *Har.* 24. See generally Hanson (1959). For *ludi scaenici* in the Circus Maximus see the account of the (in)famous games of Lucius Anicius Gallus in 167 BCE at Polybius 30.22.1–12 (Athenaeus 14.615).

69 An average imperial stage might be 50 m wide, 8 m deep and 1.5 m high. See Csapo and Slater (1995), 85. No wooden theatre of course survives, but the surviving plays of Plautus and Terence indicate a stage of very considerable width. The stage of Rome's first stone theatre, that of Pompey's Theatre, was *c.* 90 m wide.

70 The theatre of Syracuse was dedicated *c.* 460 BCE; Tarentum and Metapontum had stone theatres dating to the fourth century. The large theatre of Pompeii, with seating for 5,000, dates from *c.* 200 BCE.

71 Livy 40.51.3, 41.27.5, *Periochae* 48; Val. Max. 2.4.2; Appian *BC* 1.28; Orosius 4.21.4.

72 See p. 109.

73 Rawson (1991), 581, sees the force to be essentially a unifying one. But its social demarcations divided as well as unified, and its potential for political criticism became increasingly realised in the late republic.

74 Much is made of this in the analysis of the relationship between the Roman 'theatre and aristocratic culture' by Gruen (1992), 183–222. Gruen's focus, however, simply on the theatre as 'a setting for the articulation and propagation of aristocratic values' derives essentially from a concentration on Terence and distorts the complexity and diversity of Roman theatrical entertainment and its corresponding complex and diverse cultural effects.

75 Livy *Per.* 48; Vell. Pat. 1.15.3; Appian *BC* 1.28.

76 See Gruen (1992), 209–10.

77 Gruen (1992), 185, is appropriately cautious about drawing inferences from the politics of the theatre in the 'turbulent' last decades of the republic to the theatre of a hundred or so years earlier. Yet Cicero himself draws attention to the political use of the theatre in the days of the Gracchi and Saturninus (*Sest.* 105), and the senatorial destruction of the censorial theatre in 151 BCE shows that 'turbulent' theatrical politics existed before the age of the Gracchi.

78 The Greek inhabitants of Rome in the late second century BCE seem to have been predominantly slaves: see Kaimio (1979), 22.

79 Goldberg (1998), 13–14.

80 The conservative estimate is that of Richardson (1992), *ad loc*. Others opt for the same number of *spectatores* as *loca* in the Regionary Catalogue (= approximately 17,000 for the Theatre of Pompey, 20,000 for the Theatre of Marcellus). Goldberg (1996), 266 n. 1, (1998), 13, and Erasmo (2004), 83, seem to accept the impossible number of 40,000 for the Theatre of Pompey found in the text of Pliny (*HN* 36.115). The same Pliny passage puts the capacity of the *cauea* of the Theatre of Scaurus at 80,000. Something has clearly gone wrong with these numbers. Most estimate that even the Colosseum held only 50,000.

81 See p. 150.

82 Livy 34.44.5, 54.3–8; Cic. *Har. Resp.* 24; Val. Max. 2.4.3. On popular discontent over the seating this ancient testimony is more persuasive than the sceptical arguments of Gruen (1992), 204–5.

83 See pp. 153, 184, 262 n. 42.

Chapter 2

1 See Livy's famous 7.2 notice quoted on pp. 8–9, in which no mention is made of his namesake's Greekness and the 'Greek' *cognomen*, 'Andronicus', is omitted. Livy similarly fails to mention the Greek models of Livius' plays and the vital dramatic traditions of Greek Southern Italy and Sicily. See also Erasmo (2004), 155.

2 The ancient evidence for the life of Livius Andronicus is far from consistent. The earliest extant discussion of the chronological problems is that of Cicero, *Brutus* 72–4. For modern discussions of the conflicting *testimonia* see Gratwick (1982), 128; Drury (1982), 799–801; Kaster (1995), 48–50.

3 See Kaster (1995), *ad loc.*

4 *Antiquissimum carmen*: Charisius *GL* 1.84.6 Keil.

5 Or, at least, so the Romans thought. The issue is much debated. Varro (*LL* 5.42) connected the Saturnian verse (a short line of two cola with the first longer than the second) with the notion of Italy, esp. Latium, as the land of Saturn. At the time when Livius wrote his epic, Saturnians seem to have been used for (*inter alia*) the monumental epitaphs of Roman aristocrats and dedicatory and triumphal inscriptions. The metre may have been thought to give a 'monumental' feel to Livius' epic.

6 Prior to Livius translation seems to have been confined in the Mediterranean world to utilitarian state documents: i.e. political, religious and legal texts.

7 Cicero's employment of the word *fabula* on its own (*Brut.* 72, *Sen.* 50, *Tusc.* 1.3) is more appropriate to a tragedy than a comedy. See also Gell. 17.21.42. See Gratwick (1982), 128; Erasmo (2004), 155.

8 See also Cic. *Sen.* 50, *Tusc.* 1.3. Gellius 17.21.42 shows that the testimony is derived from Varro's *De Poetis*.

9 Dramatic performances at Tarentum are attested from the start of the fourth century BCE; the stone theatre there dates from the third century BCE. See Jory (1970), 228.

10 See also Festus 448L. The view of Brown (2002), 226, that Livy 'possibly ... refers to solo performances of some kind' seems difficult to accept in the context.

11 Cornell (1995), 68.

12 See Suerbaum (2000), 188–9.

13 See pp. 18 and 35.

14 Drury (1982), 800, is sceptical on this matter.

15 Victorinus *Ars Gram.*: *GL* Keil 6.67–8; Ter. Maur. 1931–8. Both are cited in Klotz 27. For a sceptical interpretation of the evidence, see Wigodsky (1972), 18–20. The absence of the chorus from Roman comedy is clearly related to the decline of its importance in Greek New Comedy, in which it seems to have had no relation to the dramatic action. See Hunter (1985), 9–10.

16 For the former: Warmington 2.3; for the latter: Blänsdorf (2000), 152.

17 *Noxia* and *noxa* occur in the *Twelve Tables* (e.g. *Table* 8.6 and 10; 12.2a–b).

18 I adopt *haece uostrum* of Warmington 2.4 rather than the *haec uostrorum* of Klotz.

19 The passage is quoted on p. 56.

20 Blänsdorf (2000), 150.

21 Erasmo (2004), 13, raises the possibility that Hiero's visit was motivated by 'the opportunity to see a Greek play performed in Latin'.

22 See Jory (1970), 224, who, however, exaggerates the connection between the Roman *Collegium* and the Greek Guilds.

23 So, too, Erasmo (2004), 11. But note that Cicero's Daedalus comment applies to Livius' epic, not (as in Erasmo) to the tragedies.

24 See Wigodsky (1972), 18.

25 According to Gellius, this epitaph was written by Naevius himself. Several have questioned Gellius' testimony.

26 After the Latin war of 338 BCE Roman citizenship without the vote was 'awarded' to Campanian towns (Livy 8.14.10), which, however, had not received suffrage even by the Second Punic War. See Oakley (1998), 559.

27 See Jocelyn (1969), 42, for whom, however, 201 BCE is 'a post-Varronian guess'.

28 Livy *Per.* 20; Prop. 4.10.39–44; Plut. *Marc.* 8.

29 It involves changing the ms. 'Novius' to 'Naevius' in the commentary of Servius Auctus on Virg. *Geo.* 1.266.

30 The descent of the Iulii was through Aeneas' son, Iulus or Ascanius; that of the Aemilii was through a daughter of Aeneas, Aemilia (Plutarch *Rom.* 2.3), or a grandson, Aemulus (Festus 23M). The claims may be later than the third century. The Acilii Glabriones also claimed descent from Aeneas, and many Roman families claimed descent from one of his comrades: see Jocelyn (2000), 332–4, who documents the focus on Rome's Trojan origins in the late third and early second centuries. The genealogical picture, however, is complicated by the fact that, as Jocelyn also observes, one Roman family (the Mamilii) claimed descent from the Greek Ulysses, and two (the Fabii and Antonii) from the Greek demi-god, Hercules. This did not, however, affect Rome's image of itself as 'Troy-born'.

31 See Erasmo (2004), 16.

32 Lefèvre (2000).

33 Lefèvre (2000), 181–2.

34 On further ramifications of this prologue, see Chapter 3, p. 64.

35 So Warmington (1936), *ad loc.*

36 For the former, Lefèvre (2000), 181–2; for the latter, Warmington 2.113.

37 For the dream in Sochocles' *Acrisius*, see Sutton (1984), 4.

38 *Ferat* is the ms. reading in the source for the fragment, accepted by Ribbeck, but not by Klotz.

39 Lefèvre (2000), 182.

40 Klotz begins the line with *hi*.

41 The text of this fragment has been much questioned.

42 The phrase *regalis corporis* seems modelled on such Aeschylean periphrases as *metroion demas*, 'maternal body' = 'mother' (*Eum.* 84).

43 *Pauos* is omitted by Klotz.

44 Ribbeck's conjecture *transtros* displaces *Traces* in Klotz.

45 Beard *et al.* (1998), 1.93.

46 See Beard *et al.* (1998), 1.91.

47 Livy 29.10.4–11.8; 29.14.5–14; 34.54; Ovid *Fas.* 4.247–348.

48 See Beard *et al.* (1998), 1.97.

49 Flower (2000), 28 and note 30.

50 In the late republic and early empire other occasions were sometimes used for the taking of the *toga uirilis*, but at this time (the end of the third century) the *Liberalia* was 'the regular one': Fowler (1899), 56.

51 *Praetextata* is a coinage of the later grammarians. Asinius Pollio (Cic. *Fam.* 10.32.3 and 5) as well as Horace call the literary form the *praetexta*. See the comments of Brink (1971), 320.

52 Much depends on what one thinks the 'Etruscan tragedies' (*Tuscae tragoediae*) of a certain Volnius were: Varro *LL* 5.55.

53 For a full discussion of the ancient sources, including Euanthius *De Fabula* 4.1, Festus 249L and 480L, Hor. *AP* 285–8 and scholiasts *ad loc*, see Manuwald (2001), 9–52. For a recent account of the *praetexta*, see also Erasmo (2004), 52–80.

54 See Gratwick (1982), 128.

55 The dramatic spectacle (perhaps from a *praetexta* on the Fall of Corinth) described by Horace at *Ep.* 2.1.189–93 is explicitly compared by the scholiasts to a 'triumphal procession', *pompa triumphalis*: see Brink (1982), *ad loc.*

56 The attempt of Flower (1995) to exclude funeral and triumphal games is unpersuasive.

57 Livy 27.25.6–10; 29.11.13; Plut. *Marc.* 28.1; Val. Max. 1.1.8.

58 I reached this judgement before reading Lebek (2000), 82–4, and Kragelund (2002), 23, who similarly find this context the most attractive one.

59 E.g. Bernstein (2000), who favours a production date in the especially difficult year of 207 BCE.

60 See Ribbeck (1875), 75.

61 See Ribbeck (1875), 75.

62 See Manuwald (2001), 142.

63 Petrone (2000), 118.

64 E.g. by Goldberg (2003), 29–30.

65 For details of the Romulean myth in Naevius and Ennius, see Skutsch, 212–13.

66 Marcellus' consulships: 222, 215 (suffect), 214, 210, 208 BCE.

67 An index of continuing Scipionic sensitivities about Clastidium can be seen in the account of Polybius (2.34–5) in the middle of the next century. The pro-Scipionic Polybius considerably exaggerates the role of Gnaeus Scipio in the victory.

68 Scipios: Cic. *De Or.* 2.249, Gell. 8.5–6; the Metelli: Caesius Bassus, *GL* 6.266 Keil; Ps. Asconius *ad Cic. Verr.* 1.29, 2. 215 Stangl; Jer. *Chron.* ad Ol. 144.3.

69 See the judicious discussion of Jocelyn (1969), 34–7.

70 Caesius Bassus, *GL* 6.266 Keil; Ps. Asconius *ad Cic. Verr.* 1.29, 2. 215 Stangl. For a thorough, if finally unsatisfactory, evaluation of the evidence concerning Naevius, the Scipios and Metelli, see Jocelyn (1969). The Naevian line seems to be echoed by Horace at the start of his second book of *Odes* (*motum ex Metello consule ciuicum*, 'Civil commotion from Metellus' consulship', *Odes* 2.1.1).

71 Cf. Mattingly (1960), 420: 'They publicly posted it as a pasquinade.'

72 E.g. Jocelyn (1969), 47.

73 Mattingly (1960), 432–8, also attributes it to *Clastidium*, which, however, he dates to the triumphal games of the younger Marcellus in 195 BCE with a postulated revival of the play in 115 BCE.

74 The relevant law is quoted below in Chapter 5, n. 43.

75 Because of his idiosyncratic view of *fato* (= 'with predictable disaster') Jocelyn (1969), 47, even favours 207 BCE, but does not assert it strongly.

76 The rejection of the story of Naevius' exile by Jocelyn (1969), 42, on the grounds of Naevius' low social status fails to persuade. Naevius was a *poeta cliens* of the Marcelli, and, just as an insult from Naevius was an insult from the Marcelli, so driving their *poeta cliens* into exile was a form of retribution against them. It is of interest to note that Ovid never uses his (relatively) low social status as an argument against his exile.

Chapter 3

1 Line arrangement according to Sedgwick (1960) and Christenson (2000). On the complexity of the Roman concept of *uirtus*, see Chapter 2, p. 34.

2 The *cantica* at *Bacch.* 932ff. and *Cas.* 621ff. may even parody Ennius' *Andromacha* (frag. xxvii Jocelyn, quoted on p. 68). See Hunter (1985), 121–6. On paratragedy at *Pseud.* 702ff., see Slater (1985), 134.

3 See Gratwick (1982), 133, and (for analysis of the *Amphitruo* passage quoted in the text) 130. On the *Amphitruo* passage, see also O'Neill (2003), 7–8.

4 See Hunter (1985), 114.

5 See Leigh (2000), 290. On the sophisticated audience for early Roman tragedy, see Erasmo (2004), 28–30.

6 Skutsch (1985), 1; Nepos *Cato* 1.4; Broughton (1951–60), 1.310. The scepticism of Badian (1971), 158, has not been generally accepted.

7 To regard the *amicitia*, 'friendship', between aristocrat and poet as simply reducible to the practical relationship of patron and client without any emotional bond or 'mutual fondness' seems mistaken. See Konstan (1996), 135–7.

8 For a discussion of the relevant evidence, see Badian (1971), 168–95.

9 E.g., Plautus' *Poenulus* seems to allude in its opening lines to Ennius' *Achilles*: see Jocelyn, 164–7. The Euripidean *Alcumena* referred to at *Rudens* 86 was presumably that of a Roman tragedian.

10 Some scholars argue for a single *Medea*.

11 Some of the separately titled Ennian poems, such as *Scipio*, may have been part of the *Saturae*.

12 Sil. It. 12.410; see also Lucr. 1.117–19.

13 Propertius 4.1.61: 'ragged' (*hirsuta ... corona*); Ovid *Am.* 1.15.19: 'artless' (*arte carens*). See also Horace *Ep.* 2.1. 50–2.

14 On the tragic vocabulary and syntax: Jocelyn (1972b), 1018; on characterisation (Ilia as 'one of his [Ennius'] dramatic heroines'): Gratwick (1982), 61.

15 *Origines*, written by Ennius' old patron Cato, appeared later in the 160s or even in the 150s BCE.

16 The historians even give specific (if different) dates for the onset of *luxuria*: Polybius 168 BCE; Lucius Piso 154 BCE; Sallust 146 BCE; Livy 187 BCE.

17 The senate decree of 186 BCE severely circumscribing Bacchic worship (*Senatus Consultum de Bacchanalibus*) is a case in point. So too the senate decree in 161 BCE expelling philosophers and rhetoricians from the city, and its action in 151 BCE in tearing down the (almost completed) stone theatre near the Lupercal (Vell. Pat. 1.15.3).

18 See Beacham (1999), 29, who nominates the triumphal games of Anicius Gallus in 167 BCE as an occasion where painting was most likely used on the facade.

19 See Chapter 1, n. 82.

20 For the story, see Cic. *Arch.* 22; Livy 38.56.4; Skutsch: 2.

21 That this percentage is not misleading seems confirmed by a similar percentage (67 per cent: 56 per cent recitative, 11 per cent *cantica*) of 'musical' lines in extant Plautine comedy.

22 On self and other in early Roman tragedy, see Manuwald (2000).

23 *Muttire*, 'mutter', occurs only here in extant Roman tragedy. The word occurs often in comedy, where it is primarily used of slaves: see Jocelyn *ad loc*. The 'servile' nature of the word reinforces the ideology of the whole line and its contemporary social application. Interestingly the ex-slave Phaedrus learned it as a *sententia* when a boy.

24 I have preferred the conjecture, *addecet*, of Carrio, to Jocelyn's reading.

25 Skutsch (1968), 174–6.

26 The view, too, substantially of Erasmo (2004), 9, 16, 22, 28–30, etc., who nevertheless seeks to argue a movement in the Roman tradition from 'theatre' to 'metatheatre' (44) or 'from tragedy to metatragedy' (137). The present book argues no such movement, but rather the evolution in respect of both Roman tragedy and Roman political and cultural life of an interdependent and increasing theatrical self-consciousness which was there from the start.

27 Warmington's translation (1. 289) slightly amended.

28 The observations of K. J. Reckford (1981), 10, are worth quoting. For Reckford the line suggests 'not so much terror, as a momentary sense of the mysterious riches and fascination of the underworld, much as those are depicted in an Etruscan tomb-painting'.

29 See Jocelyn, *ad loc.*

30 See Jocelyn's comments on the stated plays.

31 An interpretation first suggested by Fraenkel (1922), 238. See also Brooks (1981), 237–40.

32 Warmington 1.299.

33 Jocelyn *ad loc.*

34 For details, see Wigodsky (1972), 78.

35 *Animus* is listed as a possible substitute for the ms. *alter*, daggered by Jocelyn.

36 The opening of Catullus 64 self-consciously picks up the opening of Ennius' *Medea*. Catullus' presentation of the abandoned Ariadne in poem 64 is deeply indebted to Ennius' play; Virgil's 'dramatic' realisation of the abandoned Dido seems indebted to both Catullus and Ennius. Virgil was steeped in both Ennian epic and Ennian tragedy, and several debts to the latter are noted by imperial commentators (see, e.g., Macrobius *Sat.* 6.2.21 on *Cres.* frag. lix Jocelyn).

37 Gratwick (1982), 131–2.

38 As by Jocelyn *ad loc.* The lines were perhaps spoken to Achilles by Priam.

39 'Un poids politique': Dupont (1985), 326.

40 On the theme of cultural isolation and the political resonances of Corinth, see Vogt-Spira (2000), esp. 273–4.

41 See Wright (1931), 50.

42 So Goldberg (2000), 57, who notes that *Rhetorica ad Herennium* also cites Ennius' *Iphigenia* (*Rhet. Her.* 3.34).

43 See Erasmo (2004), 23.

44 See Vogt-Spira (2000), 270.

45 Vogt-Spira (2000), 271, also notes the importance here of *custos*.

46 The use of this word in the phrase, *gradus eliminat* ('unthresholds steps'), featured in a celebrated debate about tragic language between Pomponius Secundus and Seneca, witnessed by Quintilian. See Chapter 6, p. 185.

47 See Chapter 2, n. 42.

48 See Brooks (1981), 182–3.

49 See, e.g., Plaut. *Most.* 473; *Miles* 990. For the criticism of bombast, see Brooks (1981), 183; on the dramatic context of the line see Skutsch (1968), 172, who similarly allocates it to the Tutor early in the play.

50 Line 1 is not printed as an Ennian fragment by Jocelyn, who retains Cicero's *habebant*. Line 2, not in Jocelyn, is based on the discussion in Skutsch (1968), 168–9.

51 I read *parire* with Skutsch (1968), 188–90, rather than *parere* with Jocelyn.

52 See Skutsch (1968), 167, to whose excellent remarks on this fragment I am indebted.

53 See Jocelyn, 362. Contrast the false antithesis of Gratwick (1982), 134, who argues that 'we seem to be listening to a Roman magistrate rather than a Medea'. In the political context of Roman tragic production we necessarily hear Roman debates in the speeches of mythic figures.

54 Here I have adopted the reading of Skutsch (1968), 170–2.

55 Jocelyn, 356–7.

56 So Gratwick (1982), 136.

57 The Euripidean passage is strangely ignored by Erasmo (2004), 27.

58 For perfect subjunctives in Roman prayers, see the examples listed by Vahlen (1928), 171–2.

59 *Medea Colchis* is the conjecture of Lipsius. Jocelyn (frag. cxv) reads (*mede*) *cordis*.

60 See Tarrant (1985), 40.

61 Jocelyn, 426.

62 Jocelyn, 413.

63 I read *brabium*, 'prize', with Lindsay and Warmington, for the ms. *babium*.

64 Skutsch (1985), 314.

65 Pliny *HN* 35.66; see also Cic. *Arch.* 27, and *CIL* 6.1307.

66 Further on this temple, see Boyle (2003b), 269–71.

67 Again I find myself reaching independently a view held by Kragelund (2002), 23–4.

68 Buecheler's *domi* is preferred to Ribbeck's *minis*, accepted by Klotz. For fuller details on this difficult line, see Manuwald (2001), 162.

69 *Cunctato* of Vahlen (1928) is preferred to *cunctat* of Klotz.

70 So conjectures Erasmo (2004), 73, adding that the speaker may be Nobilior.

71 On this see La Penna (2000), esp. 249–50.

72 See Jocelyn (1972a), 82–8; on moral perversity exposed through inscription, also Eur. *Tro.* 1188–91.

73 The 'competing realities' theory of Erasmo (2004), 4–5, who differentiates sharply between so-called 'onstage reality … (= illusory drama)' and the 'offstage reality' of the audience, seems to misdescribe the relationship between Roman tragedy and its audience. Roman tragedy was always to some degree metatragic (see pp. 65–6), and, though often psychologically profound, never simply 'illusory drama'. And it had from the beginning (see, e.g, the discussion of Naevius' *Lucurgus* on pp. 47–9), a strong relationship to, and bearing on, the audience's world. A religious and social ritual, in which both *spectator* and actor participated, Roman tragedy served to figure the audience's 'reality', complementing rather than competing with it, adding to its texture. In the late republic and early empire, as Roman public life became both increasingly and more self-consciously theatricalised, the distinction between 'figure' and 'reality' began to dissolve. See especially Chapter 6, pp. 180–3.

74 Cicero (*Op.Gen.*1.2) lists Ennius as the best epic poet, Pacuvius as the best tragedian, and Caecilius as (perhaps) the best comic dramatist.

75 The name, *Pacuuius*, is Oscan.

76 The above thirteen tragedies are those accepted by Manuwald (2003), 23–6, following D'Anna (1967). Klotz and Valsa (1957) also opt for thirteen tragedies, excluding *Orestes* but including a *Protesilaus*. A *Thyestes* is also attributed to Pacuvius by Fulgentius, *Serm. Ant.* 57.

77 On Pacuvius' theatrical acclaim see Cic. *Am.* 24, *Fin.* 5.63; Pliny *HN* 35.19. For evidence that Pacuvius had his own poet-pupils: Varro *Men.* frag. 356. See D'Anna (1967), 14.

78 The main evidence for the *saturae* are Porphyrio on Hor. *Sat.* 1.10.46, and Diomedes *GL.* 1.485 Keil.

79 Compare Ennius' 'friendship' with Cato on p. 58. And see n. 7.

80 See Fantham (2003), 102, Manuwald (2003), 39.

81 For possible traces of this and the other obscure Pacuvian narratives in the visual record, see Manuwald (2003), 31–2.

82 Beacham (1992), 121, wrongly states that *Iliona* and *Medus* are based on Sophoclean originals.

83 D'Anna (1967), 21, for example, justifiably questions whether Pacuvius' *Periboea* is as dependent on Euripides' *Oeneus* as is usually asserted.

84 'La fusione di due tragedie sofoclee': D'Anna (1967), 20.

85 See Baier (2000), 297–8.

86 E.g., Fantham (2003), 114, n. 66. See also Slater (2000), 315–16.

87 First noted by Ribbeck (1875), 255–8. See also D'Anna (1967), 20, Gratwick (1982), 136.

88 Klotz reverses the (Ciceronian) order of lines 3 and 4 of the fragment.

89 E.g. Pacuvius' use of Pindar in *Armorum Iudicium*: D'Anna (1967), 20.

90 The final line has particular difficulties and is constituted variously. The reading here is that of D'Anna (1967), 79.

91 See Valsa (1957), 102, and (for Pacuvian rhetoric generally) 91–116.

92 According to Gratwick (1982), 137, n. 1, the first occurrence in extant Greek literature of the image of Fortuna standing on a ball is at Cebes, *Pinax* 7. The *Pinax* has, however, been variously dated; most scholars regard it as either Hellenistic or early imperial.

93 See, for example, the description of the triumphal procession of Paullus in 167 BCE (Livy 45.33.5–6).

94 See Plut. *Paul.* 6.8–10; 28.11.

95 See Gruen (1992), 65–6.

96 One such attempt took place in 161 BCE, perhaps a year before the performance of Pacuvius' *Paulus*: Suet. *Gram. et Rhet.* 25.1–2.

97 See Petaccia (2000).

98 See Fantham (2003), 101.

99 E.g. *Dulorestes* frags xxvi–xxvii Klotz.

100 The riddle in *Antiopa* depends on the double meaning of *testudo* as 'tortoise' and 'lyre' (tortoise-shell). It may already have been deployed in Euripides' *Antiope*: see Kambitsis (1972), 28.

101 See Slater (1992), 86–98.

102 See also Livy's use of it at 8.6.11.

103 See Beare (1964), 81, who wrongly contrasts Pacuvian practice with that of Seneca.

104 I read *hic* with D'Anna (1967) rather than *his* with Klotz.

105 *Clupeat* ('shields') only occurs here and in the Pacuvian source; *lapit* ('stones') here, in the source, and in Festus.

106 If, as some ancient and modern commentators suggest, Virgil's famous stage simile at *Aen.* 4. 469–73 is a reference to Pacuvius: see Servius *ad Aen.* 4.473, Manuwald (2003), 115.

107 The ghost rose from the recess under the stage-floor, normally used to store the curtain during performance: Beare (1964), 269; Cic. *Sest.* 126. On one notorious occasion the actor Fufius, playing Iliona, actually fell asleep: Porphyrio on Hor. *Sat.* 2.3.60.

108 On the double action of *Atalanta* and its innovative aspects, see Fantham (2003), 108.

109 Fantham (2003), 108, compares the double action of Terence's earliest comedy, *Andria*.

110 See Slater (2000), 322.

111 Bilišski (1957), 26.

112 See Flower (2000), 29.

113 For a painstaking analysis of the thematic dimension of the Pacuvian fragments, see Manuwald (2003), 43–110.

114 See Slater (2000), 318–20.

115 *Aude ecuoluere* is Ribbeck's conjecture, not adopted by Klotz.

116 See Tarrant (1978), 243.

117 See Nauck (1926), 967.

118 See Wright (1931), 60.

119 For a substantially different order, based on a tendentious reconstruction of Sophocles' *Teucer* and Pacuvius' hypothesised adaptation of it, see Sutton (1984), 132–9.

120 Sutton (1984), 135, thinks that the person arriving from Troy might be Ulysses, but the evident tone of this line tells against it.

121 A possibility raised by Valsa (1957), 47.

122 This line is variously constituted.

123 I print Hermann's conjecture, *adfligere*, cited but not accepted by Klotz.

124 Again lines which are variously constituted. This is the version of Hermann, cited by Klotz.

125 Bergk's *canunt* is accepted for the ms. *canant* in Klotz.

126 E.g. Fantham (2003), 100, who also suggests that the description might be part of a choral ode. D'Anna (1967), 229–30, seems (somewhat unclearly) to regard the speaker as Teucer.

127 Warmington 2.292–7, Klotz and Valsa (1957), 48–9, for whom they form part of Teucer's 'apologie'.

128 The quotation is from Fantham (2003), 100. For the influence on Virgil, see Wigodsky (1972), 85–6.

129 On the alliterative patterns of frag. 10, see D'Anna (1967), 229–30.

130 Ribbeck's *proliciendo* displaces the ms. *praeficiendo* in Klotz.

131 Valsa (1957), 47, attributes the remark to Oeleus, who may have been a character in Sophocles' *Teucer*. Cicero, *Tusc.* 3.71, provides very uncertain evidence for such. There is, however, no indication that Oeleus appeared in Pacuvius' play.

132 Cicero's comments are quoted in full on pp. 146–7.

133 The readings here are those of Ribbeck.

134 See Syrus *Sent.* 685: *patria sua est ubicumque uixeris bene*: 'Fatherland is wherever you have lived well'.

135 See D'Anna (1967), 167; Manuwald (2001), 181; Kragelund (2002), 44 n. 116.

136 Garton (1972), 55, opts for the triumphal games, but there is no evidence for this, as Flores (1974), 154, points out. Valsa (1957), 51, Tandoi (1992b), and Kragelund (2002), 24, favour the funeral games of 160 BCE.

137 Plutarch *Rom.* 2.3 mentions a genealogy for the Gens Aemilia which went back to a daughter of Aeneas, Aemilia (and thus through Aeneas to Venus and Jupiter). Festus (23M) traces the line back to Aemulus, a son of Aeneas' son Ascanius.

138 See D'Anna (1967), 233.

139 I have returned to the ms. reading, *sancto*, in preference to Hermann's conjecture, *sancte*, adopted by Klotz. For other readings, see Manuwald (2001), 180.

140 See Ribbeck (1875), 330.

141 Lucil. Bk 5, frag. 211, Bk 26, frags 604–6, 610–16, 620–1, 623, Bk 29, frags 842–4 Krenkel; Mart. *Epig.* 11.90.6. Persius (1.77–8) famously called Pacuvius' *Antiopa* 'carbuncular' or 'warty' (*uerrucosa*), doubly alluding to Antiopa's ragged physical appearance and the play's linguistic excrescences, which the satirist exemplified in a parodic use of the Pacuvian or Pacuvianesque adjective, *luctificabile*. On Pacuvius' later reception, see also Erasmo (2004), 42.

142 Cic. *Sest.* 126; Hor. *Sat.* 2.3.60–2; Cic. *Off.* 1.114.

143 *De Orat.* 1.246, 2.193, *Tusc.* 5.108.

Chapter 4

1 The prohibition proved short-lived. The triumphal games of Lucius Mummius in 145 BCE featured public seating. In addition to the passages cited, see Oros. 4.21.4; Val. Max. 2.4.2; App. *BC* 1.28; Aug. *CD* 1.31.

2 Syme (1939).

3 On the Jerome testimony, see Dangel (1995), 10–11.

4 See Chapter 1, n. 64.

5 Of course, some have doubted the veracity of the Gellius story: e.g., D'Anna (1967), 11–13.

6 For the date of 120 BCE see Drury (1982), 823.

7 See Horsfall (1976), 81–6.

8 See Schol. Bob. *ad* Cic. *Arch.* 27; also Val. Max. 8.14.2.

9 Cicero's term is *amicissimus*, clearly an enlargement of the usual *amicus*, often used of a relationship of association/support between social unequals. See Chapter 3, p. 58 and n. 7.

10 The following tragedies are ascribed to Accius: *Achilles*, *Aegisthus*, *Agamemnonidae*, *Alcestis*, *Alcimeo*, *Alphesiboea*, *Amphitruo*, *Andromeda*, *Antenoridae*, *Antigona*, *Armorum Iudicium* ('Judgement of Arms'), *Astyanax*, *Athamas*, *Atreus*, *Bacchae*, *Chrysippus*, *Clytaemestra*, *Deiphobus*, *Diomedes*, *Epigoni*, *Epinausimache*, *Erigona*, *Eriphyla*, *Eurysaces*, *Hecuba*, *Hellenes*, *Io*, *Medea* or *Argonautae*, *Melanippus*, *Meleager*, *Minos* or *Minotaurus*, *Myrmidones*, *Neoptolemus*, *Nyctegresia*, *Oenomaus*, *Pelopidae*, *Persidae* (*Persis?*), *Philocteta*, *Phinidae*, *Phoenissae*, *Prometheus*, *Stasiastae* or *Tropaeum Liberi*, *Telephus*, *Tereus*, *Thebais*, *Troades*. In addition Accius wrote two *praetextae*: *Brutus* and *Aeneadae* or *Decius*.

11 In comparison with one of Ennius' tragedies (*Eumenides*), none of Livius', Naevius' and perhaps one of Pacuvius' (his *Pentheus* is sometimes called *Bacchae*). Ennius' *praetexta Sabinae* is titled after its chorus, and perhaps Accius' *praetexta Aeneadae* or *Decius* owes its alternative title to the chorus. See Leo (1910), 18; Erasmo (2004), 164.

12 *Achilles*, *Aegisthus*, *Alcimeo*, *Andromeda*, *Armorum Iudicium*, *Athamas*, *Atreus*,*Clytaemestra*, *Hecuba*, *Medea*, *Stasiastae* or *Tropaeum Liberi*,

Telephus, *Tereus* have intertexts in the plays of Livius, Naevius, Ennius or Pacuvius.

13 For the multiple 'sources' of *Philocteta*, see Dangel (1995), 309–10.

14 *Rhesus* completely inverts the setting and perspective of *Iliad* 10; *Nyctegresia* seems to have dramatised the Homeric setting and perspective.

15 See Dangel (1995), 41–7, who argues strongly for Accius' 'mode de composition cyclique' (45). See also her genealogical article (1988), in which plays are assigned to different cycles and discussed in a putative chronological sequence.

16 So Dangel (1988), 64, on the Accian cycles of Argos and Thebes: 'Les deux *sagas* des maisons d'Argos et de Thèbes sont même si imbriquées l'une dans l'autre que chronologiquement on ne saurait les dissocier.' Dangel (65) even postulates that the cycles of Thebes and Argos were not only chronologically prior to the Trojan War but seem to have been written to climax in it.

17 E.g. Dangel (1988), 53 and *passim*; (2002), 109–10. She argues that Accius' cyclic composition produces a new form of historical tragedy, 'une écriture historique de la tragédie' (1988: 65) – a fusion of epic and tragedy in a self-conscious revision of Aristotle's prescriptions, 'une forme orginale d'altérité générique' (2002: 109).

18 Genealogical prologues may have been an Accian forte. *Atreus* and another tragedy (possibly *Aeneadae* or *Decius*) seem to have begun with genealogies. Notably, six of Accius' plays have patronymic titles: *Aeneadae*, *Agamemnonidae*, *Antenoridae*, *Pelopidae*, *Persidae*, *Phinidae* – note also *Epigoni*.

19 See Dangel (1995), 15–17, 21–2, 33. Like Ennius, Accius wrote a *Telephus*, although whether this was inspired by the Pergamene Altar's Telephus frieze is unknown. Certainly the importance of genealogy in the Altar's programme (Hercules – Telephus – the Pergamum dynasty) could only have confirmed Accius' own genealogical preoccupations. Note, too, Pacuvius' inclusion of the wandering Telephus in his *Atalanta* (see p. 96). If Accius did visit Pergamum, he would also undoubtedly have made use of the Pergamum Library's collection of some 200,000 scrolls, a collection second only to that of the great library of Alexandria. For a recent analysis of the Pergamene Altar, see Beard and Henderson (2001), 147–58.

20 See Wilkinson (1982), 234–6.

21 The emendations of Buecheler, which Klotz repeats, have with one exception (the opening *ibi* for the mss. *ubi*) not been reproduced.

22 Compare Aeneas' advice to his son, Ascanius, at Virgil *Aen.* 12.435–6.

23 I substitute *stagna* for *megna* and *cachinnant* for *cachinnat* in Klotz.

24 Compare Horace's epithet 'soaring': *Accius altus* (*Ep.* 2.1.56). The comment of Marcus Aper in Tacitus' *Dialogus* (20) – 'mouldy Pacuvius and Accius' – reflects the self-conscious modernity of the speaker, not the author.

25 See, e.g., Beacham (1992), 124.

26 'The three longest speeches', provided we do not accept as Accian the controversial speech from a *Prometheus* quoted by Cicero at *Tusc.* 2.23–5.

27 So, too, Erasmo (2004), 46, during an extensive discussion (45–50) of the play.

28 See Baier (2002), 56–7.

29 I restore the ms. *liquier* for *linquier* in Klotz.

30 See Rüpke (2002), 266–7.

31 Cf. Petrone (2000), 115–16.

32 I substitute Heinsius' *ostentas* for *ostentum* in Klotz.

33 At least such is argued by Dangel (1988), 60–1, in respect of this obscure play.

34 I have adopted Ribbeck's conjecture, *sento*, for the ms. *senio* in Klotz.

35 See Slater (2002).

36 Some examples: *beneficia*, *castitudo*, *contaminatio*, *decus*, *dignitas*, *discordia*, *diuidia*, *fama*, *fas*, *fidelitas*, *fides*, *gratia*, *honestitudo*, *humilitas*, *imperium*, *inpietas*, *laus*, *libertas*, *maiestas*, *nefas*, *nobilitas*, *pertinacia*, *prauitas*, *probrum*, *pudor*, *sanctitudo*, *segnitas*, *stuprum*, *uirtus*.

37 I adopt Vossius' *istuc uirile* and the ms. *ferre aduorsam* for *uirile istuc* and *aduorsam ferre* in Klotz.

38 I adopt the ms. *generi* in place of *generis* in Klotz.

39 I adopt Bothe's *quemcumque* for the ms. *quem cuique* in Klotz.

40 See, e.g. Paratore (1957), 1–7.

41 For a discussion of Scipio's behaviour here, see Astin (1967), 282–7.

42 On the 'Scipionic Circle', see Astin (1967), 294–6. Astin notes: 'Intellectual and cultural interests with a philhellenic bias were not confined to the "circle" of Scipio Aemilianus.'

43 For a contrary view, see Castagna (2002), 79–83.

44 Klotz (frag. v) also prints a one-line fragment from the raped Lucretia's speech. The Varro ms., from which this line derives, assigns the line to the *Brutus* 'of Cassius', which several have emended to 'of Accius'. I myself prefer to keep the ms. reading and give the line and the play which Varro cites to Cassius of Parma; so too Manuwald (2001), 237–43; Erasmo (2004), 100. See Chapter 5, pp. 158–9. Herington (1961), 24–5, also assigns the Lucretia fragment to Accius' play. It underlies his belief that the play ignored the so-called 'unities' of time and place, since one of the settings was Lucretia's house in Collatia.

45 Scaliger's emendation *cluat* here replaces the ms. *ciat* in Klotz. For other readings, including *fiat* 'become', see Manuwald (2001), 221.

46 Livy was certainly aware of the fundamentally 'tragic' nature of the end of Rome's monarchy. At 1.46.3, introducing his account of the murder of Servius Tullius and Tarquinius Superbus' seizing of the throne, he remarks on the *sceleris tragici ememplum*, 'example of tragic guilt', furnished by Rome's royal house.

47 See also Pliny *HN* 33.9; Dio 43.45.3–4. The statue joined those of the seven kings of Rome, and was placed next to the final king, Tarquinius Superbus, whom Brutus expelled. Richardson (1992), 369, regards the statue as 'probably early'. On Livy's theatrical narrative, Brutus' Capitoline statue and Accius' play, see Coulter (1940), to whom I am indebted.

48 See esp. Cic. *Lael.* 41; Sall. *Iug.* 31.7; Plut. *Tib. Gracch.* 14. Also Bilišski (1957), 39–43; Astin (1967), 228.

49 On all this see Dangel (1995), 15–17.

50 See Auhagen (2002) and Petaccia (2002).

51 A rare version of the myth in which Atlas and not Ares is the father of Oenomaus, Hippodamia's father. See Dangel (1988), 55.

52 Not only is Tarquin an Etruscan (i.e. one whose origins lay in the East), but the dream which he reports (quoted on p. 117) replays that of Atossa, the mother of the Persian King Xerxes, in Aeschylus' *Persae* (176–225). Poppaea's dream in the post-Senecan *Octavia* replays them both. See Erasmo (2004), 59–66. On the dynamic between tragic dramatisations of 'tyranny' and contemporary politics, see Dunkle (1967), 153: 'It was probably through the medium of tragedy that the Romans first became acquainted with the type of the Greek tyrant.' One might add that, although Accius is the last of the great tragedians of the republic, he is the one most concerned with the representation of tyranny.

53 Arcellaschi (1990), 185–93.

54 The sumptuary laws: the *lex Fannia* (161 BCE), the *lex Didia* (143 BCE), the *lex Aemilia* (115 BCE) and the *lex Licinia* (c. 103 BCE). For a discussion see Baldarelli (2002), 69.

55 Some have interpreted Accius' Bacchic plays as 'a commentary on the fall of Gaius Gracchus and his followers': Flower (2000), 29. While there is no difficulty associating such tyrants as Pentheus and Lycurgus with Gaius Gracchus, the difficulty of associating the opponents of those tyrants (i.e. Liber and his followers) with the senate makes such an interpretation difficult to accept. We do not know the date of either Bacchic play. But if Accius had wanted to choose a myth to meditate on the fall of Gaius Gracchus, he would surely not have chosen this one.

56 See Boyle (2003b), 191–2.

57 Dangel (1988), 73–4, finds a contradiction between Accius' support of the *optimates* and his 'Asianic' tragic style. There is no contradiction. The 'Asianic' style was practised by members of the Roman elite irrespective of their political affiliations. As mentioned on p. 113, one of the early exponents of the Asianic style in Roman political oratory was Sulpicius Galba, consul of 144 BCE. It was practised later by Gaius Gracchus, who, though a plebeian tribune, was a member of the senate he opposed. It was clearly a social marker, reflecting the authority/prestige of its users.

58 Biliŝski (1957), 26–49, who also argues for a conservative, pro-senatorial Accius, similarly relates (31–2) Accius' *Phoenissae* to the civil turmoil of the late republic. The next dramatisation of *Phoenissae*, of which we know, is that of Seneca.

59 See Hartkamp (2002), 161–3.

60 Cic. *De Or.* 3.217, 219; *Off.* 1.97; *Phil.* 1.34; *Tusc.* 4.55.

61 Dangel (1995), 283, scans the line differently, placing it – implausibly? – in the play's finale.

62 See, e.g., Cic. *Off.* 1.97, *Sest.* 102, *Phil.* 1.33; Sen. *Ira* 1.20.4, *Clem.* 1.12.4, 2.2.2; Mart. 4.49.3–4.

63 La Penna (1979), 130; Petrone (2002), 247.

64 See Biliŝski (1957), 36; Argenio (1961), 210–11.

65 The interpretation, for example, of Leigh (1996), 185. But one would not expect iambic senarii or (polite?) periphrastic constructions in such a Thyestean outburst. Leigh's assumption that *tyranno* here means 'tyrant' rather than 'king' begs the question.

66 Bilišski (1957), 43. If Gaius Gracchus was recalling the words of Thyestes, was this to undermine the contemporary association of the Gracchi with Atreus?

67 See Chapter 5, p. 158.

68 E.g. Bilišski (1957), 44, nominates the Marian party, most especially the tribunes Saturninus and Glaucia, as its target.

69 See Plato *Rep.* 571a–76b, on the 'tyrannical' man.

70 I read *noua* with Warmington 2.548–9 in preference to *nouus* of Klotz.

71 I adopt Ribbeck's *famae enim* in place of the ms. *famam nam* in Klotz.

72 See Oakley (2004), 27.

73 I adopt Ribbeck's *Caleti* in place of *Gallei* in Klotz. The mss. read *calleti*.

74 So, too, Manuwald (2001), 219. The third-person verb suggests that it is not the Caleti, i.e. the Gauls, who are the speakers. Erasmo (2004), 70, opts (without mentioning any other possibilities) for a chorus of Gauls.

75 I adopt the ms. *acie* and Buecheler's *lue* for *aciem* and *laue* in Klotz.

76 So, too, Manuwald (2001), 208.

77 See the excellent comments of Jocelyn (2000), 346–7.

78 Klotz reads: (disumma tibi perduellum est? quosum aut / quibus [se] a partibus gliscunt?

79 For the first interpretation: Dangel (1995), 377; for the second: Ribbeck (1875), 596, Warmington 2.553, and Erasmo (2004), 70.

80 Manuwald (2001), 217.

81 On this see Jocelyn (2000), 347–9, who cites Eur. *Heracl.* 501–2, *IA* 1375–6, 1472–6, *Pho.* 997–8, 1009–12.

82 I accept Vossius' conjecture *est is* for the ms. *essis*. Klotz reads *escis*.

83 Later commentators such as Donatus, Lydus and Diomedes view the *praetexta* as a form of tragedy. For details, see Chapter 2, p. 49. Notably, a scholiast on Cic. *Sest.* 123 actually refers to Accius' *Brutus* as *tragoedia praetextata*.

84 See Jocelyn (2000), 344, who, however, states without argument that all *praetextae* and all Roman tragedies and comedies of the third and second century BCE adhered to the single location principle. The fact that several extant Roman tragedies which we possess (Seneca's *Troades*, *Phaedra*, *Thyestes*, *Phoenissae*) and the only extant *praetexta* (*Octavia*) do not do this ought to have given him pause. Ennius' *Sabinae* may have employed different locations: see p. 86.

85 Kragelund (2002), 26–7, argues strongly for one of the purposes of *Decius* being a laudation of one of the ancestors of Accius' patron/friend, Quintus Fabius Maximus Allobrogicus.

86 Livy gives the modest figures of 8,700 Romans and 25,000 enemies killed. Others give figures three times as great. See Cornell (1994), 377–80.

87 The Samnites provided one of the two supreme military leaders of the Allied forces: Gaius Papius Mutilus, who commanded the army in the south. See Gabba (1994), 118–19.

88 For *Aeneadae* and the Decii, see Ribbeck (1875), 599, Dangel (1995), 375; and for the Fabii, see Kragelund (2002), 26–7.

89 As Dangel (1995), 375–6, argues on the basis of an unlocated fragment (Klotz *Incerta* frag. iii), which she adds to the fragments of this play.

Chapter 5

1 In the middle of 43 BCE a copy was in the hands of the poet Cornelius Gallus, which Pollio suggests to Cicero that he might request (Cic. *Fam.* 10.32.5). Despite the praise of Virgil and Horace, Pollio did not make it into Quintilian's list of Rome's foremost tragedians: *Inst.* 10.1.97–8. His style is described as 'harsh and dry' (*durus et siccus*) at Tac. *Dial.* 21.7

2 Kragelund (2002), 28, suggests that the actor Herennius Gallus, who performed in the play, may have been its author. Kragelund (28–34) discusses the play at length, and argues that this may not be the only *praetexta* to have been performed in a theatre outside Rome.

3 Accepting Ribbeck's emendation of the title.

4 The sole testimony for this *praetexta* is Varro, *LL* 6.18, where the phrase used to describe it is *togata praetexta*. Ribbeck worried whether it might have been a *togata*: see Klotz 372. For a discussion of the *Nonae Caprotinae* as paradigmatic *praetexta*, see Kragelund (2002), 18–19.

5 The attempt of Manuwald (2001), 93–4, to deny the existence of such a play is unpersuasive (see Wiseman 2002b).

6 To describe, for example, Strabo as 'dabbling in tragedy' (so Goldberg 1996: 271), given that we possess no play of his, seems more than a little prejudicial.

7 Dated performances attested: Ennius' *Andromacha* (55?, 54 BCE); Pacuvius' *Teucer* (51 BCE), *Armorum Iudicium* (44 BCE); Accius' *Eurysaces* and *Brutus* (57 BCE), *Clytaemestra* (55 BCE), *Astyanax* (54 BCE), *Tereus* (44 BCE). Undated performances attested: Ennius' *Aiax*, *Alcmeo*, *Alexander*, *Iphigenia*, *Medea Exul*, *Melanippa*, *Telamo*, *Thyestes*; Pacuvius' *Antiopa*, *Chryses*, *Iliona*, *Medus*; Accius' *Atreus*, *Epigoni*, *Philocteta*. See Wright (1931), 31–61. Even Naevius (probably) finds himself replayed: *Equos Troianus* (55 BCE). Accius' dominance of the late republican theatre is attested not only by known performances, but by the mocking of his plays in Atellan farce: see Bilišski (1957), 49.

8 See Wright (1931), 33, 48, 60.

9 Hor. *Sat.* 1.10.37ff. See Horsfall (1976).

10 On Aesopus, see Beacham (1991), 156.

11 The emphasis on, and analysis of, 'delivery' is repeated by Quintilian (*Inst.* 11.3.1).

12 See Macr. *Sat.* 3.14.12, where mention is made of the book in which Roscius compares oratory (*eloquentia*) with acting (*histrionia*).

13 Beacham (1991), 154. For a reconstruction of what such a virtuoso performance might be, at least in comedy, see Garton (1972), 170–88.

14 Roscius seems to have performed initially without the mask: Cic. *De Or.* 3.221; Diomedes *GL* 1.489 Keil.

15 Plutarch (*Cic.* 5.3) even preserves the story that, during a performance as Atreus, Aesopus in the throes of intense passion killed one of the assistants on stage with his sceptre.

16 On the professional terminology linking acting and oratory, see Fantham (2002), 362–4.

17 On the ability to sway the emotions as the most important ingredient of successful oratory, see, for example, Cic. *De Or.* 2.178.

18 On the similarity of gesture of actor and orator, see Aldrete (1999), 54–67. Quintilian offers a detailed account of the numerous and often complex hand, arm, head and face gestures available to the orator (and presumably – with the exception of face gestures – to the masked tragic actor) and the specific meanings to be attached: see *Inst.* 11.3.65–149. Sometimes the arts became almost identical when the actor played the orator or the orator adopted the *persona* of someone else, as Cicero did quadruply in *Pro Caelio* (33–8) – however much the orator tried not to seem like an actor. On the use of *prosopoeia* ('impersonation') in oratory, see Aldrete (1999), 35–6.

19 For example, by focusing on the actor's imitation of reality (*ueritas*) as compared with the orator's engagement with it: see Fantham (2002), 363 and the passages cited: Cic. *De Or.* 2.34, 2.193, 3.214. See also Corbeill (2004), 115–16.

20 Figures from Jory (1986), 144. As noted (Chapter 1, n. 43), the number of days devoted to the repetition of *ludi* improperly performed could be considerable.

21 E.g. *Rab. Post.* 42; *Att.* 1.18.2; *Fam.* 12.29.1, 13.64.2; *Fin.* 1.49; *Tusc.* 2.64. At *Amic.* 97 Cicero expressly equates *contio* (political meeting) and *scaena* (stage).

22 See Goldberg (1999), 52–7.

23 See Erasmo (2004), 53.

24 As, for example, in the mid-first century Villa of the Poppaei at Oplontis and the Villa of Publius Fannius Synistor at Boscoreale: see the discussion of Ling (1991), 30–1.

25 Designed by the architect Valerius of Ostia for the games of Libo.

26 See also Lucretius (4.75–83, 6.108–12) for a contemporary description.

27 See Beacham (1999), 31: 'Brightly colored and embroidered with design, these [awnings] pleased the eye and protected spectators from the sun, and they must have created a singular atmosphere (gently rising and falling on the breeze) as the colored rays of light played through them onto the crowd and stage.'

28 This opinion is based on Pliny's estimate of the capacity of the Theatre of Pompey, which he puts at 40,000, which modern calculations put conservatively at about 11,000. See Chapter 1, n. 80, and this chapter, n. 31.

29 See Richardson (1992), 385, to whom my comments on the Theatre of Scaurus are indebted.

30 Again I am indebted to Richardson (1992), 383–5.

31 Richardson (1992), 385. Beacham (1999), 65, is wrong in pronouncing it 'the largest Roman theater ever built'. The Regionary Catalogues attribute 17,580 *loca* to the Theatre of Pompey (for perhaps 11,000 spectators), and 20,500 *loca* to the later Theatre of Marcellus (for perhaps '13,000 spectators'): see Claridge (1998), 243; Richardson (1992), 382. These are conservative estimates. See further Chapter 1, n. 80. The Theatre of Marcellus remained the largest of Rome's three theatres.

32 Lucr. 2.416–17; Prop. 4.1.16; Ovid *Ars* 1.104.

33 On the height of the Roman stage, see Vitruvius (5.6.2), who makes clear that he wants it restricted to no more than five (Roman) feet so

that those seated in the orchestra – i.e. the senators – can see the gestures of the actors.

34 See Beacham (1991), 163–4.

35 See Rowland (1999), 245–7. Valerius Maximus (2.4.6) suggests that the curule aediles of 79 BCE (Lucius Licinius Lucullus and Marcus Terentius Varro Lucullus) introduced the *scaena uersatilis* (= *periaktos*). Cicero (*Sest.* 126) attests to the use of a trapdoor (for the emergence of a ghost) in a performance of Pacuvius' *Iliona* and (*Prov. Cons.* 14) to the existence both of the *exostra* ('device to allow the sudden appearance of the gods on high': Csapo and Slater 428) and *siparia*. Both Ciceronian passages predate the opening of Pompey's Theatre.

36 See, for example, the description of the stage curtain envisaged at Virg. *Geo.* 3.24–5.

37 For the religious nature of the *ludi scaenici*, see Chapter 1, pp. 15–6.

38 For the epigraphic evidence of the *Fasti*, see Degrassi (1963), 493–4. Richardson (1992), 411, describes the four deities as 'a small pantheon of the political rallying cries of the Sullan period'. But what they here betoken are Pompey's specific virtues. If *Felicitas* is a reference to his Sullan past, it is a reference which indexes his transcendence of it.

39 Beacham (1999), 68.

40 Vitruvius (5.9.1), for example, underscores the portico's provision of shelter for spectators and of places for the construction of stage props (*choragia*).

41 Sculptures: Pliny *HN* 7.34, 36.41; social interaction: Cat. 55.6, Prop. 2.32.11–16; also Cic. *De Fato* 8, Prop. 4.8.75.

42 For political points in a comic performance (of Afranius' *Simulans*, 'Pretender'), see Cic. *Sest.* 118. Mime, too, might be similarly charged, as the case of Decimus Laberius and Julius Caesar shows: Macr. *Sat.* 2.7.1–9.

43 The crime is noted in the *Twelve Tables*, Rome's earliest table of laws (*c.* 450 BCE), *Table* viii.1: *si quis occentauisset siue carmen condidisset quod infamiam faceret flagitiumue alteri* ('if anyone had sung or composed a song which defamed or cast a slur on another', Cic. *Rep.* 4.12). The penalty was being clubbed to death. See Warmington 3.474; and Hor. *Ep.* 2.1.150–55. See also Chapter 2, p. 54.

44 See Beacham (1991), 154–5.

45 Porphyrio, in his comments on Horace *Satires* 2.3.60, preserves the story of the actor Fufius, who was actually asleep during the prologue of Pacuvius' *Iliona*, being awakened by the repeated cry from the whole audience of the famous line: *mater, te appello*, 'Mother, I call you'.

46 Ascon. *In Pis.* 6. See Frézouls (1983), 209–14, who argues that Pompey's theatre was built in part to compensate the inhabitants of the *uici* for their lack of *ludi*. See also Beacham (1999), 55–6.

47 See Beacham (1999), 59, who presses this matter a little too strongly, citing Vanderbroeck (1987), 79–80.

48 The date is not certain, but some time in August or September seems the best guess: see Nisbet (1961), 199.

49 Apparently his voice failed at a crucial moment: Cic. *Fam.*7.1.2.

50 Cic. *Fam.* 7.1.3; Pliny *HN* 8.53, 64, 70, 72, 80; Plut. *Pomp.* 52, Dio 39.38.

51 That a predilection for large casts was in vogue in the late republic may be an inference of the anecdote in Horace (*Ep*. 1.6.41–2) that Lucullus was once asked to provide a hundred cloaks (*chlamydes*) for the stage.

52 See Plut. *Pomp*. 45.

53 Wright (1931), 73. The objections of Erasmo (2004), 87, do not convince.

54 For discussion of the political semiotics of the chosen plays, see Champlin (2003), 298, Erasmo (2004), 86–91.

55 Richardson (1992), 384.

56 See Erasmo (2004), 90, who also argues for a possible allusion in Agamemnon's triumphal procession to Pompey's adoption of the image of Alexander the Great in his own triumph of 61 BCE. On Pompey as 'Agamemnon', see also Cic. *Att*. 7.3.5; Dio 42.5.3–5; and Champlin (2003), 297–303.

57 The *ludi* were made annual and their name changed to *Ludi Victoriae Caesaris*, 'Games of Caesar's Victory'.

58 At the eastern end of the Portico of Pompey attached to Pompey's theatre was the large exedra known as the Curia Pompeii, in which the senate occasionally met, and where they were meeting when Julius Caesar was assassinated in front of them: Cic. *Div*. 2.23; Livy *Per*. 116; Suet. *Iul*. 80–1; Plut. *Caes*. 66.6–7.

59 See Beacham (1999), 89–91.

60 Suetonius' phrase *inter ludos*, 'among the shows' (*Iul*. 84.2), seems to imply performances of these plays rather than the appropriate use of individual lines during the funeral itself. Appian (*BC* 2.146), however, has the lines shouted out during the course of general lamentation.

61 See p. 97.

62 Cic. *Phil*. 1.36, 10.8; *Att*. 16.1.1, 4.1, 5.1.

63 Erasmo (2004), 97, notes the popular verse cited by Suetonius (*Iul*. 80.3):
> Brutus quia reges eiecit consul primus factus est;
> hic quia consules eiecit rex postremo factus est.
>
> Brutus, because he expelled the kings, became the first consul;
> He [Caesar], because he expelled the consuls, became the final king.

64 See Chapter 4, p. 124.

65 See Acro on Hor. *Ep*. 1.4.3, where the *opuscula*, 'little works', of Cassius of Parma are mentioned, and Porphyrio on Hor. *Sat*. 1.10.61. *Orestea* was presumably a tragedy on Orestes, not a trilogy like Aeschylus' *Oresteia*.

66 As, for example, by Warmington 2.562. See the vain attempt of Castagna (2002), 91–4, to justify reading 'Accius'; also Chapter 4, n. 44. On the importance of this *Brutus* and on Cassius generally, see Erasmo (2004), 99–101.

67 The date of this *Thyestes* is unknown. It could belong to the 40s or the 30s BCE. It is also possible that, if the play were earlier rather than later, one of its targets may have been – in addition to Octavian – Mark Antony. After the defeat of Sextus Pompey, Cassius joined Mark Antony and was with him at the Battle of Actium. This last surviving assassin of Julius Caesar was killed in Athens shortly after the battle, on the instructions of Octavian, by Quintus Attius Varus (Vell. Pat. 2.87.3; Val. Max. 1.7.7; Appian *BC* 5.139).

Chapter 6

1 For the scholiasts (on Codex Parisinus 7530 and Codex Casanatensis 1086), see Beare (1964), 374. Varius' 'gift' (*munus*) from, and friendship with, Augustus are commented on by Horace at *Ep.* 2.1.245–7. For Martial, Varius became one of the paradigms of a well-paid poet: *Epig.* 8.56.21–2, 12.4.1–2

2 A comment by Philargyrius on Virgil *Ecl.* 8.6 goes further: *omnibus tragicis praeferenda*, 'To be preferred to all tragedies'. See Leigh (1996), 171.

3 Tarrant (1985), 41, is rightly cautious on this matter, and it should be pointed out that even my spare remarks on the general plot would not receive the agreement of Lefèvre (1976), who argues quite implausibly that the part of the legend dramatised by Varius' play belongs to the period following the infamous banquet. For a refutation of Lefèvre's thesis, see Jocelyn (1978).

4 I use the name Augustus predominantly throughout this chapter, even though Octavian only received this name in January of 27 BCE.

5 For Ovid, both Varius and Gracchus 'gave cruel words to tyrants' (*darent fera dicta tyrannis, Pont.* 4.16.31). *Tyrannus* does not necessarily mean 'tyrant' in the English sense in Latin; but *fera*, 'savage', seems to indicate that here it does so.

6 The Ovidian passage cited in n. 5 seems to suggest not only that the *Thyestes* of Varius and that of Gracchus were concerned with tyranny but that their dates of composition/performance were not far apart. Erasmo (2004), 179, suggests 'the teens b.c.e.' for the date of Gracchus' *Thyestes*.

7 As Erasmo (2004), 109–10, suggests, whose theory, however, that Augustus wished to associate himself with the victorious Atreus of this play is unlikely to persuade.

8 See, esp. Cic. *Phil.* 1.33–4; 2.59, 71; 3.4; 5.22; 13.17–18. The passages are discussed by Leigh (1996), who argues that we should read Varius' play as anti-Antonian propaganda.

9 See Favro (1996), 82–95.

10 Even the Temple of Apollo Medicus built by Gaius Sosius *c.* 28 BCE contained reliefs which may have celebrated Augustus' successes in Pannonia and Dalmatia (see Galinksy 1996: 347, figs. 165, 166), and was dedicated on Augustus' birthday. For the few buildings put up by Romans other than members of the imperial family during Augustus' reign, see Boyle (2003b), 41–2.

11 See Favro (1996), 141, on this period (17 BCE–14 CE): '[Augustus] devoted the last thirty years of his life to the meticulous clarification and empowerment of an urban image directly tied to his own achievements, aspirations and memory.'

12 On the Portico of Nations, see Servius *ad Aen.* 8.721. Richardson (1992), 316, is sceptical of the Servian testimony.

13 Named after its dedicator Cornelius Balbus, the author of the *praetexta, Iter* (see pp. 143–4), who had (most unusually) been allowed to celebrate a triumph in 19 BCE. The triumph was for his 'defeat' of the Garamantes.

14 Richardson (1992), 381.

15 Caesar: Suet. *Iul.* 44.1; Dio 43.49.2. Augustus: Pliny *HN* 8.65; Suet. *Aug.* 29.4; Dio 54.26.1.

16 Ascon. *In Cic. Scaur.* 27.5–9 Clark; Richardson (1992), 382.
17 Richardson (1992), 382. On these and related numbers, see Chapter 1, pp. 22–3 and n. 80.
18 As Beacham (1999), 126, points out, the display was even 'color-coded': senators with wide purple stripes on their tunics; equestrians with narrow purple stripes on their tunics; plebeians in the central section in white togas; plebeians in the upper section in dark togas; curule magistrates in their *toga praetexta*; prostitutes dressed in red ...
19 *Periaktoi* are called *scaenae uersatiles* by Servius *ad Virg. Geo.* 3.24.
20 Depending on whether *profectus* (H) or *prospectus* (ed. Ven.) is read.
21 The evidence for *scaenae ductiles* during the Augustan period is a number of wall-paintings and Virgil *Geo.* 3.24, together with the Servian commentary *ad loc.* They are well discussed by Beacham (1992), 169–72. Similarly on Pollux' *katablemata* and on the ways of 'realising' the different stage-sets of the Vitruvius passage, see Beacham (1992), 177–8.
22 The list includes also Ennius, Naevius and Livius, but it is unclear whether Horace is talking about them simply as epicists.
23 There is, however, no indication that this play was Augustan rather than republican.
24 The phrase is that of Tarrant (1978), 259, to whose discussion of Augustan tragedy (258–61) I am in part indebted.
25 See Chapter 3, n. 36. Accius certainly had profound impact on Ovid in another play, his *Tereus* (see Chapter 4, pp. 133–4).
26 See Tarrant (1978), 59–60 and n. 191.
27 *Heroides* 4 (Phaedra to Hippolytus) and 12 (Medea to Jason) are especially mined by the later dramatist. But no less *Metamorphoses*. Two of a multitude of possible examples: *uideo meliora proboque, / deteriora sequor*, 'I see and approve the better course, / the worse I follow', says Ovid's Medea (*Met.* 7.20–1); *miserere fatentis amores*, 'Pity one confessing love', says/writes Ovid's Byblis to her brother (*Met.* 9.561); *quae memoras scio / uera esse, nutrix, sed furor cogit sequi / peiora*, 'What you say I know / To be true, nurse, but passion compels / The worse' (*Pha.* 177–9), *miserere amantis*, 'Pity a lover' (*Pha.* 671) says Seneca's Phaedra, the latter to her stepson. Even the hallmark Senecan address to parts of the body can be found in Ovid (e.g. *Met.* 9. 186). See the index in Tarrant (1985) for a list of the major debts to Ovid's *Metamorphoses* in Seneca's *Thyestes*.
28 Compare Sen. *Med.* 938–9, which may recall the Ovidian line: *uariamque nunc huc ira, nunc illuc amor / diducit* ('My wavering mind now anger drags here, now love there').
29 On the *lex Iulia theatralis*, see Rawson (1991), 508–45.
30 See Schnurr (1992), 153.
31 On the *infamia* law, see Chapter 1, pp. 17–8.
32 By 11 CE it seems that this penalty was not working as a disincentive, and permission seems to have been granted to some knights to participate in gladiatorial fights.
33 See Chapter 1, p. 18.
34 For mime and the Atellan farce, see pp. 12, 14–5.
35 On this see Lucian *De Salt.* 67–9 and *passim*. See also Sen. *Ep.* 121.6.
36 See Pylades' remark to Augustus reported by Dio (54.17.4): 'It profits you, Caesar, that the people waste their time with us.'

37 Suetonius (*Aug.* 53.1) records the story of Augustus' anger at the phrase '*o dominum aequum et bonum*' ('oh just and noble master') applied to him in a mime and accompanied by applause from the audience. Suetonius reports that Augustus was angry at the tasteless flattery, but a larger issue is an unauthorised political use of the *ludi*. Such phrases could always be applied ironically, as Pompey discovered. Compare Augustus' displeasure at the people's applause in the theatre for his adopted sons Gaius and Lucius (Suet. *Aug.* 56.2; see also under the year 13 BCE: Dio 54.27.1).

38 Esp. Hor. *Ep.* 2.1 and *Ars Poetica*. See Rudd (1989), 7.

39 See the Suetonius passages cited at n. 37. That acclamation in the theatre for imperial figures was relatively rare at this time seems indicated by Horace's references to the acclamation for Maecenas, which was clearly a unique event: *Odes* 1.20.3–8, 2.17.25–6. For the acclamation of Octavian in the theatre in 44 BCE, see Nicolaus of Damascus, *Augustus* 28. The view of Aldrete (1999), 106, that '*whenever* he (Augustus) made a public appearance, such as at the theatre, the entire audience rose in unison and applauded him enthusiastically' (my italics) lacks supporting testimony. Augustus was concerned to avoid the mistakes made by the dynasts of the late republic. The muting of the politics of the theatre seems to have been a deliberate strategy. The often-cited story of a theatrical audience rising to acclaim the poet Virgil 'as if he were Augustus' (*quasi Augustum*: Tac. *Dial.* 13) serves only to emphasise the absence of anecdotes testifying to the same for the emperor. What happened in the later empire is a different matter.

40 See Boyle (2003b), 42–3.

41 The third day of the *Ludi Megalenses* (6 April) honoured Julius Caesar's victory at Thapsus (46 BCE); the fourth day of the *Ludi Cereales* (15 April) celebrated Octavian/Augustus' first military victory at Mutina (43 BCE); the opening day of the *Ludi Florales* (28 April) was (after 12 BCE) the anniversary of the dedication of the shrine to Vesta in Augustus' house (see Ovid *Fas.* 4.949–54, *Met.* 15.864–5, and see Boyle 2003b: 226–9); the penultimate day of the *Ludi Apollinares* (12 July) celebrated (from 42 BCE) the birthday of Julius Caesar with special honorific games (see Hor. *Ep.* 1.5.9–11); the opening day of the *Ludi Romani* (September 4) was the anniversary of Lepidus' surrender to Octavian/Augustus in 36 BCE. For the evidence, see Degrassi, 437, 441, 452, 374 and 481, 507.

42 At four days longer than the *Ludi Victoriae Sullanae* (October 26–November 1), the *Ludi Caesaris Victoriae* were the longest *ludi* in the Julio-Augustan calendar.

43 From 28 BCE: *ludi* to celebrate Augustus' conquest of Alexandria, Cleopatra and Egypt (held on August 1 in 28 BCE, then every four years according to Dio: 53.1.4–6); from 13 BCE: annual *ludi* (or almost annual: Dio 54.26.2, 34.1–2; 55.6.6) on 23 September to mark the emperor's birthday; from 11 BCE: the *Ludi Augustales* (perhaps annual: Dio 54.34.2, 55.8.3, 56.29.1) on 12 October to celebrate the emperor's return. See Degrassi, 373–4.

44 Cornelius Balbus, for example, held dedicatory *ludi* at the opening of his theatre in 13 BCE. But Augustus appropriated these by having his

own imminent return from Spain announced during their performance (Dio 54.25.2).

45 See Chapter 5, p. 155.

46 On the *Ludi Saeculares*, see Davis (2001), and Schnegg-Köhler (2002).

47 See Zanker (1988), 148, for whom Augustus' whole purpose was 'to commemorate his own naval victory at Actium'.

48 Later enlarged by two days to run from 3–12 October: Degrassi, 516; also Tac. *Ann.* 1.15.2.

49 For particular demands see also Pliny *HN* 34.62 (for the restoration of Lysippus' *Apoxyomenos*); Tac. *Ann.* 2.87, 6.13 (for corn: the last mentioned when Tiberius was on Capri). For the political use of the theatre by an individual, see the case of Aemilia Lepida (Tac. *Ann.* 3.23), discussed by Beacham (1999), 160.

50 See Levick (1983).

51 Attempts to make Scaurus also the author of the anonymous *Agamemnon* are clearly misguided: see Champlin (2003), 303–5.

52 The phrase is that of Beacham (1999), 168, to whose discussion of Caligula's reign (pp. 168–86) I am much indebted.

53 Philo *Leg.* 79, 93–97; Dio 59.26.6–8.

54 Philo *Leg.* 203–06; Suet. *Gaius* 33; Dio 59.5.2.

55 Joseph. *Ant. Iud.* 19.25; Dio 59.13.3–7, 28.11.

56 Dio 59.10.3, 59.13.4; Joseph. *Ant. Iud.* 19.25–6, Dio 59.28.11.

57 On this anecdote, see Bartsch (1994), 75–6.

58 Respectively: *Ann.* 16.7, 14.15, 14.59, 64, 15.18, 14.12f.

59 See, e.g., *Ep.* 74.7, 76.31, 115.14ff.; also *Marc.* 10.1. On Stoicism and self-dramatisation, see Rosenmeyer (1989), 47ff.

60 Terms used by the sociologist Lerner (1964), quoted by Greenblatt (1980), 224ff., in his detailed discussion of the Renaissance capacity for 'improvisation'.

61 See Bartsch (1994), 2ff.

62 Strabo 6.2.6; Suet. *Gaius* 35.2, *Nero* 11.2, 12.2; Mart. *Spec.* 7, 8, *Epig.* 8.30; Dio 59.10.3.

63 It is probably the amphitheatre whose technological and decorative marvels are described in Calpurnius Siculus *Eclogue* 7.

64 Suet. *Nero* 12.3; see also Tac. *Ann.* 14.21; Dio 61.21.1–2.

65 Sen. *NQ* 7.32.3; Suet. *Nero* 11; Tac. *Ann.* 14.15.1–3; Dio 61.19.

66 Suet. *Nero* 20.3; Tac. *Ann.* 14.15.4; Dio 61.20.3–5.

67 On claques, see Beacham (1999), 213–24.

68 On this see Erasmo (2004), 117–21.

69 *Vita Persi* 8. The testimony for Lucan's *Medea* is from the 'Life' attributed to Vacca.

70 On Quintilian's dislike of Seneca, see the former's attack on the 'corrupt and dangerous' nature of Seneca's prose style (*Inst.* 10.1. 125–31).

71 So Kragelund (2002), 36, speculates.

72 *Eliminat* is used by Ennius in his *Medea Exul*. See Chapter 3, p. 73.

73 See Manuwald (2001), 244–5.

74 See Suetonius *Aug.* 74, *Dom.* 7.1; cf. Sen. *NQ* 7.32.3; Plut. *Mor.* 711Aff. For the Marius evidence, Sallust *BI* 85.13. Nor were performances of tragedy restricted to Roman interiors: note the notorious performance of Euripides' *Bacchae* at the Parthian court in 53 BCE with Crassus' head as prop (Plut. *Cras.* 33) discussed on p.157

75 The earliest explicit testimony to the *ekkyklema* and *mechane* is from Pollux in the second century CE (4.127–32). However, there seems little doubt that such simple devices (probably in a more sophisticated form) must have been in use, given the extraordinary technology of the Roman theatre. The *ekkyklema* finds a use in the final act of Seneca's *Thyestes*, the *mechane* in the last scene of Seneca's *Medea*.

76 See Beacham (1992), 181–2, for a discussion of the Pollux testimony.

77 See p. 20.

Chapter 7

1 In the Codex Etruscus *Hercules Furens*, the title given to the play in the A branch of the manuscript, is simply called *Hercules*. The A branch also gives the title *Hippolytus* for *Phaedra*, *Tros* for *Troades* and *Thebais* for *Phoenissae*. The reader needs to be aware that the bibliography on Senecan tragedy is substantial and that only a fraction of it is alluded to in this chapter. For a fuller list of important editions and studies, see Boyle (1997), 240–51.

2 *CIL* iv. Suppl. 2.6698: *idai cernu nemura* , 'I see the groves of Ida' = *Agamemnon* 730.

3 Fitch (1981).

4 Herington (1966), 429.

5 Amongst the earliest is *Consolatio ad Marciam*, composed under Caligula, and *Naturales Quaestiones* and *Epistulae Morales*, written during the last three years of Seneca's life.

6 'Die Negation der Philosophie' is J. Dingel's judgement on the tragedies (1974), 72. Recently Littlewood (2004), *passim*, has revived the unpersuasive 'negative exemplar' thesis in suggesting that the plays 'suggest the Stoic fortitude' (p. 25) which the characters might have displayed. Stoicism as life solution is severely problematised in Senecan tragedy.

7 For 'reading' see Fantham (1982), 34–49; for 'recitation' see Zwierlein (1966). The dramatic realisability of Senecan drama is strongly advocated by (among others) Herington (1966), 444, Walker (1969), Calder (1983) 184, Sutton (1986), Dupont (1995).

8 One piece of epigraphic evidence, however, is suggestive: the opening words of *Ag.* 730 (see n. 2 above), taken from the theatrically powerful clairvoyant speech of Cassandra, inscribed on a wall in Pompeii (perhaps together with a few words from *Ag.* 693: Lebek [1985]). This only 'proves' that Seneca's *Agamemnon* was known, not that it had been performed. But Pompeii had an active theatre culture, and the possibility that a performance (of some kind) influenced the graffito is difficult to resist.

9 It is customary to cite performances of Senecan tragedy in Renaissance Europe and Tudor England. More interesting is the fact that Seneca has been and is regularly performed in modern Italy, France and Switzerland. In the English-speaking world four late-twentieth-century performances may perhaps be mentioned: Seneca's *Oedipus* (adapted by Ted Hughes) at the Old Vic Theatre, London, March 1968; *Phaedra* (my translation) at the Sydney Opera House, July 1987;

Troades (also my translation) at the Alexander Theatre, Melbourne, September–October 1988; *Thyestes* (translated by Caryl Churchill) at the Royal Court Theatre, London, June 1994.

10 So Corneille had several of his plays read in public prior to performance: *Polyeucte* (1641) was read at the Hôtel de Rambouillet while still in rehearsal, and *Pulchérie* (1672) was read at the homes of the Duc de la Rochefoucauld and the Cardinal de Retz before its unsuccessful performance by the Marais company. The plays of Corneille, Racine and other Renaissance dramatists were also sometimes performed *intra domum*: so Corneille's *Horace* (1640), at the home of Cardinal Richelieu, and Racine's *Andromaque* (1667) in the Queen's apartment at the Louvre. This is not even to mention Versailles – or the Tudor and Stuart courts.

11 Among obvious problems for *recitatio*: dialogue-speaker identification; setting identification; Chorus identification; referential content of personal and deictic pronouns (e.g., *hanc*, *Tro.* 924, *hic*, *Pho.* 498, *te*, *Pho.* 652); rapid exchanges in stichomythia and *antilabai*; extensive attention to the behaviour of other characters, especially mutes (see, e.g. *Tro.* Act 4); only *occasional* stage-directions for soliloquies, the entrances and exits of characters, etc.; a multiplicity of vocal registers, as in *Medea* Act 4 (Nurse describing Medea, N. quoting M., M. herself speaking). Several of the above undermine the 'only for reading' hypothesis also. Most importantly the very randomness of textual stage-directions suggests that Seneca was not relying solely on textual or verbal means for his dramas' realisation. Stage performance alone clarifies and realises his text.

12 See Chapter 6, pp. 168–70. Seneca was undoubtedly also indebted to the Augustans for their more refined verse techniques both in the iambic dialogue line and in choral lyric. Note, however, that *Oedipus* and (possibly) *Phaedra* are six-act plays and thus exceptions to the five-act 'rule'. Seneca was no slavish follower of conventions.

13 See most esp. Sutton (1986), 28ff., 43ff., who comments on the 'sound dramaturgic principles' involved in Seneca's stage practice. On stage-setting, see Seidensticker (1969), 145; on props (in *Phaedra*), see Segal (1986), 152f. For an occasionally aberrant account of implicit stage-directions in *Phaedra* see Fortey and Glucker (1975), 699–715. On identification cues it should be observed that recitation drama requires all characters to be identified verbally at their first appearance. This does not happen in Seneca, who uses some verbal identification cues but relies in several cases on contextual and visual identification. Similarly Seneca's use of mutes (e.g. Polyxena and Pyrrhus in *Tro.* Act Four, Orestes and Pylades in *Ag.* Act Five) and textually unidentified extras is 'redolent of the stage' (Sutton 35). Disappointingly one of Seneca's recent editors reverts to the misdescriptions and worn-out prejudices of the earlier part of the last century: 'The lack of internal cohesion, the absence of constructive dialogue (as opposed to stichomythic point-scoring), the long monologues, the declamatory extravagance of the language – none of these makes for good stage drama' (Frank, 1995, 42).

14 The point is made with clarity and humour by Herington (1966), 444f.

15 Calder (1975), 32ff., favours private performance of Seneca's tragedies.

16 Cinthio, *Scritti critici* (Crocetti 1973), 184: English quotation from Charlton (1946), lxxx n.6.

17 Neville, for example, the translator of *Oedipus* (1563), expressly mentions Seneca's 'tragicall and Pompous showe upon Stage'.

18 Eliot (1951), 70. Something else from the same essay merits quotation: 'What is 'dramatic'? ... Whether a writer expected his play to be played or not is irrelevant, the point is whether it is playable' (p. 75). Since actuality entails potentiality, the history of Senecan productions entails the playability of the tragedies and thus (according to Eliot's criteria) their 'dramatic' nature.

19 Seneca regularly organises such exchanges around keywords; Seidensticker (1969, 44) terms it Seneca's 'Stichworttechnic'. Other examples: *HF* 422ff., *Tro.* 301ff., *Med.* 490ff., *Pha.* 218ff.

20 Herington (1966), 423.

21 It is an axiom of Senecan theatre, as not accidentally of Roman history, that verbal power and personal power are not coextensive. Littlewood (2004), 11, misleads in this regard.

22 Eliot (1951), 91.

23 See Sen. *Con.* 2.3.19, 3 Pref. 16, 9 Pref. 2; Quint. *Inst.* 2.2.9–12.

24 For further discussion see Boyle (1997), 18–23.

25 See Boyle (1997), 23–9.

26 See p. 99.

27 The phrase is that of Braden (1985), 62.

28 For example: *Med.* 28ff., 56ff., 439f., 531ff., 595ff., 668f., 740ff., 874ff., 1002.

29 *Med.* 56ff., 75ff., 166ff., 207ff., 319, 335ff., 365, 401ff., 531ff., 570ff., 577f., 579ff., 605f., 614f., 670ff., 684ff., 705ff., 752ff., 787ff., 817ff., 835ff., 863ff., 874ff.

30 For further discussion of the verbal and ideological texture of Phaedra, see Boyle (1985), *passim*, (1997), 58–67; also Davis (1983), Henry and Walker (1966), and Segal (1986).

31 Chief among these: master/slave, conqueror/conquered, agent/victim, Greek/Trojan, marriage-maker/marriage-breaker, truth/falsehood, justice/injustice, joy/sorrow, past/present, life/death, survival-in-death/annihilation-in-death, sacrifice/murder, ritual/barbarism, civilisation/savagery.

32 Legal imagery: e.g. *Oed.* 24f., 371, 416, 875f., 916ff., 942ff., 1026; the fate/fortune motif: e.g. *Oed.* 11, 28, 72ff., 412, 709ff., 882ff., 980ff., 1042ff.

33 For example: *Ag.* 11, 43, 63ff., 98, 138ff., 188, 219, 465ff., 580, 875., 898ff.

34 See Boyle (1983b), 228 n.60.

35 For example: *HF* 122, 882ff., 918f., 1192.

36 The structural and thematic dimensions of such analogies are explored by Calder (1976).

37 *Med.* 2f., 118ff., 225ff., 447ff.

38 Esp. *Med.* 185, 294, 579ff., 849ff.

39 *Med.* 118ff., 238ff., 272ff., 447ff., 486ff.

40 On *Medea*'s finale, see pp. 217–8.

41 Phaedra and Pasiphae: esp. 112ff., 169ff., 242, 688ff., 698f.; Hippolytus and Pasiphae's bull: cf. esp. 116–18 with 413–17, and note the sustained application of 'wild animal' epithets to Hippolytus

(231, 240, 272f., 414, 416. 798, 1064); the Minotaur and the bull from the sea: cf. 122, 171ff., 649f., 688ff., 1067, with 1015ff.

42 On the relationship of *Agamemnon* to *Troades,* see Fantham (1982); on *Phoenissae*'s relationship to *Oedipus,* see Boyle (1997), 102–6.

43 The semiotic function of which is most profitably interpreted, as noted on p. 192, as a critical placement of the latter by the former. Contrast, for example, the providential attitude to the gods in *De Ira* 2.27.1 and the attitude evident in *Pha.*, *Thy.*, *Med.* and *Oed.* (see esp. *Pha.* 1242f., *Thy.* 1020f., *Med.* 1027, *Oed.* 1042ff.). Certainly attempts by such critics as Knoche (1972) and Marti (1945) to regard the dramatic works as 'philosophical propaganda-plays' (Marti 219) are ill-founded. But see Dingle quoted in n. 6 above.

44 On which see Schiesaro (2003), 70–85, and Littlewood (2004), 195–201.

45 See Boyle (1987) *ad loc.* For the remodelling of Ovid (and of Virgil) elsewhere in *Phaedra* see that edition *passim*; also Fantham (1975), Segal (1984) and Littlewood (2004), ch. 5.

46 'Rewriting' is important. Attempts such as that of Snell (1964), 23ff., to dismiss many of Seneca's dramatic innovations in *Phaedra* as essentially derivative (generally from Euripides' lost *Hippolytos Kalyptomenos*) are now discredited. What needs also to be underscored, since some commentators badly underestimate Senecan counterpoint with Greek texts (see, e.g., Littlewood 2004), is that Seneca could expect an audience (or at least a significant part of it) to respond to the interplay between his own plays and those of the Attic tragedians. Greek tragedy and literature remained an active and formative ingredient in elite Roman education and culture: see, e.g., Sen. *Ep.* 49.12, 115.14–15, *NQ* 4.2.17; Petron. *Satyr.* 2; Stat. *Silu.* 5.3.146ff.; Quint.*Inst.*10.1.66–8. Even 'contaminatory' rewriting, such as of Euripides' *Phaethon* in *Hercules Furens* (see Diggle 1970: 96–7), would not have gone unnoticed.

47 *Pha.* 113ff., 124ff., 174., 242, 688.

48 Cf. esp. *Pha.* 330–57 with *Geo.* 3. 209–83.

49 Racine's indebtedness to Seneca's *Phaedra* is not of course confined to the messenger speech. The French tragedian models, for example, Phèdre's revelation speech (*Phd.* 2.5/634ff.) upon *Pha.* 646ff. and develops Seneca's focus on the tragic implications of the hereditary curse (*Phd.* 1.3/249f., 257f., 277f., 306; 2.5/679f.; 4.6/1289). For other intertextual connections between the two plays see the Index to Boyle (1987).

50 With *Pha.* 1256 ff. cf. Agaue's actions in the lost part of Euripides' *Bacchae* (reconstructed by Dodds 1960: 234). See also Segal (1986), 215; and this chapter, pp. 208–9.

51 See Stat. *Theb.* 3.131f.; Apul. *Met.* 7.26.

52 See Boyle (1997), 79–80.

53 See Boyle (1994) on *Tro.* 360.

54 Albeit one with large cultural ramifications. Note, too, that, although the wedding-sacrifice conflation is not central to Euripides' dramatisation of Polyxena's death, a wedding metaphor is used (ironically) by Hecuba of her daughter's death after it has occurred: *Hec.* 612.

55 See Boyle (1994), 185, 208.

56 This is no isolated occurrence. From Ennius onwards the connection between Assaracus, Rome and the Julian family is frequently rehearsed. For references see Boyle (1994) on *Tro.* 17.

57 For Caligula: Suet. *Gai.*18.3, Dio 59.7.4, 59.11.1; for Claudius: Tac. *Ann.* 11.11, Suet. *Claud.* 21.3.

58 Post-Neronian writers are equally insistent on the Troy–Rome identity: e.g. Val. Flacc. *Arg.* 1.9, Sil. Ital. *Pun.* 1.2, 14, 106, and *passim*, Juv. *Sat.* 1.100, 4.60f.

59 Tac. *Ann.* 15.39, Suet. *Nero* 38.2, Dio 62.18.1 (also 62.29.1 for other 'Trojan recitations').

60 Bloom (1973). On Senecan tragedy's self-conscious 'belatedness', see Schiesaro (2003), 223.

61 Segal (1986), 218, interprets differently: 'Tragedy is about suffering whose parts refuse to be entirely accounted for, justified, and laid to rest either by the social forms of ritual (burial) or the rationalised logic of moral explanation (justice and law).' The generalisation, however, misses the specific relevance of Theseus' failure and of *Phaedra's* ending to Senecan tragedy as such.

62 On the history of the reception of Seneca, see, e.g. Enk (1957), 282–307, esp. 288–90.

63 For valuable remarks on Senecan metatheatre, see Curley (1986), Littlewood (2004), Erasmo (2004), esp. 122–39.

64 Artaud, Gallimard edition (1964) of *Oeuvres complètes*, vol. 4, 39.

65 Erasmo (2004), 122, quoting Boyle (1997), 114, wrongly attributes to me the coinage 'actor-audience', which he uses in his analysis. It is the characters (i.e. Phaedra, Jason, Aegisthus, Thyestes, etc.), not the actors playing them, who constitute the audience for the acting of other characters (Theseus, Medea, Clytemnestra, Atreus, etc.).

66 Nor are *spectatores* confined to the living: *Ag.* 758 (the Trojan dead), *Thy.* 66 (Ghost of Tantalus).

67 My use of the term 'metatheatre' to mean theatrically self-conscious theatre, theatre which itself represents theatrical practices, is in line with current usage. Like Abel, whose 1963 book is foundational to modern treatments, I also see metatheatre as a function of an ideology of social relations. Unlike Abel, however, I do not see it as a practice or mentality originating in the Renaissance. For Renaissance metatheatre and its debts to Seneca, see Boyle (1997), 193–207.

68 See Chapter 1, p. 20. On *spectare*: see, e.g., Cic. *De Oratore* 1.18, Hor. *Ep.* 2.1.203; on *spectatores*: see Horace *Ep.* 2.1.178, 215, etc..

69 For a detailed reading of the metadramatic nature of *Thyestes*, see Schiesaro (2003), for whom the play turns its fictional and theatrical nature into 'an upfront thematic concern' (62).

70 For Atreus as model of the sublime poet of *Tranq.* 17.10–11, see Schiesaro (2003), 49–55. But note that Atreus is a dramatic poet, interested in acting in, directing and viewing his own plays.

71 The view of Littlewood (2004), 213, that 'Atreus' sadistic pleasure' is the 'dominant model for an audience's response' is too simple. Both the Thyestean and the Atrean perspectives are presented with full dramatic force and compete for the audience's engagement. On Seneca's own inspiration by the Fury, see esp. Schiesaro (2003).

72 *Tro.* 4, 95f., 371, 614, 715, 860, 870f., 884, 1055, 1067, 1075ff., 1087, 1125, 1129, 1131, 1147f. On all these passages see Boyle (1994).

73 See Boyle (1994) on *Tro.* 360.

74 See Boyle (1994) *ad loc.*

75 Aristotle *Poetics* 1449b21–8: 'Tragedy, therefore, is a representation (*mimesis*) of serious action … achieving by means of pity (*eleos*) and fear (*phobos*) the purification (*katharsis*) of those emotions'; cf. *Poetics* 1452a1ff. Tragic wonder (*to thaumaston*, cf. 'marvel', *mirantur*, *Tro.* 1148) is also associated by Aristotle with the production of pity and fear (*Poetics* 1452a4ff.). Important, too, is 'spectacle' (*opsis*), regarded by Aristotle as one of the six parts of tragedy (*Poetics* 1450a7ff.), but, though psychologically powerful, seen as least pertaining to the poet's art (*Poetics* 1450b17ff.). Indeed Aristotle considered the arousing of pity and fear by spectacle as indicating an inferior poet (*Poetics* 1453b1ff.). No Roman tragedian could have agreed. Spectacle informed Roman tragedy, as it informed Roman culture. Further disagreement with Aristotle's prescriptions (*Poetics* 1449b24ff.) is evident in Seneca's generation of pity and fear at the conclusion of *Troades* through 'narrative' (*apaggelia*) rather than through 'action'.

76 Representation of 'la fermeté des grands coeurs' in *Nicomède* succeeds according to Corneille in exciting 'l'admiration dans l'âme du spectateur' but not 'la compassion' normally produced by tragedy (*Nicomède, Examen*).

77 *Préface* to *Bérénice* (1670).

78 This is not to suggest that Hamlet's views of the purpose of 'playing' are 'coterminous' with those of Shakespeare, but rather part of the latter's more 'capacious' perspective. For an incisive discussion, see Montrose (1996), 42–4.

79 Seneca here remodels considerably Ovid *Her.* 12.160, where Medea offers her personal desolation as 'grave-offerings' (*inferiae*) to her brother's spirit.

80 For the gladiatorial language, see *Ag.* 901, *Oed.* 998; cf. *Med.* 550.

81 Willamowitz-Moellendorf (1919), III, 162.

82 The appearance of *Medea*'s final choric lines (1416–19) at the conclusions of *Alcestis, Andromache, Helen* and *Bacchae* has cast doubt on the authenticity of this 'Euripidean' ending. It was presumably, however, the ending known to Seneca.

83 Eliot (1951), 73.

Chapter 8

1 On the non-Senecan nature of *Hercules Oetaeus*, see, e.g., Leo (1878), i. 48ff., Friedrich (1954), Axelson (1964–5), 92ff.; Zwierlein (1986), 313–43. Recently Rozelaar (1985) and Nisbet (1987) have championed the Senecan authorship of the play. Their arguments have not convinced. The Senecan authorship of *Octavia* has been doubted since the time of Petrarch and is championed by few: see Ferri (2003a), 6 n.15.

2 Ferri (2003a), 50–4, argues for the priority of *Hercules Oetaeus* and the dependence of *Octavia* upon it. Zwierlein (1986), 328–38, dates *HO* to

the second century CE on the basis of its alleged imitation of Silius Italicus. Fitch (2002/04), 2.333, 512–13, dates *HO* to the last decade of the first century CE or to the early second century, and *Oct.* to 68–70 CE.

3 'Attractive' to some: Fitch (2002/04), 2.332.

4 Pease (1918), who thinks the play Senecan, lists some 400 parallels from other plays.

5 Viansino (1993), 2.2.405, who criticises the play's 'tautologie intolerabili', notes twenty-two references to Cerberus, the guard dog of the underworld.

6 For such a political reading see Viansino (1993), 413, and Nisbet (1987), 250. The latter actually reads the *belua* as a reference to Nero himself.

7 For a list of plays informed by *Octavia*, see Wilson (2003b), 2.

8 Most assessments of *Octavia* have been negative. But, since we have no other *fabula praetexta*, it is impossible to formulate appropriate criteria for evaluation. See Smith (2003), 392–3. On the generic issue, some have denied that *Octavia* conforms to generic type and is too idiosyncratic ('une prétexte devenue tragédie': Dupont 1985: 228; cf. Flower 1995: 172) to be a useful source of information on the regular form of the *praetexta*. For a vigorous defence of *Octavia* as paradigmatic *praetexta* see Kragelund (2002), who argues (10) that the play operates 'within the framework of a fairly well-defined tradition'.

9 See Herington (1961), 22; Erasmo (2004), 59.

10 On *Octavia's* indebtedness to Senecan tragedy, see esp. Herington (1961), 28.

11 Accius' *Brutus* is in fact referred to by a scholiast on Cic. *Sest.* 123 as a *tragoedia praetextata*.

12 For arguments in support of a *praetexta* on *Gaius Gracchus*, see Wiseman (1998), 52–9.

13 See Wilson (2003b), 11–12, for details of these 'competing mythical and republican and imperial paradigms'. On *Octavia* and Sophocles' *Electra*, see Herington (1961), 20.

14 For arguments in support of the continuity of the genre from republican to imperial *praetextae*, see Kragelund (2002).

15 Curiatius Maternus, whose *Cato* was clearly another anti-imperial *praetexta*; so, too, possibly his *Domitius* and/or *Nero*. See pp. 232–3.

16 The phrase is that of Goldberg (2003), 19. Similarly, Fitch (2002/04), 2.511, comments on *Octavia's* 'impoverished' language and monotonous use of personal adjectives and pronouns.

17 On non-Senecan language and style in *Octavia*, see Ferri (2003a), 31–54.

18 Hence Smith (2003), 403–5, argues for the play's essentially 'dyadic' structure.

19 Ferri (2003a) makes it a seven-act play, but, if one sticks to the convention of act-divisions by choral odes, the play has six acts (as does Seneca's *Oedipus* and, possibly, *Phaedra*).

20 So, too, Erasmo (2004), 63–6, who, however, ignores the scene's presentation of Poppaea as another victim of Nero, preferring to see her simply as a Tarquin, 'a modern-day tyrant' and 'an active participant in the political struggle between Nero and Octavia' (66).

21 The matter is discussed by Smith (2003), 412–13, esp. n. 52, who argues strongly for the interiority of the play's action. Wiseman (2001), 15–16, suggests a use of the *exostra* in *Octavia* to move from an interior to an exterior scene.

22 On the *thalamus*, see Kragelund (2002), 45–7.

23 Chaumartin (2002), 59.

24 See Ferri (2003a), *ad Oct.* 877.

25 So Wiseman (2001), 15, and (2002b) – the latter in refutation of Manuwald (2001).

26 See Wiseman (1998), 57; Kragelund (2002), 45.

27 See Ferri (2003a), 318.

28 Herington (1961), 24–5; Kragelund (2002), 42; Ferri (2003b), 107; Fitch (2002/04), 2.508.

29 For a hypothetical account of an onstage wedding, see Wiseman (2001), 19–20.

30 Fitch (2002/04), 2.509. See also Smith (2003), 415–16.

31 For this see Kragelund (2002), 48, and Fitch (2002/04), 2. 510. Ferri (2002), 67 n.159, sees the whole scene as simply imagined by Octavia in 'a prophetic hallucination'.

32 Of course, the issue of *Octavia*'s intended form of realisation is much debated. The three hypotheses – stage-production, recitation performance, private reading – have their adherents. The only arguments which have force are those based on the form of the text itself. Smith (2003), 394, n. 10, persuasively articulates the case that the play was designed for some kind of stage performance and follows this with an impressive and detailed performance critique of the whole drama. That such a stage performance took place in a private venue seems an especially strong possibility, given the increasing trend towards the private staging of drama in the early empire: Jones (1993), Csapo (1999). For a view that *Octavia* was widely known by the time Tacitus wrote the account of Octavia's divorce and execution in *Annals* 14, see Billot (2003), 141.

33 Kragelund (1982 and 1988) and Barnes (1982). See also Fitch (2002/04) mentioned in n. 2.

34 Smith (2003), esp. 426–30.

35 See Ferri (2003a), 5–30. Ferri argues strongly for the dependence of *Octavia* on the historical accounts of Pliny the Elder, Cluvius and Fabius Rusticus – and against the attempts of Kragelund (1982 and 1988) and Barnes (1982) to date the play to the reign of Galba (68–9 CE). Ferri dates the play to the last years of the Flavian principate (the 90s CE), arguing for the play's dependence on the early *Silvae* of Statius. Herington (1961), 29, uses Quintilian's evidence on the declining popularity of Seneca's prose works to argue for 90 CE as a *terminus ante quem*. Attempts to date the play after the Flavian period have persuaded few.

36 Calder (1983), 193.

37 The indebtedness to *Ad Helviam*, *De Clementia* and *De Ira* is especially marked: see Hosius (1922), *ad loc.*

38 For the former, see Williams (1994), 185, 187, Goldberg (2003), 24–5, Harrison (2003), 116; for the latter, see Habinek (2000), 296. To Fitch (2002/04), 2.507, Seneca's views are 'impractically idealistic' but presented 'in a highly favourable light'.

39 Note the pun on 'make', *faciam*: Nero made Claudius a god both by killing him and deifying him.

40 So both Poe (1989), 451, and Wilson (2003c), 86.

41 On the relationship between *Octavia* and *Thyestes*, see now the analysis of Manuwald (2003b).

42 The *lex* is preserved on a bronze plaque which came to light in the *trecento* and is now in the Lateran at Rome: McCrum and Woodhead (1961) 1 (*ILS* 244); Levick (1999) pl 12.

43 See Mellor (2003), 81. Vespasian had much to be thankful to Claudius for: see Boyle (2003a), 6. It should also be noted that Vespasian created a cultural environment favourable to at least some kinds of theatrical productions. For Vespasian's revitalisation of scenic festivals and sponsorship of actors, which – some have argued – may have provided the spur for this piece of political theatre, see Smith (2003), 427.

44 Ferri (2003a), 27–8.

45 For Domitian as a 'Nero', see Pliny *Paneg.* 53.4.

46 Ferri (2003a), 28, compares the relationship of this description to comments on senatorial subservience under Domitian by Tacitus (*Agr.* 2.3, 3.3, 45.1).

47 See Smith (2003), 396: 'We should do well to read *Octavia* not simply as an account of the crisis in the history of the Julio-Claudian dynasty ... but as a reflection of a later socio-historic climate, a distinctively Flavian climate ... which caused the playwright to look back and mythologise'. For Smith, 426, the play enacts 'a popular mandate for justified revolution, figure-headed in Octavia'. Kragelund (2002), 45, takes too positive a view of the Roman people in this play, failing to observe that, though 'nobly nostalgic', the Roman people fail.

48 See Wilson (2003c), 66.

49 See Penwill (2003).

50 Quintilian should have known; tutor to Domitian's great-nephews and heirs, he knew the circles of power (*Inst.* 4, pref. 2; Auson. *Grat. Act.* 31). On *emphasis*, see Ahl's seminal essay (1984a), and Fearnley (2003), 615–16.

51 Mason (2003), 559–60.

52 The Augustan theatre law was itself a revival and modification of the *lex Roscia theatralis* of 67 BCE (Suet. *Aug.* 44). See p. 170.

53 See Coleman (1990).

54 Mellor (2003), 81.

55 Tac. *Agr.* 2.1, 45.1; Suet. *Dom.* 10.3; Dio 67.13.2; see also Plut. *Mor.* 522DE.

56 The passage is controversial. See Kragelund (2002), 38–41.

57 See Syme (1958), 111. Bartsch (1994), 261, questions the historicity of Maternus, but a fictive Maternus would hardly have been possible, given that a great many of Tacitus' readers/audience would have had detailed knowledge of the period a quarter of a century earlier.

58 On the Capitolian festival, see Hardie (2003), 126–34.

59 See Izenour (1992), who argues that odeums, such as the Sullan Odeum of Pompei, the Odeum of Augustus at Pausilypon on the Bay of Naples, the Odeum of Nero at Cosa, were technologically advanced structures, whose sophisticated lighting, acoustics and stage sets were used for (*inter alia*) dramatic performances.

60 Hardie (2003), 130–3.
61 See Izenour (1992), 35–6, and this chapter n. 59.
62 Satirised by Juvenal, *Sat.* 7.87–92.
63 Fulgentius, *Serm.* 7 Helm, cites Rutilius Geminus and his *Astyanax*, but his date is unknown.
64 To attribute the decline of Roman tragedy to 'its very theatricality', evidenced in Senecan metatragedy (Erasmo 2004, 137–9), is unlikely to convince in the face of the increasing and increasingly self-conscious theatricality (and popularity) of the arena. The 'death of Roman tragedy', as this chapter attempts to show, is gradual, and its causes are complex and several.
65 Gunderson (2003), 643.
66 Both the writing and the performance of new Greek tragedies continued through to the end of the second century CE and the performance of revived Greek tragedies into the third century CE and possibly beyond. See Jones (1993), 48.
67 For mythological subjects (including tragic subjects such as Medea, Hippolytus, Orestes and Oedipus) on Roman sarcophagi of the second and/or third centuries CE, see Koch and Sichtermann (1982), 127–90.

SELECT BIBLIOGRAPHY

The following scholars are sometimes referred to by name alone: Clark (= Clark 1907), Csapo and Slater (= Csapo and Slater 1995), Degrassi (= Degrassi 1963), Jocelyn (= Jocelyn 1967a), Keil (= Keil 1857–80), Klotz (= Klotz 1953), Krenkel (= Krenkel 1970), Nauck (= Nauck 1926), Ribbeck (= Ribbeck 1897/98), Skutsch (= Skutsch 1985), Stangl (= Stangl 1912), Warmington (= Warmington 1935–8).

Editions of Latin texts

Astbury, R. (1985), *M. Terentius Varro: Saturarum Menippearum Fragmenta*. Leipzig.

Barbera, E. (2000), *L.A. Seneca. Ottavia*. Lecce.

Barrile, R. (1969), *Accius, Lucius: Frammenti delle tragedie e delle preteste*. Bologna.

Bonaria, M. (1965), *Romani Mimi*. Rome.

Bothe, F. H. (1834), *Poetarum Scenicorum Latinorum Fragmenta*. Leipzig.

Boyle, A. J. (1987), *Seneca's Phaedra*. Liverpool (repr. Leeds 1992).

—— (1994), *Seneca's Troades*. Leeds.

Brink, C. O. (1971), *Horace on Poetry: The 'Ars Poetica'*. Cambridge.

—— (1982), *Horace on Poetry: Epistles Book II*. Cambridge.

Christenson, D. (2000), *Plautus Amphitruo*. Cambridge.

Clark, A.C. (1907), *Q. Asconii Pediani Orationum Ciceronis Quinque Enarratio*. Oxford.

Coffey, M. and Mayer, R. (1990), *Seneca Phaedra*. Cambridge.

Costa, C. D. N. (1973), *Seneca Medea*. Oxford.

Dangel, J. (1995), *Accius: Oeuvres (fragments)*. Paris.

D'Anna, I. (1967), *M. Pacuvii Fragmenta*. Rome.

D'Anto, V. (1980), *I frammenti delle tragedie di L. Accio*. Lecce.

Daviault, A. (1981), *Comoedia Togata Fragments*. Paris.

Diehl, E. (1911), *Poetarum Romanorum Veterum Reliquiae*. Bonn.

Fantham. E (1982), *Seneca's Troades*. Princeton.

Ferri, R. (2003a), *Octavia. A Play Attributed to Seneca*. Cambridge.

Fitch, J. G. (2002/04), *Seneca: Tragedies*. 2 vols. Cambridge, MA/London.

Franchella, Q. (1968), *Lucii Accii tragoediarum fragmenta*. Bologna.

Frank, M. (1995), *Seneca's Phoenissae: Introduction and Commentary*. Leiden.

Helm, R. (1970), *Fulgentius*. Stuttgart.

Hildebrandt, P. (1907), *Scholia in Ciceronis Orationes Bobiensa*. Leipzig.

Hosius, C. (1922), *Octavia Praetexta cum Elementis Commentarii*. Bonn.

Jocelyn, H. (1967a), *The Tragedies of Ennius*. Cambridge.

Kaster, R. A. (1995), *Suetonius: De Grammaticis et Rhetoribus*. Oxford.

Keil, H. (1857–80), *Grammatici Latini*. 7 vols. Leipzig.

Klotz, A. (1953), *Scaenicorum Romanorum Fragmenta: I. Tragicorum Fragmenta, adiuuantibus O. Seel et L. Voit*. Munich.

Krenkel, W. (1970), *Lucilius Satiren*. 2 vols. Berlin.

Leo, F. (1878–9), *L. Annaei Senecae Tragoediae, accedit Octavia praetexta*. 2 vols. Berlin.

Magno, P. (1977), *Marco Pacuvio, i frammenti*. Milan.

Mueller, L. (1885), *Liui Andronici et Cn. Naeui Fabularum Reliquiae*. Berlin.

Nauck, A. (1926), *Tragicorum Graecorum Fragmenta*. 2nd edn. Leipzig.

Nisbet, R. G. M. (1961), *Cicero In Pisonem*. Oxford.

Plessis, F. and Lejay, P. (1966), *Horace: Satires*. Hildesheim.

Pociña, A. (1984), *El tragediografo Latino Lucio Acio*. Granada.

Ribbeck, O. (1897/98), *Scaenicae Romanorum Poiesis Fragmenta*.3rd edn. 2 vols. Leipzig.

Rostagni, A. (1944), *Suetonio De Poetis e Biografi Minori*. Turin.

Rudd, N. (1989), *Horace: Epistles Book II and Epistle to the Pisones*. Cambridge.

Sedgwick, W. B. (1960), *Plautus Amphitruo*. Manchester.

Shackleton Bailey, D. R. (1993), *Martial Epigrams*. 3 vols. Cambridge, MA.

Skutsch, O. (1985), *The Annals of Q. Ennius*. Oxford.

Stangl, T. (1912), *Ciceronis Orationum Scholiastae*. 2 vols. Vienna and Leipzig.

Strzelecki, W. (1964), *Cn. Naevii Belli Punici Carminis Quae Supersunt*. Leipzig.

Tarrant, R. J. (1976), *Seneca Agamemnon*. Cambridge.

—— (1985), *Seneca's Thyestes*. Atlanta.

Vahlen, J. (1928), *Ennianae Poesis Reliquiae*. 3rd edn. Leipzig.

Viansino, G. (1993), *Seneca teatro*, 2 vols. Rome.

Warmington, E. H. (1935–8), *Remains of Old Latin*. Vols 1–3. Cambridge, MA and London.

Wessner, P. (1902), *Aeli Donati Quod Fertur Commentum Terenti*. Leipzig.

Zwierlein, O. (1986), *L. Annaei Senecae Tragoediae*. Oxford.

General studies and other editions

Abel, L. (1963), *Metatheater*. New York.

Ahl, F. M. (1984a), 'The Art of Safe Criticism in Greece and Rome', *AJP* 105: 174–208.

— (1984b), 'The Rider and the Horse', *ANRW* II.32.1: 40–124.

Alcock, S. E. (1994), 'Nero at Play? The Emperor's Grecian Odyssey', in Elsner and Masters: 98–111.

Aldrete, G. S. (1999), *Gestures and Acclamations in Ancient Rome*. Baltimore and London.

Anderson, W. S. (1993), *Barbarian Play: Plautus' Roman Comedy*. Toronto.

Arcellaschi, A. (1990), *Médée dans le théâtre latin d'Ennius à Sénèque*. Rome.

Argenio, R. (1961), 'Retorica e politica nelle tragedie di Accio', *RSC* 9: 198–212.

Astin, A. E. (1967), *Scipio Aemilianus*. Oxford.

Auhagen, U. (2002), 'Accius' Antenoridae: Zwischen Aitiologie und Tagespolitik', in Faller and Manuwald: 19–38.

Axelson, B. (1964–5), *Korruptelenkult: Studien zur Textkritik der unechten Seneca-Tragödie Hercules Oetaeus*. Lund.

Badian, E. (1971), 'Ennius and his Friends', *Fondation Hardt Entretiens* 17: 149–208.

Baier, T. (2000), 'Pacuvius, Niptra', in Manuwald (2000): 285–300.

—— (2002), 'Accius: *Medea siue Argonautae*', in Faller and Manuwald: 51–62.

Baldarelli, B. (2002), 'Enomao, il re povero? Alcune ipotesi sulla possibile rappresentazione des contrasto povertà-richezza nell' Oenomaus di Accio', in Faller and Manuwald: 63–78.

Balsdon, J. P. V. D. (1969), *Life and Leisure in Ancient Rome*. London.

Barnes, T. D. (1982), 'The Date of the *Octavia*', *MH* 39: 215–17.

Barton, C. (1993), *The Sorrows of the Ancient Romans*. Princeton.

Bartsch, S. (1994), *Actors in the Audience*. Cambridge, MA.

Beacham R. C. (1992), *The Roman Theatre and its Audience*. Cambridge, MA.

—— (1999), *Spectacle Entertainments of Early Imperial Rome*. New Haven.

Beard, M. and Henderson, J. (2001), *Classical Art: From Greece to Rome*. Oxford.

Beard, M, North, J. and Price, S. (1998), *Religions of Rome*. 2 vols. Cambridge.

Beare, W. (1964), *The Roman Stage*, 3rd rev. edn. London.

Bernstein, F. (1998), *Ludi Publici: Untersuchungen zur Entstehung und Entwicklung der öffentlichen Spiele im republikanischen Rom*. Stuttgart.

—— (2000), 'Der römische Sieg bei Clastidium und die zeitgeschichtliche Praetexta des Naevius', in Manuwald (2000): 157–73.

Betts, J. H., Hooker, J.T. and Green, J. R. (eds) (1986), *Studies in Honour of T. B. L. Webster*. Bristol.

Bieber, M. (1961), *The History of the Greek and Roman Theatre*. Princeton.

Biliŝski, B. (1957), *Accio ed i Gracchi: contributo alla storia delle plebe e delle tragedia romana*. Rome.

Billot, F. (2003), 'Tacitus Responds: *Annals* 14 and the *Octavia*', in Wilson (2003a): 126–41.

Blänsdorf, J. (ed.) (1990), *Theater und Gesellschaft im Imperium Romanum*. Tübingen.

—— (2000), 'Livius Andronicus und die Anverwandlung des hellenistischen Dramas in Rom', in Manuwald (2000): 145–56.

Bloom, H. (1973), *The Anxiety of Influence: a Theory of Poetry*. Oxford.

Bonner, S. F. (1949), *Roman Declamation*. Liverpool.

Bowman, A. K., Garnsey, P. and Rathbone, D. (eds), *Cambridge Ancient History XI: The High Empire AD 70–192*. 2nd edn. Cambridge.

Boyle, A. J. (ed.) (1983a), *Seneca Tragicus. Ramus Essays on Senecan Drama*. Berwick, Vic.

—— (1983b), '*Hic Epulis Locus*: the Tragic Worlds of Seneca's *Agamemnon* and *Thyestes*', in Boyle (1983a): 199–228.

—— (1985), 'In Nature's Bonds: a Study of Seneca's *Phaedra*', *ANRW* II.32.2: 1284–1347.

—— (1997), *Tragic Seneca: an Essay in the Theatrical Tradition*. London.

—— (2003a), 'Introduction: Reading Flavian Rome', in Boyle and Dominik: 1–67.

—— (2003b), *Ovid and the Monuments: a Poet's Rome*. Bendigo. Vic.

Boyle, A. J. and Dominik, W. J. (2003), *Flavian Rome: Culture, Image, Text*. Leiden.

Braden, G. (1985), *Renaissance Tragedy and the Senecan Tradition: Anger's Privilege*. New Haven.

Braund, D. and Gill, C. (eds) (2003), *Myth, History and Culture in Republican Rome: Studies in Honor of T. P. Wiseman*. Exeter.

Braund, S. M. and Gill, C. (eds) (1997), *The Passions in Roman Thought and Literature*. Cambridge.

Bremmer, J. and Roodenburg, H. (eds) (1991), *A Cultural History of Gesture from Antiquity to the Present Day*. Oxford.

Broccia, G. (1974), *Ricerche su Livio Andronico epico*. Padua.

Brooks, R. A. (1981), *Ennius and Roman Tragedy*. New York.

Broughton, T. R. S. (1951–60), *The Magistrates of the Roman Republic*. 3 vols. New York.

Brown, P. G. McC. (2002), 'Actors and Actor-Managers at Rome', in Easterling and Hall: 225–37.

Brunschwig, J. and Nussbaum, M. (eds) (1993), *Passions and Perceptions: Studies in Hellenistic Philosophy of Mind*. Cambridge.

Buecheler, F. (1915/1927), *Kleine Schriften*. 2 vols. Leipzig and Berlin.

Calder, W. M. (1975), 'The Size of the Chorus in Seneca's *Agamemnon*', *CP* 70: 32–5.

—— (1976), 'Seneca's *Agamemnon*', *CP* 71: 27–36.

—— (1983), '*Secreti loquimur*: an Interpretation of Seneca's *Thyestes*', in Boyle (1983a): 184–98.

Canter, H. V. (1925), *The Rhetorical Elements in the Tragedies of Seneca*. Urbana.

Caratello, U. (1979), *Livio Andronico*. Roma.

Casaceli, F. (1976), *Lingua e stile in Accio*. Palermo.

Castagna, L. (2002), 'Osservazioni sul *Brutus* di Accio', in Faller and Manuwald: 79–103.

Cebe, J.-P. (1960), 'Le Niveau culturel du public plautinien', *REL* 38: 101–6.

Champlin, E. (2003), 'Agamemnon at Rome', in Braund, D. and Gill: 295–319.

Charlton, H. B. (1946), *The Senecan Tradition in Renaissance Tragedy*. Manchester.

Chaumartin, F.-R. (2002), 'Comments' on Kragelund (2002), *SO* 76: 57–60.

Claridge, A. (1998), *Rome: an Oxford Archaeological Guide*. Oxford.

Coffey, M. (1986), 'Notes on the History of Augustan and Early Imperial Tragedy', in Betts, Hooker and Green: 46–52.

Coleman, K. M. (1990), 'Fatal Charades: Roman Executions Staged as Mythical Enactments', *JRS* 80: 44–73.

Conte, G. B. (1994), *Latin Literature: a History*. Baltimore and London.

Corbeill, A. (2004), *Nature Embodied: Gesture in Ancient Rome*. Princeton.

Cornell, T. J. (1994), 'The Conquest of Italy', in Crook, Lintott and Rawson: 351–419.

—— (1995), *The Beginnings of Rome*. London.

Costa, C. D. N. (ed.) (1974), *Seneca*. London.

Coulter, C. C. (1940), 'Marcus Junius Brutus and the *Brutus* of Accius', *CJ* 35: 460–70.

Cova, P. V. (1989), *Il poeta Vario*. Milan.

—— (1989), 'Sulla datazione del Tieste di Vario', *Athenaeum* n.s. 66: 19–29.

Crocetti, C. G. (1973), *Giambattista Cinthio Giraldi: Scritti critici*. Milan.

Crook, J. A., Lintott, A. and Rawson, E. (eds) (1994), *The Cambridge Ancient History: IX. The Last Age of the Roman Republic: 146–43 b.c.* 2nd edn. Cambridge.

Csapo, E. (1999), 'Performance and Iconographic Tradition in the Illustrations of Menander', in Porter *et al.*: 154–88.

Csapo, E. and Slater, W. J. (1995), *The Context of Ancient Drama*. Ann Arbor.

Curley, T. F. (1986), *The Nature of Senecan Drama*. Rome.

Currie, H. MacL. (1981), 'Ovid and the Roman Stage', *ANRW* II.31.4: 2701–42.

Dangel, J. (1988), 'La place de l'Orient dans le théâtre d'Accius', *REL* 66: 55–74.

—— (1990), 'Les généalogies d'Accius', *Euphrosyne* 18: 53–72.

—— (2002), 'Accius et l'altérité à l'oeuvre: théâtre idéologique et manifeste littéraire', in Faller and Manuwald: 105–25.

Davis, P. J. (1983), '*Vindicat omnes natura sibi*: a Reading of Seneca's *Phaedra*', in Boyle (1983a): 114–27.

—— (2001), 'The Fabrication of Tradition: Horace, Augustus and the Secular Games', *Ramus* 30: 111–27.

Degrassi, A. (1963), *Inscriptiones Italiae*. 13.2. Rome.

Delarue, F. (1985), 'Le *Thyeste* de Varius', in Renard and Laurens: 100–23.

Diggle, J. (1970), *Euripides Phaethon*. Cambridge.

Dingel, J. (1974), *Seneca und die Dichtung*. Heidelberg.

Dodds, E. R. (1960), *Euripides Bacchae*. 2nd edn. Oxford.

Dorey, T. A. and Dudley, D. R. (eds) (1965), *Roman Drama*. London.

Drury, M. (1982), 'Appendix of Authors and Works', in Kenney and Clausen: 799–935.

Duckworth, G. E. (1952), *The Nature of Roman Comedy: a Study in Popular Entertainment*. Princeton.

Ducos, M. (1990), 'La condition des acteurs à Rome', in Blänsdorf: 19–33.

Dunkle, J. R. (1967), 'The Greek Tyrant and Roman Political Invective of the Late Republic', *TAPA* 98: 151–71.

Dupont, F. (1985), *L'acteur-roi: le théâtre dans la Rome antique*. Paris.

—— (1988) *Le théâtre latin*. Paris.

—— (1995), *Les monstres de Sénèque*. Paris.

Easterling, P. and Hall, E. (eds) (2002), *Greek and Roman Actors: Aspects of an Ancient Profession*. Cambridge.

Edwards, C. (1993), *The Politics of Immorality in Ancient Rome*. Cambridge.

—— (1994), 'Beware of Imitations: Theatre and the Subversion of Imperial Identity', in Elsner and Masters: 83–97.

Eliot, T. S. (1951), *Selected Essays*. 3rd edn. London.

Elsner, J. and Masters, J. (eds) (1994), *Reflections of Nero: Culture, History and Representation*. London.

Enk, P. J. (1957), 'Roman Tragedy', *Neophilologus* 41: 282–307.

Erasmo, M. (2004), *Roman Tragedy: Theatre to Theatricality*. Austin, Texas.

Faller, S. and Manuwald, G. (eds) (2002), *Accius und seine Zeit*. Würzburg.

Fantham, E. (1975), 'Virgil's Dido and Seneca's Tragic Heroines', *G&R* ns 22: 1–10.

—— (1989), 'Mime: The Missing Link in Roman Literary History', *CW* 82: 153–63.

—— (1996), *Roman Literary Culture*. Baltimore.

—— (2002), 'Orator and/et Actor', in Easterling and Hall: 362–76.

—— (2003), 'Pacuvius: Melodrama, Reversals and Recognitions', in Braund, D. and Gill: 98–118.

Favro, D. (1996), *The Urban Image of Augustan Rome*. Cambridge.

Fearnley, H. (2003), 'Reading the Imperial Revolution: Martial Epigrams 10', in Boyle and Dominik: 613–35.

Ferri, R. (2002), 'Comments' on Kragelund (2002), *SO* 76: 60–8.

—— (2003b), '*Octavia* and the Roman Dramatic Tradition', in Wilson (2003a): 89–111.

Fitch, J. G. (1981), 'Sense-Pauses and Relative Dating in Seneca, Sophocles and Shakespeare', *AJP* 102: 289–307.

Flores, E. (1974) *Letteratura latina e ideologia del III–II a. C.* Naples.

Flower, H. I. (1995), '*Fabulae Praetextae* in Context: When Were Plays on Contemporary Subjects Performed in Rome?', *CQ* n.s. 45: 170–90.

—— (1996), *Ancestor Masks and Aristocratic Power in Roman Culture*. Oxford.

—— (2000), '*Fabula de Bacchanalibus*: The Bacchanalian Cult of the Second Century bc and Roman Drama', in Manuwald (2000): 23–35.

—— (ed.) (2004a), *The Cambridge Companion to the Roman Republic*. Cambridge.

—— (2004b), 'Spectacle and Political Culture in the Roman Republic', in Flower (2004a): 322–43.

Fortey, S. and Glucker, J. (1985), '*Actus Tragicus*: Seneca on the Stage', *Latomus* 34: 699–715.

Fowler, W. W. (1899), *The Roman Festivals of the Period of the Roman Republic*. London.

Fraenkel, E. (1922), *Plautinisches in Plautus*. Berlin.

Frank, T. (1931), 'The Status of Actors at Rome', *CP* 26: 11–20.

Frassinetti, P. (1953), *Fabula Atellana: saggio populare latino*. Pavia.

Fredericksen, M. F. (1965), 'The Republican Municipal Laws: Errors and Drafts', *JRS* 55: 183–98.

Frézouls, E. (1983), 'La construction du theatrum lapideum et son contexte politique', in Zehnacker: 193–214.

Friedrich, W. H. (1954), 'Sprache und Stil des Hercules Oetaeus', *Hermes* 82: 51–84.

Futrell, A. (1997), *Blood in the Arena: the Spectacle of Roman Power*. Austin.

Gabba, E. (1969), 'Il *Brutus* di Accio', *Dioniso* 43: 377–83.

—— (1994), 'Rome and Italy: The Social War', in Crook, Lintott and Rawson: 104–28.

Galinksky, K. (1996), *Augustan Culture: an Interpretive Introduction*. Princeton.

Garelli-François, M. H. (1998), *Rome et le tragique*. Toulouse.

Garton, C. (1972), *Personal Aspects of the Roman Theater*. Toronto.

Gentili, B. (1979), *Theatrical Performances in the Ancient World*. Amsterdam.

Gilula, D. (1989), 'Greek Drama in Rome: Some Aspects of Cultural Transposition', in Scolnicov and Holland: 99–109.

Gleason, M. (1994), *Making Men: Sophists and Self-Representation in Ancient Rome*. Princeton.

Goldberg, S. (1986), *Understanding Terence*. Princeton.

—— (1995), *Epic in Republican Rome*. Oxford.

—— (1996), 'The Fall and Rise of Roman Tragedy', *TAPA* 126: 265–86.

—— (1998), 'Plautus on the Palatine', *JRS* 88:1–20.

—— (1999), 'Cicero and the Work of Tragedy', in Manuwald (2000): 49–59.

—— (2003), 'Authorizing Octavia', in Wilson (2003a): 13–36.

Graf, F. (1991), 'Gestures and Conventions: The Gestures of Roman Actors and Orators', in Bremmer and Roodenburg: 36–58.

Gratwick, A. S. (1982), 'Drama', in Kenney and Clausen: 77–137.

Greenblatt, S.J. (1980), *Renaissance Self-Fashioning: From More to Shakespeare*. Chicago.

Griffin, M. T. (2000), 'The Flavians', in Bowman *et al.*: 1–83.

Grilli, A. (1965), *Studi Enniani*. Brescia.

Gruen, E. S. (1990), *Studies in Greek Culture and Roman Policy*. Leiden.

—— (1992), *Culture and National Identity in Republican Rome*. Ithaca, NY.

Gunderson, E. (2003), 'The Flavian Amphitheatre: All the World as Stage', in Boyle and Dominik: 637–58.

Habinek, T. N. (1998), *The Politics of Latin Literature*. Princeton.

—— (2000), 'Seneca's Renown: Gloria, Claritudo and the Replication of the Roman Elite', *CA* 19: 264–303.

Hanson, J. A. (1959), *Roman Theater-Temples*. Princeton.

Hardie, A. (2003), 'Poetry and Politics at the Games of Domitian', in Boyle and Dominik: 125–47.

Harrison, G. W. M. (ed.) (2000), *Seneca in Performance*. London.

—— (2003), 'Forms of Intertextuality in the *Octavia*', in Wilson (2003a): 112–25.

Hartkamp, R. (2002), 'Evander im *Atreus*: Die Selbstdarstellung des Tragikers L. Accius und der antiexemplarishche Gehalt seiner Stücke als Ausdruck von Alterität', in Faller and Manuwald: 161–72.

Henry, D. and Henry, E. (1985), *The Mask of Power*. Warminster.

Henry, D., and Walker, B. (1966), 'Phantasmagoria and Idyll: an Element of Seneca's *Phaedra*', *G&R* n.s. 13: 223–39.

Herbert-Brown, G. (ed.) (2002), *Ovid's Fasti: Historical Readings at the Bimillenium*. Oxford.

Herington, C. J. (1961), '*Octavia Praetexta*: a Survey', *CQ* n.s. 11: 18–30.

—— (1966), 'Senecan Tragedy', *Arion* 5: 422–71.

—— (1982), 'Senecan Tragedy', in Kenney and Clausen: 519–32.

Heurgon, J. (1964), *Daily Life of the Etruscans*. London.

Horsfall, N. (1976), 'The *collegium poetarum*', *BICS* 23: 79–95.

Hose, M. (1999a), 'Anmerkungen zur Verwendung des Chores in der römischen Tragödie der Republik', in Riemer and Zimmermann: 113–38.

—— (1999b), 'Post-Colonial Theory and Greek Literature in Rome', *GRBS* 40: 303–26.

Hunter, G. K. (1974), 'Seneca and English Tragedy', in Costa: 166–204.

Hunter, R. L. (1985), *The New Comedy of Greece and Rome*. Cambridge.

Izenour, G. C. (1992), *Roofed Theaters of Classical Antiquity*. New Haven.

Jocelyn, H. D. (1967b), 'The Quotations of Republican Drama in Priscian's Treatise *De Metris Fabularum Terentii*', *Antichthon* 1: 68–9.

—— (1969), 'The Poet Cn. Naevius, P. Cornelius Scipio, and Q. Caecilius Metellus', *Antichthon* 3: 32–47.

—— (1972a), 'Ennius as a Dramatic Poet', *Fondation Hardt Entretiens* 17: 39–95.

—— (1972b), 'The Poems of Quintus Ennius', *ANRW* 1.2: 987–1026.

—— (1978), Review of Lefèvre (1976), *Gnomon* 50: 778–80.

—— (1980), 'The Fate of Varius' *Thyestes*', *CQ* 30: 387–400.

—— (2000), 'Accius' *Aeneadae aut Decius*: Romans and the Gallic Other', in Manuwald (2000): 325–61.

Jones, C. P. (1991), 'Dinner Theatre', in Slater, W. J. (1991): 185–98.

—— (1993), 'Greek Drama in the Roman Empire', in Scodel: 39–52.

Jory, E. J. (1970), 'Associations of Actors in Rome', *Hermes* 98: 224–53.

—— (1986), 'Continuity and Change in the Roman Theatre', in Betts, Hooker and Green: 143–52.

Kaimio, J. (1979), *The Romans and the Greek Language*. Helsinki.

Kambitsis, J. (1972), *L'Antiope d'Euripide*. Paris.

Kenney, E. and Clausen, W. (eds) (1982), *The Cambridge History of Classical Literature, II: Latin Literature*. Cambridge.

Koch, G. and Sichtermann, H. (1982), *Römische Sarkophage*. Munich.

Konstan, D. (1996), *Friendship in the Classical World*. Cambridge.

Kragelund, P. (1982), *Prophecy, Populism, and Propaganda in the 'Octavia'*. Copenhagen.

—— (1988), 'The Prefect's Dilemma and the Date of the *Octavia*', *CQ* n.s. 38: 492–508.

—— (2002), 'Historical Drama in Ancient Rome: Republican Flourishing and Imperial Decline?', *SO* 76: 5–51.

La Penna, A. (1979), *Fra teatro, poesia e politica romana*. Turin.

—— (2000), 'Le *Sabinae* di Ennio e il tema della concordia nella tragedia arcaica latina', in Manuwald (2000): 241–54.

Lebeck, W. D. (1985), 'Senecas Agamemnon in Pompeji (*CIL* iv 6698)', *ZPE* 59: 1–6.

—— (2000), 'Livius Andronicus und Naevius: Wie konnten sie von ihrer dramatischen Dichtung leben?', in Manuwald (2000): 61–86.

Lefèvre, E. (ed.) (1972), *Senecas Tragödien*. Darmstadt.

—— (1976), *Der Thyestes des Lucius Varius Rufus: Zehn Überlegungen zu seiner Rekonstruktion*. Mainz.

—— (ed.) (1978), *Das römische Drama*. Darmstadt.

—— (2000), 'Aitiologisch-politische Implikationen in Naevius' *Danae*', in Manuwald (2000): 175–84.

Leigh, M. (1996), 'Varius Rufus, Thyestes and the Appetites of Antony', *PCPS* 42: 171–97.

—— (2000), 'Primitivism and Power: The Beginnings of Latin Literature', in Taplin: 288–310.

—— (2004), *Comedy and the Rise of Rome*. Oxford.

Lennartz, K. (1994), *Non uerba sed uim. Kritisch-exegetische Untersuchungen zu den Fragmenten archaischer römischer Tragiker*. Stuttgart and Leipzig.

Leo, F. (1910), *De Tragoedia Romana*. Göttingen.

Levick, B. (1983), 'The *Senatus Consultum* from Larinum', *JRS* 73: 97–115.

—— (1999), *Vespasian*. London.

Lightfoot, J. L. (2002), 'Nothing To Do with the *Technitai* of Dionysus?', in Easterling and Hall: 209–24.

Ling, R. (1991), *Roman Painting*. Cambridge.

Littlewood, C. A. J. (2004), *Self-Representation and Illusion in Senecan Tragedy*. Oxford.

MacDonald, W. L. (1982), *The Architecture of the Roman Empire I: Introductory Study*. 2nd edn. New Haven.

—— (1985), 'Empire Imagery in Augustan Architecture', in R. Winkes (ed.), *The Age of Augustus (Archaeologia Transatlantica 5)*: 137–48. Louvain-la-Neuve.

Manuwald, G. (ed.) (2000), *Identität und Alterität in der frührömischen Tragödie*. Würzburg.

—— (2001), *Fabulae praetextae. Spuren einer literarischen Gattung*. Munich.

—— (2003a), *Pacuvius. Summus tragicus poeta. Zum dramatischen Profil seiner Tragödien*. Munich and Leipzig.

—— (2003b), 'The Concepts of Tyranny in Seneca's *Thyestes* and in *Octavia*', in Wilson (2003a): 37–59.

Mariotti, I. (1960), *Introduzione a Pacuvio*. Urbino.

Mariotti, S. (1986), *Livio Andronico e la traduzione artistica*. Urbino.

—— (1991), *Lezioni su Ennio*. Urbino.

Marti, B. M. (1945), 'Seneca's Tragedies: A New Interpretation', *TAPA* 76: 216–45.

Mason, S. (2003), 'Flavius Josephus in Flavian Rome: Reading On and Between the Lines', in Boyle and Dominik: 559–89.

Mastrocinque, A. (1983/84), 'La cacciata di Tarquinio il superbo: tradizione romana e letteratura greca', *Athenaeum* n.s. 61: 457–80; 62: 210–29.

Mattingly, H. B. (1960), 'Naevius and the Metelli', *Historia* 9: 414–39.

McCrum, M. and Woodhead, A. G. (1961), *Select Documents of the Principates of the Flavian Emperors, Including the Year of Revolution: a.d. 68–96*. Cambridge.

Mellor, R. (2003), 'The New Aristocracy of Power', in Boyle and Dominik: 69–101.

Mette, H. J. (1964), 'Die Römische Tragödie und die Neufunde zur Griechischen Tragödie', *Lustrum* 9: 5–211.

Mommsen, T., Krueger, P. and Watson, A. (eds) (1985), *The Digest of Justinian*. Philadelphia.

Montrose, L. (1996), *The Purpose of Playing: Shakespeare and the Cultural Politics of the Elizabethan Theater*. Chicago and London.

Moore, T. J. (1994), 'Seats and Social Status in the Plautine Theater', *CJ* 90: 113–23.

—— (1998), *The Theater of Plautus: Playing to the Audience*. Austin.

Morelli, G. (1974), *Poesia latina in frammenti*. Genoa.

Murray, O. (ed.) (1990), *Sympotica: A Symposium on the Symposion*. Oxford.

Nicolet, C. (1980), *The World of the Citizen in Republican Rome*. Berkeley.

Nisbet, R. (1987), 'The Oak and the Axe: Symbolism in Seneca, *Hercules Oetaeus* 1618ff.', in Whitby *et al.*: 243–51.

North, J. A. (1983), 'These He Cannot Take', *JRS* 73: 169–74.

Nussbaum, M. (1993), 'Poetry and the Passions: Two Stoic Views', in Brunschwig and Nussbaum: 97–149.

Oakley, S. P. (1998), *A Commentary on Livy Books VI–X: II, Books VII–VIII*. Oxford.

—— (2004), 'The Early Republic', in Flower (2004a): 15–30.

Ogilvie, R. M. (1965), *A Commentary on Livy Books 1–5*. Oxford.

O'Neill, P. (2003), 'Triumph Songs. Reversal and Plautus' *Amphitruo*', *Ramus* 32: 1–38.

Paduano, G. (1974), *Il mondo religioso della tragedia Romana*. Florence.

Panayotakis, C. (1995), *Theatrum Arbitri. Theatrical Elements in the 'Satyrica' of Petronius*. Leiden.

Paratore, E. (1957), *Storia del teatro latino*. Milan.

Pease, A. S. (1918), 'On the Authenticity of the *Hercules Oetaeus*', *TAPA* 49: 3–26.

Penwill, J. L. (2003), 'Expelling the Mind: Politics and Philosophy in Flavian Rome', in Boyle and Dominik: 345–68.

Perna, R. (1978), *Livio Andronico, poeta di Puglia*. Bari.

Petaccia, M. R. (2000), 'Der Orestes-Mythos in der lateinischen archaischen Tragödie und im politisch-religiösen Zusammenhang der römischen Republik', in Manuwald (2000): 87–112.

—— (2002), 'Gli *Antenoridae*', in Faller and Manuwald: 229–43.

Petrone, G. (2000), 'La *praetexta* repubblicana e il linguaggio delle celebrazione', in Manuwald (2000): 113–21.

—— (2002), 'L'Atreo di Accio e le passioni del potere', in Faller and Manuwald: 245–53.

Plass, P. (1995), *The Game of Death in Ancient Rome: Arena Sport and Political Suicide*. Madison.

Poe, J. P. (1989), '*Octavia Praetexta* and its Senecan Model', *AJP* 110: 434–59.

Porter, J., Csapo, E., Marshall, C. W. and Ketterer, R. C. (eds) (1999), *Crossing the Stages: The Production, Performance and Reception of Ancient Theatre. Syllecta Classica* 10.

Potter, D. and Mattingly, D. (eds) (1999), *Life, Death, Entertainment in the Roman Empire*. Ann Arbor.

Rawson, E. (1991), *Roman Culture and Society*. Oxford.

Reich, H. (1974), *Der Mimus*. Leipzig.

Renard, M. and Laurens, P. (eds) (1985), *Hommages à Henri Bardon*. Brussels.

Ribbeck, O. (1875), *Die römische Tragödie in Zeitalter der Republik*. Leipzig. (Repr. Hildesheim 1969).

Richardson, L. Jr. (1992), *A New Topographical Dictionary of Ancient Rome*. Baltimore and London.

Riemer, P. and Zimmermann, B. (eds) (1999), *Der Chor im antiken und modernen Drama*. Stuttgart.

Rosalia, A. de (1982), *Lexicon Accianum*. Hildesheim.

Rosenmeyer, T. G. (1989), *Senecan Drama and Stoic Cosmology*. Berkeley.

Rousselle, R. J. (1987), 'Liber-Dionysos in Early Roman Drama', *CJ* 82: 193–8.

Rowland, I. D. (1999), *Vitruvius: Ten Books of Architecture*. Cambridge.

Rozelaar, M. (1985), 'Neue Studien zur Tragödie Hercules Oetaeus', *ANRW* II.32.2: 1348–1419.

Rüpke, J. (2002), 'Accius als Theologe', in Faller and Manuwald: 255–70.

Schiesaro, A. (1994), 'Seneca's *Thyestes* and the Morality of Tragic *Furor*', in Elsner and Masters: 196–210.

—— (1997), 'Passion, Reason and Knowledge in Seneca', in Braund, S. M. and Gill: 89–111.

—— (2003), *The Passions in Play: Thyestes and the Dynamics of Senecan Drama*. Cambridge.

Schnegg-Köhler, B. (2002), *Die augusteischen Säkularspiele*. Munich and Leipzig.

Schnurr, C. (1992), 'The *Lex Iulia Theatralis* of Augustus: Some Remarks on Seating Problems in Theatre, Amphitheatre and Circus', *LCM* 17: 147–60.

Scodel, R. (ed.) (1993), *Theatre and Society in the Classical World*. Ann Arbor.

Scolnicov, H. and Holland, P. (eds) (1989, *The Play out of Context: Transfering Plays from Culture to Culture*. Cambridge.

Scullard, H. H. (1972), *Roman Politics 220–150 B.C.* Oxford.

Segal, C. P. (1984), 'Senecan Baroque: the Death of Hippolytus in Seneca, Ovid and Euripides', *TAPA* 114: 311–26.

—— (1986), *Language and Desire in Seneca's Phaedra*. Princeton.

Segal, E. (1968), *Roman Laughter: The Comedy of Plautus*. Cambridge, MA.

Seidensticker, B. (1969), *Die Gesprächsverdichtung in den Tragödien Senecas*. Heidelberg.

Shackleton Bailey, D. R. (1965–7), *Cicero's Letters to Atticus*. 6 vols. Cambridge.

—— (1977), *Cicero: Epistulae ad Familiares*. 2 vols. Cambridge.

Skutsch, O. (1968), *Studia Enniana*. London.

Slater, N. (1985), *Plautus in Performance*. Princeton.

—— (1992), 'Two Republican Poets on Drama: Terence and Accius', in Zimmermann: 85–103.

—— (2000), 'Religion and Identity in Pacuvius' *Chryses*', in Manuwald (2000): 315–23.

—— (2002), 'Some Accian Women', in Faller and Manuwald: 289–303

Slater, W. J. (ed.) (1991), *Dining in a Classical Context*. Ann Arbor.

—— (ed.) (1996), *Roman Theater and Society*. Ann Arbor.

Smith, J. A. (2003), 'Flavian Drama: Looking Back with Octavia', in Boyle and Dominik: 391–430

Snell, B. (1964), *Scenes from Greek Drama*. Berkeley and Los Angeles.

Strzelecki, W. (1963), 'Naevius and Roman Annalists', *RIFC* 91: 440–58.

Suerbaum, W. (1968), *Untersuchungen zur Selbstdarstellung älterer römischen Dichter: Livius Andronicus, Naevius, Ennius*. Hildesheim.

—— (2000), 'Religiöse Identitäts- und Alteritätsangebote im *Equos Troianus* und im *Lycurgus* des Naevius', in Manuwald (2000): 185–98.

Sutton, D. F. (1983), *The Dramaturgy of the Octavia*. Königstein.

—— (1984), *The Lost Sophocles*. Lanham, New York and London.

—— (1986), *Seneca on the Stage*. Leiden.

Syme, R. (1939), *The Roman Revolution*. Oxford.

—— (1958), *Tacitus*. 2 vols. Oxford.

Szemerényi, O. (1975), 'The Origins of Roman Drama and Greek Tragedy', *Hermes* 103: 300–37.

Szilágyi, J. (1981), 'Impletae Modis Saturae', *Prospettiva* 24: 2–23.

Tandoi, V. (1992a) *Scritti di filologia e di storia della cultura classica*, 2 vols. Pisa.

—— (1992b), 'Il dramma storico di Pacuvio: Restauri e interpretazione', in Tandoi (1992a): i. 39–59.

Taplin, O. (ed.) (2000), *Literature in the Greek and Roman Worlds: A New Perspective*. Oxford.

Tarrant, R. J. (1978), 'Senecan Drama and its Antecedents', *HSCP* 82: 213–63.

Traina, A. (1970), *Vortit barbare: Le traduzioni poetiche da Livio Andronico a Cicerone*. Rome.

Valsa, M. (1957), *Marcus Pacuvius, poète tragique*. Paris.

Vanderbroeck, P. J. (1987), *Popular Leadership and Collective Behaviour in the Late Roman Republic*. Amsterdam.

Venuti, L. (1995), *The Translator's Invisibility: a History of Translation*. London.

Verrusio (1977), *Livio Andronico e la sua traduzione dell' Odissea omerica*. Rome.

Versnel, H. S. (1970), *Triumphus: an Inquiry into the Origin, Development and Meaning of the Roman Triumph*. Leiden.

Veyne, P. (1990), *Bread and Circuses*. London.

Vogt-Spira, G. (2000), 'Ennius' Medea: Eine Fremde in Rom', in Manuwald (2000), 265–75.

Walker, B. (1969), Review of Zwierlein 1966, *CP* 64: 183–7.

Waszink, J. H. (1948), 'Varro, Livy and Tertullian on the History of the Roman Dramatic Art', *Vigiliae Christianae* 2.4: 224–42.

Weber, E. (2000), 'Die ältere Tragödie in Rom und die Legende von der trojanischen Abstammung', in Manuwald (2000): 135–41.

Welch, K. (1994), 'The Roman Arena in Late-Republican Italy: a New Interpretation', *JRA* 7: 59–80.

Whitby, M., Hardie P. and Whitby M. (eds) (1987), *Homo Viator: Classical Essays for John Bramble*. Bristol.

Wigodsky, M. (1972), *Vergil and Early Latin Poetry*. Wiesbaden.

Wilkinson, L. P. (1982), 'Cicero and the Relationship of Oratory to Literature', in Kenney and Clausen, 230–67.

Willamowitz-Moellendorf, U. von (1919), *Griechische Tragödie*. Berlin.

Williams, G. D. (1994), 'Nero, Seneca and Stoicism in the *Octavia*', in Elsner and Masters: 178–95.

Wilson, M. (ed.) (2003a), *The Tragedy of Nero's Wife: Studies on the Octavia Praetexta*. Auckland.

—— (2003b), 'Introduction: The Importance of the *Octavia*', in Wilson (2003a): 1–12.

—— (2003c), 'Allegory and Apotheosis in the *Octavia*', in Wilson (2003a): 60–88.

Winkes, R. (ed.) (1985), *The Age of Augustus*. Louvain.

Wiseman, T. P. (1993), *Historiography and Imagination: Eight Essays on Roman Culture*. Exeter.

—— (1998), *Roman Drama and History*. Exeter.

—— (2001), *The Principal Thing (Classical Association Presidential Address)*. Sherborne.

—— (2002a), 'Ovid and the Stage', in Herbert-Brown: 275–99.

—— (2002b), Rev. of Manuwald (2001), *BMCR* 2002: 06.13.

Wright, F. W. (1931), *Cicero and the Theater*. Northampton, MA.

Wright, J. (1974), *Dancing in Chains: The Sylistic Unity of the Comoedia Palliata*. Rome.

Zanker, P. (1988), *The Power of Images in the Age of Augustus*. Ann Arbor.

Zehnacker, H. (ed.) (1983a), *Théâtre et spectacles dans l'Antiquité*. Leiden.

—— (1983b), 'Tragédie prétexte et spectacle romain', in Zehnacker: 31–48.

Zimmermann, B. (ed.) (1992), *Antike Dramentheorie und ihre Rezeption*. Stuttgart.

Ziolkowski, A. (1992), *The Temples of Mid-Republican Rome and their Historical and Topographical Context*. Rome.

Zorzetti, N. (1980), *La pretesta e il teatro latino arcaico*. Naples.

—— (1990), 'The *Carmina Convivalia*', in Murray: 289–307.

—— (1991), 'Poetry and the Ancient City: The Case of Rome', *CJ* 86: 311–29.

Zwierlein, O. (1966), *Die Rezitationsdramen Senecas*. Meisenheim am Glan.

—— (1986), *Kritischer Kommentar zu den Tragödien Senecas*. Mainz.

INDEX

Abel, L. 272n67

Accius, Lucius 21, 52, 71, 79, 88, 108, 109–42, 143, 144, 145, 147, 149, 152–3, 154, 156, 157, 158, 166, 167, 173, 177, 179, 205, 223, 224, 225, 243n53, 245n64

Achilles (Ennius) 58, 243n53

Achilles (Livius Andronicus) 28, 30

Acilii Glabriones 247n30

actors and acting 8, 9, 16–18, 19–20, 23, 145–8, 152–4, 171, 176, 177, 178, 179, 180, 183, 242n39

Aegisthus (Accius) 122

Aegistus (Livius Andronicus) 28, 30–3, 93

Aemilii (family) 38, 107

aemulatio (rivalry concept) 12

Aeneadae or *Decius* (Accius) 115, 119, 125, 137–42, 223, 255nn10,11, 256n18

Aeschylus 31, 42, 49, 73, 89, 100, 112, 128, 129, 145, 224, 248n42, 258n52, 263n65

Aesiona (Naevius) 37

Aesopus, Claudius 128, 145, 147, 148, 152–3, 155, 171

Afranius, Lucius 166, 184, 241n35, 262n42

Agamemnon (Seneca) 31, 32, 79, 189, 190, 198, 199, 201, 205, 221, 268n8

Agamemnonidae (Accius) 112

Agathon 79

Agrippa, M. Vipsanius 162

Agrippa, Postumus 175

Aiax (Ennius) 58, 67, 89

Aiax Mastigophorus (Lucius Andronicus) 28, 33–4

Alcmeo (Ennius) 58, 67, 69

Alcumena 250n9

Aldrete, G. S. 266n39

Alexander (Ennius) 59, 63–6, 67

Alexander, the Great 156, 263n56

Ambracia (Ennius) 59, 83–5, 124

amicitia 58, 88, 255n9

Amphitruo (Plautus) 56

Andromacha (Ennius) 59, 62, 64, 67, 68, 145, 152, 153, 154, 205, 249n2, 260n7

Andromacha (Naevius) 37, 205

Andromeda (Accius) 119, 120, 121

Andromeda (Ennius) 59

Andromeda (Livius Andronicus) 28, 29

Anicius Gallus, Lucius 245n68, 250n18

Annales (Ennius) 38, 50, 59, 61, 66, 84, 85

Antenoridae (Accius) 125

Antigona (Accius) 120

Antiopa (Livius Andronicus?) 28, 29

Antiopa (Pacuvius) 87, 91, 92, 93, 94, 95, 98, 108, 154, 255n141

Antiphilus 152

Antiphon 145

Antonii (family) 247n30

Antonius, Gaius 158

Antonius, Marcus 162, 263n67

Apelles 178

Aper, Marcus 256n24

Apollodorus, of Athens 29
Apollodorus, of Tarsus 79
Apollonius, of Rhodes 112
Appian 239nn1,3, 240n17,
  263n60
Appian Way 61
Apuleius 236
Archias, Aulus Licinius 112
Argonautae (Accius) *see Medea*
Argonauts 88, 112, 199–200
Aristarchus 243n53
Aristophanes 106
Aristotle 214, 256n17
Armorum Iudicium (Accius) 114
Armorum Iudicium (Pacuvius) 87,
  89, 91, 97, 100, 108, 158,
  253n89, 260n7
Artaud, Antonin 210
Artists or Artisans of Dionysus 12,
  18, 29, 35, 179, 244n59
Arulenus Rusticus 233
asides 99, 196, 224
Astin, A. E. 257n42
Astyanax (Accius) 112, 114, 121,
  122, 205, 260n7
Atalanta (Pacuvius) 87, 93, 96,
  256n19
Atellan farce 9, 10, 12, 18, 19,
  171, 176, 179, 184, 240n21,
  244n59, 260n7
Athamas (Ennius) 59, 70
Atilius, Marcus 144, 158
Atreus (Accius) 111, 115, 119, 120,
  125, 127–33, 145, 154, 179,
  256n18
Atreus (house of) 112, 125
audiences 20, 21, 22–3, 60, 110,
  153–5, 164–5, 170–1, 182
Augustan tragedy 144, 160–76, 193
Augustiani claque 183–4
Augustus 144, 145, 157, 159, 208,
  228, 243n51, 244nn57,58

Bacchae (Accius) 126
Bacchae (Pacuvius) *see Pentheus*
Bacchic cults 14, 70, 98, 126,
  250n17; Accius 135; Naevius
  42–9
Badian, E. 249n6
Balbus, Cornelius 143–4, 225,
  264n13, 266n44

Barnes, T. D. 275n35
Bartsch, S. 276n57
Bassus, Caesius 233
Bathyllus 172
Battle of Carrhae (53 bce) 157
Battle of Pydna (168 bce) 106, 107,
  108
Battle of Sentinum (295 bce) 137
Beacham, R. C. 245n64, 250n18,
  253n82, 261nn27,31, 262n47,
  264n18, 267n52
Beare, W. 253n103
Bellum Poenicum (Naevius) 50, 51
Bergk 254n125
Bernstein, F. 248n59
Bilišski, B. 258n58, 259n68
Bloom, H. 208
Boethius 106
Bothe, F. H. 32, 257n39
Bourdieu, Pierre 63
Braden, G. 270n27
Brooks, R. A. 241n25
Brown, P. G. McC. 244n59,
  246n10
Brutus (Accius) 52, 117–19, 123–4,
  134, 140, 141, 147, 149, 152,
  153, 158, 223, 224, 225,
  255n10, 260n7
Brutus, Marcus Junius 158,
  242n39
Brutus Callaicus, Decimus Junius
  111–12, 123, 124, 147, 242n47
Buecheler, F. 252n68, 256n21,
  259n75
Burrus, Sextus Afranius 191

Caecilius Statius 58, 166, 252n74
Caelius Rufus, Marcus 104
Caesar, Gaius Julius 23, 144, 145,
  157–9, 160, 164, 242nn46,47,
  244n57, 262n42, 266n41;
  funeral 108, 144, 158, 239n1
Caesar Strabo, Julius 110, 111,
  143, 144, 260n6
Caligula, emperor 130, 176,
  177–9, 186, 190, 208
Calpernius Siculus 208, 267n63
Campus Martius 151, 157, 162,
  164, 183
Carcinus 79
Carneades 91

Carthage: destruction 110, 123; *see also* First Punic War; Second Punic War

Cassius, of Parma 79, 143, 158–9, 161, 257n44

Castagna, L. 257n43, 263n66

Cato 'Censorius' the Elder, Marcus Porcius 38, 50, 58, 64, 84, 85, 91, 92, 127, 181, 239n7, 240n19, 250n15

Cato Licinianus, Marcus Porcius 108

Cato Uticensis, Marcus Porcius 233

Catullus, Gaius Valerius 69, 72, 148, 167, 205

Catulus, Lutatius 148, 149

Chaeremon 79

choragus 19

chorus 19; Accius 112, 138, 142; Augustan drama 169–70; Livius Andronicus 29; Naevius 42, 49; *Octavia* 225; Pacuvius 105; Seneca 105

Chryses (Pacuvius) 87, 89, 90, 91, 95, 96, 98, 99, 154

Cicero, Marcus Tullius 3, 18, 21, 143, 144, 145, 146, 147, 148, 149, 152–3, 154, 155, 156, 158, 159, 162, 239n7, 243nn48,49,55, 245n77, 261n18, 262n35; and Accius 110, 111, 116, 123, 124, 129, 130, 133, 256n26; and Ennius 58, 68–9, 71, 76, 79, 86, 251n50; and Livius Andronicus 27, 36, 246nn2,7; and Naevius 50, 51, 52, 53, 54, 55; and Pacuvius 87, 88, 89, 95, 97, 99, 100, 105, 106, 108, 254n131

Cicero, Quintus 144, 145

Cimber 145

Cincius Alimentus, Lucius 127

Cinthio, Giraldi 193

Circus Maximus 21, 155, 157, 171, 175, 178

circuses 171, 175, 230; *see also ludi circenses*

civic identity *see* national identity

civil war 85–6, 110, 126

claques *(fautores)* 20, 158, 183–4, 230

Clastidium (Naevius) 50–2, 53, 54, 55

Claudius, emperor 179, 185, 190, 191, 208, 227, 228, 275n39

Claudius, Appius 138, 149

Cleophon 79

Cluvius 275n35

Clytaemestra (Accius) 21, 156, 173, 260n7

Codex Etruscus 189

collegium, scribae et histriones 16–17,

collegium poetarum 17, 84, 111, 143 35

Colosseum 230, 231–2, 235

contaminatio (combination concept) 12, 37, 39, 67, 89, 112, 241n35

Coponius 156

Corneille, Pierre 192, 214

coturnus (raised boot of tragedy) 19, 188

Crassus Dives, Marcus Licinius 157, 267n74

Crates, of Mallos 91

Cresphontes (Ennius) 59

Critolaus 91

Curiatius Maternus 79, 223, 232–3, 241n30, 274n15

Curio, Gaius Scribonius 21–2, 150

Danae (Livius Andronicus) 28, 29, 39

Danae (Naevius) 37, 38–42

dance 8, 10, 14, 171–2

Dangel, J. 256nn15–17, 257n33, 258nn57,61, 259nn79,89

D'Anna, I. 101, 252n76, 253nn83,84,90,104, 254n126

Datus 184

Decius (Accius) *see Aeneadae*

Decius Mus, Publius 13, 137–42

Deiphobus (Accius) 112

Demetrius 229

Didascalica (Accius) 110, 125

Dingel, J. 268n6

Dio 172, 175, 177, 178, 180, 184, 235

Dio Chrysostom 229

Diodorus Siculus 239n1

Diogenes, of Sinope 79

Diogenes, the Stoic 91

Diomedes (Accius) 113, 122

Diomedes 13, 49, 241nn30,32, 252n78, 259n83
Dionysiac actors' guilds 12, 18, 29, 35, 179, 244n59
Diphilus 145, 153
Diribitorium 178
Domitian, emperor 228, 230, 234, 235
Domitius Ahenobarbus 157
Donatus 49, 259n83
Drusus, Marcus Livius 142
Dulorestes (Pacuvius) 87, 88, 90, 91, 94, 95, 96, 98, 253n99
Dunkle, J. R. 258n52

ekkyklema 187–8
Eliot, T. S. 193, 196, 218
emotion 7, 147, 172; Accius 113, 120–1; Ennius 66, 67; Pacuvius 95, 96, 97, 100, 105, 108; Seneca 214
emphasis (layered speech) 229–30
Ennius, Quintus 27, 29, 38, 50, 56, 57–87, 88, 89, 92, 99, 100, 112, 124, 128, 129, 133, 145, 147, 152, 153, 154, 161, 167, 205, 243n53, 248n65, 249n2, 255n11, 259n84, 265n22
epics: Ennius 59, 61; Livius Andronicus 27–8; Naevius 36, 37, 42, 50, 51
Epictetus 229
Epicureanism 91
Epigoni (Accius) 119
Epinausimache (Accius) 112, 122
Equos Troianus (Livius Andronicus) 28–9, 34–6
Equos Troianus (Naevius) 21, 37, 38, 156, 173, 260n7
Erasmo, M. 239n6, 246n80, 247n21, 250n26, 252nn57,70,73, 256n27, 259nn74,79, 263nn53,56,63, 264nn6,7, 272n65, 274n20
Erectheus (Ennius) 59, 66
Eriphyla (Accius) 120
Etruscan culture 7, 8–9, 10, 49
Euaretus 100
Eumenides (Ennius) 59, 255n11
Euripides 29, 39, 61, 64, 67, 70, 71, 72, 73, 74, 77, 79, 86, 88,

89, 95, 110, 112, 128, 134, 157, 223, 253nn83,100, 267n74; compared with Seneca 202–6, 208, 214, 217, 218
Eurysaces (Accius) 113–14, 125, 147, 152–3, 260n7
exodia (after-pieces) 9, 12
exostra 151, 187, 274n21

Fabii (family) 142, 247n30
Fabius Maximus Aemilianus, Quintus 107
Fabius Maximus Allobrogicus, Quintus 112, 142, 259n85
Fabius Maximus Rullianus, Quintus 137, 142
Fabius Pictor, Quintus 10, 38, 50, 59, 127
Fabius Rusticus 275n35
fabula Atellana see Atellan farce
fabula crepidata 11, 13; *see also* Roman tragedy
fabula palliata 11, 13, 19
fabula praetexta 10, 12–13, 19, 61, 143–4, 149, 156, 166, 173, 232, 233, 238; Accius 110, 113, 117–19, 123–4, 137–42, 147, 255n10; Balbus 143–4; Ennius 59, 83–7; Naevius 12, 36, 37, 42, 49–55; Pacuvius 87, 106–8; Pollio143; Pomponius Secundus 184; *see also Octavia*
fabula togata 13, 19, 184
Fantham, E. 253n109, 254nn126,128
fasti triumphales 7
fatal charades 231–2, 238
Faustus 236
fautores see claques
Favro, D. 264n11
Ferri, R. 273n2, 274n19, 275nn31,35, 276n46
Fescennine jesting *see* jesting
Festus 7, 243n52, 254n137
First Punic War (264–241 bce) 10, 17, 28, 36, 38, 55
Fitch, J. G. 273n2, 274n16, 275nn30,31,38
Flaccus, Verrius 243n52
Flavian tragedy 221–38
Flores, E. 254n136

Flower, H. I. 240n13, 248n56
Fraenkel, E. 251n31
Frézouls, E. 262n46
Fronto, Marcus Cornelius 235
Fufius 253n107, 262n45
Fulgentius, Fabius Planciades
    252n76
Fulvius Nobilior, Marcus 58, 59,
    60–1, 83, 108, 242n39
funerals 3–5, 7, 18, 50, 106–7,
    108, 125, 150, 158, 175

Galba, emperor 233
Galba, Servius Sulpicius 113,
    258n57
Galba, Sulpicius 58
Gallus, Cornelius 259n1
Garton, C. 254n136, 260n13
Gellius, Aulus 36, 57, 240n19,
    246n8, 255n5
Geminus, Rutilius 276n63
genealogy: Accius 113, 125, 127,
    128, 142, 256n19; Rome's
    claim to Trojan origins 38, 142,
    207–8
Gentili, B. 241n25
Glauchia, Gaius Servilius 259n68
Goldberg, S. 246n80, 251n42,
    274n16
Gracchi 17, 123, 126, 130, 245n77
Gracchus, Gaius 110, 113, 126,
    133, 142, 223, 258nn55,57
Gracchus, Sempronius 79, 161,
    166
Gracchus, Tiberius 110, 123, 124,
    128
Gratwick, A. S. 251n53, 253n92
Greek cities of southern Italy 10,
    11, 18, 21, 27, 29, 38, 58
Greek comedy 57
Greek culture 7, 9, 10–12;
    Pacuvius 91; revival in imperial
    Rome 229, 237–8
Greek drama 14, 19; remodelling
    11–12; see also Greek comedy;
    Greek New Comedy; Greek
    tragedy
Greek epics see Homer
Greek New Comedy 11, 95, 169,
    240n21, 247n15
Greek tragedy 18, 167, 169, 233,

236, 237–8, 243n53; Accius'
    adaptation of 112, 128, 141;
    Ennius' adaptation of 61, 63–4,
    67, 69, 70; influence on Livius
    Andronicus 27–36; influence on
    Naevius 37–49; influence on
    Pacuvius 88–9, 99; Seneca and
    193, 202–6, 208–9, 214,
    217–18; see also Aeschylus;
    Euripides; Sophocles
Greenblatt, S. J. 267n60
grex (acting company) 19, 123
Gruen, E. S. 242n43, 243n49,
    245nn74,77, 246n82
Guild of (Dramatic) Poets 17, 111,
    143
Guild of Writers and Actors
    16–17, 35

Habinek, T. N. 240n15, 241n28
Hadrian, emperor 238
Hannibal 15, 39, 41
Hector Proficiscens (Naevius) 37
Hectoris Lytra (Ennius) 59, 66, 67,
    70
Hecuba (Accius) 205
Hecuba (Ennius) 59, 66, 67, 88, 205
Heinsius 257n32
Helvidius Priscus 230, 233, 235
Hercules Furens (Seneca) 189, 190,
    198, 199, 201, 221
Hercules Oetaeus (Senecanesque drama)
    189, 221–3, 228, 229, 232
Herennius Gallus 260n2
Herennius Senecio 233
Herington, C. J. 193, 257n44,
    275n35
Hermann 254nn123,124,139
Hermiona (Livius Andronicus) 28
Hermiona (Pacuvius) 87, 90, 91, 93,
    94
Hermogenes, of Tarsus 230
Hesiod 112, 125
Hiero II, of Syracuse 34
history 231, 232, 233; Accius 113;
    Naevius 37; Octavia 223; Seneca
    199–201, 206, 208
history play see fabula praetexta
histriones see actors and acting
Homer 27, 28, 37, 59, 112, 123,
    125, 205, 256n14

Horace 11, 13, 20, 49, 93, 119, 143, 145, 152, 165, 166, 167, 168–9, 172–3, 188, 217, 240n22, 241nn28,32, 248nn51,55, 249n70, 262n51; and Accius 256n24; and Livius Andronicus 28, 36; and Pacuvius 108; Seneca's rewriting 205
Hortensius 100, 104, 147, 154
Hyginus 29, 78, 79

identity 182; Ennius 59–60, 61, 70, 71; Pacuvius 95–6, 98; *see also* national identity
Iliona (Pacuvius) 87, 88, 94, 96, 98, 108, 154, 253n82, 262nn35,45
imitatio (imitation concept) 12
imperialism 96, 110, 240n15
infamia law 171
Ino (Livius Andronicus) 28, 29
instauratio rule 15, 148
Ion of Chios 100
Iphigenia (Ennius) 59, 66, 67, 205
Iphigenia (Naevius) 37
irony 67, 84, 124, 266n37
Iulii (family) 38
Izenour, G. C. 276n59

Jerome 36
jesting 8, 9, 10, 11
Jocelyn, H. D. 67, 71, 76, 77, 78, 79, 80, 81, 82, 243n53, 249nn70,75,76, 251nn50,51, 252n59, 259n84
Jory, E. J. 244nn56,60, 247n22
Jugurtha 110, 134
Julian *see* Salvius Julianus
Justinian, emperor 17
Juvenal 234, 236, 237, 276n62

katablemata 166
Klotz, A. 31, 52, 84, 101, 106, 107, 131, 137, 252n76, 253n88, 254nn123,125,127,139, 257n44, 259nn78,82
Knoche 271n43
Kragelund, P. 241n30, 248n58, 252n67, 254n136, 259n84, 260n2, 274nn8,14, 275nn31,35, 276n47

Laberius, Decimus 244n57, 262n42
Laelius, Gaius 88
Laenas 243n48
Latin 10, 22, 28
Lebek, W. D. 248n58
Lefèvre, E. 264n3
Leigh, M. 258n65, 264n8
Lentulus Crus, Cornelius 144
Lentulus Spinther, Cornelius 149
Lepida, Aemilia 267n49
Lerner 267n60
lex Iulia theatralis 164, 170, 230
lex Roscia theatralis (67 bce) 23, 149, 276n52
Liberalia 8, 14, 48
Lindsay 252n63
Lipsius 252n59
Littlewood, C. A. J. 268n6, 270n21, 272n71
Livius Andronicus, Lucius 8–9, 16, 27–36, 37, 38, 39, 58, 59, 69, 93, 100, 112, 127, 133, 240n21, 255n11, 265n22
Livy 7, 8–9, 10, 12, 18, 21, 165, 244n59, 250n16, 259n86; and Accius 124, 138, 139, 140, 141; and Ennius 85; and Livius Andronicus 27, 29, 35; and Naevius 38, 51; and Pacuvius 107
Lucan 71, 184, 190, 207, 208, 229
Lucian 236
Lucilius 64, 69, 92, 101, 104, 108, 111, 123, 181
Lucretius 148, 205, 261n26
Lucullus 262n51
Lucullus, Lucius Licinius 261n35
Lucullus, Marcus Terentius Varro 261n35
Lucurgus (Naevius) 37, 38, 42–9, 51, 98, 126, 252n73
ludi 61, 154, 173–6, 179
Ludi Apollinares 14, 15, 78, 79, 134, 144, 149, 152, 153, 158, 162, 242n39, 243n48, 245n68, 266n41
Ludi Augustales 176, 266n43
Ludi Capitolia 234
Ludi Ceriales 14, 243n48, 266n41
ludi circenses 15, 235

Ludi Compitalicii 155, 174
Ludi Florales 14, 15, 242n48, 266n41
Ludi Magni 14
ludi magni uotiui 16
Ludi Martiales 174, 175
Ludi Megalenses 14, 15, 157, 243n48, 245n68, 266n41
Ludi Plebii 14, 242n43, 243n48
Ludi Romani 14, 16, 23, 28, 37, 50, 60, 157, 164, 242n43, 243n48, 266n41
Ludi Saeculares 163, 164, 173, 175, 179, 185
ludi scaenici 8, 9, 13–16, 21, 22, 29, 51, 60, 106–7, 109, 144, 148, 155, 175, 178, 179, 235
ludi sollemnes 16
Ludi Veneris Genetricis 157
Ludi Victoriae Caesaris 162, 173, 174
Ludi Victoriae Sullanae 266n42
Ludus (Naevius) 53
Lupus (Naevius) *see Romulus*
Lusus Troiae (Troy Game) 175, 208
Lydus 49, 259n83
Lynceus 166

Macro, Naevius Sertorius 177
Maecius Tarpa, Spurius 155
maeniana (spectator balconies) 9
Maenius, Gaius 9
maiestas concept 33
Mamilii (family) 247n30
Manuwald, G. 252n76, 260n5, 274n25
Marcelli (family) 53
Marcellus, Marcus Claudius (hero of Clastidium) 37, 50, 51–2, 53
Marcellus, Marcus Claudius (nephew of Augustus) 164, 170
Marius, Gaius 110
Marti, B. M. 271n43
Martial 108, 221, 229, 230–1, 232, 233–4, 237, 235, 264n1
masks: dramatic 19, 50, 147, 184, 188; funeral 4, 50
Maternus *see* Curiatius Maternus
Mattingly, H. B. 249nn71,73
mechane 187–8
Medea or *Argonautae* (Accius) 71, 112, 115–17, 119, 121, 125

Medea (Ennius) 59, 71, 86–7, 88
Medea (Ovid) 167–8
Medea (Seneca) 71, 189, 190, 194–5, 197, 198, 199–200, 201, 209, 210, 215–18, 221, 267n75, 269n11, 271n43
Medea Exul (Ennius) 59, 70, 71–8
Medus (Pacuvius) 71, 87, 88, 92, 94, 96, 98, 108, 253n82
Melanippa (Ennius) 59
Melanippus (Accius) 112
Meleager (Accius) 121
Memor, Scaevus 233–4
Menander 180
metatheatre and metatragedy 11, 51, 65–6, 116, 208–18, 252n73
Metelli (family) 36, 37, 53, 54, 55
Metellus, Quintus Caecilius 54, 55
mime 14–15, 171, 172, 231, 232, 235, 236, 244nn57,60, 262n42
miriones 245n64
Mithridates, of Pontus 110, 126, 134
Mnester 178
moral comment: Accius 121–2, 123, 126, 141; Ennius 60, 61–2, 70–1, 75, 86–7; Livius Andronicus 33; Naevius 42; *Octavia* 226; Pacuvius 96–9; Seneca 197–9, 204–5, 209, 218
moral values *see* Roman elite, values of
Moschion 49
Mueller, L. 32
Mummius, Lucius 255n1
munera 16, 235
music 4, 6, 8, 10, 14, 18, 19; Accius 120, 128, 130, 141; Ennius 61, 64, 81; Livius Andronicus 29; Naevius 40, 41, 44, 45; Pacuvius 95, 103, 105, 108
Musonius 229
Mussato, Albertino 223
Myrmidones (Accius) 122

Naevius, Gnaeus 11, 12, 14, 28, 29, 36–55, 56, 59, 69, 98, 112, 126, 127, 156, 173, 205, 225, 241n25, 252n73, 255n11, 260n7, 265n22
national identity 10, 70; Ennius 59–60, 61; Naevius 42, 50–1

national myths 10, 37, 38, 39, 127, 142, 207–8
naumachia 157, 175, 179, 230
Nemea (Ennius) 59
Neoptolemus (Accius) 114
Nero, emperor 23, 179, 180–8, 191, 206–7, 223–9, 233, 234, 274n6
Nerva, emperor 237
Neville, Alexander 269n17
Newton, Thomas 189
Nicias 152, 156
Nicomachus 100
Niptra (Pacuvius) 87, 89, 99
Nisbet, R. 273n1, 274n6
Nobilior *see* Fulvius Nobilior, Marcus
Nonae Caprotinae 144
Nonius 70
noxa legal term 30
Nyctegresia (Accius) 112

Octavia (Senecanesque *fabula praetexta*) 141,181, 189, 221, 223–9, 232, 233, 235, 258n52, 259n84
October Horse ritual 29
odeums 230, 234
Odusia (Livius Andronicus) 27–8
Oedipus (Seneca) 189, 190, 196, 197, 198, 199, 201, 209, 221, 268n9, 269nn12,17, 271n43
Opimius, Lucius 126
Oppian Law (215 bce) 85
oratory 72, 97, 99, 113, 115, 126, 145, 147–8, 182, 229, 258n57; Seneca's oratorical style 193–7
Orestes (Pacuvius) 87, 91, 94
Oscan and Oscans 9, 12, 58, 87, 155, 242n39
Otho's Conspiracy (69 ce) 181
Ovid 48, 71, 115, 124 133, 134, 135, 136, 137, 144, 161, 166, 167–8, 169, 171, 175, 197, 201–2, 205, 207, 218, 221, 230, 242n38, 249n76, 273n79

Paccius 236
Pacuvius, Marcus 31, 71, 87–108, 109, 111, 112, 145, 146–7, 154, 158, 166, 225, 255n11, 256n19, 262n35

painting 10, 88, 149, 152, 156, 182, 188; *scaenae frons* 60, 149, 151, 163
Panaetius, of Rhodes 91, 123
pantomime 171–2, 176, 235, 236
Parasites of Apollo 244n60
Paris (pantomime actor) 235
partheneion (expiatory hymn) 35
Parthia, confusion of drama and reality 157, 267n74
Paullus Macedonicus, Lucius Aemilius 61, 91, 106, 239nn1,4, 253n93
Paulus (Pacuvius) 87, 106–8, 225
Pease, A. S. 273n4
Pelopidae (Accius) 119
Pentheus or *Bacchae* (Pacuvius) 87, 94, 98, 255n11
Pergamum, influence on Accius 113
Periboea (Pacuvius) 87, 93, 98, 99, 253n83
Persidae or *Persis* (Accius) 112, 122
Persius 108, 184, 208
Petronius 182, 207, 208
Phaedra (Seneca) 189, 190, 196, 197, 198, 199, 200, 201–5, 207, 208, 259n84, 268n9, 269nn12,13, 271n43
Phaedrus 250n23
Philargyrius, Junius 264n2
Philo 177
Philocteta (Accius) 112, 115, 119
philosophy 229; Pacuvius 91–2; Seneca 181–2, 190, 192, 198; Stoic 91, 181–2, 192, 198, 223
Phinidae (Accius) 114–15
phlyakes farces 11
Phoenissae (Accius) 119, 126–7, 258n58
Phoenissae (Seneca) 189, 190, 201, 259n84
Phoenix (Ennius) 59, 62
Phrynichus 49
Pindar 253n89
Piso, Gaius Calpurnius 183
Piso, Lucius 250n16
Pisonian Conspiracy (65 ce) 180
Plautus 11, 14, 18, 20, 34, 39, 53, 54, 56–7, 58, 61, 62, 64, 96, 108, 110, 124, 166, 243n53, 245n69, 250n21

playwrights: Augustan tragedy
166–8; Flavian tragedy 232–4;
republican 12, 16–18, 123; *see
also individual writers*
Pliny, the Elder 88, 150, 246n80,
275n35
Pliny, the Younger 188, 236
Plutarch 107, 147, 157, 229,
239n4, 254n137, 260n15
poetry 7, 11, 59, 111, 229–31
political comment 152, 173, 176,
177, 179–80, 184, 230, 232–3,
235, 238; Accius 122–42;
Curiatius Maternus 233;
Ennius 61, 70, 71, 76, 79,
85–7; *Hercules Oetaeus* 223;
Naevius 39, 42, 47, 50, 51,
53–5; *Octavia* 223, 225, 226–9;
Pacuvius 96, 97–9, 107;
Pomponius Secundus 186;
Seneca 218, 223
political display 3–7, 16, 151–2,
162–4, 178; *see also* spectacle
Pollio, Gaius Asinius 143, 145,
248n51
Pollux 166, 167n75
Polybius 3–4, 15, 91, 96, 107,
123, 180, 245n68, 249n67,
250n16
Polygnotus 152
Pompeii: *Agamemnon* graffito 189,
268n8; wall-painting 188
Pompey 23, 144, 150, 151, 152,
153, 154, 155–7, 266n37
Pompilius 144
Pomponius Secundus, Publius 79,
184–6, 192, 251n46
Porphyrio 252n78, 262n45,
263n65
Portico of Pompey 151–2,
263n58
Postumius (consul in 173 bce)
243n48
Postumius, Publius 7
praefica (chorus-leader) 4
Publilius Syrus 242n40
pulpitum (stage) 21
Punic Wars *see* Carthage; First
Punic War; Second Punic War
Pupius 144, 166
Pylades 172, 265n36

Quintilian 72, 87, 92, 113, 115,
145, 161, 167, 168, 184–5,
186, 189, 229–30, 251n46,
260nn1,11,18, 275n35

Racine, Jean Baptiste 202, 215,
269n10
Rawson, E. 245n73
recitatio 145, 186, 192, 193, 235,
236
Reckford, K. J. 250n28
religion 8, 12–13, 15, 23, 151,
226, 235; Accius 126, 140, 141;
Ennius 70; Livius Andronicus
34, 35; Naevius 42–9, 50;
Pacuvius 98–9; *see also* Bacchic
cults; funerals
Renaissance drama 189, 268n9,
269n10, 272n67
Rhesus (pseudo-Euripides) 112
Rhetorica ad Herennium 72
Ribbeck, O. 48, 52, 248nn38,44,
253n87, 254nn115,130,133,
257n34, 259nn71,73,79,
260nn3,4
Richardson, L. Jr 246n80, 257n47,
262n38, 264n12
Roman comedy 10, 11–12, 13, 18,
56–7, 58, 61, 92, 93, 95–6,
166, 172, 186, 234;
disappearance of 236; Ennius
58, 59; Livius Andronicus 29,
36; Naevius 36–7, 54
Roman drama: early republic 3–23;
political function of 61, 152–5,
158–9, 172, 176, 178, 236–7
(*see also* political comment,
political display); production *see*
theatres; staging 18–21, 110,
186–7, 192–3 (*see also* actors and
acting); varieties 10–16; *see also*
playwrights; Roman comedy;
Roman tragedy
Roman elite 4–5, 10–11, 16, 22,
50, 91, 125, 142, 170, 178,
179, 182, 183, 230, 238; as
authors 143–4, 145; Ennius and
59, 60–1, 63; *Octavia* and 228;
values of 22, 30, 33, 34, 48, 52,
60, 61–2, 66, 70–1, 97, 98,
121, 124, 126, 134, 142

Roman Forum 4, 9, 21, 39, 110, 112, 126, 147, 148, 157, 162
Roman identity *see* national identity
Roman tragedy 10, 11–12, 13, 14, 231, 232; Augustan 160–76; disappearance of 236–8; end of the republic 143–59; Flavian 221–38; Julio-Claudian 176–88; recitation 145, 186, 192, 193, 235, 236
Rome: cultural production in late empire 236–8; Flavian 229–38; myths of origins 10, 37, 38, 39, 127, 142, 207–8; palimpsestic nature of Julio-Claudian 206–8, 218; political crisis 109–10, 122–7; theatricality and power 3–7, 23, 97, 178; theatricality and reality 148–9, 156–7, 180–8, 229, 252n73
Romulus or *Lupus* (Naevius) 37, 50, 52–5, 225
Roscian Law (67 bce) 23, 149, 276n52
Roscius Gallus, Quintus 18, 145, 146, 147, 148, 171, 260n14
Roscius Otho, Lucius 149
Rozelaar, M. 273n1
Rubrenus Lappa 79, 236
Rupilius 145

Sabinae (Ennius) 59, 70, 85–6, 255n11, 259n84
Saguntum 39, 41
Salinator, Marcus Livius 27, 35
Sallust 250n16
Salvius Julianus 17
Santra 144, 166
Saturnalia 11
Saturnian verses 27, 36, 54, 112
Saturninus, Lucius Appuleius 123, 245n77, 259n68
satyric drama 10, 13, 42, 166, 240n16
scaenae ductiles (drawn scenery)166
scaenae frons 21, 60, 149, 151, 163
Scaliger 257n45
Scaurus, Aemilius 150, 152
Scaurus, Mamercus Aemilius 79, 177, 179

Schiesaro, A. 272n69
Scipio (Ennius) 58, 59
Scipio (family) 53–5, 61
Scipio, Gnaeus 53
Scipio, Lucius 61, 242n39
Scipio, Publius 61
Scipio Aemilianus Africanus Numantinus, Publius Cornelius 88, 107, 110, 123
Scipio Africanus Major, Publius Cornelius 5–7, 23, 54, 55, 58, 60, 64
Scipio Nasica 58
Scipio Nasica Corculum, Publius Cornelius 107, 109
Scipio Nasica Serapio, Publius 124
Scipionic Circle 91, 123
Second Punic War (218–201 bce) 14, 15, 38, 48, 51, 58, 85
Sedigitus *see* Volcacius Sedigitus
Segal, C. P. 272n61
Seidensticker, B. 270n19
sellisternium ritual 15
Seneca, Lucius Annaeus 31, 32, 69, 71, 79, 99, 105, 115, 121, 129, 130, 131, 132, 133, 167–8, 169, 177, 181, 184, 185, 187, 189–218, 251n46, 253n103, 258n58, 259n84, 265n27, 267n75; declamatory style 193–7; form and meaning in 197–201; intertextuality 201–5; metatheatre 208–18; in *Octavia* 223, 224, 226–7, 229; palimpsestic texts 205–8; performance 192–3; post-Senecan drama 221–9
Seneca, (Lucius) Annaeus, the Elder 168, 190, 196
Servius Auctus 127, 247n29
Servius Tullius, king 124, 153
Shakespeare, William 215, 241n31
Sibylline books 48
Sicilian slave revolts 98
Silius Italicus 5–6, 7, 229
singing 7, 186
siparia 151, 166, 187
Skutsch, O. 251nn51,54
Smith, J. A. 274nn18,21, 275n32, 276n47
Snell, B. 271n46

soccus (slipper of comedy) 19
social comment 11; Accius 122–8, 142; Ennius 70, 75, 86–7; Pacuvius 97–9, 107; Seneca 209, 218
social hierarchy, theatre as mirror of 23, 60–1, 63, 149, 164–5, 170–1, 230–1
Social War (91–89 bce) 110, 142
soliloquy 69, 99–100, 196, 224
Sophocles 29, 31, 33, 39, 41, 63, 78, 79, 89, 100, 112, 120, 128, 133, 205, 221, 222, 223, 253n82, 254nn119,131
spectacle 4, 9, 16, 160–2, 172, 173–6, 178, 179, 234–5, 236, 273n75; Accius 119–21; avoided in *Octavia* 224; Flavian 230, 231–2; Neronian Rome 180–8; Pacuvius 94–5; Seneca 217–18; *see also* funerals; political display; triumphs
Stasiastae or *Tropaeum Liberi* (Accius) 126
Statius, Publius Papinius 229, 275n35
Stoicism 91, 181–2, 192, 198, 223
Strabo *see* Caesar Strabo, Julius
Suetonius 27, 36, 37, 57, 58, 97, 160, 170, 173, 178, 179, 184, 206, 233, 235, 236, 260n6, 263nn60,63, 265n37
Sulla, Lucius Cornelius 18, 110, 148
Sutton, D. F. 254nn119,120, 269n13
Syme, Ronald 110, 233
Szilágyi, J. 240n18

Tacitus 161, 176, 177, 180–1, 183, 185, 186, 207, 208, 228, 229, 232, 233, 236, 237, 241n30, 256n24, 275n32, 276n46
Tandoi, V. 254n136
Tarentilla (Naevius) 54
Tarquinius Superbus 124, 125, 257n47
Tarrant, R. J. 264n3, 265nn24,27
Telamo (Ennius) 59, 100
Telephus (Accius) 122, 256n19
Telephus (Ennius) 59, 62

Temple of Fortuna Huiusce Diei 106
Temple of Hercules Musarum 59, 83–4, 111, 143, 145
Temple of Honos et Virtus 50
Temple of Magna Mater 152
Temple of Minerva 17, 35
Temple of Venus Genetrix 149, 157
Temple to Mars 111–12, 123
Temples of Concord 85–6, 126
Terence 11, 15, 17, 19, 37, 61, 67, 92, 96, 106–7, 108, 123, 166, 241n35, 245n69
Tereus (Accius) 111, 115, 133–7, 158, 260n7, 265n25
Tereus (Livius Andronicus) 28, 100, 133
Teucer (Pacuvius) 31, 87, 93, 97, 98, 100–6, 108, 145, 146–7, 260n7
Theatre of Balbus 164
Theatre of Gaius Scribonius Curio 150
Theatre of Marcellus 22–3, 157, 163, 164, 179, 230, 261n31
Theatre of Pompey 21, 22, 38, 150–2, 155–7, 158, 163, 173, 179, 183, 234, 242n39, 245n69, 261n28, 262n46
Theatre of Scaurus 23, 150, 164, 246n80
theatres 21–3, 60, 61, 149–57, 163–6, 187–8; Flavian 230; repression and control 22, 23, 109, 111, 170–2, 176, 178, 179, 230–1, 235; staging of drama 18–21, 110, 186–7, 192–3; *see also* spectacle
Thebes 29, 88, 112
Third Macedonian War 79, 106
Third Samnite War 137, 142
Thrasea Paetus, Publius Clodius 183, 233
Thyestes (Cassius of Parma) 79, 143, 159, 161
Thyestes (Ennius) 59, 70, 71, 78–83, 128, 161
Thyestes (Sempronius Gracchus) 161
Thyestes (Seneca) 79, 129, 130, 131, 132, 133, 189, 190, 196, 197, 198, 199, 201, 210–13, 226, 227, 267n75, 268n9, 271n43

Thyestes (Varius Rufus) 161, 167, 175
Tiberius, emperor 163, 166 176–7, 183, 186, 190, 228
Titius, Gaius 144
Titus, emperor 231, 233
tragicomoedia (tragicomedy) 56–7
tragoedia see Roman tragedy
tragoedia cantata 186, 192
tragoedia saltata 186, 192, 236
Trajan, emperor 237
triumphs 5–7, 37, 50, 106, 123, 157, 161, 226, 255n1
Troades (Accius) 120, 205
Troades (Seneca) 189, 190, 193–4, 196, 198, 199, 200, 201, 205, 207, 208, 210, 213–15, 259n84, 268n9
Trojan theme 10, 28–9, 37–8, 59, 63, 69, 70, 88, 112, 142, 207–8
Tropaeum Liberi (Accius) *see* Stasiastae
Troy Game (*Lusus Troiae*) 175, 208
Tudor drama 193, 197, 268n9, 269n17
Turranius 166
Twelve Tables 262n43

Ulpian 17

Vahlen, J. 252n69
Valerius 229
Valerius, of Ostia 261n25
Valerius, Lucius 85
Valerius, Marcus 7
Valerius Maximus 147, 239n10, 261n35

Valsa, M. 252n76, 254nn121,127,131,136
Varius Rufus, Lucius 79, 161, 166, 167, 169, 175
Varro 8, 12, 15, 28, 36, 37, 97, 111, 144, 155, 158, 233, 240n18, 246nn5,8, 257n44
Versnel, H. S. 239n5
Vespasian, emperor 228, 230, 231, 232–3, 234
Viansino, G. 273n5, 274n6
Virgil 143, 148, 167, 168, 207, 256n22; and Ennius 69, 72; and Livius Andronicus 36; and Pacuvius 103, 253n106; and Seneca 201, 202, 205
Vitellius 182
Vitruvius 13, 119, 151, 165–6, 261n33, 262n40
Voconian Law (169 bce) 85
Vogt-Spira, G. 251n45
Volcacius Sedigitus 36, 37, 58, 69
Volnius 248n52
Volscian 242n39
Vossius 257n37, 259n82

Wall-painting *see* painting
Warmington, E. H. 45, 46, 82, 84, 107, 138, 140, 247n18, 252n63, 254n127, 259nn70,79, 263n66
Wilson, M. 274n13
Wiseman, T. P. 240nn13,17, 274nn21,25
women 85; actresses 15; female pain in Accius 120–1
Zanker, P. 266n47
Zwierlein, O. 273n2

Greek Tragedy in Action
Oliver Taplin

'A reissue of Greek Tragedy in Action couldn't be more timely: here is a book that championed new trends in the study of Greek drama, offering fresh readings of old texts and above all a dynamic sense of theatre. Oliver Taplin's viewpoint has proved to be both prophetic and influential.' - Professor Pat Easterling, University of Cambridge

Oliver Taplin's seminal study was revolutionary in drawing out the significance of stage action in Greek tragedy at a time when plays were often read purely as texts, rather than understood as performances.

Professor Taplin explores nine plays, including Aeschylus' Agamemnon and Sophocles' Oedipus the King. The details of theatrical techniques and stage directions, used by playwrights to highlight key moments, are drawn out and related to the meaning of each play as a whole. With extensive translated quotations, the essential unity of action and speech in Greek tragedy is demonstrated.

Now firmly established as a classic text, Greek Tragedy in Action is even more relevant today, when performances of Greek tragedies and plays inspired by them have had such an extraordinary revival around the world.

Pb: 0-415-30251-X

Available at all good bookshops
For ordering and further information please visit:
www.routledge.com